TRADITION AND FUTURE SHOCK:

VISIONS OF A FUTURE THAT ISN'T OURS

Askr Svarte

(Evgeny Nechkasov)

PRAV PUBLISHING

2023

PRAV Publishing
www.pravpublishing.com
prav@pravpublishing.com

Originally published for private circulation in Russian by Svarte Publishing
(Novosibirsk, 2020), text copyright © 2020 Evgeny Nechkasov

Translation copyright © 2023 PRAV Publishing

Cover images:
"Woman of the Mursi tribe with Kalashnikov gun,
Omo Valley, Ethiopia" (3 December 2013), Lost Horizon Images,
Cultura Creative RF via Alamy Stock Photo; "Successful team",
G-Stock Studio via Shutterstock.

ISBN 978-1-952671-80-7 (Paperback)
ISBN 978-1-952671-81-4 (Hardcover)

"Future Shock", per Alvin Toffler, is the fear and repulsion that
a human being and society experience in the face
of rapidly increasing progress, a shock conditioned by a loss
of any understanding of the nature of progress and the direction
of societal development.

***

The "uncanny valley" effect is when overly naturalistic humanoid
robots or synthetic objects which copy the things of the natural
world in detail incite a person's reaction of disgust and rejection.

***

The main points of this book were formulated and thought through
on Yule days to the sound of a crackling wood stove
in an old wooden shack on the outskirts of a small,
half-dead Siberian village.

TABLE OF CONTENTS

TRADITION AND FUTURE SHOCK:

VISIONS OF A FUTURE THAT ISN'T OURS

Preamble

Over the past several decades, scientific-technological progress has accomplished yet another qualitative leap and radically transformed the social, political, international, cultural, and anthropological landscapes. It follows that any critical futurological works, like any analyses of the current moment, stand on the shaky, fluid ground of the volatility and mutability of this world which such accounts attempt to register or outline in its trajectories. The present book is no exception. Moreover, already upon its release this book will have become obsolete — in the time that this book travels from the author's manuscript to readers, one popular neural network application will have already gone out of fashion, one messenger or social network will have been supplanted by others, and new generations of youth will have buried and reinvented a whole layer of their previous subcultures and signs.

The sudden and rapid eruption of the COVID-19 pandemic into our lives also turned out to be high-octane fuel for accelerating mankind's migration into virtual reality, for the development of numerous online services, remote work and entertainment, and for serving as a classic sanitary and biopolitical pretext for strengthening digital surveillance-and-punishment over the populations of many countries.

On the other hand, new programs, entertainment avocations, trends, breakthroughs in gadgets, new pop icons of the "new Enlightenment" and "science hipsters", and new movies, games, and books have already appeared and created an atmosphere of electric tension-and-attraction around the image of a positive future guaranteed by scientific progress and imminent singularity.

Paradoxically, commendatory rhetoric on ongoing technological changes can be heard from circles who otherwise *a priori* consider themselves to be Traditionalists or conservatives critical of progress, among circles of pagans of different traditions, political movements of a conservative bent, populists, and others fighting for identity and religiosity. Their midst, too, has come to host delusions as to the essence of technology and progress alongside false understandings of the course of time. Such has led them to various attempts at synthesizing Traditionalist-conservative values with technological progress and futurism, ranging from the "Archeofuturism" of Guillaume Faye to the so-called "Dark Enlightenment" of Nick Land. This also includes all those ideas of a spiritual-occult-technological synthesis in the spirit of New Age, which remain just as exotic and irrelevant from the point of view of Tradition as they are from the point of view of science. The suggestive magic of the positive, progressive future has ensnared pagans and soft Traditionalists in its web of illusions, ranging from the uncritical and inertial, i.e., everyday school-based perception of progress as an "objective natural process of Nature", to conscious apologetics for a "high-tech paganism" and other projects, such as migration into virtual reality, which is supposed to allow for the creation of a "magical" and "miraculous" world of Tradition without ever leaving one's chair and monitor.

All of this poses a most serious problem for understanding what "paganism" is, what "Tradition" is, what the "human" is, and what "time" and "our world" are as such. Falling under the (Post-) Modern spell of flashing updates, upgrades, and innovations, pagans and soft Traditionalists have been drawn into a whirlwind and have lost the unshakable vertical orientations of Eternity and the Sacred. In other words, they have lost their essence and self, carried away by the digital stream of simulacra.

For these reasons, first and foremost, we urge readers not to seek in our work any entertaining hermeneutics of culture or some critique of specific scientific achievements or technological solutions, but to understand behind the facade of mutating forms the common message, mood, and vector of movement as we see it. The world is rapidly approaching technological singularity and tectonic shifts in social structures, but the final forms remain difficult to survey and imagine. Forms are the essence of mutability, or that which we observe constantly, but their kaleidoscope hides from tired eyes precisely where all of this is leading and from what preconditions all of it has been unfolding. The examples we have chosen for the sake of clarity of evidence may become outdated, but their essence which we expose will remain unresolved, alarming like an open wound and threatening the future of all peoples, their identities and pagan traditions, and the originality of their Being.

Finally, our endeavor is, among other things, to pose extremely uncomfortable, aggravating, disturbing, and deeply existential questions about things and situations which did not exist at all in the world of Tradition, or which were always left in the background draped under numerous veils. In this respect, in our days, Traditionalism has a paradoxical priority before Tradition in its Golden Age. In our work, we take some of the intellectual and metaphysical intentions of Traditionalism to their very limits, and in some places we overstep them to enter previously untouched and taboo lands.

It would be a mistake to perceive the posing of such questions as idly irritating the surrounding public, since we are posing these questions first and foremost to and for ourselves. It would be wonderful if they deeply resonate with you, external observers and readers. Indeed, through participating and being involved in these questions, you will already become internal accomplices following through the night with us.

***

PART I:
TECHNOLOGY AS FATE

Tekhne and Gestell

Poiesis and Mythos

The world in which we exist, the ordered Cosmos in its unfolded complexity, is a beingful world, being in its openness. The nature of this being is *physis* (φύσις[1]), i.e., growing, sprouting, bringing up and forth, nurturing and cultivating. The Divinities order *physis* through arranging and ranking the levels of the hierarchies of the Cosmos in correspondence with the *Logos* (λόγος[2]).

The human belongs to the beingful world as part of it. Traditions tell of the divine origin of man: the Divinities create and bring proto-mankind to completion, as is vividly expressed in the Eddic myth of the creation of man and woman (Ask and Embla, the Ash and the Yew) by the triad of Divinities, Odin, Hoenir, and Lóðurr (or Odin, Vili, and Vé in the *Younger Edda*), out of logs found on a shore. These humanoid logs are in essence matured *physis* spiritualized by the divine Logos to ultimate completeness. A similar plot is known in the Hellenic tradition, where Zeus or Athena intervenes upon Prometheus' flawed clay creatures and refines them to human status.

Man's primordial perception of the surrounding world-structure and his place in it is characterized by an openness to Being and a capacity for wonder, amazement, and sacred awe. Yet, human nature also includes the possibility of turning away from Being, closing off and turning away one's view solely towards the dimension of the extant world and beings.

---

1   Hence "physics", the "physical" world, and τὰ μετὰ τὰ φυσικά, "meta-physics" as "above physics." The Latin translation of *physis* as *natura*, "nature", already narrowed and concealed the primordial fullness of the Greek term. The sprouting of being and the beingful world as *physis* is very close to the doctrine of manifestationism, but entails a number of differences, especially in the terms of Heideggerian thought and the hermeneutics of *das Geviert*.

2   The word λόγος encompasses dozens of meanings and interpretations, among which we can highlight "harvest" (in the sense of "gathering"), "word", "teaching", "thought", "notion", "order", and "lightning."

The kinship of the Divinities and man is revealed in the capacity to create and transform the world of beings, to create things within it. Myths tell of the divine origins of crafts and occupations: the Divinities reveal to man the ways to hunt and to work the earth, trees, and metals. Just as Odin, Vili, and Vé accomplish the demiurgy of man out of wood ($ὕλη^3$), so does man inherit such and work to bring stone, wood, or metal to its needed form, thereby embodying the idea which he has beheld. Openness to Being manifests itself in all of this as the capacity to see a potential thing in another actual and in its own way amazing thing. A tree is beautiful in and of itself, it is pleasing to the eye and is the focal point of rich forest symbolism, yet the human, illuminated with inspiration (open to inspiriting, which in Tradition is described in terms of being blessed and visited by the Muses), can see another thing or things that might be concealed within the tree and proceed to engage in just as symbolically rich and partly ritualized transformation of the self-sufficient tree into handmade products consecrated by the patron Deity of his craft. Man thus reveals his likeness to the Divinities: to Zeus, Hephaestus, Vulcan, and Odin in the act of creating, or in hunting to Artemis, in agriculture and herding to Demeter, Freyr, and Veles, in seafaring and fishing to Njörðr, etc. This was the case in our distant ancestors' each and every act. There was no void in their space of life: all deeds, crafts, and spaces were consecrated and occupied by Divinities, spirits, past ancestors, demons, or Titans. Sacrality had its fullness and its shades — from the solar-Apollonian through the ecstatic-Dionysian to the chthonic-Titanic dimensions of life. Blacksmithing, for instance, was considered to be an occupation touching the lower worlds by virtue of the subterranean mining of ore and the close connection between the furnace and fire and the metamorphosis of raw ore into the final product. For this reason, as well as in connection with the heightened danger of fires, the blacksmith's craft was often conducted in the village outskirts, indirectly proximate to the "chaos" beyond

---

3   ὕλη - *húlē, hyle* - literally means "wood", and in Aristotle's works was transformed into the category of matter.

the village enclosure. In the Germanic-Scandinavian tradition, blacksmithing was the lot of the dwarfs, the masters of the mountain depths who created divine artifacts.

For Aristotle, the origin of a thing is linked to four main causes:

1. *Causa materialis* - the substance, the matter (ὕλη) out of which a thing is made (the log in the myth of Ask and Embla, the clay out of which Prometheus' creatures are made);

2. *Causa formalis* - the form of a thing which the material takes on, i.e., the shape of a blade which a metal takes on;

3. *Causa finalis* - the aim, the assignation of a thing, its *telos* (for a blade to cut and pierce an enemy, which guides the use of certain alloys and the process of forging);

4. *Causa efficiens* - the force which creates the thing itself, i.e., the craftsman, the master, the human (in the case of the first humans, this would be the Divinities who accomplish creation).

On the metaphysical scale of demiurgy and cosmogony, the fourth cause casts a shade of "madeness" over the whole beingful world, a point which can be attributed to an obvious and tragic minus of Aristotle's philosophy. It is no coincidence that precisely Aristotle's ideas found resonance in creationist religion in the face of Christianity and then constituted the foundation of Scholasticism. Nevertheless, Aristotle himself still belonged to the Ancient World, where the context of the creation of things was still otherwise and still retained traces of manifestationism and the presence of an immediate, all-pervading, all-binding manifestation of the sacred in deeds, matter, and ideas.

In a block of marble, a master can see the prototype and silhouette of a statue trapped inside it (the *eidos* + form) and chisel away all the unnecessary parts, thus releasing (bringing into light) a beautiful image of one of the Divinities. Or a smith can take an ore in which there are absolutely no proto-forms of a future blade and process it, cast its mold, and forge it into a sword. A thing is a place of manifestation and being.

Like the Divinities' ordering of the Cosmos as a whole (λόγος), man's being open to the Divinities in his harmonious creating of things not out of raw resources, but out of other things of nature (φύσις), constitutes the essence of the organic manifestation of τέχνη (tekhne). Tekhne is not strictly limited to the sphere of crafting, i.e., transforming marble, pine, or clay into something else, but also includes the sacred sciences, music, and is in a most intimate way related to poetry. If tekhne is in essence human activity and creation (craft demiurgy as imitatio Dei or μίμησις, mimesis, "imitating" the Demiurge), then poiesis (ποίησις) literally means "to bring out into the light", "to work out", "to form and set out here." Thus, tekhne already stands in the shadow of poiesis as the more noble art. Martin Heidegger emphasized that φύσις is ποίησις in its higher sense, i.e., the manifestation of the world and human creation are equally absorbed in the essence of "bringing out into the light."[4] Heidegger indicates elsewhere that understanding τέχνη only as crafting means narrowing its domain. Rather, tekhne is all art, including philosophy and poetry, it is knowing and seeing, beholding an image-form of creation in the mind.[5] Still, this Greek notion is ambiguous, and in ancient literature it also means "cunning" (literally "knowing how to do something"), and this cunning bears a mark of "deceit" which would later come to be understood as "villainy." This allowed Heidegger to translate such into German as Machenschaft, "machination", to describe nihilism and the form of wielding the power of the beingful world in his era. Here we are already dealing with emancipated τέχνη-technology, as opposed to poetry, philosophy, Being, and myth.

Poiesis as poetry is intimately linked with language and the oral transmission of traditions. Traditions point out to us that

---

4   See Martin Heidegger, On Time and Being, trans. Joan Stambaugh (New York: Harper Torchbooks, 1972).

5   See Martin Heidegger, "The Origin of the Work of Art" in Poetry, Language, Thought, trans. Albert Hofstadter (New York: Perennial Classics, 2001).

the Divinities particularly patronize poetry and songs, as is expressed in the poetic structure of sacred texts and the foremost poets of antiquity (the Eddas, the Iliad, the Odyssey, etc.). In the case of Odin, the Divinities bestow - riskily and transgressively - poetry upon humans, elevating the skalds and belittling would-be-storytellers lacking the gift (the myth of the Honey/Mead of Poetry). Poetry is also found in the practice of theurgy, or magical ascendance to reality through rhythmic incantations and charms. In the latter cases, the connection between *poiesis* as *tekhne* and ancient man's creation and influencing the world is especially clear. Poetry, song, and incantations are the language in which people communicate with the Divinities and transmit teachings and customs. Rationalistic and positivistic argumentations on the origin of song, i.e., claiming that ancient people invented such on a whim or that it emerged by chance out of the cries of the first people, are impossible. It is much more probable (let us use this slippery word) to say that song was discovered or heard in the silence of night, in the communal circle in the light of fire — it was heard, "listened" or "caught on to", and "sung along-with" by peoples. Thus the Divinities bestowed the gift upon men.

Song and poetry did not emerge out of a need for communicating and transmitting information, but are a way of human being, a testimony of the being of things and the world as they were revealed to ancient man in his mythological sight and as testimony to Being (*Sein/Seyn*) as such. *Poiesis* and poetry are not limited to songs, hymns, and poetry as a form of versification and text formulation. As Heidegger emphasizes, *poiesis* is man's main way of dwelling (*Wohnen*) in the world. To this we might add a poetic maxim by Evgeny Golovin[6]:

И с обнаженного лезвия	And from the naked edge
Теки, моя кровь, теки.	Stream, my blood, stream.
Я знаю: слово «поэзия» —	*I know: the word "poetry"*
Это отнюдь не стихи.	*Is by no means only verses.*

---

6   Evgeny Golovin, *Ortanz*. Our italics.

Poetic creation can be in the form of prose or poetic verse, it can be a craft, war, everyday life, or any act in its sacred authenticity. *Poiesis* is life and death and man's path between them. Finally, as Heidegger remarked, poets and philosophers are equally close in their insights into Being, as they sit across from each other on equal, neighboring peaks.

The special dimension of a "thing" is revealed if we turn to the etymology of the very word for "thing" in Russian, *veshch'*, and *ding* or *thing* in German and English. The common root of *ding* and *thing* is *þing*, i.e., the assembly of free, armed people that discussed issues and adopted decisions, such as the old Icelandic Things and Althings. An analogous semantic array is found in the Russian word *veche* (and the Czech *vece*), from which *veshch'* also derives. As follows, *veshch'*/*veche* go back to the root **vekt'*, and further to the Indo-European **wek*, meaning "to speak, to say, to utter." A thing (*veshch'*) is something that is proclaimed (*vozveshcheno*), uttered, and of which speak (*veshchaiut*) those few who have been admitted into the sacred circle around the fire, i.e., the free men bearing arms, warriors, elders, priests, and skalds. A thing and its primordial origin are thus closely connected with a certain organic, traditional, sacrally sanctioned collectivity, even aristocracy. Poetry and craft demiurgy originally co-participate like *imitatio Dei*, as man acts as the *causa efficiens* for things just as the Divinities are the *causa efficiens* for the world and man within it. At the same time, the creative impulse for crafting and the knowledge of crafts are bestowed upon man by the Divinities and Muses through openness to the sacred in the ecstasy of illumination.

A divergence from poetic being and world-feeling in the direction of a more "technical" relation towards the cosmos was already pronounced in Plato. A technical, mechanical motif can already be traced in the *Republic*'s description of the structure of the ideal city and society. Poets are already unwelcome in the logic of Platonism and in the state presented in the *Republic*. Yet, Plato still did not reject the Divinities and did not postulate anything of the sort that might be taken for later deism or atheism. In Plato, the Divinities are fully present, fulfill their roles, and are offered sacrifices. Myth and poetry, however, are displaced into the periphery and marginalized as fairy tales and fables which corrupt the conscience of youth. The poet's freedom to create and carefully circumvent hierarchy and order in language poses a threat to the hierarchy of the state and the Platonic pedagogy for ideal citizens. In the *Phaedrus*, Socrates is made to place poets at nearly the very bottom of the hierarchy of people, while philosophers are deemed the best of men by right (although here we would not dispute Socrates-Plato). In Platonism, thus, we can register a rift between the positions of the philosopher and the poet — not to mention the figure of the priest, so integral to archaic societies, whose functions and practices are seemingly "divided" or "dispersed" between philosophers, poets, and, in some societies, shamans. *Logos* as order, hierarchy, law, and *ratio* becomes a regime of dominance over myth, poetry, ecstasy, and openness-to-Being. Instead, Plato built a referential metaphysics of the beingful world as a world of copies/embodiments above which stands the higher world of supra-being, the world of ideas whose being in its idealness, unencumbered by matter, is superior to the ordinary material world. In other words, there are things given to us in material presence, and there is the world of the ideas of things, which is immaterial and exists on the higher ontological level. Things in the world are the embodiments of ideas, to which matter brings diversity, distortions, and imperfections. In this optic, we can speak of the ontological quality of things and of degrees of "ideality" among them in relation to the pure ideas.

Following his teacher, Aristotle attributed *tekhne*-craft to the sphere of the lower estates' occupations. The laws of Aristotle's logic would be successfully incorporated into the foundations of the science of Modernity (New Time). We have already grasped the link between myth and *poiesis*/poetry; now it bears adding "symbol" to this semantic range, as a synonym or as another expression of holism. The first law of logic, A=A, is opposed to symbolism as such, which it reduces to the level

23

of a sign with one specific meaning.[7] A symbol, like holism in general, encompasses numerous meanings and interpretations, and its essence lies in this semantic pluralism: a symbol is always something referring to something else, harboring a reference to another meaning, or a symbol's different meanings might be connected through still others. The "logical" law of the symbol could be conventionally described as "A=A + the possibility of something else", whereby the symbol in and of itself does not exclude the situation of the first law of logic, but encompasses it as one among many individual hermeneutical cases in different contexts (or in one and the same at once), and this essentially casts a shadow over the remaining two laws of logic.

One textbook example of such can be seen in the disputes among both scholars and ordinary pagans over the authenticity of myths about one or another Deity, or over some legendary tale whenever there are several versions featuring different details. Modernist rationality quite logically says that only one variation of a non-contradictory synthesis of all the known versions can be true, with the inevitable exclusion of some fragments and elements which cannot possibly fit into a common picture without contradictions. We can observe a similar situation earlier in history, during the formation of the Christian canon and the numerous apocrypha with varying degrees of credence. From the point of view of Modernity and its logic, which many pagans unconsciously share, a diversity of accounts of one or another myth is taken to be evidence of its falsity, naivety, and the "inventedness" of all mythology as such.[8] The lack of any strict truth in the likes of A=A demands either working through knowledge of the truth (scientifically and logically demonstrating that one version of a myth is true, while

---

7   See Askr Svarte, *Gods in the Abyss: Essays on Heidegger, the Germanic Logos, and the Germanic Myth*, trans. Iliya Koptilin and Daniil Granovskiy (London: Arktos, 2020).

8   This also explains the pathological secularism present in pagan milieux when issues of values and morality are resolved on the basis of tradition all the while as physical reality and the laws of nature and society are explained through physics, positivist science, and materialism rather than through myth.

others are false or apocryphal), or discarding myth as a language and paradigm altogether, as a system incapable of logical correspondence and truthfulness. From the point of view of myth (holism → symbolism → poetry), all variations of myths of the Divinities or heroes are true and are facets of complex figures and plots in which differences in details only underscore the fundamental holism and openness of Being. Diversity does not demand reduction to correspondence or one truth, but creates a broad palette of hermeneutics and finds resolution on the higher metaphysical planes. It could be said of the Divinities that their superiority over the manifest world allows them to exist beyond logical frameworks, to be supra-logical. Let us say even further: our ancestors had access to a different kind of thinking, one which we call poetic or mythological, within the scope of which the strictness of identity was a special case of ecstatic Being. Today, such openness is difficult for us to reach; we see the world as if through a keyhole, whereas our ancestors stood on the tops of mountains with endless mytho-poetic expanses opening up before their gaze.

Despite the marks of technicism and craftsmanship in the cosmic demiurgy of Plato and Aristotle, the Neoplatonic school of thought of Plotinus, Proclus, Iamblichus, and Damascius accomplished a synthesis of all of Hellenic philosophy into a single system, brought such into vertical harmony, and, most importantly, revealed the upper apophatic dimension of the Intellect (*Nous*, νοῦς), the One (ἕν), embracing all and annulling all the contradictions of the many (πολλα). The Neoplatonists interpreted Plato's *Parmenides* dialogue as laying the foundations of the doctrine of the One and its relation to the many. The essence of this dialogue, upon which the whole ensuing rethinking of the Platonic legacy was based, boils down to five hypotheses on the relationship between the One and the many as constituting the ontological hierarchy of levels of Being[9]:

---

9   See the appendix "*Kommentarii Damaskiia i traditsiia neoplatonicheskoi ekzegezy dialoga Platona 'Parmenid'*" [Damascius' Commentary and the Tradition of Neoplatonic Exegesis of Plato's *Parmenides* Dialogue] in L.Y. Lukomsky, *Kommentarii k "Parmenidu" Platona* [A Commentary on Plato's *Parmenides*] (Mir, 2008).

1) ἕν

2) ἕν πολλα

3) ἕν και πολλα

4) πολλα και ἕν

5) πολλα

The first hypothesis speaks of the One, which is above the world of beings and is strictly apophatic. The One ecstatically comes to be known as the Intellect goes beyond its boundaries, i.e., through induced altered states of consciousness (e.g. intoxication) or by going beyond the logical frameworks and laws of thinking, which leads us to the conclusion that the poetic perception of the world is *a priori* closer and open to the One. *Poiesis*, however, does not mean permanently remaining in intoxicated ecstasy in beholding the One beyond the world of beings, but rather underscores the organic and "light" quality of the possibility of gesturing and gazing at the One, of which the second hypothesis speaks.

The second hypothesis, ἕν πολλα, "the One-many" emphatically "lacks" any of the syndetic unions between any two parts that establish hierarchy or relations as in the case of the third and fourth hypotheses. The level of ἕν πολλα is the manifestation of the One of the first hypothesis (which is in pure from the Nothing) in its cataphatic aspects as the many, or as true Being, for instance in the expression "God is Being." Ἕν πολλα is the play and intersecting dynamic of the One-many. Any attempt at introducing some kind of fixation or stasis upon the One-many would lead either to the many falling away, leaving the One, ἕν, of the first hypothesis (which simply is not in the many), or the bare πολλα of lower matter (nihilism).

The level of ἕν και πολλα, "the One and many", fully corresponds to the creationist metaphysics of the Only-One, which entails a distancing of the world across an ontological rift from the nature of God (Jehovah, Yahweh, Allah). A maximal expression of this closed topography can be found in

Gnosticism, where the Demiurge is the embodiment of cosmic evil and his perverted creation is a dungeon of souls.

The antithesis to the latter is "the many and the One", πολλα και ἕν, which corresponds to the gnoseology and ontology of Modernity, i.e., the supremacy of the material many (matter, atoms), positivism, conventionalism, and the atomic civil society. The "One" here is society as a sum of individuals, the conventional truth and taxonomy of types and forms as generalized ascensional categories, i.e., the "One" is constructed as the sum of the many below. We described the relation between creationism and Modernity in another one of our works and in other terms as the relation between father and son, between the source and the outflowing river.[10] In this light, the turn from ἕν και πολλα to πολλα και ἕν is logical and reflects Nietzsche's ascertainment of the death of God and the rise of nihilism.

The final hypothesis speaks of the lowest ontological horizon of being: πολλα. Here there is only the many, lacking any One from the preceding hypotheses, i.e., there is neither supra-Being, nor the Divinities, nor conventional generalizations, but only the infinite process of the fragmentation of matter (the sub-atomic level of strings, branes, virtuality, simulacra, etc.). The level of πολλα is the chthonic space of pure Titanism and its poverty.

The mythopoetic reality of Tradition is most tightly linked to the doctrine of manifestationism as the originary ontological matrix of all paganism as such. From one approach, it could be said that manifestationism is mythopoiesis, i.e., the two are synonyms which reflect one and the same idea in different ways. The essence of the doctrine of manifestationism is reflected in the word itself, the Latin *manifestare* meaning "to manifest", "to make appear". The doctrine of manifestationism holds that the Cosmos, all worlds, beings, phenomena, and man are in essence manifestations of the Divine principle. The Divinities create

---

10 See Askr Svarte, *Polemos: The Dawn of Pagan Traditionalism*, trans. Jafe Arnold (PRAV Publishing, 2020); *Polemos II: Pagan Perspectives*, trans. Jafe Arnold (PRAV Publishing, 2021).

the worlds, create the first people, establish order in the world and society, give people crafts and knowledge, and command the elements and phenomena. Between the Divine principle expressed in the many Divinities, daimons, and lesser spirits, and the world, peoples, and humans, there is no fundamental ontological rift of natures. There is no qualitative difference, only differences along the initiatic hierarchy of the levels of Being and comprehensions of the sacred depths. The sacred holism of manifestationism discloses reality in such a way that any and every thing and creation in the world is in one way or another (whether lucidly or concealed from uninitiated eyes) connected with the Divinities.

The peak of manifestationism is sacred monism, or treating the world as the manifestation of one supreme Divinehood, whereby the various Divinities are often faces and manifestations of its multifaceted essence. Monism in manifestationism directly refers us to the One of Neoplatonism, the first hypothesis of the *Parmenides*, and Julian the Faithful's Helios. Monism is most developed of all in the Indian schools of non-duality - Advaita-Vedanta, Tantra, Shaivism, and Shaktism.[11] Divine monism closes the circle of all ontology unto the Divine element (Theo-ontology) which outpours into the world, whereby the world is in essence the "body of the Divine" in its most direct, empirical (mythopoetic) givenness.

In other cases, when a tradition does not directly declare a Supreme Divinity of whom the universe is a manifestation, the all-embracing nature of the Divine and sacred is nevertheless present. The worlds of Tradition know no emptiness or unoccupied places. Rather, every locus of space is connected with the Divinities or other lesser mythical beings, sometimes even of a demonic character. The Divinities are patrons of cities (Athena and Athens) and have dedicated sacred groves (Baldr's grove), fields (Makosh), rivers, and mountains. Even

11 We outlined the horizon of monism in the Germanic-Scandinavian tradition in our book *Gods in the Abyss: Essays on Heidegger, the Germanic Logos and the Germanic Myth* (London: Arktos, 2020).

Earth itself is at times under the aegis of a Goddess or is her expression, as is the case of Jörð among the Germanics, Gaia among the Greeks, the Slavs' Mother-Earth, etc. The same case stands with the figure of the Sky-Father, such as Tyr or, even more vividly, Tengri in the shamanism of the Turkic peoples. Younger Divinities and spirits are the patrons of forests (the Slavic *leshi* and *rusalki*), bodies of water like swamps, rivers, and lakes (the Slavic *vodyanoy*), fields, roads, hills, and lowlands.[12] In peasant life, one finds spirits of the house (Slavic *domovoy*), the bathhouse (Slavic *bannik*), the barn (Slavic *ovinnik*), etc. All of them are the *genii locorum*, the spirits of places, guardian-spirits of specific spots, trees, boulders, etc. All of the spaces of nature are populated by beings which are today deemed with a tinge of disdain "fabulous", "fairy-tale creatures." Thus, the whole universe is the fabric of the sacred, a hierarchy of beings and their dwellings. Here there are Divinities, over there are *genii*, spirits, *leshi*; here is a person's home and its *domovoy*; here is a village and its patron, over there are the spirits of the mountains and ancestors; over our heads are the Sky-Father and the Divinities; under our feet is Mother-Earth, the ancestors, and the lower worlds. Nowhere is there any unoccupied, empty place. A wandering person is always a guest passing through others beings' homes and dwelling places, hence the rich arrays of protective practices, the sacred fear of foreign spaces and of traveling through forests, and the practice of hospitality. This is another manifestation of holism, of the fullness of the sacred saturation of the manifest world.

The notion of *manifestare* is lexically and semantically very close to φύσις as the self-sprouting and self-manifestation of the beingful world, and this is analogous to the Divine's self-disclosure in the form of the universe. Thus, ποίησις is the bringing-forth-out-of, the manifesting-out-of the beingful world and order by the Divinities, the ordering of the cosmos

---

12 See N.A. Krinichnaya, *Krest'ianin i prirodnaia sreda v svete mifologii. Bylichki, byval'shchiny i pover'ia Russkogo Severa* [The Peasant and the Natural Environment in the Light of Mythology: Tales and Beliefs of the Russian North] (Moscow: Dmitry Pozharsky University/ Russian Academy of Sciences, 2011).

and human societies, and the gifting of language, poetry, and crafts. In the latter case, the Divinities act as *Logoi* which do not contrast but rather express *Mythos*. Priests, shamans, and poets partake of them in such.

An altogether different ontology was put forth by creationism (from the Latin *creatio*, as in *creatio ex Nihilo*, or "creation out of nothing"). Such is the dogmatic premise of Christianity and the essence of all Abrahamism. Creationism is built around a radical, essential difference in cause between God and the creation of the world and man. God does not manifest himself as the world, but creates it out of nothing like a creature, a handicraft that is radically different from himself. Creation is conferred meaning and ontology only tangentially by the Creator, out of his intention and implication (as in "using" creation) in the fate of his work of production. If manifestationism is non-duality between the Divinities/God and the world and man (or the illusion of duality, cf. Leela and Maya), then creationism is rigid doctrinal dualism. Monism, the pinnacle of pagan holism and theology, is in creationism opposed by monotheism. The figure of the One (the Supreme Divinity or the all-embracing oneness of the world by the sacred) is in the Abrahamic religion shifted to the lower register of "the Only." The positive pole of Being, of fullness and the sacred, is embodied in one God who imparts the world with his intervention, involvement, movement, predestination, and miracles — like a craftsman pouring wine into a vessel he has manufactured. The priority form of relationship between God and peoples, God and the human, is the Covenant in the form of sacred books (the Torah, Bible, Quran, etc.), i.e., there is a contract of relations as opposed to the organic manifestation of hierarchies, Dharma, the Due, and an order of the universe that is obligatory for the Divinities and all beings in manifestationism.

The Abrahamic God's creation of the world out of nothing, the ontological difference between the Creator and creation, and the relationship of Covenant and Design — all of this captures the obviously technical character of creationist demiurgy and the ensuing vector of development towards the "cooling down of creation", that is towards the paradigm of Modernity. One of the most radical versions of creation left by its Creator can be found in the Gnostic sects, where the world is likened to a sealed vessel from which all the wine has been dried out and only a vague scent of the Spirit remains. In this optic of a world deprived of the genuine God while subordinated to false "Divinities" (the Demiurge-Fool and his archons), the world is of no value whatsoever to the chosen pneumatics, and hence any blasphemy and operations aimed at destroying or transforming it are permissible. This very same imperative is present in milder form in Abrahamism, where God entrusts the earth and all creatures to man for his use.

The genesis of Abrahamism, and Christianity in particular, came about amidst the desert territories of the Middle East and Near Asia. The poverty of the lands inhabited by the Semitic tribes was imprinted into creationism as *creatio ex Nihilo*, and later in nihilism, with which it was altogether fraught from the beginning. The spread of Judeo-Christianity in Europe was a conquest by a non-Indo-European Logos and ontology over the Logos of Europe and its own peoples. This conquest resulted in the deformation of all the structures of European peoples' traditions and cultures, leading to "Christianization" on the surface and a re-coding of values in the very depths of thinking. Manifestationism and its structures passed into the periphery and into the underground, but with the passing of time and the rediscovery of ancient thought, its strategies gradually penetrated and took root on the upper intellectual level of "dual faith" as well as in Christian mysticism and theology.[13]

Yet another most important innovation introduced by creationism was a change in the paradigm of time. Intrinsic to Tradition is cyclical time, which reflects eternity in the world of phenomena as well as the idea of likeness between the lower and the higher. From the cycle of the day (morning, day, evening, night) to the cycle of the year, cyclicality is the paradigmatic

---

13   See Askr Svarte, *Polemos II: Pagan Perspectives.*

matrix of the sacred hermeneutics of Tradition. The Winter Solstice is the point of death and birth, Spring is the season of becoming and growth, the Summer Solstice is the flourishing peak of energy, and Autumn is the time of harvest and old age, followed again by winter — the setting of the sun, decline, dying, and transition. Human life, the emergence and dying of things, and the annual agricultural cycle with its cultural-cultic framework are all seen through this cyclical framework. More broadly, the cosmos itself, like the whole structure of the world, is subject to cycles of manifestation and concealment. The end of each cycle sees an eschatological resolution accomplished in the form of a final conflict between the Divinities and Titans, after which the world is destroyed only to be reborn again, as the Divinities re-create the world and eternity manifests itself in the eternal return.[14]

In creationism, time is constructed in a completely different way, one which largely predetermined the whole subsequent history of Europe and the formation of technology. Creationist time is linear, it is thrown forth from the point of creation through the Covenant and history to the point of eschatology, the triumph of the Messiah (the Moshiach for the Jews, Christ for Christians, and the Mahdi for Muslims), the Final Judgement, and the subsequent end of history. In fact, modern historiography, concerned as such is with the duration and content of a separate slice of time, appeared precisely thanks to the linear time of creationism. Creationist doctrine posits a specific starting point for the world, from which one can determine a fully specific and reliable countdown of years, and a very specific endpoint, albeit with an unknown date. This endpoint, framed by a period of tribulations and Christ's battle with the Antichrist, is ultimately resolved through the Final Judgement as the end of history, as the completion of the line of time with the restoration of the Garden of Eden from before the Fall. Pious believers will then abide with Christ and God,

---

14 See Sergei Zhigalkin, *Metafizika vechnogo vozvrashchenniia* [The Metaphysics of the Eternal Return].

while sinners will be finally cast into Hell. Thus, creationism asserts a linear historial, one that is finite and whose end point is positive in meaning. The historial of creationism is, in the final analysis, the anticipation of a positive future following all trials and tribulations. This "one-off" history, or history as such, is earthly, concrete, and runs from point A to point B.

Noteworthy in this respect is the fact that Abrahamic theology and apologetics are tightly bound to the idea of the material and historical evidence and proof of events in the Bible (or the Torah and Koran), that is proving the actual existence of their characters and their deeds. In their polemics first with pagans and later with science, Christian theologians have actively striven to prove the reality of what is told in Scripture. For pagan manifestationism, the embodiment of a myth in material presence is only one level, sometimes completely unnecessary, of its manifestation and hermeneutics. For creationism, however, the historicity of all events is irrefutable proof of the rightness and truth of their morality and metaphysics. This is used to argue for their superiority over pagan "fairy tales" or to substantiate the weight of religion in the eyes of secular science. Historical-archaeological confirmation of the existence of Christ and the events of the Bible are *ergo* supposed to completely scientifically prove everything else. Here, in the linear historial of creationist theology, originates the predominantly materialistic interpretation of myth and its reduction to the immanent level of the real, the factual, versus the "mythical" which otherwise always implies openness and "something else" higher than reality.[15] This principle is well known in its laconic formulation as "Ockham's razor": entities are not to be multiplied beyond necessity. This reductionist principle formulated by the Franciscan William of Ockham in the 14th century laid the foundations for modern epistemology.

---

15 See Evgeny Nechkasov, *"Polemika iazychestva i khristianstva: vopros bogovoploshcheniia"* [The Polemic between Paganism and Christianity: The Question of Divine Incarnation] in idem, *Identichnost' iazychnika v XXI veke* [Pagan Identity in the Twenty-First Century].

At the initial stage, Christians' strong eschatological and messianic moods practically neutralized the open possibility of the active development of technology. Fear of God and expectations of the imminent Second Coming of Christ at times prompted believers to turn away from "perishable" earthly life in anticipation of the impending end of the world.

The Marginality of the Enlightenment

The counterpoint to this early situation would become one of the most important, epochal moments in European history: the Renaissance. Retrievals of the heritage of Antiquity, particularly Plato and the Neoplatonists, led to a flourishing of philosophy and the arts, freed out from under the shadow of rigid Catholic censorship. In the spirit of a Platonist humanism, theologians, mystics, philosophers, sculptors, architects, and artists turned to the human being, to his intellectual world and beauty, and thereby also ennobled the Church with new views. Christian mystics especially enthusiastic about the heritage of Ancient Greece, such as Nicholas of Cusa, expressed ideas of a Christian-pagan synthesis. The ontological rift between God and the world was substantially reduced, the intellect and imagination drew out the magical-aesthetic horizons of the soul's ascent to and merging with the high, and matter and corporeality were consecrated.[16] Imbued with a magical sense of the cosmos' inspiration (the Platonic World Soul) and the interconnection of every being and every thing, the arts and sciences, including the natural sciences, blossomed. Scientific and engineering achievements were supposed to illustrate or confirm occult theses and the doctrines of alchemists, magi, and Renaissance creators. Technology was on the rise, but it was occult technology and a matter of noble arts and craft guilds with their own secrets and mysterious language.

According to one scholar of the Renaissance, Francis Yates, it was precisely in this era, in Renaissance magic, that modern

---

16 See Ioan P. Couliano, *Eros and Magic in the Renaissance* (Chicago: University of Chicago Press, 1987).

secular science began to take shape.[17] The giants recognized by secular science, such as Nicholas Copernicus, Giordano Bruno, and Isaac Newton, were de facto engaged in confirming their own occult and Kabbalistic seekings with scientific operations and theories, a point which scientific historiography usually passes over in silence. At the same time, the breakthrough of Renaissance Neoplatonist humanism shifted into a lower direction, thereby opening up the way for secular humanism and negative freedom, i.e., the freedom of science and method, freedom from clerical dogma, and then freedom from the irrationalism of alchemy, Kabbalah, and spiritualism in the Enlightenment era.

The imperative of emancipation from the old authority of the Church and God which appeared in the works of the Enlightenment encyclopedists and ideologues — Descartes, Rousseau, Voltaire, Locke, Hume, Kant, and others — led to the installation of the paradigm of Modernity, whose axial lines were formulated around deism/atheism, secularism, the subject-object landscape of Cartesianism, causality and determinism, skeptical rationalism, a new temporality, and progress.[18] Religious faith was reduced to mechanical deism, a viewpoint from which God is held to be a craftsman, a watchmaker, who created the mechanism of the world's laws, giving it the impulse of movement and then no longer participating in its fate. The scientific-technological outlook of deism represented the idea of *creatio* taken to its extreme, turned toward the mere immanent level of creation, subordinated not to the will and design of God, but to the material laws of Nature which were once upon a time fixed by God and which continue to function as objective natural-physical reality. God himself is henceforth not "objectively" real as in the religious world picture; his being is now

---

17   See Frances Yates, *Giordano Bruno and the Hermetic Tradition* (Chicago: University of Chicago Press, 1964); idem, *The Rosicrucian Enlightenment* (London: Routledge, 1972).

18   In the emergence of Modernity, one cannot ignore the significance of the French Revolution of 1789 and its slogan, "Freedom, Equality, Fraternity", which had a decisive influence on the socio-political aspects of the new paradigm.

a consequence of variously convincing rational demonstrations of his existence and necessity as the grounding "first mover" of the world. The next step would be proclaiming religion to be a source of obscurantism and superstitions. Henceforth, man with his rational mind and methods of reasoning opens the way to cognizing the world, the laws of nature, and truth.

Atheism took shape practically simultaneously alongside deism and would become ubiquitously established not much later. The notion of God as a watchmaker who created the world-mechanism, cocked its springs, and then left his creation, logically led to the next step of discarding the figure of God as an inessential detail de facto playing no part in the mechanism's functioning, i.e., in the physics of the laws of nature. In the absence of empirical evidence for the reality of God and his participation in the movement of earthly matter, logical demonstrations of the existence of God become insufficient. Liberation from God thus became an act of autonomizing the mechanicism of the natural-scientific world-perception. Atheism's radical form, anti-theism, casts its scientific criticism against not only religion, but all forms of myth, the sacred, and "superstitious beliefs." Henceforth, religion is the "naive childhood of mankind" overcome by science and its methodological presentation of genuine knowledge about the world of things. Thus, Modernity recognizes and affirms its opposition to any form of tradition, both Abrahamic and pagan. The place of religiosity is in the periphery of society, as the lot of the unenlightened masses, obscurantists, and clericalists. In the best case scenario, it is the private affair of individuals located on the lower social rung and functions within the framework of secularism.

Secularism formed a rift in the integrality of social life, at the center of which had earlier stood the Church, and before it, the Divinities and myth. The condition of secularism meant dividing up social institutions and spheres and subjugating the religions that had hitherto determined their whole worldview and worldly legislation. Religion is left as merely one source of morals and with the function of fulfilling spiritual needs in isolation from authoritative influence on other spheres of society. An important role in the rise of secular order in Europe was played by the Reformation and Protestantism. The pathos of Protestant theology was based on the imperative of cleansing Catholicism of its authoritative and intermediary layers between man and God, as well as adapting religious texts to popular perception, including translating the Bible into regional languages. The clash between Catholics and Protestants in the Thirty Years' War was resolved by the Westphalian system of world order in Europe, within which freedom of religion was enshrined as a personal choice. Protestantism's victory yielded yet another downward shift of register to a lower floor, closer to the level of materiality and the "disenchantment of the world" (per Max Weber's expression). Protestant ethics introduced severe restrictions on corporeality in morality (Puritanism), abolished church grandeur and the spiritual ecstasy of services, and appealed to a minimalist aesthetics. In the social sphere, extreme Protestant positions spoke of a radical predetermination of those who would be saved in the Final Judgement, and of how such people are already distinguished by success and wealth during their lifetimes. According to Max Weber, the peculiarities of Protestant ethics laid the basis for capitalism and opened the way for the formation of accumulation and production, which implicitly became another act in the emancipation of technology and its withdrawal from the restraining shackles of the spiritual orientation of man.

The nature of Protestant theology *vis-à-vis* Modernity would be fully disclosed only considerably later by the modern philosophers and theologians Rudolf Bultmann and Paul Ricoeur. The new Protestant theology proposed to consider religion as a fraction: its denominator is the structure (approximately 95%), which embraces everything irrational and conventionally "mythical" in religion, while the numerator contains the approximately 5% of "*kerygma*", that is the dry, rational residue of the essence of religion. Kerygma is contrasted to the structure, and, according to Ricoeur and Bultmann,

Protestantism's aim consists in eradicating this structure and cleansing Christianity of all superfluous irrational ballast, i.e., the maximal possible adaption of Protestant ethics to Modernity. This is a mechanical view of religion which sees the latter as consisting of modifiable parts that can be changed or discarded in optimizing and modernizing the whole mechanism. The integrity of religion as it is given in Revelation (or Tradition as expressed in pagan myth in all its diversity) is abolished and divided into parts completely subject to the will of man and the needs of the current social moment.

Modernity owes its subject-object topography to René Descartes. At the core of Cartesianism lies rationalism, skepticism, and the dualism of subject and object — *res cogitans* ("thinking thing") and *res extensa* ("extended thing"). The holistic unity of traditional epistemology, wherein the knower merges with the known, is thus broken up into two poles: the cognizing actor-manipulator and the set of things spread out in front of and existing independently of him, which he cognizes (up to certain limits, whence the Kantian problem of the "thing-in-itself") and manipulates. Descartes' doctrine was yet another downwards shift toward the many (πολλα) and effected a consolidation of dualism in the mental structures of rational thinking.

Time itself also underwent metamorphosis. The cyclical time of eternity, of Tradition, was replaced by the linear time of the Abrahamic religions. In Modernity, time breaks out of the historical segment stretching between the point of Creation and the point of the End of History and becomes two endless beams emanating into the past and the future from the con-temporary point (Modernity), the "here and now" in the history of human development. Coming to consciousness of and reflecting on this contemporary moment, European humanity, freed from traditional eschatology or the positive reign of the Kingdom of God, acquired the endless horizon of the future, sanctified by utopian ideas whose realization was entrusted to social and scientific-technological progress, development, and economics.

The future is not guaranteed to be positive, but it ought to be so, and must be made so. In the chronological dimension, the horizons of the future incomparably exceed all known periods of human life or the lives of previous civilizations, which is taken to mean that "there is [still] time." Analogously, the past is opened up virtually to the state of an infinite beam turned backwards along the scale of time. The spans of time between the "now" and the times targeted by scientific theory on the origin of the universe (the Big Bang) are so immense compared to the human world that they are perceived as "eternity." Fundamental physics, meanwhile, seeks to break through this temporal boundary and ask questions about the state of the universe in the period before its unfolding.

The infinity of the past and the horizon of the flow of time into the future "in sum" speak to an objective infinity, i.e., the eternity of the flow of time. Our human "now" is contemporaneity, moving along a line forward with time, within the common bosom of eternity-infinity. But here we are dealing with a substitution of notions. In Tradition, Eternity is not the infinite duration of time, but its "canceling out", its "revocation" in the "moment" of timelessness, the "moment" of going beyond the cycle in rituals and holy days, when the sacred and the Divinities ecstatically irrupt into the world. Eternity is the lot of the Divinities and myth over and above time. In Modernity, eternity over time is replaced by eternity as the sum of infinity. And here lies the forgery, the simulacrum of eternity, for in Tradition the whole always precedes and is always greater than the sum of its parts, whereas Modernity claims that the sum of the constituent parts in composition is whole and nothing more. We can set aside an infinite number of points on the infinite line of con-temporal time, and we can do this truly forever, but this would be a false and ill eternity. In the traditions of different peoples, meanwhile, only one point is enough: the point of genuine Eternity sanctifying all of time, astonishing and whisking man out of the whirlwind for a moment of the sacred. This point is usually the most sacred holiday, such as harvest, the Winter Solstice, when the Sun dies and is reborn, a day of great mysteries, or any other event of myth which serves as the matrix and starting point for all other rituals and holidays in the annual cycle.

Time as con-temporary infinity is the realm of pure materiality and the many, πολλα. The infinity of time is the infinite fragmentation of a moment into days, hours, and seconds, through which humanity drags itself along in its enduring experience of time and in its aspiration to give time meaning.[19]

This brings us to the problem of determinism and causality in the modern era (the epoch of "New Time"). Various notions of causality, cause-and-effect relations, and the predetermination of phenomena and events were widespread throughout traditional societies, but they never exhausted the entire picture of the world and were of a rather different explanatory character. In Tradition, logical consistency bore a mythological and magical character, was more flexible, and at the same time was localized on a certain level of being. Certain actions, for instance sacrifices, incantations, rituals, and mysteries, were supposed to provide harvest, protection, or a person and society's initiatic transformation. The causal logic of events was explained with this language of myth: an insufficient sacrifice meant a poor harvest; neglecting an amulet meant conflict with other beings; a falling star meant an ancestor's spirit's desire to visit the world of the living; the cause of lightning is Zeus' wrath, etc. The nature of myth is broader and freer than strict logical laws, hence the cause-and-effect relationship in tradition is a form of play and "fairytale" narrative. It can easily be torn apart, revised, or rearranged in accordance with the structure of myth. The ancient Germanic hero might defy the "determination" of fate and come out victorious. Here we can draw a semiotic analogy with symbols and signs. A symbol always

---

19 Here it would be appropriate to recall Zeno's aporia about Achilles and the tortoise as a metaphor for man's fruitless, mocking striving towards a positive future of progress. Utopia will always be one step ahead and out of reach.

has branching semantics, a wide range of meanings, while a sign has a specific signified. When we interpret or decipher a symbol in a specific meaning, we bring it closer to a sign. It may be said that determinism is acceptable in the mythological picture of the world as a form of reducing symbolic polysemantics to one or another signifying instance, but there always remains the possibility of metamorphosis or performing a magical gesture that will change the chain of events in a "supernatural" way.

In the Enlightenment, the world was subject to disenchantment and flattened down to a material slice of being and a correspondingly disenchanted and flattened interpretation of what was unfolding. The rules of myth were discarded in the wake of the time of mechanical determinism and the world's enslavement in its logic. In Modernity, causality is quantified and calculated, it is the predetermination of linear and non-linear calculus, formulas, and computing power. No space is left for theophany, miracles, or mystical metamorphosis; there remain only unusual attractors, previously unaccounted factors, lack of data, etc. This is the logical-mathematical desert of the thinnest material slice of being. The principles of cause-and-affect and the interconnectedness of phenomena were taken to be the scientific methods and foundations of classical physics, their influence being just as clearly visible in the theory of the evolution of species as in the psychology of behaviorism and Pavlov's conditioning.

An immense contribution to desacralization was brought by Marxism, which affirmed materialism and a scientific method of cognition based on evolutionism shifted into the sphere of socio-economic relations and determinism. Economic relations and labor became the matrix for interpreting the course of history, human behavior, and the division of society into feuding classes. Metaphysical or idealistic phenomena and teachings, including any form of religiosity, were explained through matter and human operations, that is to say they were built from the bottom up, as the cultural superstructure over the base and as the means for keeping the lower classes in a state of exploitation by the upper classes. The development of materialistic sciences, technology, extensive and intensive production, and the inculcation of atheism make up Marxism's "positive" program in most of its ideological variations.

As myth is abolished, the trap of the mechanical worldview clamps shut. For the man of Modernity, for the positivist, Marxist, scholar or adept of science, there is no way out of this system. One can only refine, adjust, and rescale its complexity, its quantity of factors, actors, and lines of connection and development. Whatever goes beyond these limits is placed in the semantic nest of "fairy tales", the "unscientific", or is marginalized as psychopathological nonsense. Then appear synergetics and chaos theory which, while aiming to describe nonlinear dynamic systems which are extremely sensitive to the smallest changes in their parameters, bifurcations, and attractors, are nevertheless merely a reconceptualization of the very same cause-and-effect relationship on a new paradigmatic level.

A significant step towards overcoming determinism and causality was taken by Postmodernity with its rhizome and total relativism. In Postmodernist reality, cause-and-effect relationships and logical patterns are constructed in an arbitrary, kaleidoscopic way in accordance with a person's desires. A chain of events and connections can unfold in literally any direction, contrary to any determinants and logic, or not unfold anywhere at all, instead forming an atomic chaos of incoherent evens, the "link" between which is established by any DJ-trendsetter (blogger, fashion, media). If in Tradition determinism had mythological, Divine grounding, had a localized position in the hierarchy of the levels of Being, and was flexible, and if in Modernity determinism is the only thing that exists at all and is the basis of science, then Postmodernity is tired of all of this and decides to solve the problem with a drowsy thesis: "If you want it so, then so be it, and if you don't, then it isn't so, or here's 'so' and 'so' at the same time for whatever."

Previously, the Enlightenment also revived and elevated such a figure from Antiquity as Democritus of Abdera. This philosopher's teaching was practically identical to the views of the Enlighteners and scientists of Modernity. Democritus rejected the Divinities and was an atheist, he devised his own doctrine of a primordial vacuum, and he was the first to "discover" or allege that everything that exists is made up of atoms. It is extremely telling that there is a legend that Plato ordered that all of Democritus' books be bought up and burned. Alongside Democritus, the teachings of the atomists and materialists Epicurus and Lucretius Carus have also been resurrected. According to atomism, the ἄτομος is the smallest indivisible unit of which, like a constructor, all things and nature consist. The world is not a manifestation of the Divine from above, but is a collection of the smallest possible units from below. Since Ernest Rutherford's successful experiment, science has gone beyond atoms and has broken even deeper into matter, to protons, quarks, quanta, strings, and branes. Moreover, according to Karl Reinhardt, already in ancient times sophistry became the field where the *poiesis* of *mythos* was replaced by the pure *tekhne* of rhetoric and the methodology of relativistically persuading opponents. In other words, thinking, philosophizing, is turned into a set of pragmatic techniques, methods, and templates. Truth is not the Good (as per Socrates/ Plato), but that which is momentarily, conveniently, profitably demonstrated in polemic.[20]

Turning to analytical philosophy, we find yet another opponent of *poiesis* in the face of Ludwig Wittgenstein with his concept of the atomic fact, i.e., the simple, self-identical statement or object. The analytical approach to language and ontology (for Wittgenstein, the grammar of language is the ontological structure of the world) is in essence the reign of positivism in language. The atom of matter is reflected in the atomic fact of the simplest statement that cannot possible be interpreted otherwise than meaning that which it means. Hence the pathos of purging language of its "games" and layers of meanings, of striving to turn language into a form of logico-mathematical

---

20 See Karl Reinhardt, *Mify Platona* [Plato's Myths].

formulas for achieving the transparent clarity of statements, translations, and analysis. The rigor and unambiguity of the atomic fact is reflected in the acceleration of communication, whereby everything that goes beyond "A=A" is discarded. The paucity of the atomic fact-statement contrasts not even so much deliberate ambiguity as the very richness and ripeness of the word-symbol as such. The neopositivist analytical approach to language and philosophy embodies an absolute sterility of thought and closing-off from Being, unlike the bringing-into-being of *poiesis* and *mythos*.

Over the course of the historical involution of human perceptions and society, we have come to find ourselves in our moment of the Western European (and, with some reservations, global) historial. It bears recognizing that a paradigm shift does not occur strictly consistently and all-embracingly all at once and over and over again. Part of society, ranging from ordinary people to scholars and philosophers, still lives in the paradigm of Modernity and wages apologetics for the ideals of the Enlightenment with small drops of new data. Media and the vast majority of young people float quite freely on the waves of the virtual rhizome and do not find themselves beset by fundamental questioning. Beyond the West (the US, Europe, and part of Russian society), the paradigms of Modernity and Postmodernity are sporadically blooming in the former British colonies, in Latin America, and in the developed countries of Asia, especially in Japan. To this day, sometimes in the same neighborhood, "progressive humanity" exists alongside traditional societies which still live, to the extent such is possible, outside of the materialist and progressist paradigm and culture, still worshipping their Divinities and spirits and following their customs. The world is more complex than the limited concept of "universal values of progress and development" — more complex, but this does not mean better. What the majority of the ordinary population now considers to be "objective reality" is nothing more than a relatively new and synthetic paradigm of thinking, a pair of glasses firmly placed over their eyes. But our ancestors — mine, yours, and the ancestors of neighboring and distant peoples — thought of the cosmos in a radically different way. The etymology of the word "radical", the Latin *radix* ("root"), tells us that their thinking and their traditions were rooted in an altogether different soil and sprouted from an altogether different seed — a noble one — than that of Modernity.

The World as Ready-to-Hand

Perceptions of the world and relations and attitudes towards it have changed. Everything that exists, all things, objects, and matter in the world — the world in its all-encompassingness and man as part of it — is the beingful world as a whole. But now, man perceives the beingful world not as the Divinely-constructed cosmos with its inherent holism, hierarchy of beings, order, and saturation by the light of the sacred, but as a dark material at hand, a piece of clay which must be reshaped in accordance with will, a resource waiting to be extracted from the bowels of the earth and processed. Man perceives the beingful world as a whole as raw material, an absolute object prostrated before him like a target site for exploitation.

This fundamental break between the sacred and the world, between the Divine and the mortal (and, more broadly, between Heaven and Earth, leaving the latter to become a fiefdom for man torn away from God), was first accomplished by creationism, which postulated a radical duality and difference between the Creator and creation. Alain de Benoist sees the roots of the modern resource and consumption approach to nature and the planet as a whole in Christianity.[21] In the Abrahamic paradigm, the world appears as creation, and the main qualities of craftwork are utility and service. The onto-theology of creationism emphasizes the crafting operation of creation not out of itself — for then it would be an ideo-variation of manifestationism (*creatio ex Deo*) — but out of nothing, which underscores a gap and relation of subordination.

---

21 Alain de Benoist, *Vpered, k prekrashcheniiu rosta! Ekologo-filosofskii traktat* [Forward, to the Cessation of Growth! An Ecologico-Philosophical Treatise].

In other words, in the hands of the Christian theologians in Europe, creationism finally put the whole beingful world at the disposal of pragmatism, leaving nihilism as the "driving force" or alienating cause of this framing.

As the "father" of Modernity in Europe, Christianity also laid the basic preconditions for what would over time develop into the secular-humanist and scientific-technological paradigm. As Martin Heidegger noted, science is always secondary in relation to truth, because its sphere of interest and operations is the extant world as such, its classifications, moving parts, development, reconfiguration, and transformation.[22] The scientific method is the basic presupposition of interpreting the world to be something that can be subjected to experiment and calculation as such. In and of itself, science has no relation to the disclosure of truth, to *poiesis* and craft understood as primordial *tekhne*.

To Heidegger also belongs one particularly famous example which illustrates modern man's relation to nature. One of Germany's foremost rivers is the Rhine — the river sung of in legends and fought over by the Germanics, Celts, Romans, and later the French, the Rhine exalted in the hymns of Hölderlin, who was for Heidegger one of the most important poets of all time. Now, Heidegger notes, man arranges a hydroelectric power station along the river. The constructed station changes not only the landscape, but also the essence of the river. Now, it is no longer the Rhine of the Song of the Nibelungs, no longer the blood-stained border between the Germanics and the Celts and the French in the West, but merely an appendage of the power station. Engineering the river towards itself, transforming it, the Rhine is now the engine, an element of its engineering structure consigned to flowing and rotating the turbines that is now its "work." The installation of the hydroelectric power station makes the Rhine built into the plant's structure, transforming it from a legend into a worker. The antithesis to such a station

---

22 Heidegger, "The Origin of the Work of Art."

is the bridge, which connects the banks, "crowning" the river without reducing it to such a negative metamorphosis.

The example of the Rhine can be extended to encompass nature as a whole, to the beingful-world-as-a-whole, of which man is a part and in which man dwells. Earth becomes a storage bin of useful materials that must be taken out and used. Rivers, the winds, and the tides of seas and oceans are supposed to do useful work for energy extraction; forests are supposed to supply materials, as are flora and fauna supposed to supply food. If a land is not rich in anything, then it can always be used as (= it should provide) space for storage, logistics, and waste management. In the end, even man and whole peoples come to be evaluated and ranked according to economic indices, "workforce", costs, and services.

In their culture and in their metaphysics, peoples always reflect the climate, landscape, and scenery in whose midst they live and flourish. This has been spoken to by the organicist school of Friedrich Ratzel and finds reflection in the Neoplatonist thesis that the birth of philosophy in Greece was partially predetermined by its favorable climate. The question of whether the surrounding environment conditions a people's metaphysics, or if it is a people's surrounding environment that is the manifestation of their metaphysical structure, is a hermeneutic circle. The landscape surrounding a people is in essence a unique imprint of the Divine in the surrounding reality, of the idea in the matter of nature. Turning one's place of life, so exalted in tradition, into ready-to-hand resources leads to its destruction — to the disenchantment of rivers by hydroelectric power stations, the cutting down of sacred forests, the leveling of enigmatic mountains for the sake of extracting chthonic ores and coal.[23] Surrounding nature is supposed to work and/or be re-worked in the industrial paradigm, and in the post-industrial

---

23   One illustrative example is the destruction of one of the four *shikhany* (limestone mountains), Shakhtau, in Bashkiria, Russia. It was stripped down to a pit for the sake of the industrial production of soda. Local residents associate the *shikhany* with beautiful legends and beliefs, such as that the mountains are ancestors who met to make decisions.

paradigm peoples' cultures and even people's data become additional resources and raw material for production.

Thus happens the disenchantment of the world.

Tekhne and Technology

The involution of eras is reflected in the transition from *poiesis-tekhne* to the dominance of technology and production. *Tekhne* was originally bound to *poiesis* as a form of craft, art, and production. At any mention of "production", modern man hears the noises of machines and imagines a conveyor belt, i.e., the modern fabrication process. Here, however, we urge hearing in the word "production" the word "pro-ducing", i.e., "bringing-out" into the light, into the world, *poiesis*. The inspired artisan (the creator, artist, musician, skald), open to the being of the thing, releases the form of the thing out of present-at-hand material. Man acts as the "pro-ducer", the "bringer-out" and "author." Man "dis-closes" the thing, and in Tradition this process was always framed by a complex array of ritual practices, from the simplest to the lengthiest, multi-level ceremonies. Thus, producing participated in the light of the sacred through the creator's openness to Being.

Modernity is found in the dark shadow of the dominance of technology as the opposite principle and relation to the beingful world. The conveyor-belt, industrial, shop, mechanical production of monotype, standardized things is the opposite pole to *tekhne*. To designate this negative phenomena of emancipated technology, Heidegger introduced the compound word *Ge-stell*, or "en-framing", from the German *erstellen*, i.e., to create, to erect, to install, to frame. "Technology" in the modern understanding of Enframing is ambivalent, since it is essentially connected with *tekhne*. It can be said that in Modernity, technology as Gestell has unfolded and revealed its negative face to us (and we are enveloped, overwhelmed by it), but in its depths it still harbors the imprint of its original state. The essence of Enframing lies in the following key provisions:

- A peculiar way of producing truth and knowledge which corresponds to the final stage of the oblivion of Beyng and the proliferation of machinations upon the beingful world.

- Relegating the whole beingful world to the status of ready-to-hand raw materials and resources for extraction and processing. The whole world becomes a warehouse and workshop. The beingful world is appropriated and put at the disposal of the subject.

- Man becomes — for the meanwhile — the master of the world, a creator and manufacturer with a sphere of interests on the material plane of progress and development through technology, and later he himself becomes a source of raw materials and resources.

- The mass, mechanical Enframing (modern production) of things (products) replaces artisanal creation.

Instead of openness to Being and the positive will to disclosure, there is negative will, or will to close-off from Being. An authentic thing always bears the marks of the hand's work, slight imperfection of symmetries, roughness of surfaces and forms, and behind it lies illuminated insight and a reflection of light. Ananda Coomaraswamy pointed to how, for archaic art, the ideally precise, "perfect" thing is akin to something dead, and hence craftsmen never aspired to absolute symmetries or verified standard copies. Moreover, maximal naturalism and copying the real external appearance of products is a sign of the primitive thinking of the urbanite.[24] A horse figurine made out of a precise plastic mold with faux mane and tail is qualitatively inferior to a symbolic, wooden carved horse. Enframing supplies mass things, technologically verified copies with perfect symmetry produced in large quantities with unified standards and minimal human participation. Michel Foucault has described the formation of technological knowledge as a realization of four procedures: (1) selection, or the exclusion of the useless and peculiar; (2) normalization, whereby knowledge becomes interchangeable

---

24   See Ananda Coomaraswamy, *Vostok i Zapad* [East and West].

like modules; (3) hierarchization, entailing formalization, classification, and standardization; and (4) centralization, i.e., the control of technological knowledge. A qualitative difference is thus revealed: each of the many chalices or pairs of shoes co-created by the craftsman has been produced, "brought-out-forth", and is originally of its own being, whereas not a single one of the millions of industrial things is unique and co-created.

The beingful world is no longer brought out into the light and dis-closed. Instead, man as the king of the world devotes himself to manipulating the present-ready extant world. Only the cycle of processing raw materials, recyclables, and yesterday's things into new products and consumption remains. The connection between the emergence of Enframing and the development of the capitalist economy with its intrinsic attitude towards production and societal structure is obvious.

In the era of Modernity, traditional demiurgy finally passes into the form of industry, and in Postmodernity to semiurgy, or the production and consumption of signs and simulacra. As the machinery of Modernity leads to uniform mass products for consumption, their "individuality" comes to be "furnished" through their trademarks, branding, and signs. De facto identical things and goods are marked and distinguished by brands and trademarks which gradually push the material things themselves into the background, instead bringing to the fore the differences between their labels, marketing "wars" between goods, the ideology of consuming certain brands, and the development around such of consumer niches and subcultures (the "fan community"). The sign, label, and brand becomes more significant than the thing itself, acquiring autonomy from the real world of things. This is connected with the emergence and spread of the phenomenon of simulacra, or bad copies of things, shiny fakes, clones, and, finally, absolute simulacra, i.e., "copies without originals", signs which hide the fact that they mean nothing and do not refer to anything.

If in Modernity the forge of Gestell becomes the conveyor belt and factory, then in Postmodernity the Enframing picks up speed and emancipates even more for itself in the sphere of virtuality, information technology, mass media, and the related entertainment and consumer industries. The possibility of endlessly and easily copying and replicating "file-things" on the absolute plane of the Internet or the localized screen, and the possibility of creating non-existent worlds, creatures, and deep spaces on screens — such is the ideal sphere of semiurgy and the recycling of simulacra. But this is not limited to the strictly digital sphere, as capitalism with each new round masters, appropriates, and exploits people's exhaustion with conveyor stamps and marketing "wars" between sign-brands by offering the simulacra of "neo-craft" and "neo-artisanal" goods instead of the genuinely "enduring" or "long things" of Tradition.

So-called "craft" and "handmade" products are designed to attract the attention of the tired consumer by allegedly being handcrafted piece-by-piece and containing a deliberate roughness of forms and design which are positioned on the market as an antithesis to mass industrial products. In fact, the vast majority of such "handmade" products are pastiche "compilations" (typical methods of the Postmodernist game) of previously industrially produced casts purchased in specialized shops. A similar situation obtains with so-called "craft" goods, which are made in a manner reflecting the manufacturing cycle, only in miniature, and entailing the same investment in signs — only now the role of the sign is fulfilled by the label "craft made", which is supposed to indicate to the consumer that the good is "non-industrial." This is not to mention the analogous use of mass-produced casts, as in the case with "handmade" products, and the hopes which local producers pin on the rise of mass home 3D printers and personalized micro-manufacturing. Instead of authenticity, the consumer (the converse anthropological type of the producer) is offered "authentic fakes" or sets of signs that are supposed to indicate that before them are "genuine" handicraft and artisanal creations. Thus is successfully sold the simulacrum of craft and *poiesis*, copies of lost or altogether nonexistent originals, and even further, copies which are better than the originals.

As the Enframing — encompassing modern philosophy, science, and technology — is closed off from truth and deals only with the already present, ready-to-hand, extant world (i.e., it does not engage in bringing being out into light, but operates purely with what is already here), it is only logical that the notion that the whole beingful world is a raw material awaiting productive manipulations extends to include the human being as well. Since man also fully, concretely, objectively exists, and given that part of his nature is material, then from the point of view of the Gestell he himself represents a special form of material. Hence begin speculations and machinations on the very nature and selfhood of man, the very limits of the human being and being human. Unlike nature-as-raw-material, in the case of man the Gestell encounters a special kind of being amidst the beingful-world-as-a-whole. Man, according to Heidegger, is "world-forming" (*Weltbildend*[25]), and he in particular is the bearer of the primordial *tekhne* of which Gestell is a negative variation. In man, Gestell faces not an object in the form of a weak-willed rock or wood, but a volitional subject who can be open as well as closed-off to the truth of Being and *poiesis*. Traditional doctrines would say of this that man practices *imitatio Dei* or mimesis, i.e., demiurgy framed by the sacred. Moreover, the material, corporeal aspect of man is but only one part of human nature, not all of it as such. Otherwise, man would be just another empty matter. Man is presence; he exists, thinks, wills, creates, and bears the special imprint of the sacred.

In the face of man, Gestell-technology comes into open conflict with existence. The negative will previously projected outwards now collides with the willing subject, the special being that is Dasein. Inlaid in human nature, however, is a fundamental freedom of choice: being open to the truth of Being or being closed-off. The Gestell's aim towards the human is to convince and lure him to the side of closing-off, to negative will. Enframing calls into question the original being

---

25 See Martin Heidegger, *The Fundamental Concepts of Metaphysics*, trans. William McNeill and Nicholas Walker (Bloomington: Indiana University Press, 1995).

of human corporeality, intellect, and uniqueness. Among other things, Enframing redefines its position amidst the beingful world by "fitting" the latter into its process of supplying and producing in the same way that the erection of a power plant changes the essence of the Rhine. Man originally acted as the creator of technology, but over the course of time he is turned into a servant and repairman of the machines and conveyor belts of industry, then into a consumer of goods who creates the very demand that provides for the machine's work, and finally he becomes a consuming re-transmitter of the signs and simulacra of semiurgy. Man is turned into an organic appendage of mechanical technology that guarantees technology's own production and recirculating of production. It is not technology that satisfies man's needs, but now it is man who by the sweat of his brow ensures uninterrupted Enframing.

At different historical stages, this was hampered by the presence of the Divine order in the cosmos and the natural fear of the otherworldly, the Titanic and "demonic" in the societies of Tradition, as well as authentic existence and openness to Being. Later, in the Christian period, there was inertial adherence to customs and the neglect of matter, despite the fact that creationism takes to its limit the ontological difference between man and the world on the one hand, and God on the other. This is to say that the basic prerequisites for the nihilism of the negative will of Enframing were already laid then, but did not come out into the fore until later. Finally, in our contemporary era, already deep in the bosom of science, the frontier of restraint remains only in bioethics and public discussions on the vectors and boundaries of transhumanism. Here it is important to point out the primordially weak character of this barrier. Bioethics, whose purview now encompasses arbitrating questions on the limits of technological interference with the human body between the scientific community and society, has set before itself the task of formulating the gradual and weighed advance of progress by taking into account social and cultural factors. The task at hand, questioning the very idea of progress and questioning treating the human as a being to be modernized, is no longer even taken up.

Technology is *a priori* not a neutral phenomenon and "only a tool in man's hands." Technology as Enframing inevitably turns towards man and his being, imposing itself and its regime of existing (being closed-off) and enveloping humanity in the comfort of its accomplishments and dreams of new horizons. Technology is not existential in its essence; it alienates man from his own authenticity and from the problem of being present, and it alienates man from tradition and the sacred overall. Technology is the embodied ideology of Enframing.

Looking around today, we see the decisive dominance of Gestell in practically all spheres, both on the outside, i.e., on the front of processing nature as raw material into products, as well as inside, in the trajectory of society and man. The emancipation of technology (Gestell as the dark double of τέχνη, technology and production as the embodying of Enframing) has become the accomplished fate of mankind, and it is disclosing and increasing its power right before our very eyes, a point which complements and resonates with the eschatological doctrine of Traditionalism.

***

Progress from the Point of View of Tradition

In order to understand the fate being accomplished before our eyes, it is necessary to determine as accurately as possible our position in time, which is defined by the general metaphysical context.

In Tradition, the symbol of time is the circle, the cycle. As a structural symbol in the traditions of different peoples, it has variations pertaining to the peculiarities of cultures, their beliefs, and the cycles of agrarian work. The idea of cyclical time is most expressively exhibited by the annual circle of the change of seasons. At northern latitudes, the year is divided into two pronounced seasons: the polar day and polar night, and thus the primordial circle is divided into two parts by a vertical line. Moving southwards, there are four seasons: winter, spring, summer, and autumn, hence the circle's division by a cross, the so-called "solar cross." Depending on the culture and climatic-geographical environmental conditions, some peoples have autumn blend with winter or summer begin in spring, which thus accentuates a tripartite structure of time (such as among the Slavs).

The paradigmatic hermeneutic key is the solar cross, of which other two-part, tripartite, or otherwise partial symbols are ideo-variations. The circle, or the Year-Wheel, expresses the idea of cyclicality at all levels of the cosmos. The yearly seasons begin with the Winter Solstice, the point of the sun's rebirth and the beginning of the new year for many peoples, then comes into spring, the awakening of life, then to summer, the peak and highest point of the sun in the sky, then to autumn, the season of harvest, and then to winter, to the fading and concealing of the yearly night. An analogous structure can be observed in the daily cycle: morning, day, evening, and night are used as metaphors for both the year and human life, i.e., birth and childhood as spring, growth and maturation as summer, the transition into fall and then the old age of winter, which borders on departure into the afterworld. The vertical division of the circle into spring-summer (light) and autumn-winter (dark) parts of the year adds a horizontal division into the manifest world of people and the Divinities above, and the lower, subterranean world of the Titans, chthonic monsters, as well as some of the underworlds of the dead.[26] Thus, the Celtic Cross can express not only the traditional concept of time, but also a map of sacred topography.

The symbolism of the Celtic Cross describes the cosmogonic cycles and the metaphysics of eras in an analogous way, from the manifestation of the primordial beingful world out of Chaos to its ultimate destruction and dissolution. The most well-known doctrine expounding this is that of Hesiod's five generations of people, which are identified with five key eras:

- The Golden Age - the generation of people who live alongside the Divinities without knowing labor and worries.

- The Silver Age - the generation of people who live in pride and forego sacrifices to the Divinities.

- The Bronze Age - the generation of people who worship Ares and war.

- The Age of Demigod-Heroes, which is akin to the pre-decline, pre-sunset streak of the light of heroic spirit in man who can still prove his dignity before the Divinities.

- The Iron Age - the fifth generation of people who are deeply submerged in the vanity of toil and suffering (Hesiod himself exclaims that he does not wish to live with them in this epoch).

---

26 Different traditions have distinctive notions of the number and location of the worlds of the afterlife. The Scandinavians distinguish Valhalla as a place for worthy warriors in the halls of Odin, and Helheim to be an underground, poor, monotonous, gray kingdom of souls. Indian traditions conceive of the afterlife worlds as akin to hell (*Naraka*). Among the Slavs, the world of the dead is parallel to the world of the living and is therefore everywhere, which is similar to the etymological meaning of the Greek Hades as the "invisible" world.

In Hinduism, there is a widespread quadruple division of the cosmic cycle, the Maha-Yuga, into four epochs, each of which lasts shorter than the preceding:

- The Satya-Yuga - the Golden Age, the longest epoch, when harmony and order reign and the metaphysical conditions of the cosmos are luminous and light.

- The Tretya-Yuga - the epoch in which piety and the purity of the cosmos decrease, but people and the world are still generally elevated overall, and due sacrifices are still made to the Divinities.

- The Dvapara-Yuga - the third epoch in which the general metaphysical qualities of the cosmos are even further in decline. Diseases, catastrophes, and wars appear.

- The Kali-Yuga - the fourth and final epoch, whose name is associated with the Goddess of Death Kali, who destroys Shakti. The name *Kālī* means "Black", which corresponds to the qualities of this part of the cycle.

The Kali-Yuga is the shortest era in the Maha-Yuga, but it embodies the densest submersion into time, which is experienced as an unending, dragging persistency and as the cosmos' simultaneous submersion into cause-and-effect determinism (the law of karma and rebirths). All spheres of human life decline, and sacrifices and praises to the Divinities cease.

The Germanic-Scandinavian tradition in the *Elder Edda* says that humanity awaits the future coming of Fimbulvetr, the Great Winter, which will see the falling the World Tree to the point of the onset of Ragnarök, the eschatological battle between the Divinities and the Jotunns (the Titans) and monsters, which ends with the death of the world. Descriptions of the end times are extremely similar across Indo-European traditions. For instance, one verse from the *Elder Edda* is almost identical to a fragment in Hesiod's *Works and Days*:

Völuspá, Elder Edda:

Brothers will struggle and slaughter each other,
and sisters' sons spoil kinship's bonds.
It's hard on earth: great whoredom;
axe-age, blade-age, shields are split;
wind-age, wolf-age, before the world crumbles
no one shall spare another.[27]

Hesiod, *Works and Days:*

For this race now is iron indeed, and never, night or morn,
Will leave off from their suffering, worn down by toil and woe.
The Divinities will give them harsh and grievous cares, but even so,
They too shall have a share of good, mixed though it be with pain
Also, Zeus will eradicate this race of mortal men:
In such a time when at their birth babies turn out to be
Gray at the temples; when fathers and sons have lost all harmony;
When the relation of comrade to comrade fails, and of host to guest;
When brother no longer is friend to brother, as formerly in the past.
They'll treat their parents with disdain as soon as they are old,
Heartlessly finding fault with them in accents harsh and cold;
And ignorant of the punishment the Divinities mete, as they are,
They'll not be likely to repay their parents for their care.
Taking the law into their hands, they'll pillage and destroy
Each other's cities...[28]

The tripartite, descending division of time among the Slavs is also associated with generations of people, as in the famous folklore proverb: "In old times there were *bozhiki*, but we people are *tuzhiki*, and the next people will be *pyzhiki*: it will take 12 people to lift a straw, whereas the former people lifted trees that today not even a hundred could lift." In other words, in the past, people, i.e., "we", were mighty and handsome "godlings" or "little Divinities", whereas now we are "strainers" (*tuzhiki*),

---

27 Translation by Henry Adam Bellows (1936).

28 Hesiod. *Theogony and Works and Days*, trans. Catherine Schlegel and Henry Weinfield (Ann Arbor: University of Michigan Press, 2007), lines 176-190.

we "strain" (*tuzhimsia*), which is to say we already have to exert great effort, only to be succeeded in the future by altogether weak *pyzhiki*, or "dwarves."

The shamans of Siberia believe that the very first ancient shaman was all-powerful, like Erlik-khan, and could in one step ascend to the heavens, but he limited his own powers, with which each subsequent generation of shamans would be weaker than the preceding.

Chronologically dating the beginning of the decline and change in eras is an open question. The Indian tradition speaks of cycles lasting dozens and hundreds of thousands of years and entailing a compacting of time. The nominally longest cycle, the Satya-Yuga, was presumably not perceived as any duration of time at all. On the other hand, the shortest cycle, the Kali-Yuga, is felt like infinite duration. According to one version, the turning point in history was the battle between the Pandavas and Kauravas at Kurukshetra as described in the *Mahabharata*, with which began the Kali-Yuga lasting to this day. Historical datings of the battle at Kurukshetra differ, but their general trajectory takes us back several thousand years. This concords with Hesiod's conviction that he was already living among the fifth generation of people.

Drawing on the data of the profane sciences, some propose the countdown of the "fall" to have begun with the Neolithic Revolution (approximately 10,000-3,000 years ago), others with the appearance and spread of Christianity at the turn of the millennia, and others with the Enlightenment, which saw the rapid ascent of the scientific worldview and the direct manifestation of the anti-traditional rhetoric of Modernity (the acceleration of Gestell and the disenchantment of the world). However, it would be more correct to consider these points to be milestones along the way of a much more general involution.

These doctrines of time and universal regress are a reflexive effect of the transition from the Golden Age to the Silver Age, when time itself began to be *felt*[29] and thereupon formulated into the doctrine of descending cycles. Out of this crystallized the fundamental message of the pagan and Traditionalist understanding of time as moving from better to worse, from the beginning (flourishing, spring, birth) to the end (sunset, winter, death). We find ourselves in the final part of the solar cross. All the sources of the heritage of Tradition that are available to us are at best imprints from the Silver Age, yet it can be said with confidence that a large part of the history of mankind unfolds in the era of the End.

Our future is negative. The doctrine of cycles speaks of renewal and rebirth, but preceded by a final removal from the source, the disappearance of the world in winter-night fog, and passage through the point of death. The time of Fimbulvetr projects onto the topography of descent into the lower worlds and underscores the growing role and necessity of honoring those Divinities who are associated with Death and Destruction, both in the dimensions of the manifest world of people and on the whole universal scale of the cosmos.

The eschatological theme is inseparably linked with the topic of the *Endkampf*, or final battle between the Divinities, people, and the Titans and monsters. Pushed forth into time, the world lives in the shadow of this conflict. One of the most important remarks on how we ought to understand the myth of the war between the Divinities and Titans was issued by Friedrich Georg Jünger, who pointed out that the Titanomachia is a meta-historical, hiero-historical confrontation. The war between the Olympians and the Hecatoncheires and Titans at the dawn of time did not end, but is seen in the logic of myth as an "eternal" plot that unfolds throughout history in different variations and decorations. The Indian clash between the Devas and Asuras as well as the Germanic-Scandinavian opposition between the Aesir and Vanir on the one hand, and the Jotuns and Thursa on

---

29 Hence the interpretation that sacred rituals and solar festivities are points of ruptures of time and breakthroughs into Eternity-above-time (vertical time), when the state of the Golden Age is restored or the annual cycle is renewed on Yule or the Winter Solstice.

the other, also fit onto this canvas. The meta-historical approach to the confrontation between the Divinities and Titans allows for capturing the chronological asymmetry which can be found in the Greek and, for instance, Germanic traditions. In the case of the Greeks, the Titanomachia is localized at the dawn of history and de facto crowns the cosmogony and triumph of the Olympians, of Apollo over Python, whereas for the Germanics, the decisive battle takes place in the end times and is of a more tragic character for the Divinities and the world as a whole. The clash of the Divinities, heroes, and people with monstrous beings is an echo or flash of the confrontation unfolding over the world.

The essence of Titanic nature is expressed by hubris (ὕβρις), that is excess, pride, anti-divine pathos. In the case of the heroes, such as Odysseus, Achilles, or Heracles, their boldness proves their heroic and demigod nature or leads to the restoration of harmonious relations with the Divinities after their heroic odyssey. In the case of Titanism, however, things end with the tragic fate of Prometheus, Oedipus, or Sisyphus, who undergo punishment for their unauthorized and eternally condemned audacity in challenging the Divinities. Other traits of Titanism include poverty or depravation, greed (cf. the Old Icelandic *Jötunn* means "devouring"), foolishness, simpleness (as in the case of Epimetheus), incapacity for cunning and higher spheres of intellect[30], deformity or a disharmony of forms (monsters, giants, chimeras). The Titans are located on the level of earth or in the underworlds, which reflects their chthonic nature, their "processualism", i.e., their immersion in processes, the eternal incompletion of their deeds and undertakings (*"immer noch nicht"*), and their theomachism, as in their conflict with the Olympians, the Aesir or Devas, heroes, and people.

Turning to the contemporary situation, it is obvious that in the theatre of meta-historical combat operations the advantage is now on the side of Titanism and hubris as embodied in the

---

30 See *Havamal* 164: "Here are the saying of the High One / in the hall of the High / needed by people / woeful to Jötuns." [Translated from author's Russian - trans.]

Gestell. The Titanic forces are storming Olympus, the Jotunns are converging on Vígríðr, while the Divinities — as Martin Heidegger and Friedrich Georg and Ernst Jünger noted — have withdrawn into concealment; the subtle Divinities no longer tolerate the mechanical noise of jackhammers and conveyor belts. Technology and production are the attire of the Titans, they are at home amidst workshops and factories. "Where there are no Gods, there are Titans", Friedrich Georg Jünger summated.[31]

We dwell in the period of universal nighttime winter. We are nearing the point of midnight on the year circle, which corresponds to metaphysical submersion below earth, submersion in the viscous, dragging-on, vacuous time of the lower worlds of Hades and Helheim. This location in time and space substantiates an eschatological optimism, for it confirms the truth of ancient predictions. Today we clearly see that the due is being fulfilled. The metaphysical order of the course of time, the general involution of the cosmos and man, is unfailingly observable.

Proceeding from the above exposition of the Traditionalist view of the course of history as decline, we can see how further metamorphoses of notions of time have unfolded up to our moment. The notion of cyclical time was closed in creationism with the advent and establishment of the dominance of Christianity in Europe. Creationism shifted the whole picture of the cosmos to a lower level, plunging into historiography and materiality. The very act of *creatio ex Nihilo* laid down the principle of an absolute "counting point" before which there was nothing (or more precisely, there was the nothing, void of Being). The notion of history therefore changes essentially. The Edenic period of Adam and Even, an age of prosperity, did not yet know history. History begins with the Fall of the first humans, their first dressing in "clothes of skin" (Genesis 3:21) and their exile from Eden. Humanity is henceforth condemned to ordeals until the end times — and in this

31 See Friedrich Georg Jünger, *Grecheskie mify* [Greek Myths].

one can still trace echoes of the traditional notion of time as involution. Eschatological pessimism is cleaved by prophecies of the coming of the messiah, the savior, and therefore history — the future — acquires a positive horizon. The coming of the messiah in the figure of Christ renews the concept of history, dividing it into periods of before and after. The appearance of the "Son of God" confirms the truth and rightness of the Old Testament prophecies and is a guarantee of the truth of the doctrine of the Second Coming at the end of time. The line of history connected with the New Testament and the Church that seized power in diminishing Rome and formally baptized all of Europe — and which also, according to prophecy, awaits a period of apostasy — unfolds between Christ's Resurrection on the third day and the end of the world. Fundamental to creationism is this notion of "positive eschatology" or a positive future. Despite the seal of sin, apostasy, the brief reign of the Antichrist (as promised by John the Theologian) and the Final Judgement, the most important reference points of this historial are linked to the anticipation of positive events (the incarnation of God in the Son, Christ's victory over the Antichrist, the salvation of the righteous) and the restoration of absolute good in the end. This is the foundation of the positive teleology of time which is preserved in the scientific picture of the world of Modernity. With respect to pagan cyclical time, it cannot be said that the *telos* of the year is winter, while summer, for instance, is not, for every season is to a certain extent self-sufficient and bears its own cultural set of rituals, practices, works, and songs, and this does not give rise to any boredom.

A decisive contribution to the lucid articulation of linear time and progressive development came in the work of the Christian theologian Blessed Augustine of Hippo, who elaborated the doctrine of the Earthly City and Heavenly City. One fragment from his work is altogether telling:

> The whole family of God, most high and most true, has therefore a consolation of its own,—a consolation which cannot deceive, and which has in it a surer hope than the tottering and falling affairs

of earth can afford. They will not refuse the discipline of this temporal life, in which they are schooled for life eternal; nor will they lament their experience of it, for the good things of earth they use as pilgrims who are not detained by them."[32]

For Augustine, the normative and truly good, blessed paradigm is the life and history of the City of God, whereas the Earthly City is transitory. Man here is a passer-by who relates to the world as if to a foreign country. The consequence of this perception of the world (in which one can also discern a slight Gnostic flavor) is treating the world and objects as if they are ready-to-hand.

The cyclicality of time on the scales of life, the year, and the cosmos embodies the complicity of eternity in every new turn and every moment.[33] In creationism, there is a revolution of time against pagan tradition, whereby history becomes "one-off time" and assumes the shape of a slice of historical time into which humanity is plunged (sent into exile). The beginning of "history" in paganism (insofar as it is at all legitimate to ascribe to the ancients the modern historiographical understanding of time[34]) is rooted in mythological eternity, whereas for Christians history begins altogether conventionally and "documentarily." The documented historicity of events that actually happened acquires ever greater significance in this sacred history, as opposed to the cyclical meta-history of myth.[35] Having a specific beginning in a distant past (Augustine proposes 5551 BCE), the Abrahamic historial has a specific end point in its distant future, after which there will be no new beginning, neither

---

32 Aurelius Augustine, Bishop of Hippo, *The City of God*, trans. Rev. Marcus Dods (Edinburgh: T&T Clark, 1871).

33 See Zhigalkin, *Metafizika vechnogo vozvrashcheniia* [The Metaphysics of the Eternal Return]; idem, *Ob inykh gorizontakh zdeshnego. Apologiia vechnogo vozvrashcheniia.*

34 The ahistoricism of the ancients is underscored by their indifference to the exact dating of military treaties or the records of dates in the chronicles. The ancient Hindus especially stand out on this.

35 This notion is especially pronounced in the Western Christian traditions of dispensationalism and chiliasm/millennialism, i.e., the doctrine of the thousand-year reign of Christ on earth.

of a cycle nor a segment. An extraordinary event will happen: the end of history altogether. The Second Coming of Christ, victory over the Antichrist, and the Final Judgement will put an end to the historical course of time. Sinners will be cast into Hell, and the righteous will be raptured to Heaven (i.e., they will return to Eden or, in an anthropological sense, man will be restored to the state of Adamic perfection).

This very same idea is reflected in the early Utopians (More, Campanella), who illustrated ideal cities or states constructed according to human reason here on Earth. The idea of the "end of history" would subsequently be inherited by the leading ideologies of Modernity. Karl Marx wrote of the end of history in the form of the triumph of dialectical communism, and the liberal ideologue Francis Fukuyama proclaimed the end of history in the form of the triumph of Western Liberalism and unipolarity that onset in the 1990s.[36] The Christian idea of the end of history was also reflected in German Nazism in the concept of the "thousand-year Reich".

We can thus see how, in accordance with the doctrine of universal regress, the relation to time has changed: from eternity reflected in cyclicality, humanity descends to the historical segment localized in time. The overall picture changes essentially, and subsequent Western thought in the era of Modernity only restructures this Christian notion, boiling it down to deism and then to secularism and psychologism. In the era of Modernity, starting with the Enlightenment, the principal idea of the linearity of time is not disputed, but its sacred dimension is gradually emasculated.[37] The world is a manifestation of the Divine or God's creation, hence it was important for Modernity to eliminate the mythical and the

---

36 See Francis Fukuyama, *The End of History and the Last Man* (New York: Free Press, 1992). This author later admitted the extreme prematurity of his theses.

37 This is associated with such names as René Descartes, Gottfried Wilhelm Leibniz, Charles-Irénée Castel de Saint-Pierre, Nicolas de Condorcet, Johann Gottfried Herder, Jean-Jacques Rousseau, Voltaire, Charles Fourier, Herbert Spencer, Auguste Comte, etc.

sacred as the primordial causes of the emergence of the world and time. Ockham's maxim formulated at the very dawn of the Renaissance — "there is no need to involve the superfluous to explain essence" — becomes the methodological "razor" thanks to which unnecessary, irrational superstructures are discarded. Instead of changing the qualitative status of the world, there arises the idea of social development, increasing complexity, and improving the well-being of society and individuals as its members. The harmony and balance of Tradition (the Golden Age) are replaced with an aspiration for a better tomorrow extended into the future.

Already in deism, God is imagined to be a demiurge-watchmaker who creates the world like a mechanism, inlaying its physical laws and subsequently acting as *Deus otiosus*. Deism sought to reconcile the presence of God as the creator with scientific, rational knowledge of the world, and the image of a mechanism, a mechanical watch, became symbolic and somewhat paradigmatic of Modernity. If God created the world like a watch, setting the necessary mechanics for motion and laws, and then withdrew, then the very fact and value of his former presence can be neglected as in no way influencing the physical, natural-scientific picture of the world.

Watches With and Without Chains

The reduction of God to the status of a creator who has left his creation eliminates the Christian version of positive eschatology. Linear history and progressive development in the spiritual sphere are displaced by the unfolding of progress on the strictly material plane of this world, to which speak evolutionism, historiography, humanism, and psychologism (anthropocentrism). The world is turned into a raw map, and the idea of socio-political development illuminated by rational reason takes center stage. In Abrahamic history, understood as a segment of universal time, the rightward side of the line is opened up into infinity.

With regards to the future, the idea of onward progress as a permanent process, whereby the formula that "the future kingdom/utopia will be a better place than this one" is replaced by the more mundane "tomorrow will be better than yesterday." Seeing history from the point of view of progress leads to describing all preceding times, eras, states of society, culture, etc., as less perfect and primitive, but which over the course of time (as we approach in a straight line the point of today) evolutionarily or revolutionarily improve, become more complex, and develop for the better. Mythopoetic existence in the world is in this new optic of progress deemed the "naive childhood of mankind" or the "religious obscurantism of the Church" slated to be overcome.

Progress as a process in the scientific-technological and socio-political spheres treats yesterday as worse than today. It implicitly admits that today, the current state of society and level of development, will tomorrow become obsolete, imperfect. Following this logic, we arrive at a collision: progress claims that tomorrow will bring improvement and development, innovations and transformations, but already upon the day after tomorrow this "tomorrow" will have already become the passed, imperfect "yesterday", which, as one can work out in their head, allows for the future to be interpreted as "insufficiently future", as progress still in need of further improvement. This process turns yesterday's segment into a forward-directed infinity, where the futurological image of the ideal future dissipates with each new step toward it, disappearing on the horizon of future technological and digital singularity.[38]

Thus, the contemporary moment is to be understood as con-temporaneity, i.e., moving-with-time in an interval from the imperfect yesterday to the more developed tomorrow. This movement "in step" with progress ensures the hypnotic engagement of the masses in the process of development, as well

---

38   This is a distant echo of the idea of the "end of history." The question as to the nature and properties of time at the point of or after the Singularity remains open, including in connection with revisions of the parameters of corporeality.

as fixates their focus on the narrow slice of the contemporary and actual. Entrancement with the grand narrative of the future towards which scientific progress strives remains the lot of the fascinated, hypnotized stratum of scientists, engineers, futurologists, and futurists, while the world of Tradition and the values of the past are written off to the whim of socio-humanitarian archaeology.

The segment opened up towards the future turns into a ray with a beginning point, but since the religious picture of the world presupposes not only Divine teleology, but also demiurgy, then in the era of Modernity the segment logically moves away from the left, i.e., the direction of the past and the emergence of the world. One-time linear history in the likes of the Abrahamic segment, framed by beginning and end and entailing progress between, opens up in both directions into an infinite timeline while maintaining a progressive trajectory of development. The appearance of the world is therefore shifted from the dating of Christian theologians into the depths of the cosmic past, to the era of the Big Bang or some cosmological singularity when all of the universe's matter was compressed into a single point outside of time. It is important to note that in the scientific picture of the world, cosmogony is concerned only with material aspects, a point which underscores the general material character of the Iron Age. The proposed age of the universe is more than 13 billion years, which, compared to the recorded history of Earth as a whole and mankind in particular, represents a value which we perceive as "infinity", since in everyday life a person does not operate with and does not encounter any such proportionate quantity. In other words, there is no essential difference for a person between the astronomical antiquity of the universe's origin and abstract "eternity." Movement along the straight line stretching from infinity to infinity is marked by time, and here we return to the image of a mechanical watch on a chain.

Let us imagine the following picture. A certain gentleman alpinist decides to leave his pocket watch in a mountain crevice as a memento. He sets its beautiful, well-adjusted mechanism and hangs it in a secluded place, protected from adverse weather conditions. He heads back down and tells no one about the evidence left of his ascent. The gears, springs, and quartz bearings confidently rotate the clock hands around the dial. Time is ticking. Our gentleman dies, and no one else in the world of men knows that somewhere on the mountain the mechanism continues to run. For the whole world, this watch in the crevice simply does not exist. Sheltered from the world, it continues to count time. But the paradox lies in that from now on, the course of the watch's hands and their correspondence to the numbers on the dial no longer mean anything. No one watches the watch tick, and it does not tell anyone the time. It runs for the sake of running, runs out for the sake of running out, and is pure movement along a straight line, devoid of the cultural context of human attention.

Mechanical watches embody the mechanism of a winch which moves inexorably and measuredly from left to right along the stretched string of time. The running of a mechanical watch is pure movement through sterile time. The chain ties a person to this "winch" like shackles. The mechanical clock drags a person through the viscous density of time. Comprehending time and experiencing it as such is the field of conventional semantics and history in the disenchanted era.[39] The watch guarantees the process of man's movement from one infinity of the past to another infinity of the future through a series of fleeting moments of infinity here and now. Since conceptualizing the content of images of the future and theories of the universe's origin depends on the dominant scientific theory and paradigm of knowledge, i.e., the conventional superstructure, sooner or latter the watch will exhaust its supply, the clock will stop in the middle from de facto nowhere to de facto nowhere.

The mechanical watch is an idealistic image of Modernity, a metaphor of deism. We can deepen this metaphor even further by descending to the hypochthonic, subterranean level

39   See George Woodcock's essay, "The Tyranny of the Clock" (1944).

of understanding time. We are talking about atomic clocks, in which the passage of time is measured by the vibrations of atoms, such as cesium or mercury. The stability and accuracy of atomic clocks is extremely high (10^{-14}–10^{-17}), i.e., with respect to all of human history they can be considered absolutely accurate. Atomic clocks express the simple idea, fully resonant with the doctrine of cycles on the metaphysical conditions of the last epoch, that time is an accidental fluctuation of matter. Time is not created by the Divinities. Even the Christian God of deism did not cock the mechanics of such universal clocks. Time is the endless oscillation of atoms, ions, and quanta, the fluctuation of strings and branes below the subatomic level.

In Tradition, time is counted in various ways: the burning of a wax candle, a torch or oil lamp, bamboo-water or hourglasses, the shadows of poles, the cycles of days and nights, or the order of the night watchmen. The clock is the absolute symbol of hellish worlds: just molecules, just the frequency of vibrations, just time-as-matter and its equal segments.

Here, the problem of the "end of history" finds resolution, as it concerns only social time and the history of human society. Ended history still continues its journey through the space-time of the empty cosmos, just as clocks tick without history. Atoms vibrated for millions of years before man and consciousness, and they will continue to do so indefinitely long after the latter have been washed away by the waves of times.

Atomic vibrations are theoretically supposed to cease at absolute zero temperature, but in reality the laws of thermodynamics prevent absolute zero from ever being reached, and quantum theory speaks of the conservation of "zero" oscillations even at zero kelvin. The cessation of the vibrations of matter is associated with the world of absolute ice, cooling, and closing off from light. This is the world of chthonic spaces, of vertical time falling into infinity as an increasingly viscous deceleration of oscillations directly proportional to the process of cooling at subatomic levels.

One of the traditional images of Shiva-Nataraja dancing in the Deity's ring of fire is about just this. Shiva's dance and the flare of the fire are the movement and upholding of the life of the world and the fire of Dharma. The cessation of his dance is death and destruction, extinguished fire, the immovable corpse of the Deity, and the liberation of the Asura Apasmara.

In Tradition, the predominant notion is that mankind dwells in the middle world (the manifest world, e.g., Midgard), where Apollonian harmony and the perfection of Eternity are in a Dionysian way intertwined with becoming, time, and the Earth. The Divinities are immortal, for they reside in Eternity beyond and above time. This fundamentally differs from human mortality and "eternity" falsely conceived as an unceasing, infinite duration of time. The Divine and Eternity are complicit in societies of Tradition through the sacred opening-up of time in rituals, rites of excess, ecstasy, and numinous horror embracing the life of the sacred. Such is the vertical time of Eternity (outside of time), whose Titanic double is descending time, falling into the infinity of thickening time like the clock hands' illusion of "eternity."

The Contemporal Rhizome

The linear time of Abrahamism, although still harboring an existential-eschatological tensions, unfolds into a less substantive straight line in the middle of a cosmic vacuum and material bodies. The conception of time undergoes further dissolution in Postmodernity, starting in the second half of the 20th century.

The fundamental scientific conception of time dissipates. Contemporality as progressive movement in step with time and development collapses into a rhizome-like canvas of variable temporalities. The image of a line stretching in both directions gives way to the image of a rootstock, a rhizome, or a plane with folds and branches. Every locality on the overarching fabric can now postulate its own voluntaristic time, which can

71

be measured in any kinds of units, have any structure, and move in any direction. The grand narrative of universal time dissolves into small and disconnected temporalities, modules, intersections, and folds on the surface, like fungi growing out of one mycelium which slicing does not damage. In social life, this means that neighbors can literally believe and live in different chronological paradigms, be they mythical, natural-scientific, pseudo-scientific, fantasy, or hallucinatory. Virtual time, which a Network user plugs and connects to, can go faster or slower than time observed outside the window, and vice versa: the value of real time can depend on the length of play time, which itself is converted into a status ranking. More broadly, different social groups, strata, subcultures, sects, and individuals can privately obtain their own "aeonic time" (Gilles Deleuze). Fundamental here is that there is no common universal time for all, no "bigger time" as an idea, for every time or chronological concept is equal to others and coexists in play.

The metaphor of a surface, a plane, refers to corporeality, to experiencing time as a totality of fleeting feelings and impressions that are either accepted (the imperative of duration) or discomforting (the imperative of avoiding pain or interpreting pain to be pleasant). This superficiality also excludes any deeper or higher dimension, just as a rhizome moves along the surface topography of its foldings and branching without penetrating any deeper and without breaking upwards (transcending). Here we face the last step into the abyss, a fall into time that is so deep that it ceases to be perceived as such, as any course of time, as falling, as a feeling of duration common to all. This is the final stage of the ductility, subterranean inertia, cooling down, and closing of time, the feeling that there is no time at all, that time has stopped. Mankind no longer moves anywhere, whether towards an eschatological end or a positive future or utopia. Each individual moves wherever they wish and lives within a today cast out into a "tomorrow."[40]

---

40 Cf. Zygmunt Bauman's term "liquid modernity".

Traditionalists find themselves in a paradoxical situation. In these conditions, our paradigmatic discourse is on one plane "equalized" with the scientific world picture as well as with any other subcultural, pseudo-scientific, or schizoidic concept. Everything attains legitimacy — but a playful, unauthentic legitimacy. Time and the serious questions of "when and where?" are discarded as a dictatorship of grand narratives, as the dictatorship of a need for genuinely locating oneself within a grand picture of time on the circle of the universal cycle. The Postmodernist replies to this question, "Whenever you want, even now if you want", but these words mean nothing genuinely serious and do not lead to any events, as they flowingly glide along the surface of smooth superficiality and do not call for any genuine *response*.

On the other hand, such a situation can be tactically supportive, as it allows for fencing off our paradigm and waging an offensive against all others while they are busy constructing their own micro-enclaves and filling their time with whatever forms of empty activity keep them from being bored.

The Excess and Monotony of Novelty

Non plus ultra - "nothing beyond measure." According to legend, this maxim was inscribed on the Herculean columns on the cliffs of the Gibraltar Strait, symbolically marking the limits of the Mediterranean ecumene. On the philosophical dimension, *non plus ultra* expresses the idea of perfection, harmony, and balance between Heaven and Earth. Harmony and order (one of the meanings of the Greek word κόσμος) were established by the Divinities at the beginning of time and the cosmos. In Hinduism, the universal law of the due is called Dharma. The notion of the due is also tied to the greater fate of the world, as in the Germanic-Scandinavian tradition's *Wyrd* (an analogue of Dharma) and *orlog* (fate and prescribed debt, the due) or Ragnarök, the Fate of the Lords (the Divinities, the Aesir). The Germanic example especially emphasizes the eschatological and dramatic character of the world's fate and is directly linked to the loss of harmony, regularity, measuredness, and law.

A world that has lost the Divine dimension (or more accurately, has been closed off from it) is ruled by the Titanic powers that seduce and ensnare the human being. As Friedrich Georg Jünger aptly summed up this situation: "Where there are no Gods, there are Titans." The essence of the Titanic is unbound hubris, excess, greed, disharmony (chimeras, imperfections), materiality, all manifest in mechanicism and endless processualism (the curse of Sisyphus). With regards to craft and *poiesis*, the matter at hand is the Gestell, which is expressed in a permanent striving for the new. Titanism is *plus ultra* - above and beyond all measure.[41]

But the "new" becomes problematic. The latter sense of the "new" should not be confused with a "newly" produced, handcrafted thing which in essence reproduces one and the same thing that has lost its functionality. The creation of another or "one more" thing is not yet the creation of a novelty. The essence of novelty is connected with the idea of progress, with the notion that what is new is qualitatively superior to the old, i.e., the "new" is something better, a qualitative category associated with the era of Modernity, in which whatever is new is superior to the imperfect, rough handicraft. Complexity turns from a technical characteristic into an axiology, which in turn leads to a moral-ethical assessment of things (moral obsolescence) and innovations, including society itself. Ultimately, the new strives towards a polarity with regards to the old, that is the "already former", to the framing of what has never been, to the absolute novelty of the unprecedented, whereby the problem of "novelty" is transferred from the domain of technical and axiological complexity into the sphere of emotions, hype, and hysterical delight with the "unprecedented." The semiurgy of the post-industrial era greatly simplifies the introduction, multiplication,

---

41 It is interesting to note that in the 16th century, when the active conquest of the New World and the installation of the era of Modernity began, Charles V changed the motto *"Non plus ultra"* on the Spanish coat-of-arms to *"Plus ultra"*.

and circulation of the new, as it separates novelty from the immediate thing and its characteristics, instead placing ever greater emphasis on the sign and PR-hype around the event of a novelty's premiere. Products themselves — cars, phones, gadgets, updates, add-ons, etc. — might not contain any fundamental novelty, but instead only augment the functions they already carry out, or they might even offer the old under the guise of the new.[42] This is no longer of importance, for the focus of attention is shifted to the consumerism of signs, to the demonstration of consuming products that mark lifestyle, status, subculture, and complicity in all current trends.

The Traditionalist approach to solving the problem of introducing the new is reflected in the verses of the German poet Stefan George's *Das Wort*, in which we see a succinct expression of *poiesis* and the matrix of any demiurgy as such — poetic, artistic, and handicraft:[43]

Из далей чудеса и сны Я нёс в предел моей страны	Wunder von ferne oder traum Bracht ich an meines landes saum	Wonder or dream from distant land I carried to my country's strand
Ждал норны мрачной чтоб она Нашла в ключе их имена —	Und harrte bis die graue norn Den namen fand in ihrem born —	And waited till the twilit norn Had found the name within her bourn —
Схватить я мог их цепко тут Чрез грань теперь они цветут...	Drauf konnt ichs greifen dicht und stark Nun blüht und glänzt es durch die mark...	Then I could grasp it close and strong It blooms and shines now the front along...
Раз я из странствий шёл назад Добыв богатый нежный клад	Einst langt ich an nach guter fahrt Mit einem kleinod reich und zart	Once I returned from happy sail, I had a prize so rich and frail,

---

42 Such is "pseudo-event-dispensing".

43 Martin Heidegger, "The Nature of Language" in *On the Way to Language*, trans. Peter D. Hertz (New York: Harper & Row Publishers, 1982), 60.

Рекла не скоро норна мне: «Не спит здесь ничего на дне»	Sie suchte lang und gab mir kund: So schläft hier nichts auf tiefem grund	She sought for long and tidings told: "No like of this these depths enfold."
Тут он из рук моих скользнул Его в мой край я не вернул...	Worauf es meiner hand entrann Und nie mein land den schatz gewann...	And straight it vanished from my hand, The Treasure never graced my land...
Так я скорбя познал запрет: Не быть вещам где слова нет	So lernt ich traurig den verzicht: Kein ding sei wo das wort gebricht.	So I renounced and sadly see: Where word breaks off no thing may be.

Heidegger draws attention to this poem with a question: "What are words, that they have such power?"[44] Heidegger then conveys: "But the word does not give reasons for the thing. The word allows the thing to presence as a thing."[45] In this lies the special magic of the word: bringing a thing to presence as such, allowing a thing to be as it is in the word. Yet, the origin of a thing might be altogether fabulous, fantastical, or dreamlike (*traum*).

In the second stanza, someone addresses "the gray-haired Norn" (*die graue norn*), one of the three woman who weave the threads of fate, so that she find at the bottom the key of the word for a thing brought from afar or from a dream. This old Norn is possibly Urðr, whose name means "Became" (the grammatical past perfect) and is related to the Old Icelandic verb *verða* - "becoming", "being." From the very same word comes the name of the second Norn, Verðandi, or "Happening" (present continuous), while the third Norn is Skuld, or "Following." As soon as the Norn first finds and raises the word from the bottom, the thing becomes present. The new, unknown thing can come into being, become a being, come into its own; after all, the words at hand are about bringing it from somewhere into its

---

44 Heidegger, *On the Way to Language*, 141.

45 Ibid., 151.

native land ("*mein land*") if the appropriate word can be found for it from the past, from Tradition. Otherwise, in the case that no suitable word is found at the bottom, the thing dissolves and, we can assume, it is already a new thing which has no equivalent in Tradition, or it is an empty, exposed simulacrum.

The aspiration for constant, uniform improvement, the growth of quantitative and qualitative factors and the nomenclatures of goods, and the complication of processes and mechanisms was accounted for and described by Gregory Bateson as the "monotonic process", akin to a strictly monotonic function in mathematics, which is always increasing.[46] We often encounter such functions as illustrations of the growth of indices on graphs and charts. The monotonic function is the idealistic expression of progressist aspirations: constant, stable, unlimited, irreversible growth and expansion. In the socio-political sphere, this is first and foremost the capitalist system, which ensures production and financial speculation, as well as the extremely progressist ideologies of Liberalism and Marxism. The broad spectrum of Third Way ideologies is also in solidarity with the idea of progress, but tries to clothe or reconcile such with traditionalist and conservative settings, which is a false path of compromise.

One textbook example of a monotonic process is the ascending graph representing the onset of scientific and technological singularity. Moving to the right end of the time scale, i.e., into the future, the quantity of scientific discoveries and the implementation of new technologies, as well as their cost and size reductions, will increase over ever decreasing periods of time. When the curved line straightens upwards into vertical take-off, we have the moment of singularity, the convergence of all scientific, technological, and socio-economic branches and relationships in the shortest possible instant of time (per Raymond Kurzweil). After this point, neither man nor human society will ever again be the same as they were right up to this instant.

---

46   See Gregory Bateson, *Mind and Nature: A Necessary Unity* (1979).

Bateson pointed out that in real life monotonic processes are fatal, leading to the death of both organic systems and mechanisms. For example, a constant increase in steam pressure in the boiler of a steam locomotive leads to an imbalance in its mechanisms, and hence to explosion. The increasing rate of a structure's vibrating elements leads to a destructive resonance. In reality, thus, monotonic processes and progress, understood as broadly as possible, need to be compensated for, such as when steam is released, fuel supplies are paused, excess energy is diverted, and vibrations are stopped. The point of technological singularity can be seen as the desired achievement of maximal monotony and the refined balancing of the system in order to reach "design capacity."

However, it is the vertical trajectory of development that always remains fundamental. On the coordinate grid, from the lower left corner to the upper right, a moral-evaluative scale is immediately set up: from the lower, inferior past to the higher, superior future. The very idea of progress and its ideal monotonic tempo are not questioned or revised. Sure, there might indeed arise problems, the adepts of development say, but these are problems of expenditures, balancing, and stress relief within the system (whether of an engineering or social structure), and not problems of the system itself and its scale of values. This is the domain of the axiom of science-intensive faith.

Another example of monotonic processualism is the theory of biological and social evolution, starting with Democritus and moving forward with Lamarck, Darwin, Engels, and the synthetic theory of evolution. To compensate for some of its gaps, modern evolutionary theory includes such actors as catastrophes (as in catastrophe theory), extinctions, and mutations in order to clarify the evolutionary process and let off the steam of contradictions and gaps along the classic hyper-linear scale. Evolutionist theories demonstrate, among other things, a vivid example of the usurpation of history by ensnaring it in a web of interpretations. The entire history of life on Earth is seen as the more or less progressive evolution of organisms and, later, social systems. The world, living organisms, people, and societies have throughout history striven towards the present day, to the bright lights of screens, comfort, and the achievements of science. Consciousness of this striving is attributed to the thinking of the ancients and is imposed upon the historical development of all societies, just like Eurocentrism. The contemporal moment of the modern West, starting with Durkheim, Spencer, and Comte, who ideologically replicated the imperative of creationism's exclusivity, is declared to be a universal, general ideal to which all societies aspire. The West and Modernity are idealized chronologically: the history of European peoples led to Modernity, to the contemporary moment, because it could not lead elsewhere, for such was an objective, logical process. It is also idealized spatially: the barbaric and underdeveloped non-Western peoples of the colonies are subject to modernization and Westernization. Migration from poor peripheries to the more developed metropolitan centers also derives its grounds and justification from this outlook.

Thus, the *"plus ultra"* and ὕβρις are emancipated. The ideas of universalism, progress, and development, first inlaid by Judeo-Christian creationism and matured in the Enlightenment, are sporadically diffused into all other societies as a universal norm. The thought of the possibility of some other, original, unique way of development, or the idea of no development in any direction, is discarded as irrelevant. Everyone wants to be the West, because it represents the modern, highly developed civilization on a planetary scale. This false historial, based on selective factology, marginal ancient thinkers, reductionism, and sadistic ethno-cultural genocide against the original identities of any and all peoples, whether European or non-European, has been planted over the centuries through education systems. The ordinary student or exceptional pupil, or simply any person with a modern secular education, is a devout epistemological racist and psychopathic maniac in their mental setup as adepts of progress. The triumph of globalization as the expansion and spread of the West in its (Post-)Modern version means the destruction of local identities (and the simulacrum of "glocalization"[47]) and a variation of the end of history. (Post) Modernity is everywhere and forever, the space of the globe has been engulfed and "ended", and the future is cancelled, for it has already arrived in the form of "today drawn out into tomorrow."

In the world of Tradition, we find images of monotony in the figure of Sisyphus and somewhat in repeated "monotonous" episodes of incessant suffering, such as the Titanic torments of Tantalus and Prometheus. Monotonic processes are essentially "sick" infinity, just like falling time. Upon accelerating, they ultimately expose monotony to be a form of all-consuming boredom of timelessness. The flow and consumption of new things, TV talk shows and series, games, and other media products are designed to distract the human from the essential questions of meaning and Being, to distract a person from being themself, i.e., Human. The flow of the new dilutes boredom and diverts attention, streaming people into the pleasant, womb-like slumber of a calmed mind.

False chronology can also be found in the history of the origins of the sciences and technologies, which are artificially made ancient, projected back into Antiquity. The fact that between the world of Modernity ("New Time") and the world of Antiquity (Tradition as a whole) lies not just a chronological distance, but a qualitative difference of radical opposites, is overlooked. For example, the roots of psychology are presumed to lie in Aristotle's teaching, or the basics of mechanics in Archimedes, just as modern mathematics is seen in Pythagoras' number (number as Divine). These are gross mistakings of qualitatively different substances and phenomena originating from different premises and living according to different laws and in different noetic universes and cultures. The origin of the modern sciences lies no deeper than the Renaissance, but the

---

47 Glocalization is the simultaneous combination of the opposite processes of globalization and localization/regionalism, i.e., global networks, logistics and technologies + local values, culture and aesthetics. Such de facto implies a gradual, mild form of colonization and hybridization, not the preservation of local identity and tradition amidst the modernization of the production sphere.

logic of progress indicates that the aspiration for the developed and modern is "objective", and therefore eternal. Thus, facts are adjusted to fit the ideology of development, while all the facts which indicate that the great scholars and godfathers of the sciences were most deeply involved in occult, spiritual, and metaphysical mysteries and studies are ignored.[48]

If we turn from the problem of false treatments of history to spaces, we see a projection - or retrojection - of the progressist approach onto the historials of archaic cultures and peoples, like the anthropologists of the colonial era did. In their studies of "primitive" societies, anthropologists projected their own intellectual structures, stereotypes, and misconceptions regarding the historical process onto other cultures and traditions which had developed from altogether different premises and moved along their own authentic trajectories. If the 18th-19th century anthropologist saw hints or semblances of social relations, technological solutions, and behaviors similar to the new European ones, then he placed such into a hierarchy of the development of peoples in terms of their proximity to "civilization" and degree of involvement in development (or, conversely, their degree of "backwardness"). Thus, he retrojectively recreated, attributed, and sketched into a network of interpretations his reality in the past. Coupled with the false chronology of progress is the false understanding and ranking of the Other / Others, i.e., peoples, cultures, traditions, and religions, who are forced to submit to a foreign idea and suffer for their insufficient compliance with foreign ideals.[49]

Monotony opposes life as such, which it drives into the procrustean bed of progress, excluding as "primitivism" and

---

48 See E.R. Dodds, *The Ancient Concept of Progress and Other Essays on Greek Literature and Belief* (Oxford: Oxford University Press, 1973); V.A. Gutorov, *"Poniatie i kontseptsiia progressa v strukture antichnoi politicheskoi teorii"* [The Notion and Concept of Progress in the Structure of Ancient Political Theory]; R.V. Svetlov, *"Fukidid i illiuzii idei progressa"* [Thucydides and the Illusions of the Idea of Progress].

49 This situation mirrors and replicates the process of creationism's rise and spread throughout Europe and the world, only now in a new secular and scientific framing.

"childish naivety" the fundamental maxim that "societies do not develop, societies live."

Modernity appears before us as an upside down picture of the world. From the point of view of determinism, from the point of view of mechanics and chains, poetry and myth are an invasion of disorder, a violation of the design and integrity of a mechanism and its functioning, especially because they go beyond the logic of A=A. Defending myth and the sacred and rejecting the universalism, progress, and monotony of the Gestell is seen as obscurantism, as a desire for barbarism, as a radical form of "traditionism" and for all intents and purposes "fascism." The modern world, like the hypochthonic level of being, appears before us as a closed system which resists any higher standards (the original norms of unconcealment and harmony), demagogically interprets sacred order to be an invasion of chaos, shifts discourse onto moral and socio-political planes, and consistently represses the last normal humans still oriented towards higher values.

Titanic mechanicism serves progress as processualism aspiring towards monotony, whereas tradition and the sacred remove the problem of the "race for the production of goods and signs" by instead granting harmony and tranquility in ecstatic eternity and the moderation and cyclicality of life. Rushing into the abyss of things, progress cannot conceive of its own stop, which for it would mean death, madness, delirium, while traditional craft and life are in no hurry.

Progress persistently tries to convince us that it is destiny, that it is forever. But it is not. Ancient and still living archaic societies did not and do not know progress. Progress literally does not exist in their picture of the world and thinking. Attributing to such societies any aspiration for development is an obsessive suggestion and falsification of the history of ideas. Progress is one of the local and temporal ideas of the "New Age" of Modernity in accord with the law of universal involution, which has now attained planetary scale. Heidegger remarked that progress moves from the great to the little, and that the little can be inflated to enormous proportions while retaining littleness as its essence. Progress is not forever, it was not here before, and this means that it might not be in the future, and this further means that it can be overcome and discarded as an idea and a bad toy already right now.

For people oriented towards the sacred and towards authentic existence in the conditions of the incoming End, progress does not exist now. Blind faith in progressive development and a positive future is, among other things, the anthropological marker of those whom Friedrich Nietzsche in *Thus Spake Zarathustra* called the "last people."

Against Reality

The word "reality" that we use in everyday life to designate the whole beingful world, as a synonym for "world" in all of its dimensions, comes from the Latin word *"res"*, or "thing." Reality is derived from "thing", i.e., "thinghood", "substance", the "essence" of all that is.[50] Let us recall that the Germanic *ding* and Russian *veshch'* go back to the aristocratic Thing and Veche and are most intimately connected with *poiesis*. When speaking about the world of Tradition, we understand "reality" to mean myth, being oriented to the higher and sacred, the hierarchy of cosmic levels and estates in society, as well as a person's degree of spiritual perfection and realization.

We shall sharpen our attention to this notion not least because the very use of the word "reality" immediately, harshly delineates the real from the *unreal* (*irrealis*) and the *surreal* (*surréalisme*, the supra-real), i.e., the real as the empirically and physically given as opposed to the fairy-tale, the legendary, mythical, and imaginal. In the sense that we understand it in ordinary situations, reality is the modern concept, the reality

---

50 Let us clarify that the Greek term οὐσία, which was translated into Latin as *res*, means not only things as objects, as items, but beings as such. For example, the Divinities are beings (they exist, they are), but it cannot be said that they exist as items like Cartesian material objects.

of Descartes and Newton, the world of *res extensa* (of mere objects), and reality is "objectness", "objectivity", the world of physical energies, the natural laws of evolution and common sense. The real is what can be verified and is unfalsifiable (per Karl Popper). Creationism also has pretensions to "reality" with its hard apologetics for the historicity of Christ and the events described in the Bible. This impression is also grounded by the fact that Modernity is based on the secular and atheistic development of the basic premises already inlaid in creationism.

Looking at reality as an idea, as a concept, we can trace a number of its metamorphoses. In the world of Tradition, there is no "reality"; "reality" does not exist. And the converse is true: when we say "this is real" or "reality", we are not dealing with Tradition whatsoever, and in the "best" case such concerns the events of sacred Biblical history which have been confirmed by history and archaeology. This is the case because Tradition knows no division into "real" and "unreal", the latter understood to be everything fairy-tale-like and mythical. We might conditionally express this in the following manner: Tradition's "reality" is myth, i.e., permanent wonder and miracle, metamorphosis, talking animals, sacred groves of the Divinities inhabited by fauna, leshy, rusalki, the great Yule Cat, and the wandering spirits of the dead. It could be said that if everything is real, then there is no negative referent with respect to which one could construct some kind of division into real and unreal.

The strict delineation of real and unreal takes place in Modernity and bears the moral stamp of progressism. Tradition as the qualitative content of past epochs is cast off as unreal, as the tales of mankind's naive childhood, as a world of imagined beings, stories, Divinities, etc. In the best case, such is allotted a place in children's literature and fantasy, when in leisurely moments the rational mind can indulge in the fun of reading about imaginary, fantastical things that never happened. Only children and the elderly believe in such fairy tales and devilry - the young because they are uneducated and dumb, and the old because they have already lost their mind. Reality, as we have already said, is Newton's substance, Descarte's objectivity, the world of *ratio* and sober reason, the laboratory-world. The implantation of reality in the Enlightenment era was an offensive and mass genocide against traditions. Whoever appeals to reality is acting, consciously or not, against Tradition.

In Postmodernity, the next round of metamorphoses of the real takes place with the emergence of virtuality, from the Latin *virtualis*, "that which is possible." The fundamental trait of virtual reality is that it is created, and its existence depends on technology, computing power, gadgets, and interfaces for plugging in, connecting and communicating with a person. Virtual reality is a broad notion that includes visual interactive products (computer games, entertainment content), educational services, network environments, and the Internet as a whole. Within virtual spaces, it becomes possible to stimulate any fantastical and absolutely new landscapes, topographies, spaces, types of creatures, characters, laws of physics, societies, and development — all of which never existed in the real world of Modernity or in the myths of Tradition. Or, following the style of realism, virtuality can thoroughly replicate the real world down to the smallest details.

It would be more accurate to see virtual reality not as an interactive media add-on to computer technology, but as an actual parallel reality, where everything that is potentially possible (virtual in the ontological sense) can be (and with a high degree of probability already has been) embodied in a specific locus of virtual space. At the same time, the reality of the virtual remains a form of illusion, a hallucination, since the realms and objects of the virtual world are not objects, but the derivatives of computational processes (physical reactions on a panel or board) and rendering. The realest part of the virtual world is the hardware. In an altered state of consciousness, such as during a psychedelic experience, everything illusory is perceived by the delirious person as real, beholdable, and tactile. Everything is extremely convincing: even UFOs, even gravity, even human rights, even 3D avatars in a computer game, even a falling apple.

Virtuality is the ideal embodiment of the rhizome in the form of the screen and its false imaging depth (the projection of 3D computing onto a 2D plane). It feeds on the possibility of the impossible and the reality of the unreal without violating physical laws and common sense; it allows for "surfing" without friction and a nature of playful interaction.

Just as the concept of reality in its time demarcated the real from myth, displacing the latter into the margins and periphery, so does virtuality in Postmodernity attack the real of Modernity, but it does so in a different way. Modernity dealt with Tradition directly and harshly, treating it like obscurantism and ignorance of the mind, whereas Postmodernity acts gently, playfully, and friendly. It says: Yes, there is natural reality, the material world, and here is virtuality; you can relax in it, dive into it and escape; or, even better, here is augmented reality, a combination of the real world and virtual projections on screens, glasses, and mirrors. And here is the interactive contact of QR codes and layouts, the export of real life into a virtual newsfeed, the mutual integration of smart services and spaces, online information panels, real-time references about an object when you point a smartphone camera at it, an audio guide application, a fitness tracker synchronizing your physiological data with a sever, and so on and so on. Augmented reality is treated as improved reality, while the old reality of Modernity is unobtrusively marked as morally obsolete. Think about it: it is not a thing that is being declared morally obsolete, but fundamental reality, even if only that of Modernity.

Looking back, we find an analogous pattern in deism, which is subtly predominant among many contemporary pagans. For example, when the latter defend and justify the truth of the pagan heritage, the truth of the mythical and metaphysical provisions of Tradition, they often do so by drawing upon the theories and discoveries of fundamental physics. Zen koans and the paradoxes of the correlation between Being and Becoming (Parmenides and Heraclitus) are justified with reference to quantum entanglement. The Buddhist idea of Śūnyatā, the

Great Void that is the foundation and essence of the universe, is explained to be an ancient premonition of the void that reigns between the atoms of matter. Heraclitus' teaching that fire is the source of everything is deemed a prediction of the Big Bang. The Germanic Thor's Megingjord is the asteroid belt around Saturn (his Roman counterpart) after whom the planet was named. And the statue of Shiva-Nataraja at CERN symbolizes the endless motion of the particles of matter that maintains the universe just like the Deity's endless dance. And so on and so on.

The general pattern is such that ancient thinkers and their ideas are presented as exactly the same as we contemporary people and our ideas, as if they already knew both common and avant-garde scientific truths but simply described them in a different language — "and now that science has reached its highest stage of development, we see that ancient knowledge and scientific knowledge finally coincide." Here lurks the substitution and ignorance of deism, wherein the self-sufficient and total paradigm of myth and Tradition is reduced to an historically early analogue of modern scientific knowledge. In deism, the truth of something traditional is based in and justified only through science, hence the very "reality" of Tradition (of myth) ends up in the position of something inferior, incapacitated, and flawed, something that needs any and all crutches of scientific reinforcement. Myth is reduced to literary allegories for *a priori* dominant scientific knowledge. The scale of values is set by Modernity, and the concept of progress is thrown onto and into the past.

Here is an absolutely analogous structure: "Yes, Tradition is real, but let us improve and ground it through science, then it will be better, more pleasant, and won't irritate us with its contradicting of the scientific method." Postmodernity simply takes this logic to the end, turning it around on Modernity itself. Postmodernity proposes something better than reality itself. Such is not a return to Tradition, but rather is, among other things, a toying with relicts and fragments of traditional forms, simulacra, and hallucinations.

Man lived and inhabited this world poetically: through wonder, astonishment, horror, and being oriented towards the sacred, creation, art, and war. Instead of the deeply entrenched word "reality", which imperatively divides and dictates what there genuinely is and what there is not, we can employ the Heideggerian *existential* of Dasein's "*in-der-Welt-sein*", "being-in-the-world."[51] In Russian there is also the word "*Yav'*" and its etymological derivatives - *iavnyi* (the manifest), *iavlennyi* ("manifest", "phenomenal"),and *iavit'sia* ("to appear"), i.e., to come out into the world, to find and disclose oneself.

Man now lives and inhabits ecosystems of global digital services like Google, Yandex, the Chinese WeChat and Baidu, etc., which present a broad spectrum of online services, "real" gadgets, and offline services that close the lifeworld and everyday practices unto them. Also in this line are the sectors of online games like *Second Life*, which create an improved analogue of the world of the real in virtuality, or the numerous fantasy MMORPG alternatives to this world. Such ensure the circulation of traffic, data, signs, attention, money, time, and people in the closed-off niches of corporations which blur the boundaries between the strictly online and offline world (the best augmented reality).

From this follows a natural, logical conclusion for Traditionalists: revolting against the modern world means revolting against reality. It is a fundamental gesture of rejecting the "real" and, accordingly, augmented reality in favor of another. This is not because we are missing something in "reality", such as miracles, which we can add in and then be satisfied with and accept this world, but because we do not need "reality" as such, installed as it is on absolutely alien ontological foundations.

The imperative of every pagan is to re-enchant the world. Every pagan now finds themself facing the problem of will to the sacred in a post-sacred world.

---

51   See Martin Heidegger, *Being and Time*.

Waking Up Before Midnight

Of fundamental importance to a people and a human being is the notion of a homeland: a place whence originates one's kind, space, and nature, in whose maternal womb his people came about and which they reflect in their culture. A homeland is a person's home, a place of authentic rootedness in the land under its own sky, surrounded by its Divinities and loved ones, including one's deceased ancestors.

But, in addition to the spatial dimension of a homeland corresponding to the spatial question of "Where?" and the embodiment of *topos* (τόπος) with respect to the existential of being-present-in-the-world, a homeland also has a temporal dimension corresponding to the question of "When?", the embodiment of *chronos* (χρόνος), that is the temporal dimension of being present. Dwelling in one's homeland is dwelling in authentic space and time.

On the basis of diverse teachings, it can be said that the core of temporal authenticity in the mythological pictures of different peoples can be constituted by different events. For the Greeks, this would be the Golden Generation of Hesiod and the Divinities' victory over the Titans in the Titanomachia, the establishment of order in the cosmos. For the predominantly agricultural culture of the Slavs, this would be the agrarian cycle of being, being in the cycle of dying and resurrecting time. For the Germanics, the nerve lies on the horizon of eschatology, in the final battle between the Aesir, the Einherjar, and the Jotunns and army of the dead.

Looking around us, we see that spatially we are now "nowhere", in "no place" (α-τόπος, or, in Heidegger's words, which we will discuss later, in a state of homelessness). The surrounding industrial reality and technology, especially screens, replace the genuine environment of the manifest world. The Gestell is an alienating mediator between people and between people and nature. Temporally, we finds ourselves amidst the "never", the "not-ever", in the timelessness and historiography of empty time (and even foreign calendars and hierohistories), of bored Dasein in the absence of the Event of Coming-to-Be.

In the teachings of Zen, *satori* (enlightenment, awakening, cf. *samadhi* in Hinduism) is described as the direct experience of one's genuine nature *present here and now*. With regards to our situation and path, we can speak of "*black satori*", "Black Awakening", or awakening and residing in a not-here and not-now - *not where we must be, and not when we must be.* We speak of a negative self-determination in space and time with respect to authenticity, of a *black mode of awakening*, an experiencing of genuine nature when our localization in space and time are conducive to the total opposite.

All of the above-said, as well as what we have considered many times in other places, leads us to describe our current moment in a series of issues and imperatives for understanding:

I. Finding ourselves in the lower left sector of the Year-Wheel, we nevertheless cannot clearly say how far away the point of the End is from us. The thickened, vacuous time of night could continue for infinitely long, and everything will end without the onset of the End itself (i.e., the end would not be an event, but a process, an eternal "not yet") until the last individuals, after all the rest around them, forget about any movement in any direction, about time and teleology, about eschatology, remaining instead in the hypnotic captivity of one or another futurological concept or the fantasy world of role-playing games.

II. On the other hand, the infinite dragging on of time might conceal the opposite: the incredible nearness of the End. The End might come about literally any second, in any instant amidst the here and now. This is the enigma of time, and a pause between this second of the here "not-yet-End" and the next second of the not-here "already-happened-End" might constitute the very qualitative emptiness of the duration from the first point. The density of time reaches its maximal significance in the very last instant, like the darkest night before sunrise.

90

III. Hence the fundamental imperative of our situation: we live in the interlude of a great "between" in the End of Times, in the midst of the darkness of night, always a second before Midnight. To presume that the End will come about in our age would be extreme optimism. It is more likely that not even our distant great-grandchildren will see the End.

IV. The "rebirth" of paganism and Traditionalism in our days finds itself in the situation of waking up in "hell", in the midst of the unleashed and unfolding abyss of chthonic and Titanic powers and concealed Divinities. Paganism's current awakening is akin to coming back to consciousness right before one's moment of death, the eschatological end of which traditions speak. Hence the fundamental posing of the cornerstone question of the death of the world and the position of paganism/Traditionalism towards this world and its death.

To live and practice Tradition while pretending that "everything is normal, nothing has changed", or to claim that "there is no fundamental problem, Tradition and Modernity are fully compatible", is the grossest mistake, a lie, and a complete misunderstanding of both Tradition and the current moment.

On a somewhat different matter and in a different context, Heidegger put forth a phrase which can rightly be applied to this situation: "The flight into tradition, out of a combination of humility and presumption, achieves, in itself, nothing, is merely a closing the eyes and blindness towards the historical moment."[52]

Yet, the majority of pagans, even those familiar with these questions and problems, confidently tend towards conformism — "we have to live in the present moment, and we need to live well." Such a paganism has next to no prospects for authenticity.

V. The aspiration to flee into the past, which is understood literally, as if a human could go back in time like they go down

---

52   Martin Heidegger, "The Age of the World Picture" in idem, *Off the Beaten Track*, 72.

a forest path, is impossible. On the other hand, the utopianism of the Enlightenment and all possible versions of a positive future based on *ratio* are irrelevant to us.

VI. The situation of the instant before death, the instant before Midnight (the Yule of the universe) poses the question: which Divinities are responsible for this moment? The Divinities of Midnight, i.e., those who in the Tantric Trimurti correlate with the era of of the Kali-Yuga, the Divinities of Destruction and Death. The Divinities of the sphere of Thanatos, as well as the Divinities of the Dionysian circle, i.e., those who descend into the lower worlds of the dead, go into concealment, die and resurrect. In the Greek tradition, the world of the dead, Hades (Ἀΐδης), means "unseen", and the Deity Hades is depicted on bas-reliefs with his face turned away from the viewer. And there is Dionysus, the suffering, dying Deity who returns into the world. In the Indian tradition, this is Shiva, Bhairava, Kali, and Durga. In the Germanic-Scandinavian tradition: Wotan/Odin, the ecstatic Deity of Death and Wisdom who sacrifices himself to himself, as well as the Goddess Freya, the Mother of the Fallen.[53]

The Divinities of Death reign in the World Night. Today, therefore, their cult is the most legitimate. Due destruction happens with their sanction. Moreover, the Divinities of Death are almost always also Divinities of Wisdom, which leads one to suspect the *special eschatological character of this knowledge.*

VII. The doctrine of monism postulates that the world is the manifestation of the Divine. Consequently, in the era of the End, the world is the manifestation of the Divinity of Death, and the world itself is a corpse. Hence a number of risky and seizing hypotheses, such as: (a) if the world is simply a corpse, like a dead, rotting human, then everything has de facto already ended and is simply decomposing until some final point when the bones scatter as dust; or (b) the corpselike state of the world

---

53   See Askr Svarte, *Gods in the Abyss.* One of Odin's names is *Bǫðgæðir* ("Promoter of Battle"), that is the patron of strife and war, which coincides with the description of the Wolf Age presented in the Prophecy of the Völva (*Vǫluspá*).

refers us to an image that is widespread in shamanism, where a shaman who has obtained initiation or departed on a journey (a variation of concealment) lies down for several days as if he were dead and does not react to anything. The Germanic-Scandinavian tradition says that Odin went on such journeys, on which he would lie down as dead.[54]

VIII. In any case, this leads us to the necessity and inevitability of perceiving today's world and time like a *shmashan*[55] or kurgan, which demands from us a due and correct conceptualization of everything happening around us, of the place and position in which we — me, you, paganism, and Traditionalists — find ourselves. The due is due to be fulfilled, the world must head to its End, to death and destruction. For now, there is only protracted cooling down and falling. It is impossible to tolerate this as hitherto — and it will no longer be as it is. The new Golden Age or Other Beginning lies behind the veil of infinite endlessness.

Whoever does not understand and share these imperatives, whoever turns away and brushes off such questions, does not understand the whole problem of time and the essence of Tradition all the way to the end. In essence, they do not (yet) represent anything. *Fata volentem ducunt, nolentem trahunt.*[56]

***

The reader who is encountering such a posing of questions for the first time might have the false impression that our position on the fulfillment of the due and eschatological inferno is equivalent to that of Gnosticism, which rejects the world. It bears briefly dispelling this misconception by turning to the structural points of dissonance between our positions and those of Gnostics:

---

54 See the *Younger Edda* and Mircea Eliade's *Shamanism: Archaic Techniques of Ecstasy.*

55 In India, a *shmashan* is a place for ritual cremation as well as a dwelling for radical Aghori ascetics who worship Shiva in his most terrifying forms.

56 "Fate leads the willing, drags the unwilling."

I. Gnostics deny the world any value in any period of time or at any stage of the cycle, since it was originally created by a false and foolish Demiurge-God (Saklas or Yaldabaoth).

Pagan Traditionalism does not deny the value of the world as such. Moreover, we do not consider our Divinities to be stupid bastards and demonic beings. Our Divinities are good and powerful, some of them are subtle and gentle, while others are frightening and menacing.

It can be asserted with full confidence that we reject the value of the contemporary world of Modernity and Postmodernity as a form of decline, degradation, and deformation of the primordially blessed, good, and Sacred-full world when and wherein people and the Divinities lived without hiding or concealing themselves from one another. We reject these paradigms' claim to totality and to a lack of alternative to their interpretations and machinations.

II. Gnostics insist on a radical and irreducible dualism between ignorant creation (the Sethians' *kenoma*) and the divine plentitude of the pleroma, the realm of Barbelo and the God Abraxas.

Radical and insurmountable dualism is a feature of the ontology of creationism, and it is thus quite logical that Gnosticism would manifest itself in subsequent history as a multiplicity of both Christian and anti-Christian sects. Such is a purely inner-Abrahamic problem. The early Gnostics were actively exposed as dualists by the Neoplatonists.

The doctrine of manifestationism holds that the world is a manifestation of the Divine. The positions of holism and monism indicate to us the need for harmony between the spiritual and the material dimensions.

III. Characteristic of Gnosticism is the notion that there is a limited number of special people (pneumatics) who will escape the world and return to the *pleroma*, while all the rest, including the world itself, will be left on their own like an empty, sealed pot.

The idea of "salvation" as escape from this world to some other, radically different and perfect world, while this world is left as some separate object left to its own fate, is not characteristic of paganism. There are hierarchies, both estate and spiritual, and degrees of initiation in accordance with which wisdom is revealed to a person. In some sense, the fate of this world is a knot of the fates of peoples, Divinities, and natures. When speaking of the Other, we do not mean a space outside of some seeming "prison", but rather we understand such to be something that is revealed here instead of what exists now.

IV. Knowledge of one's divine nature, of the illusoriness of matter, passions, and the falseness of other Divinities (such as the archons who rule the world and enslave people in spiritual fetters) is the essence of gnosis, which provides a person with an outcome.

In the Gnostic picture of the world, the pagan Divinities are archons who keep souls in this world and do not allow the elect to be freed. In paganism itself, however, the Divinities are good and each of them patronizes their own craft, space, and is responsible for certain "functions" in the overall cosmos. Gnostic teachings on the illusoriness of matter and on true Divinehood are somewhat similar to the teachings of Advaita-Vedanta and Tantrism, but the latter do not have any insurmountable dualism, "chosenness", or demonization of various Divinities as "servants of a bastard deity." Therefore, such superficial comparisons do not wield any deep identity.

In speaking of the fact that our moment in time is under the patronage of the Divinities of Death, which means that the world must die and everything must end, we are never saying that we ourselves should flee or escape to another, higher world and therefrom observe the infernal torment of the rest of humanity and "cursed" creation. On the contrary, our place is in the world, and by recognizing its fate we recognize our own. In this lies the essence of reconciling with the world: common fate instead of the pathology of fundamental rejection (as in Gnosticism) or striving for endless improvement (Titanic processualism).

It is also necessary to issue a remark that goes beyond the strictly Gnostic and which concerns an alleged equivalence between our approach and radical creationism. We do not insist on the destruction of the pole of the Earth, the pole of matter and the space of chthonic powers, as the supporters of a radical Apollonian position do. We do not want only Heaven to be left without Earth. We want measure and patriarchal, hierarchical order. Heaven is above. The Earth is below. Man and peoples are children of the Divinities symbolized by the Tree, a Dionysian unification of poles.

Manifestationism thus differs from the radical dualism of the Gnostics and creationism (Uranopolitism in Orthodoxy or the messianic-eschatological expectations of the Mahdi in Islam, etc.). The pole of the Earth is important for paganism in many respects, from the metaphysical and authoritative (the space of the Sovereign) to the artisanal (the matter of a thing per Aristotle) and agrarian. It is also necessary to take into account the ideology of the third estate, which upholds the structural integrity of Tradition. Even when we are completely focused on questions of Heaven and the One, it bears keeping in mind and in the horizons of sight love for the Earth, for the feminine metaphysical poles expressed by the figures of Aphrodite and Freya, Demeter and Frigga.[57]

***

Archetypal Figures

The idea of progress and treating the world as ready-to-hand can be associated with several archetypal figures and Gestalts (per Ernst Jünger) which became leading and iconic in the European culture of Modernity. They have inspired supporters of both liberalism and Marxism, the *a priori* progressive ideologies, as well as supporters of the "Third Way" and conservatives. They have been used for apologetics for the paradigm of Modernity with reference to Antiquity, and upon them have been built

---

57 See Julius Evola's *Eros and the Mysteries of Love: The Metaphysics of Sex* on the Aphroditic and Demetric types of femininity.

a false historial of objective, successive progress and the special role of modern man with his creation of development and civilization in the world. In their times and contexts, some of these figures were marginalia, tales of Titanic failure followed by inevitable punishment (Prometheus, Icarus), while others illustrated transitional movements in modern history (Goethe's Faust, Jünger's "Worker"). Through these examples, we can trace how hubris-based inferiority, failure, and the Gestell have been installed and raised to the norm of archetypes, and how the genuine heroism of Achilles and ecstatic or ascetic sacrality have been replaced by altogether modern production types.

Prometheus and his Humans

The name Προμηθεύς means "thinking ahead", "fore-thinking." Prometheus is the brother of Epimetheus ("after-thinking"), the son of the Titan Iapetus and the Oceanid Clymene (according to Hesiod).

Hesiod's *Theogony* sets forth a late mythological tradition of plots about Prometheus in the context of the regression of human generations and the changing of metaphysical ages. Prometheus, who acts on the side of the Divinities in the Titanomachia, took favor to humans and decided to deceive Zeus in the dividing up of the carcass of a sacrificial bull at Mekone. By cunning, he made Zeus choose the worst part of the offering (the bones and fat), leaving the good meat for people. For this deceit, Zeus deprived people of fire, which Prometheus stole back and gave to humans, thereby violating the will of the Thunderer.

In the *Protagoras* dialogue, Plato retells this story in the following way. Prometheus' brother, Epimetheus, distributed qualities and gifts to all living beings, but out of a misunderstanding he gave the wrong lot to man. Prometheus then stole fire and the skills of Hephaestus and Athena, and gave the knowledge of crafts to people. But he could not give them the law of living together in community which Zeus processed. Seeing the increasing lawlessness and quarrels between men who could not live together, Zeus sent Hermes to establish truth and shame among men to strengthen their relations and become law. Athena and Hephaestus' skill and Zeus' truth together made people complicit in the Divine lot.

Prometheus' sympathy for mankind is revealed in the story of the origin of the last (fifth) human generation with whom Hesiod wished he did not have to spend his time. According to this myth, after the flood that destroyed the previous generation, Prometheus created people out of fire, earth, and clay, but they turned out to be defective and imperfect. Athena or Zeus then breathed Spirit into them, thereby finally making them into humans, hence their twofold nature and the name of their generation, "Promethean." Prometheus loved and cared for this mankind (the "last people"), but his rebellion against the law and will of Zeus for humans' sake only caused them more suffering. For the theft of fire, Zeus sent Pandora and instructed Hephaestus to chain Prometheus to a cliff in Colchis, where an eagle pecks at his liver every day.

Prometheus' punishment is the subject of the famous tragedy by Aeschylus, *Prometheus Bound*, which radically differs from the Greek's predominantly solar-Divine orientation versus anti-divine Titanism. Aeschylus sings praises of Prometheus and exalts his feat, but remains silent on the grief that he brought to people. Aeschylus therefore differs radically from Hesiod, in whose work Zeus sees Prometheus' tricks in advance. Hesiod's story is a story of the fall, whereas Aeschylus is optimistic about progress and Prometheus' gifts to people:

> One short word sums up all you need to know:
> all human arts derive from Prometheus.[58]

Prometheus continues to taunt Zeus and predicts his fall — as the Seer, he knows this secret. For refusing to give it up and for his impudence towards Hermes, Zeus casts Prometheus into Tartarus, whither he falls while uttering words typical of a genius of deceit and lies:

---

58 Aeschylus, *Prometheus Bound*, trans. Deborah H. Roberts (Indianapolis: Hackett Publishing Company, 2012), 516-517.

This onslaught from Zeus
comes at me openly
to fill me with fear.
O my revered mother,
O sky, whose encircling
light we all share,
you see:
how unjustly I suffer![59]

The figure of Prometheus, with his message of rebellion against the supreme power of the Deity Zeus and his proximity to human suffering, gained popularity in the age of the Enlightenment. Prometheus became a symbol of struggle against tyranny and authority, including religion. Prometheus was seen as a humanist, the giver of reason (*ratio*), Modernity, and the patron of progress. He was praised by Percy and Mary Shelley, and Byron's "Prometheus" depicted the idea of the light of rational reason and development leading humanity to prosperity:

Thy Godlike crime was to be kind,
To render with thy precepts less
The sum of human wretchedness,
And strengthen Man with his own mind...[60]

Here, the Titan's gift of crafts to man are identified with progress in the field of technology and the Industrial Revolution. Enthusiasm for Prometheus was also expressed by Karl Marx, who went on to author a thoroughly materialist philosophy. Prometheus was also proclaimed to be a role model by Adolf Hitler, and in the United States of America the figure of his brother Atlas became the personification of the radical liberal-capitalist ideas of Ayn Rand's objectivism. According to Friedrich Georg Jünger, Prometheus is the eternal instigator, the embodiment of incessant, active becoming and the desire for the new (without completing the old, the already initiated). The passage of the prophecy of Zeus' fall is often interpreted

---

59   Ibid., 1106-1113.

60   Lord Byron, "Prometheus", *Poetry Foundation* [https://www.poetryfoundation.org/poems/43843/prometheus-56d222b61d799].

as the onset of the *"Gestalt of the Worker"*, to use Jünger's term, that is the era of machines in whose Titanic noise the Divinities do not dwell and from which they withdraw:

> *Such is the challenger he's making ready*
> *for himself, a marvel difficult to fight,*
> *who will find a flame more powerful than lightning,*
> *with a noise that overwhelms the thunderclap, a*
> *nd will break to bits the trident of Poseidon,*
> *earth-shaking sea spear. Dashed against this evil,*
> *Zeus will learn how far rule is from slavery.*[61]

Friedrich Georg Jünger writes of Prometheus thusly:

> Compared to his father Iapetus, Prometheus appears an innovator. He stands out from his circle and he stands alone. Although he belongs to the Titans, he advises Zeus in the battle waged against him. He moves way from his Titanic essence in its original form, diverges from it. But he is just as distant from the Divinities, and in connection with this stands the fact that he appears a loner; from all sides he is illuminated by light.[62]

Where there are no Divinities, there are Titans. He who takes the technological message-gift of Prometheus to the extreme in the light of the *ratio* of Modernity is Zeus' adversary.

Icarus

Another figure of this sort from antiquity was the great master engineer and craftsman Daedalus, the creator of the labyrinth in Crete where the bastard son of King Minos, the Minotaur, was imprisoned. Languishing in captivity at Minos, Daedalus decided to flee the island to his native Hellas. "The heavens are free, let us fly aloft them!", the master exclaimed as he proceeded to create something unprecedentedly new: wings made of wax and feathers in the likeness of birds. Having crafted the wings, Daedalus instructed Icarus on how to fly with them:

> *"Let me warn you, Icarus,*
> *to take the middle way,*

---

61 Aeschylus, *Prometheus Bound*, 925-930.

62 Friedrich Georg Jünger, *Grecheskie mify* [Greek Myths].

100

in case the moisture weighs down your wings,
if you fly too low,
or if you go too high,
the sun scorches them.
Travel between the extremes…"[63]

Daedalus and Icarus successfully leave Crete, and while flying over the other islands, people mistake them to be unknown Divinities. Winged and inspired, Icarus violates his father's order to stay in the middle space and, playing too far, rises steeply up towards the sun. The fiery disk of Apollo burns his wings and melts the wax that holds the feathers together, and Icarus falls into the sea.

The story of Icarus, the son of the great artisan Daedalus, is very revealing. Firstly, it emphasizes that people belong to the middle world. Even while in flight, Daedalus instructs his son to keep to the mid space and not descend to the water (the hypochthonic level) or ascend too far up to the sun. Secondly, for the Greeks, the sun was the face of Apollo. The Neoplatonists interpreted the Greek name *Apollon*, Ἀπόλλων, to be α-πολλα, that is "not-many", or the One, ἕν. Thirdly, Icarus' tragic case shows us how fascination with artificial wings, which are otherwise appropriate and function in the world of people as long as they are not taken to overstep limits, leads a person to approach excess and blindly attempt to rise to the Sun-Apollo. It is not artificial wings that ascend to the Divinities, but ecstatic inspiration of the mind and spirit. There is divine potential within man that no technology is capable of revealing, for technology is deeply rooted in the chthonic depths. In some sense, man ascends to the One only naked, i.e., cleansed of material aberrations and attachments. The illusory power of technology is fraught with deceit. For being entranced by technology, mankind pays with scorched wings and a grave in the depths of waters.

---

63   Ovid *Metamorphoses* VIII.183, trans. A.S. Kline.

Doctor Faust

The legends of Dr. Johann Faust outstripped the real figure already in the Reformation, around which time they became part of German culture and were often mentioned by diverse authors. But the story of Faust found its most complete and famous form in what would be the *opus magnum* of Johann Wolfgang von Goethe. Goethe himself is also reflected in *Faust* as a person who expressed his era and its contradictions. Like Johann Wolfgang himself, Goethe's scientist Faust is seized with passion over progress, the rigorous sciences, and the new picture of the world, but at the same time he is well-versed in alchemy, a connoisseur of grimoires, and even practices the invocations of theurgic magic. Thus, he correlates with the paradigm of the "Rosicrucian Enlightenment" described by Frances Yates, who attributes to the "founding fathers" of the natural sciences and Modernity a dualism of interests and aspirations, a state of transition and/or rift between the occult-mystical Renaissance and secular Modernity. The story of Faust illustrates man's final liberation from nostalgia for the past and how he finally comes to stand on the side of the New Time of Modernity.

At the beginning of *Faust*, the doctor is depicted as a man who has become "jaded" with knowledge, whom little satisfies anymore. In yet another attempt to overcome his apathy, Faust takes on translating the New Testament into German, and it is in this fragment of the work that the changes in the thinking and worldview of Enlightenment man are fully revealed. In the spirit of the deism of *Naturphilosophie*, Faust begins to not simply translate Scripture, but to correct it in the spirit of the times.

> It is written, "In the beginning was the Word. "
> How soon I'm stopped! Who'll help me to go on?
> I cannot concede that words have such high worth
> and must, if properly inspired,
> translate the term some other way.
> It is written: "In the beginning was the Mind. "
> Reflect with care upon this first line,

and do not let your pen be hasty!
Can it be mind that makes all operate?
I'd better write: "In the beginning was the Power!"
Yet, even as I write this down,
something warns me not to keep it.
My spirit prompts me, now I see a solution
and boldly write: "In the beginning was the Act."[64]

This passage reflects the shift in perceptions of the sacred (in this instance, in the context of Christianity) from philosophical and priestly (word and thought) to martial (strength) and, finally, artisanal (deed). Faust's interpretations echo the first steps of Ernst Jünger's "Worker", who is enraptured by the affairs of production and interprets everything else through this lens.

The doctor is distracted from further translating Scripture by an obsessive spirit, whose advice Faust follows to invoke Mephistopheles. Goethe portrays the Devil in this figure, but he also bears the markings of the Enlightenment. He enters the room dressed as a student, and he is slippery and not as omnipotent and unstoppable as some of the Titans. The Mephistopheles of Goethe's *Faust* is closest of all to a human and acts as a complete double of Faust himself. Mephistopheles introduces himself thusly:

I am the Spirit of Eternal Negation,
and rightly so, since all that gains existence
is only fit to be destroyed; that's why
it would be best if nothing ever got created.
Accordingly, my essence is what you call sin, destruction,
or — to speak plainly — Evil.[65]

Mephistopheles appears as the embodiment of nihilism: the line "spirit that is always used to denying" speaks not about the completion of negation at some point, but an endless process of negating and denying again and again, an eternal "no." Here the Devil mirrors the Titanism of becoming in the process of the nihilation of the beingful world, its taking-into-nothing.

---

64 Johann Wolfgang von Goethe, *Faust I & II*, trans. Stuart Atkins (Princeton: Princeton University Press, 2014),1224-1237.

65 Ibid., 1338-1344.

Mephistopheles proposes Faust a deal: the spirit promises Faust the fulfillment of all his desires, which are different from the dreams of ordinary people, but on the condition that he is to play this game forever. Faust and Mephistopheles agree that death will overtake the doctor at the height of his fame as soon as he exclaims "Moment, stop!" But the evil genius of nihilism knows no pauses and stops. Only the Divinities, who reside in eternity in heaven, far from the world of becoming, do. Man, freezing for a moment, is destroyed by the flow of time descending into the abyss. The connection between Mephistopheles and the New Time of Modernity is emphasized by the fact that, having changed his appearance, he instructs a student who accidentally looks at Faust on how to comprehend science, and at the same time explains how, in general, such is a pointless engagement. At the end of the conversation, he leaves the thirsty student an autograph that is a quotation from the Book of Genesis: "And you will be like God, knowing good and evil." Mephistopheles thus equates the science of the Enlightenment with the apple of the serpent of Eden.

Faust and the Devil embark on journeys to the edges of the world, visiting countries and eras and meeting along the way different people, mythical beings, Divinities, demons, emperors and kings. Over the course of their wanderings, Faust loses the nobility for which he had been revered by ordinary people at the beginning of the story, and indulges in deceit, adultery, lies, and so on. By the end of the drama, we meet already our contemporary Faust, who says of himself:

> I wish to rule and have possessions!
> Acts alone count — glory is nothing.[66]

Faust is already obsessed with pure action and realizing the will to power and property — fully in the spirit of the Protestant ethics of capitalism. He calls himself not a "likeness of God", but a "king of nature" who has rejected the desire to get rid of boredom in an impulse towards God, opting instead to remain within the element of matter. The combination of positive and

---

66 Ibid., 10187-10188.

negative will is resolved by the latter's victory, as the doctor closes himself off to Being, with which phase begins his fast track to death. Faust embraces the industrial idea of conquering the forces of nature. Watching the ebb and flow of the waves — a "useless waste of strength" — the spirit of the *Arbeiter* says:

> It can be done! - Although the tides may flood,
> when there's a hill they gently press beyond it;
> however arrogant their motions,
> the slightest mound confronts them proudly,
> the slightest depth attracts them to itself.
> And so I quickly worked out plans,
> resolving to obtain a precious satisfaction:
> to bar the shore to the imperious sea,
> narrow the limits of the ocean's great expanse,
> and force the waters back into themselves.
> I've worked out every step within my mind;
> this is what I want, what you must help me do![67]

Faust adventurously acquires for himself some coastal lands, where he unfolds a grandiose construction site to remodel the coast. Mephistopheles' servants, lemurs, build a huge palace, drain the swamps, and construct a dam. Faust is delighted by the sounds of shovels and the sight of crowds of workers, all the while as Mephistopheles has already given the order to dig his grave. Looking over his achievements, Faust pronounces the last dithyramb for man free from everything and capable of achieving happiness on earth by his own will. Wishing to stop the highest moment, Faust drops dead.[68]

In Goethe's *Faust*, with God's permission, angels save Faust's soul from Mephistopheles. Goethe's drama thus reflects the spirit of the times: for his merits as a worker wishing to ennoble a person with will and freedom, angels save him from the Devil. This unthinkable substitution of sin for virtue in Goethe's work is sanctioned by the God of deism and rationalism. Having lost the dispute over Faust's soul, Mephistopheles in fact won all of

---

67 Ibid., 10223-10233.

68 Not so much to "stop", but to prolong beyond measure the moment of triumph, which refers us back to the nuances of the interpretation of time.

humanity. Man aspired to become God, but was content to be the king of nature. Negative will wins out, opening the way for Modernity and its strategies. But the modern Faustian man is not quite yet the "last one", despite his anti-theistic struggle and progressism. He dreams of grand projects and transforming the natural world in accordance with his own (albeit Titanic) will. This is the proportionate antithesis to the Divine transfiguration. Faust is still struggling with boredom, still trying to inspire his being with engineering projects.

But when it comes to the contemporary man of the 21st century, we can recognize how he has largely lost the spirit of Faust and his passion. The last global projects of humanity, largely fueled by the worker ideology of socialism and the property of capitalism, ended with the first explorations of space. Thereafter, man gradually stepped back from global projects to local concerns with the "lifeworld" (Alfred Schutz). Even the space programs are already commonplace relicts. The world of media, virtuality, social networks, and the "Internet of things" (the third and fourth industrial revolutions) are today more important, more powerful, and more significant than the ideals of the second "classical" industrial revolution.

Active negative will dissipates into negative lack of will, or "willessness." Postmodern man is a tired Faust; he has not yet died, but the boredom has overcome him. The routine of daily operations, messaging, Internet surfing, and consuming signs constitute his familiar and cozy, meaningless world in an endless stream of news feeds, pics, quote fragments, and reposts.

In retrospect, we cannot imagine Faust abandoning his engineering vision and his own militant way of transforming nature for the sake of a new TV series, or exclaiming "Stop, moment!" when his pic or post on Facebook gets 1000 likes. This is inconceivable and does not match his scale, but it is completely complementary to the last humanity that Mephistopheles wins and inherits. His eternal spirit of negation becomes embodied in the endless streams of social networks and media.

The Faustian spirit of insatiable desire for knowledge and transformation became a kind of archetype of the man of Modernity, who turned the beingful world into ready-to-hand raw materials. This was remarkably described by Oswald Spengler in the following words:

> The peasant, the hand-worker, even the merchant, appear suddenly as inessential in comparison with the three great figures that the Machine has bred and trained up in the cause of its development: the entrepreneur, the engineer, and the factory-worker. Out of a quite small branch of manual work - namely, the preparation-economy - there has grown up (in this one Culture alone) a mighty tree that casts its shadow over all the other vocations - namely, the economy of the machine-industry. It forces the entrepreneur not less than the workman to obedience. Both become slaves, and not masters, of the machine, that now for the first time develops is devilish and occult power.[69]

The enlightened creator type, that of the engineer and science expert who transforms the world and revels in progress, has penetrated the European mind so deeply that today even conservatives of various kinds, including those among the "New Right" and Traditionalists, right-wing anti-globalists, or even such parodies as the virtual Alt-Right, all strive to preserve this figure and somehow revive it. Apologetics for the Faustian spirit can be found expounded by Alain de Benoist's former student, Guillaume Faye, the theorist of "Archeofuturism", who proposes to "saddle" the beast of technology and affirm a compromise between pagan values and the ancient understanding of *tekhne* on the one hand, and modern technology, transhumanism, and futurism on the other.[70] Exalting praise for machines and man's fusion with automata could already be found in the Italian futurism of Marinetti as a common feature of the obsession with technology prominent in early 20th-century aesthetics and culture.

---

69 Oswald Spengler, *The Decline of the West*, Volume II, 504.

70 See Guillaume Faye, "*Novye ideologicheskie vyzovy*" [New Ideological Challenges] in the volume *Evropeiskaia Identichnost'* [European Identity].

Lack of consistency and due depth of reflection on one's own history and "evolution" hinders the the so-called "(new) Right" from calling into question the spirit of Faust and the allegedly positive role of Prometheus. From this follows the obvious fact that modern conservatism (which as a term and phenomena is already extremely ephemeral) is rooted in the paradigm of Modernity and cannot step beyond it; it is not able to take the one more fundamental step towards greater consistency and authenticity in defending the interests and values of the world of Tradition. Contemporary Rightists are right to reproach, expose, and fight the absolute adepts of progressism — the cultural-Marxist Left, the feminist episteme, and partially the propagandists of technological singularity — but their positive program de facto does not mean overcoming the discourse of Modernity and progress, but rather returning to earlier positions within the same linear-progressive paradigm. Whereas, in truth, what both contemporary radical Traditionalists and right-wing conservatives do not like is, in essence, a refraction of the same Promethean and Faustian aspirations and platforms, only on other planes (let us recall that Prometheus was an exemplary figure for all three of the political theories of Modernity). This is comparable to a beam of light which, falling into a prism, is scattered into a wide spectrum of shades. Therefore, calling to discard, for instance, radical social constructivism, gender theory, and cultural Marxism in the social sphere and values, while at the same time emphasizing and supporting scientific-technological progress, is nothing more than a contradictory rollback and compromise, one that will once again take us back to square one due to the inevitability and irreversibility of progress, which always touches and affects all spheres of human life.

It is worth remembering that Faust concluded his pact with the Devil, a point which should be especially relevant to those on the Right who consider themselves champions of Christian values. From a pagan point of view and by analogy with Aeschylus' drama, this refers us to the Titanic pole of the cosmos. In other words, *casus Faust* is the question: the Divinities or the Titans?

The Sacred or the Gestell? Negation or compromise? This is Europe's great problem.

The Worker

Formulating the Gestalt of the Worker and the era of late Modernity is the merit of the German philosopher and writer Ernst Jünger. A veteran of the two World Wars and an ideologue of the Conservative Revolution, Jünger articulated the idea of the Worker on the basis of his own experiences and testimony. The early 20th century was marked by the collapse of bourgeois society and its values, which were replaced by an even more crude nihilism and the next step of regression (Jünger's contemporary, Julius Evola, predicted the coming to power of the new, fourth, proletarian estate). Amidst an even greater dehumanization of the world, technology came to the fore with all its strength and power, plainly demonstrating its power in the First World War. The title of Jünger's memoirs from this war is telling: *Storms of Steel*. This refers to the transition to the widespread and excessive use of automatic weapons in combat operations, and especially artillery, which tore up earth under the incredible density of volleys of fire. The use of long-range and automatic firearms changed the configuration of the battlefield with respect to "soldier-weapons." The sword and bayonet were no longer an extension of the hand, but rather the soldier became the machine gun's operator. The duel and clash of armies was replaced by the destruction of an enemy's living masses at a distance. Armored vehicles came into the vanguard, to which the rear was also enslaved with all the factories, plants, and industry needed to provide supplies of steel, bullets, shells, tanks, and aircraft. "Total mobilization" came about at the confluence of technology, science, and human masses. All kinds of activities, including recreation, entertainment, and even escapism, became forms of "work" and ideology.

In such a situation, a new existential type, or rather a figure that relegated the individual to the background, enslaving and erasing him in a mass, revealed itself: *"der Arbeiter"*, "the

Worker." The Gestalt of the Worker, as a manifestation of unleashed nihilism and will, mobilizes humanity at the service of technology and the will to power. At the same time, however, the Worker is not identical to the figure of the proletarian as such, but rather embraces wider strata and classes in society.

During this period of his writing (Jünger wrote *The Worker* in the Weimar period between the two World Wars), Jünger treated the Worker with sympathy, seeing in him the potential of mobilization as well as some inevitability as the Gestalt of the era.[71] It is extremely telling that Ernst's brother, Friedrich Georg, subsequently subjected the figure of the Worker to criticism, exposing him to be the awakening and restoration of Titanic power and the Promethean spirit.[72] Friedrich Georg saw in technology and machinery a manifestation of the hunger and thirst of the womb of furnaces and machines. Such a comparison directly refers us to the Scandinavian Jotunns (Titans), whose name etymologically means "devouring", "hungry." In other words, technology is poverty and lack, and the Worker mobilizes humanity to serve this poverty in vain attempts to satisfy the endless hunger of conveyor belts.

We are indebted to Friedrich Georg Jünger for two more apt formulations regarding technology. Firstly, he clearly showed that technology is the attire of the Titans, their uniform, and it is in the noise of machines that they find comfort and pleasure, whereas the Divinities flee from such rough commotion and noise. Secondly, he gave the most precise determination that follows from such: "Where there are no Gods, there are Titans."

After the Second World War, Ernst Jünger revised his views and in his diaries increasingly expressed agreement with his brother as to the Titanic nature of the late 19th and early 20th century, and later he turned to pointedly anti-Modernist subject matter altogether.

---

71 Jünger later formulated and put forth two other Gestalts, the Anarch and the Forest Rebel, to which we will turn in later chapters.

72 See Friedrich Georg Jünger, *Grecheskie mify* [Greek Myths]; idem, *The Failure of Technology: Perfection Without Purpose*, trans. F.D. Wieck (Der Schattige Wald, 2021).

Dizzied Achilles

The confrontation between two of the ancient Greek philosophical schools, the Platonists and the Sophists, is well known. For the Platonists, philosophy meant "love of wisdom (*Sophia*)", whereas Sophistry was the degeneration of knowledge into a form of word games, substitutions of notions, and technically proving any given position, i.e., pseudo-philosophical dizzying of the mind. One of the Sophist techniques was to formulate various aporias (irresolvable contradictions) that were logically valid, but impossible in the manifest world of situations. One of the most famous of such was Zeno of Elea's aporia of Achilles and the tortoise.

According to this aporia, Achilles will never be able to catch up with the tortoise in front of him, even if his speed is greater. While Achilles runs his part of the distance to the tortoise, the tortoise will have time to "get away" ahead for some distance. Achilles will catch up to it again, but the tortoise will again inch ahead a little, and so on, gradually and infinitely reducing the insurmountable gap between the hero and the tortoise. This aporia underscores the insurmountability of the infinite yet small distance to victory in a strange race. This situation can easily be seen as a problem of time and the gap between the "not yet" or *epokhe* (ἐποχή - "cessation", "pause") in the face of the End. The hero Achilles' attempt to outstrip the tortoise is the futile attempt to catch up and adapt traditional and heroic ideals to the world of Modernity and progress, which will always Titanically outpace and deceive Achilles. Zeno's aporia dizzies the hero and us. It places us in a situation of false wisdom, in a space of crooked mirrors, where the advantage is on the side of the chthonic and is reinforced by the infinite subdivision of infinitesimal numbers of distance which directly pertain to monotonous processes and functions.

Numerous rational and mathematical solutions to this aporia have been proposed throughout history, but the question is still not "closed." From our point of view, there is no need to solve this aporia logically and based on *ratio*. Instead, it should be seen as a kind of Zen koan, to be solved not gradually, but harshly, with a leap forth and to the side at once.

Achilles' task is to restore his heroic daring, to stop chasing after the tortoise and staying behind it. All the hero has to do is step over the tortoise. *Ergo*, if we see this aporia as a metaphor for our situation, it is necessary to overcome the idea of progress as such and to step over the idea of the future. In this case, "the future" is the problem of the forthcoming imposed by progress, futurism. Whoever constructs plans for the future (how to outrace the tortoise when it is a step ahead) will always lose. We should not be interested in "how to equip the future" or "how to make things better", and paganism should not at all see itself as part of one or another futurological scenario within the linear progressive paradigm.

We draw nearer to a solution to the problem of the "future" as soon as we cease talking about future scenarios and methods for "saving" us tomorrow or in *n*-years. The very idea of the "future" is sick infinity whose formula is "the end that will never finish ending." In any version and any scenario of the "future", any paganism — and that means all paganism, without exception — is doomed to self-parody.

The first horizon of real perspectives and prospects for paganism (which for us is "equal" to the authenticity of human being, even the most tense and tragic) begins beyond the "future."

The hero must show his Divine nature, overstep time, and head into Eternity.

Baldr Slain

The Germanic myth of the young Deity Baldr expounded in Snorri Sturluson's *Younger Edda* as well as the *Vegtamskviða* in the Elder Eddic corpus gives us a language for paradigmatically describing the triumphant rise of technology in the European context.

In the *Gylfaginning*, Odin himself describes Baldr and his halls with epithets which allow us to draw a comparison of his being to that of Hesiod's Golden Age. Baldr is the most luminous, innocent, good, and pure Deity who radiates beauty. Vice and evil never touched the halls of his Breiðablik. Baldr's youthfulness also associates him with the Spring of the Year, the manifestation of dawn.

Yet, it was written into Baldr's line and fate that none of his lots would come true, and dreams of his own death gradually began to haunt him. Assembled at the Thing, the Aesir decided to shield Baldr from danger. His mother, Frigg, had a word with every thing in the world, that they were not to harm the young Deity, and thus his purity took on the obverse of invulnerability. Still, there was one thing that Frigg did not dare disturb with her good will: a small bush of mistletoe with white berries.[73] Seen paradigmatically, the mistletoe is the Greek τέχνη in its authentic form, being the edge of ποίησις. *Tekhne* as *poiesis* did not seem to Frigg to pose any danger, and it would have been left to itself if not for the intervention of a vengeful force — the figure of Loki[74], who embodies the Titanic pole of hubris, daring excess.

Having cunningly extracted from Frigg the location of the mistletoe to the west of Valhalla, Loki plucked the mistletoe and cultivated it into a strong rod. Then, coming to the Aesir's sacred place, where all the Divinities were hurling spears at the invulnerable Baldr, Loki found the blind Höðr, who wasn't playing along in the martial entertainment. He put the rod in his hands and directed him with his gaze. At the hands of Loki-Höðr, Baldr fell slain on the mount of all the Aesir, thus marking the end of the Golden Age and youth.

---

73 The whiteness of Baldr's hair was compared to white flowers, perhaps the Edelweiss, hence the white fruits of the mistletoe might have played the role of some kind of metaphysical guarantor that does not hurt others like it. Frigg also calls the mistletoe "young for oaths."

74 The story of Loki's vengeance and problematic metaphysical character, as well as the events ensuing after Baldr's death, have been expounded in detail in our work *Gods in the Abyss*.

In order to understand the paradigmatic quality of this myth, it bears presenting its necessary correspondences with the metaphysical picture in the manifest world. The mistletoe in the West is the *poiesis-tekhne* that grows in the *Abendland*, the Country of Sunset, Evening, and Decline, that is the etymological "West" (in Russian, "West is *zapad*, literally the "falling" [of the sun]). This is consonant with the metaphysics of the Year and the eschatological anticipations associated with the metaphysics of the symbols of Night, Winter, Sunset, and dying. In the invasion of the Titanic will of Loki, who is the Germanic counterpart of Prometheus-Faust, we can recognize the rise of Christianity and its ontology of creationism (the rift between God and the world, God and man) that laid the foundations for the further metaphysical divergence of poetry and technology towards the dominance of the Gestell. The inoculations and appropriations of Hellenic wisdom in the form of Aristotelian and Neoplatonic metaphysics did not heal and overcome this rift (the "era of madness" in Pavel Florensky's terms[75]) rooted in the core of Judeo-Christian ontology.

Loki's Jotunic hubris forms a pair with Höðr's blindness, which is the reflection and final imperfection of the One-Eyed Deity. Wotan's one eye is interpreted as his ability to see and gain insight into the realms of chthonic and feminine metaphysics and practices. Such does not reflect mere semi-blindness, but rather doubled vision (non-dual presence). Höðr is deprived of the capacity to see light, including the light of Baldr the Sun, and this means that he is fully immersed in the darkness of indiscernibility. His subjectivity lies in that he is nevertheless present among the Aesir in their sacred place, which reflects his desire to participate in their game and make a throw. Such is reflected in the modern might of 19th-20th-century Germany in industry, war, and philosophy. Such is Germany enveloped in the spirit of Faust, like Höðr led by the hands of Loki, yet still

---

75 See Pavel Florensky, *The Pillar and the Ground of Truth: An Essay in Orthodox Theodicy in Twelve Letters*, trans. Boris Jakim (Princeton: Princeton University Press, 2004).

close in the flickering presence of the spirit of Wotan, which led Carl Jung to draw the erroneous conclusion that Germany was then possessed by his spirit.

Baldr's ensuing fate is withdrawal, abidance in the netherworld beyond, where he awaits the final death of the whole cosmos. He will then return from the forests and take his promised kingdom, which will be the beginning of the new cycle, the new Golden Age and Spring.

***

Our Nature

The metaphysics of shifting cycles speaks of a successive regress of eras entailing an involution of mankind. Hesiod said that every new era essentially meant a new generation of people with different qualities (the Golden generation, the Silver, etc.) who yield different visions of society and relations between one another and the Divinities. Plato argued that a person's estate identity belongs to the metal predominant in their soul. Those whose souls consist of gold are inclined towards philosophy and the defense of truth. Those whose souls have silver mixed in become warriors and rulers. The same applies to arts and crafts.

The regression of ages and the alteration of mankinds can be viewed not only diachronically, but also synchronically: every society has an estate structure that puts golden, silver, bronze, and iron people in their places in accordance with the divine hierarchy. The involution within the cycle reflects a shift in estate dominance downwards to the destruction (democratization, liberalization, development) of the whole structure of society. Those who previously occupied the higher levels of the hierarchy (warriors, kings, priests, philosophers, and ascetics) are denigrated and displaced into the periphery of society, while the lower, marginal elements rapidly rise on the waves of "enlightenment" and social progress.

We can take the human being as the point of view and departure for interpreting the ongoing shift in cycles and change in the world picture. We noted above that man occupies a twofold position in his relation to the beingful world: on the one hand, the attitude towards the world as ready-to-hand depends on him; on the other hand, he himself is a special being, a volitional element in the manifest world. Therefore, when man begins to see the beingful world as raw material, he necessarily begins to attribute himself (as a human and as society) to this category, i.e., the human comes to look upon himself as clay.

The anthropocentrism of the Enlightenment was centered around replacing God with man as the "crown of nature", i.e., secular humanism. We propose to look at man from the point of view of "before", that is in the world of the Divinities, and "after", amidst the prospects of post-human horizons. Therefore, with a certain share of generalizing conventionalities, we will speak of three types of humanism.

The Man of Tradition: Maximal Humanism

At the core of traditional societies stands the sacred. The Divinities are the sources or figures of the maximal concentration of the sacred. The social structure and concept of the human are no exception. Widespread throughout Tradition is the idea that a whole people or large lineages (*rod*, clans, theods) originate from a progenitor-Deity or a sacred animal, whence totemism and a number of animal names and surnames from deep antiquity, for example the Ynglings and their progenitor, Yngvi-Freyr, among the Scandinavians, or Tuisto among the continental Germanics, and later the practice of tracing royal genealogies to the Divinities.[76] It is telling that Tuisto, the progenitor-Deity or first man, is the son of Earth, the Goddess Jörð. This connection between man, Earth, the Heavens, and the Divinities is underscored in the spirit of Martin Heidegger's *das Geviert* (the "Fourfold").

A maximally theocentric view of society is expressed in the Vedanta, where the whole structure of society is seen as the large, organically articulated body of the Deity Brahma. The estate of Brahmin-priests embodies the head and mouth of Brahma, the Kshatriyas represent the hands, the Vaishya the stomach and thighs, and the Shudras the feet. The outcasts of society, the Chandalas and Dalits, are the dust under Brahma's feet. This division corresponds to the basic roles and functions of estates in Indo-European societies, which have been lucidly expounded

---

76 Divine genealogy should not be equated with strictly material euhemerism, according to which the Divinities are essentially deified legendary ancestors, i.e., from an anthropological view ordinary people exalted by their descendants in sagas and legends.

by Georges Dumézil: the Supreme Divinities, the Divinities of War, and the Divinities of Agriculture are "doubled" in the manifest world by priests, the warrior nobility, and farmers and artisans. Each estate, in turn, can consist of a number of castes covering various narrow specializations, varieties of crafts, or groups of servants, warriors, and mystical-philosophical darshanas.

It is extremely important to understand that the estate system of Varna is not "repressive" as the adepts of liberal democracies tend to make it out to be. The arrangement of varnashrama has its origin in the Divine. All of society is the symbolic body of the Deity in direct manifestation. Here it is appropriate to speak of an organic integrity and unity in which everyone has and takes their own place in the hierarchy.[77] This could be called "maximal humanism." There is no individual in the modern, autonomous sense here; rather, every person is a hierarchical incarnation of his *rod*, estate (if the estate has a patron Deity, then the person is his reflection as well), and at most the supreme Divinity of the pantheon, including along the genealogical, horizontal line of inheritance from the progenitor-Deity. A person acquires their maximal identity in the Divine; the center of the "I" is located in the higher worlds.

This humanism covers not only the community of the living, but also includes all the deceased ancestors and their spirits (what could conditionally be called the "varna of the dead"). A specific person in a *rod* is a link in a large chain of the

---

77   Unlike the "classless" societies of the ancient Slavs or Germanics, caste stratification is especially pronounced in India. It is not always the case that an estate can be singled out in terms of a separate "professional" stratum, as sometimes it is enough for certain things that cannot be done by just any person, but must be done by a worthy person or a representative of a *rod* or family in which this knowledge (priestly, healing, artisanal) has been passed down since ancient times. Instead of an estate-stratum, clan-lines can be assigned the functions and duties of being shamans, of dispensing rituals, being healers, or affairs proper to different sexes, as is the case with the specification of purely female and purely male occupations. The fourfold system of varnashrama can also be correlated with European triadic social systems in which the role of artisans and farmers is otherwise combined. The medieval emergence of an intermediate bourgeois class between the aristocracy and farmers was an anomaly of Modernity.

rebirths of souls extending into the worlds beyond. The cult of the *rod*, the veneration of ancestors, and regular communication with the dead (visits, offerings, wakes) inscribe a person into the larger sacred context associated with *thanatos*.

Within the scope of maximal humanism, we can speak of the "absolute individual" who harbors the minimum of his own "I" and the maximum of the Divine and power. The King or Emperor (or in the very least the warrior leader of a community, the head), for instance, is an absolute individual who is the personal embodiment of the warrior Deity on earth, a living figure of power, and, in essence, a person-State, the Sovereign. This line can be found in the sacralization of the pharaohs in Egypt, or in Asia in the sacred figure of the Emperor, and on a smaller scale in Melanesia, where the leader, in the event of external exchange relations, acts as the face of the whole tribe, and, vice versa, providing for the leader means that the tribe is providing for itself through a complex supply chain. Another example of the absolute individual is the ascetic who, being to some extent excluded from the life of the community (for example, the Greek μοναχός, whence "monk", meaning "alone", "solitary"), nevertheless concentrates within himself the maximal sacrality, spiritual height, and Divine-realization (Jivanmukti in Hinduism) otherwise unattainable to the ordinary person.

As a metaphor for maximal humanism, we can take a circle with a point in the center, the circumpunct, which is, among other things, the most ancient symbol of the Sun. At the center is the line of the Divinities or a cult's central Deity which emanates from itself the world, order, and the sacred in all directions, thereby creating and enchanting the entire circumference of society. As follows, the periphery of the circle is inhabited by the castes of outcasts who are further removed from the divine light, while closer towards the center are saints, ascetics, priests, and philosophers.

The symbol of the circle with a point in the center accounts for the metaphysical structure of society, just as a tree can be considered a symbol of the human being. Rooted in its native soil (the space of development; Heidegger's Earth), the tree grows and stretches upwards towards the sky (the Divine, spiritual initiatic horizons, the normative conception of the Good in society; Heidegger's Sky and Divinities). The Earth also acts as an analogue of the periphery, the surrounding circle, and the sky as the enchanting center, whereby this symbol can be extended to the whole of society, implying that the voice of a people is that of their leader/king, their philosophers, poets, and artists.

With regards to the last generations of people, we are no longer dealing with the symbolism of the tree, but with the people created out of clay or mud by Prometheus. Such is not organic growth out of the Earth into the Light of the Logos of the Divinities, but anguished and unsuccessful Titanic forgery enlivened only upon the intervention of Zeus or Athena.

The image of an inverted tree whose roots reach out into the sky while its branches stretch down towards earth is widespread in mystical schools. Here we are confronted with a metaphor of the Divine emanating downwards into the boundaries of matter (Plato's *khora*; Aristotle's ὕλη-wood). The superimposition of these two symbols onto each other — the tree growing out of the earth and the tree growing out of the sky — gives us an exhaustive symbol of the human being, depicting his middle position in the world and his fundamental freedom to move upwards (towards the transcendent and the Divinities) or downwards (into the embrace of dark matter). Metaphysics explains this through the passage of initiations, wherein a person is transformed, losing their earthy roots and acquiring heavenly ones.[78]

Initiation is the basic social structure of traditional societies which determines the inclusion of people into a single "organism" on different levels of hierarchy. When young men and women pass through a ritual of initiation, their anthropological status is qualitatively changed, as they are introduced into the boundaries of the circle or rooted in the soil. Before this point,

---

78 Various mysticisms also emphasizes the analogy between man as a tree and the idea of the World Tree as a symbol of the cosmos, akin to the formula "as below, so above." This is another allegorical motif of maximum humanism.

they generally tend to be some kind of ephemeral, borderline creatures who could simply die at an early age. The process of initiation was often accompanied by receiving a first or new name, by which a young man, or rather already a man and husband, became known to society. It is the rite of initiation that makes a person into a human being, a human of our *rod*, our community, included in our tradition and reflecting a certain facet of it.[79] There could be a number of initiations in a person's life, as nearly every life change was framed by a ritual of transition: birth, initiation into the community, initiation into a craft, marriage, change of age status, and death. Death and rebirth in a qualitatively new form is the main structure of rites of initiation. In addition to "social" initiations, there were also initiations of spiritual growth, mysteries of higher knowledge that changed the initiate's socio-anthropological status and their whole view of the world (turning the trees roots upwards to the sky). Such, for example, were the Eleusinian mysteries in ancient Greece, which were predominantly a priestly-philosophical path.

Over the flow of time, nearing the lower part of the circumference of the Year-Wheel, society degrades and collapses. The Divine center is concealed or removed and the centrifugal forces of disorder (unrestrained hubris) destroy the circle's harmony. In such a scene, what used to be sacred and ordering can no longer be found in the center (where there might be found, for instance, man as the "king of nature" or a mobile banking application), but is scattered throughout the periphery. Initiation becomes a foremost problem for adherents of tradition and Traditionalists.

In René Guénon's view, initiation presents itself as a chain of the transmission of tradition running through time, akin to the Christian ritual of ordination going back to the Apostles and Christ himself. For a Traditionalist, according to Guénon, what is important is being incorporated into this chain, since the very

79 See Mircea Eliade, *Rites and Symbols of Initiation: The Mysteries of Death and Rebirth* (Thompson: Spring Publications, 1984).

fact of participating in it is capable of spiritually transforming a person. Hence Guénon's own numerous attempts to find a truly initiatic organization, which made him into a kind of "collector of initiations." We call this approach "horizontal", since here the connection with the transcendent is guaranteed and simultaneously mediated through a temporally horizontal line of transmission, through secret societies and organizations.

Guénon's student, Julius Evola, already called into doubt this concept of his teacher. For Evola, the most important point in the cause of initiation is a "rupture of levels", i.e., a qualitative change in the nature and thinking of an adherent of traditional metaphysics, his passage onto a higher plane of being and understanding of the world. According to Baron Evola, such an event can seize a person not only through consciously entering a thousand-year-old chain of esoteric knowledge, but can also be caused by other factors. This picture of initiation is more dramatic, bears the influence of Tantrism, and at the same time is more suitable to the conditions of the Kali-Yuga. According to Tantric notions, the decisive role is ultimately played by the adept's degree of Divine-realization (spiritual perfection), not his position in the Varnas and castes (or his "social status" in the language of Modernity). There are three such levels in Tantra: the *pashu*, or level of the carnal person, the animal; *vira*, or the hieratic type of ascetic; and *vidya*, or the realized adept. If the estate system of Vedanta is conceived vertically, then the Tantric one either parallels it or is sometimes described in the spirit of an intellectual paradox, i.e., as a vertical in relation to a vertical. In other words, a simply hereditary Brahmin might stand on a lower position relative to Brahma than a radical Aghori ascetic who is close to outcastes in the social hierarchy but in the spiritual hierarchy is already one with Shiva. In Indian culture, these two paths coexist in a certain harmony and balance, for which it is difficult to find relevant analogues in European traditions. Evola essentially prescribed the Tantric path for precisely the most adverse conditions.

Intense experiences in war, the horror of a brush with death, the bottomless bitterness of injury or loss — all such experiences, according to Evola, can bring a person into a borderline state, to a point at which he can take a step upwards out of this state of higher tension (and thus collapse the previous state of being and push off from it), or he might regret and not take advantage of the moment. This is how Evola justified the possibility of self-initiation as a very rare opportunity for a person in our days. This is what we call "vertical initiation." If for Guénon belonging to a long chain of succession in this world is of principal importance, then the Evolian approach consists of only one link: its bottom embraces a person, and its top link connects with the transcendent, the sacred. Such initiation does not introduce a person into some kind of esoteric society and does not attach them to a divine-social whole, since traditional society has long since been destroyed. Rather, a person is initiated into another level of being and is personally transformed. Their situation in the modern world can be described with the tragic image of people among ruins — those who are real people amidst a destroyed world.[80]

There is a famous Hermetic metaphor for two ways of igniting a flame. We can identify the first with the Golden Age of the world of Tradition, when the flame of the sacred burns so powerfully and brightly that anything profane that falls into it is set alight. The blazing figure burns even damp logs. This can be illustrated with the thought experiment of throwing an ordinary modern person into the world of Tradition. The initial shock would gradually give way to astonishment, and the suggestion and veil of the scientific worldview would fall from his eyes. He will take his place among people and will see the miraculousness of the world and everything unfolding around him. In other words, he will be "re-enchanted", re-enter the circle, and be enchanted by the Divine ("initiated" per Guénon).

A different situation is described with the image of flashing sparks in the midst of boundless, thick ice. If in the first case the inner fire is ignited due to contact with an exterior flame, then in this case the inner fire is ignited due to its own awareness of its

---

80   See Julius Evola, *Men Among the Ruins.*

total difference from the surrounding environment of ice. Such a spark (a person, its bearer) does not know Tradition, its light and heat, but existentially and deeply, tragically feels that they do not belong to the entire surrounding reality. This is a flash of rejection in favor of an unknown light and fire. Such a spark cannot return to Tradition, and its bearer might not even know anything of such a "reality" beyond Modernity and will simply tragically burn out.[81]

The second way is complementary to Julius Evola's views and the eschatological conditions of the End Times. Such is awakening on the eve of death, finding oneself in the midst of decline and decay, in the center of an inert, cold environment of ice.[82] The nature of this spark raises a number of deeply enigmatic questions. Why does this spark flare up at all? What brings it to shine? Is this flame amidst ice the same as the outer flame of the traditions of the past? What does the spark amidst the world of ice have to do with the fact that it flares up right on the eve of the eschatological moment?

Intermediate Forms

The Abrahamic religions differ from pagan traditions already on the level of ontology, which in turns finds its specific reflection in anthropology and humanism. Hesiod tells of how, over the course of time, human generations decline down to the final, fifth mankind molded of clay. Clay-matter is the lower limit of human involution in traditional society, the flat person living on the thin material slice of being. The point in Tradition where the human being ends, where mankind comes to its end, is where creationism only begins. The crafted, clay-created human is taken to be the normative anthropological type in the Abrahamic traditions. A human and their soul were never gold

---

81 Such brings to mind the figure of the saint or trickster who finds himself in the periphery, in the marginal strata of society, a tragic witness to the Sunset-Decline (Emil Cioran) akin to decadents (Baudelaire, Rimbaud), or gloomy visionaries (Lovecraft, Poe, Mamleev). See Evgeny Golovin (ed.), *Bezumie i ego Bog* [Madness and its God].

82 These are typical characteristics of subterranean netherworlds.

or even bronze, but were immediately made of clay — this is the starting position of the Abrahamic faiths.

In creationism, mankind is close to the spirit of Prometheus, and this is manifest in the fact that it is none other than creationism that opened the gates for ensuing Modernity and affected thinking in such a way that the beingful world came to be perceived as ready-to-hand, rather than as disclosed, flourishing Being.[83] On the estate level, the adherents of the Abrahamic religions were originally from the border of the third estate (farmers and artisans) and outcasts. The Hindus saw the metaphysics and morality of Christianity and Islam, despite the latter's militant terror, to be a manifestation of third-estate Dharma, and even perceived Christ as one of Krishna's faces turned towards the lower classes of society.

The establishment of creationism led to the destruction of traditional societies which expressed their own myths. By the Middle Ages, the Indo-European structure of society had undergone metamorphosis and was expressed in three estates: the Christian estate (predominantly the Catholic clergy), the warrior nobility and court aristocracy, and the lower strata of lay peasants. This structure no longer expressed maximal humanism. This is not yet the problem of the individual, but, as Alain de Benoist aptly notes, monotheism was the basic premise for the monohumanism of Modernity, the emergence of the individual, and speculations on human rights. Creationism postulates an intermediate or median humanism, within which the human being is no longer part of a universal unity, but is part of one large estate.

This can be expressed in terms of the metaphor of the circle with a point in the center thusly: one sector along the circle opposes itself to the whole circle and expands from the periphery into the center. The maximal scale of humanism is limited by the institution of the Church and its dogma. The approach to

83   See Alexander Dugin, *Postfilosofiia. Tri paradigmy v istorii mysli* [Post-Philosophy: Three Paradigms in the History of Thought] (Moscow: Eurasian Movement, 2009); Askr Svarte, *Polemos*.

infidels is arranged accordingly: the norms of humanity do not extend to them at all. The principle of defining a person through baptism (or in Islam through belonging to the Ummah) becomes dominant. In Tradition, the divine principle emanates itself into the world (and emanates the world out of itself in monism), and is therefore complicit in it, just as society is its manifestation. In the Abrahamic religions, God and the world are separated by an insurmountable abyss, and the "body of Christ" in the form of the Church is assembled from the bottom up out of its constituent parts, i.e., parishioners and the priesthood. In Orthodoxy, the Church consists of the clergy and the laity, whereas Catholicism is more consistent with creationism in that only the clergy makes up the body of the Church.

This median humanism is even more distinctly expressed in the ensuing history of the emergence of a radically new phenomenon — the class of the bourgeoisie, consisting of city dwellers cut off from the earth, a strata of urbanites, merchants, servants of the nobility, technical artisans, and entrepreneurs. The bourgeoisie represents a conglomerate of disparate people torn from their traditional roots and mixed with the characteristically non-Indo-European social types of the merchant and lackey, whose higher status at first lies only in their access and service to the nobility. This is aggravated by the fact that the bourgeoisie does not and cannot have any sacred grounding in view of its composite nature. From the point of view of Tradition, the bourgeoisie represents the degeneration and disintegration of the lowest castes, a society of lackeys and freed slaves, but from the point of view of intermediate humanism, it is a legitimate estate and something greater than the individual. Moreover, at the initial stages, the bourgeoisie did not come into conflict with the Church.[84]

---

84 It is worth noting how, in the vast majority of cases, Western conservatives advocate restoring bourgeois conservatism in one version or another, or in different emphases, without paying attention to the truly radical horizon of conservative ontology. See Alexander Dugin, *Chetvertyi put': Vvedenie v Chetvertuiu Politicheskuiu Teoriiu* [The Fourth Way: An Introduction to the Fourth Political Theory] (Moscow: Academic Project, 2015).

As Alain Soral has shown in his polemical correction of Julius Evola and René Guénon, it is precisely the morality and values of the bourgeoisie, not the third estate of peasants, that underlies the humanism of Modernity.[85] The Baron said in his writings that the degradation of anthropological types did not end with the bourgeoisie, that still ahead lurks the coming of the fourth estate and its moralities — that of the proletariat, a degenerate type of laborer who is maximally subordinated to technology. Class theory is also a bare example of intermediate humanism: a person's views, values, and everyday way of life are derived from his class affiliation (another form of "greater community") and relation to the means of production. This would later be repeated by stratification theory in sociology, which is based on a more complex array of socio-economic relations.

Thinking about intermediate humanism and remaining within the boundaries of the Middle Ages and the Renaissance, we are still somewhere close to Tradition, we still remember Tradition very well, since it was still here just yesterday, its warmth and light are still felt. Christianization was not an instant process, but stretched out throughout Europe over long centuries, and its penetration into broad layers of the population proceeded only with great difficulty. Peasants longest of all preserved an enormous, complex array of rituals and everyday pagan beliefs (for example, so-called "folk Orthodoxy" in Russia). The knightly ethos flourished in the warrior estate, and such was inconceivable without the influence of the Germanic, closed male societies and special form of the expression of Eros in culture. Even Christian theology assimilated a complex array from pagan philosophy and translated it under the guise of Christian mysticism (Eckhart, Tauler, Pico della Mirandola, Ficino).

Real submersion into the sub-anthropological and hypochthonic levels of humanism began in the transition from

---

85 Alain Soral, *Poniat' Imperiu: Griadushchee global'noe upravlenie ili vostanie natsii?* [Understanding Empire: Impending Global Governance, or an Uprising of Nations?] (Moscow: Global Revolutionary Alliance, 2012).

the Renaissance to the Enlightenment, when the bourgeois masses undertook to see to their own emancipation.

The Humanism of the Last People

At the core of minimal humanism lies the notion that the individual is an indivisible, finite subject in the Cartesian sense. It is precisely in minimal humanism and in the individual that we encounter the idea of "man as such", i.e., when people say "person", "man", or "human" in everyday speech as part of "common sense", then, whether consciously or not, they are appealing to the modernist concept of the individual. In our philosophy, a person is never given "by themself" in any positive sense, but always stands in the light of the sacred, estate, and initiation (in Tradition); otherwise, they represent a problem, a trauma, a task, a troublesome point of being-here in terms of historical regress and the flight of the Divinities.

In Modernity, man does not ascend to his roots in the sacredly understood Sky and Earth with the Divinities. Instead, his ground is based on convention. Here is an interesting point: determining what and who is "human" is an act of reflection, one being's thinking about its essence, its fundamental definition. Reflection on the essence of the human determines a person's position in the general taxonomy, the nomenclature of species of living organisms (class - mammalian, order - primates, etc.). The human chooses to regard themself as the final derivative of the evolutionary process, the individual, i.e., the product of strictly material evolution later supplemented by social development (which does not change the biological nature of man overall).

Thus, "human" or "person" is but a name that some individuals (the humanists of the Enlightenment, the scientific community) invented in agreement among themselves to denote the common feature of individuals in general. The minimal foundations of humanism fit into several criteria: genetic and physiological identification, i.e., having the appearance of a person regardless of race and gender, the possession of reason (*homo sapiens* and "common sense") and capacity, and minimal education irrespective of culture and religion.

Minimal humanism, or "monohumanism", *a priori* asserts universal "common human" values, the biophysiological level of identity and interests, and universal cultural norms and human rights granted to a person from birth simply by virtue of the fact of belonging to the species.[86] In the paradigm of minimal humanism, it is enough to be born to be a human. There is no sense of initiation and effort towards being a human, and culture and tradition are leveled to a set of optional and fluid socio-cultural parameters. This fundamental stake in the lowest biological criteria of identity excludes huge layers of folk cultures and the diversity of structures of thinking (the plurality of Logoi), and reduces the world-forming role of Tradition and the sacred in all of its diversity down to secular ethics, morals, and aesthetics. However, insofar as the concepts of the individual, natural human rights, and minimal secular humanism are not objective universal reality, but rather a product of the degeneration (progress) of European civilization, which has in turn claimed and imposed its universality by way of cultural genocide, we can expose and demarcate minimal humanism as the most primitive form of biological and gnoseological racism, one which spreads not only extensively — to other peoples — but also intensively, transforming European society itself from within.

If we understand "human" identity and corresponding "humanity" in precisely such a manner, through minimal criteria, then from our position we can boldly reject "the human" as a form of universal humanistic and biological identity. Whoever believes in a tradition is not a human, but a member of one or another *rod* on the way to ascending to a mythical ancestor, whether Tuisto or a Totem-Bear. The human (in the form in which it is presented by modern natural and social sciences) does not exist in the world of Tradition and maximal humanism.

---

86   See Alain de Benoist, *Beyond Human Rights: Defending Freedoms*, trans. Alexander Jacob (London: Arktos, 2011).

The philosophical and political substantiation of minimal humanism is centered around the idea of constantly liberating the human from greater identities. On this is based the idea of liberalism, which is the correlate of progress. The atomic society of free individuals, centered around the consumer economy, technology, social programs, and humanism, can be regarded as a compromise between the interests and values of the bourgeoisie and proletariat.[87]

With regards to liberalism, it bears emphasizing a most important distinction between two types of freedoms as they were defined by the theorist of liberalism and emancipation, John Stuart Mill: liberty and freedom, or negative and positive freedom. Negative freedom, or "freedom from", "liberty", postulates the imperative of emancipation from any external interference and coercion (from the state, the Church, the military, other major social institutions), from the framework and conditions of normative society. The imperative of "freedom from" entails liberation from all large collective identities, whether estate, tradition, religion, hereditary occupation, morality, societal customs, etc. Belonging to something larger, for instance to an estate or hereditary occupation, predetermines a person's life path and sets the appropriate framework, prescribing a certain ethics and common set of values and rituals. Liberalism demands the right to "terminate the contract of belonging" to an estate or any other collective category at the wish of the individual as the source and bearer of an autonomous morality (Rousseau's "noble savage"). The logical consequence of negative freedom is that it is neither a given nor reclaimed as a perfect state of freedom, but reveals itself to be an infinite process of emancipation. In other words, it is not so much "liberty" as "liberating." Here is manifest and disclosed the complete homology between monotonic processes and progress, as well as a direct connection with the Titanic

---

87 The latter generally disappear in the post-industrial society, thereby leveling the classical agenda of class struggle. Nevertheless, the general materialistic imperative and scientific methodology remain as constituents of scientific knowledge and have been successfully incorporated into the liberal paradigm.

complex of theomachism and the destruction of the sacred order of things. Liberation begins with a consciousness of privation, a lack of freedom (understood as permissiveness and self-will) among a certain category of people, and this consciousness nurtures growing hubris.

The figure of the autonomous individual unbound by the obligations of sacred estate duty, society, and ritual can be found in the world of Tradition only among outcasts. The Chandalas, pariahs, criminals expelled from society, and violators of taboos are freed from the focus of society, from the obligatory fulfillment of its rules. They are even forbidden from entering society, initiations do not apply to them, and they live on the periphery of society or far outside of it. They have no destiny and no due. From the point of view of Tradition, the liberal individual is not a human at all — the fact that he has arms and legs and a human appearance is no grounds for considering him "one of our own", because behind him do not stand, or more precisely, through him are not manifest the sacred figures of the Divinities, his *rod*, and his inclusion in the whole body of the "greater human" that is society. Instead of an estate or clan, outcasts form masses and herds. Friedrich Nietzsche wrote of this type:

> You call yourself free? Your dominating thought I want to hear, and not that you escaped from a yoke. Are you the kind of person who had the right to escape from a yoke? There are some who threw away their last value when they threw away their servitude. Free from what? What does Zarathustra care! But brightly your eyes should signal to me: for what?[88]

Negative freedom ultimately exposes its nihilism as liberation for the sake of liberation (process for the sake of process) without any aim towards affirming anything higher and ruling.

Unlike negative freedom, "freedom for" is aimed at manifesting the will-to-create, the will to the heroic act. Positive freedom is the freedom to dedicate one's life to the embodiment

---

88 Nietzsche, *Thus Spoke Zarathustra*, trans. Adrian del Caro (Cambridge: Cambridge University Press, 2006).

of an idea which transcends the terms and scale of earthly live and overcomes the level of everyday life.

The question of the correlation between liberty and freedom in the light of the autonomous individual and Modernity is problematic with respect to yet another pole of individuality in Tradition: the figure of the monk, the ascetic hermit who is entirely focused on the sacred and on spiritual realization. The minimal individual problematizes the maximal individual of traditional societies.

In ancient times, in maximal humanism, the individuation of a community member took place against the background of his distinction *vis-à-vis* the common social structure. The king or leader occupied the pinnacle of worldly power (the focal point of all of society), and the priest or shaman personified a special entity in the sacred hierarchy. Ascetic hermits, including the Aghori and Kapalikas in India, the Cynics in Greece, the wandering jesters (*skomorokhi*) and holy fools in Rus, moved into the periphery of society, fell out of estate hierarchies and obligations, and violated taboos, but such was compensated for by the fact that they became focal points of the sacred (even a path of rather transgressive and dark versions) in possession of strong magical and healing abilities, wisdom, and direct proximity to the Divinities. Holy hermits crystallized as specific pearls of society, drawing towards themselves at once neglect, apprehension, fear, reverence, and expectations of granting grace to ordinary members of the community.

But the estate system of traditional society has been abolished. The "holy hermit" today does not reveal himself against the background of the "greater man" of normal society but, as it were, is present among outwardly all the same extroverted individuals. Outwardly, according to the criteria of minimal humanism, this type does not differ at all from the last people. Thus arises the problem of distinguishing between negatively liberalized, non-classed and non-estate individuals, whose horizons are focused on hedonism, consumerism, and freedom of speech, and the person who devotes themself to the sacred. A glance from the outside is hardly likely to be able to distinguish them from among the conventional crowds of people, hence we can only speak of such loners as having a special look and deep inner distance amidst so many surrounding atoms. While surrounding people are de-humaned, these persons who are "co-present" in contemporary society (or more precisely, who claim such a status) find themselves in the very same position of the spark in the middle of ice or amidst anthropological ruins. The question of initiation is problematic, the question of maximal individuation is problematic, and all that is obvious and experienced literally on one's own skin is alienation from the contemporal "here" alongside a craving and drawnness towards something Other.

Dividing the Indivisible

The human is a word written in sand to be washed away by the first incoming wave. This is how Michel Foucault, one of the key thinkers of the paradigm of Postmodernity, defined the future of the human. Since progress and liberation are endless processes gravitating towards monotony, the modernist moment of the "simply human", i.e., the individual Cartesian subject, was doomed in advance to become but a page in history. Since the mid-20th century, we have fully moved into the fields of posthumanism. Here is the moment of coincidence between the Postmodernist and Traditionalist views of the "human." Postmodern posthumanism is the next step of progressive ideology, the new act of the spectacle of liberation, whereas for Traditionalist the "post-" here means that we have descended ever deeper into non-human or para-human anthropology. If Modernity defined the human through minimal humanism, then Postmodernism is not about the human at all, but the spheres of transhumanism and posthumanism, of a world after or without man even in his biologically egalitarian identity. Modernity liberated itself from Tradition, and now Postmodernity liberates Modernity from itself.

The foundations of posthumanism were laid by a constellation of philosophical and political schools. These include the poststructuralism and postmodernism of Michel Foucault, Gilles Deleuze and Felix Guattari, Roland Barthes, and Jean-François Lyotard, the descriptions furnished by Jean Baudrillard, the revisionism of Freudo-Marxism in Jacques Lacan, and the Frankfurt School (Theodore Adorno, Herbert Marcuse, Max Horkheimer). Postmodernism is constituted by its extension of the liberal vector of liberation, now enriched by a revised Marxism. Since the class approach of Marxism failed in Western societies due to the dissolution of classes into a single egalitarian mass, the Left shifted the "oppression-exploitation-rebellion" structure onto the spheres of culture and sexuality, whereby all possible minority groups became the "new proletarians", the new oppressed under the paradigm of Modernity with its ideas of norms. This was accomplished through postulating a total relativism and social constructivism. The very concept of "norm", albeit of the type built in accordance with the blueprints of the Enlightenment, humanism, and scientism, is abolished as such. Any states and combinations are emancipated and legitimized. Insofar as there is no referential norm, the very notion of "deviating from the norm" no longer has any meaning.

If we turn to the question of the human, then one of the first notions to collapse was the idea of the individual. Instead of individuality, there is now dividuality, i.e., the indivisible subject of Modernity becomes divisible and divided. One of the first to point in this direction was Sigmund Freud with his account of the two-leveled *topos* of consciousness and the unconscious, by which he intended to "bring light into the basement of the mind." Freudo-Marxism in its new editions appeals to this structure with the aim of emancipating and releasing irrational subconscious desires, primarily related to the sphere of sexuality, and irrational emotions, all of which are now socially rehabilitated. Freudianism wanted to heal a person from their passions through the power of the reasoned mind, whereas Postmodernity proposes healing by freeing passions from the shackles of the mind.

Gilles Deleuze and Felix Guattari relativized the concept of psychiatric and psychological norms for the individual, calling instead for the rehabilitation of schizophrenia and mental disorders as various "alternative norms." In so doing, they sought to level the criterion of sanity and capacity, including in the legal sphere, that was hitherto important to the society of Modernity. Consciousness is now open to be deconstructed by psychedelic substances used outside of a ritual-shamanic context and for the purpose of recreation and relaxation as in Western pop culture following the "drug revolution" of the 1960s.

Along with the waves of development in the technological means of communication — mobile phone connection, the Internet, social networks, and interactive gadgets — the individual undergoes dissolution. Dividuality is the momentary intersection and overlapping of different practices and signs summarily and temporality collected into the subject or personage. This is the bricolage technique described by Deleuze and Guattari, the momentary schizophrenic compilation of the "whole" out of what is at hand in a given moment. The human being is not a whole, but a constellation of streams of desires: hunger, thirst, sex, violence, entertainment, impressions, adrenaline, sleep, narcotic intoxication, economic relations, athletics, programming, and subcultural sectional identities like punk or fitness. All of these can be fluid and represent a set of fashion trends dispersed over time (the identity of the buyer, the fashionista). To this is added the "spraying out" of the "I" onto objects, such as gadgets, phones, cars, or virtual things like social media accounts, profile pictures, and bundles of subscriptions and services. The human becomes the sum of desires, account posts, what they consume, the brand of their phone or car, what they eat and share on social networks, what brands they wear, etc. The "I" or ego is only one of the actors in this process, perhaps still too totalitarian and restricting of the stomach's desire to eat, the eyes' desire to look, the penis'

135

desire to penetrate, and the desire of things to be accumulated. Since all the actors of this assemblage are impermanent, fluid, and coexist in a complex, dynamic network (cf. chaos theory; the rippling pulsations of the rhizome) of relationships and influences, fashions and trends, there is no static person at all, who instead is redrawn from tide to tide. Key terms associated with this include the "body without organs", the "desire machine", and "schizo-masses."

Any subcultures, collectivities, and identities are in Postmodernity's optic mere "imagined communities" in the spirit of Benedict Anderson's sociology, where an imaginary concept that only weakly correlates with reality comes to the forefront. No unity is actually experienced, but is constantly fantasized as if present. The minimal grounds for the institutionalization of imaginary communities are provided by daily practices of micro-iterations, communications, and everyday life (e,g., the hippy commune or gay ghetto), i.e., what Schütz described as the "lifeworld" (in minimal sociology) and around which Thomas Luckmann developed his theory of social constructivism. One typical case of imagined community is "geeks fandom", the community of fans of one or another global pop culture phenomenon (a musician, band, computer game, movie, etc.) who in reality might never interact with each other at all, but at the same time imagine and declare their "love" for a band or movie, which imparts them with some particular distinctive features and gives them some kind of identity. This corresponds to Parmenides' fifth hypothesis that there is only the many, πολλα, and no One beyond or ensuing. The "one" of the masses is only a situational occasion, for example a stadium during a game, a concert, or watching an online stream. As soon as the attractor of attention finishes, the "unity" dissolves like a mirage and scatters across other points of attraction.

The species identity of the human disappears with the individual, opening up the way for freedom for interspecies transactions and transformations (chimeras, animal-people[89,]

89   See Erik Sprague and Tom Leppard's "Lizardman" and "Anver D."

alien aesthetics[90]), currently on the level of culture and body modifications (tattoos, piercings, plastic surgery). The principle of the beingful world being ready-to-hand like raw material is now applied to the human in full measure, opening up endless series of options for reassembly.

Biopolitics/Necropolitics

One of Michel Foucault's most important discoveries in contemporary society was his description of the mechanisms of biopower and biopolitics.[91] From our philosophy's point of view, the phenomenon of biopolitics clearly illustrates the degradation and disintegration of the people, the folk, and organic power relations into the dominant Gestell's "treatment" of "populations" (nations/masses/citizens).

The essence of biopolitics lies in that the political technologies and power relations which previously covered social life are transferred and applied directly to the physiology and biology of a population. Here, it bears emphasizing, a people is turned into a faceless population, a workforce on the labor market, a taxable base of potential hires and recruits. In other words, the people and its people are dehumanized. "Population" is an extremely egalitarian notion that levels cultural, racial, ethnic, and other differences, in essence gravitating towards a mass of "naked life" (Giorgio Agamben) which governmental authority turns to "handle."

Considering a population to be a mass of raw materials, government authority undertakes to "sculpt" the desired types of

---

90 The cult futurological comic *Transmetropolitan* predicts that a genetic drug will be popular in the society of the future. It literally turns an addict into a half-beast or a fully-fledged animal for several hours. But some have gone even further and developed a serum that turns people into semi-aliens (from an alien ghetto in Eastern Europe) on a permanent basis, and they begin to fight for their rights. We are seeing an almost identical situation today.

91 See Michel Foucault, *The Birth of Biopolitics: Lectures at the College de France, 1978-1979*, trans. Graham Burchell (New York: Palgrave Macmillan, 2008); idem., *Discipline and Punish: The Birth of the Prison*, trans. Alan Sheridan (New York: Vintage Books, 1995).

citizens and instill them with the needed qualities. Propaganda depicting images of the normative citizen is disseminated alongside sanitary-hygienic and medical programs and institutions, militarism, the promotion of healthy lifestyles, the regulation of citizens' diets, control over childbirth and abortion ("planned parenthood"), drug programs, and education on emancipated, previously taboo practices (such as face mask and social distancing mandates), and so on.

Biopolitics is embodied in all three of the political ideologies of Modernity. Fascism and Nazism broadcasted the normative image of the "blonde Aryan", propagated the radical ideal of positive eugenics, and encouraged selective childbearing in institutions like the Lebensborn[92], as well as engaged in physically eliminating marginal and handicapped elements of the population. We find biopolitics in the USSR in the "Ready for Labor and Defense" program aimed at physically transforming the population, as well as the "Liquidation of Illiteracy" program. Health became a matter of class homogeneity dealt with by the relevant commissariat. Elements of radical biopolitics were also present in Pol Pot's regime in Cambodia. Liberalism also practiced eugenics and racial segregation in the 20th century, but later switched to implicit, soft biopolitical strategies in the spirit of "freedom from", through the emancipation and normalization of body modifications, body positivity, and transhumanism. In general, each modern ideology engages in breeding and selecting its "new human" to achieve its ends. In this respect, Modernity took over the Enlightenment's bio-evolutionary approach to man. From the point of view of Traditionalism, the matter at hand is the dehumanizing of society, turning it into a clay mass out of which Titanic power can mold anything, and appealing to subhuman, irrational passions emotions, fears, and impressions.

Michel Foucault's doctrine of biopolitics has been developed by the Cameroonian post-colonial philosopher Achille Mbembe, who expands the horizons of biopower to include the sphere

---

92 See A. Vasil'chenko, *Ariiskii mif III Reikha* [The Aryan Myth of the Third Reich] (Moscow: Yauza Press, 2008).

of "necropolitics." If biopolitics brings biological life into the sphere of politics and governmental practices, then necropolitics subordinates death itself and related practices and discourses to such authority. Necropolitics means that governmental authority's policies determine who should die, how, when, and on what scale. The manifestations of necropolitics are quite diverse and account for a number of characteristic types and situations, including those pertaining to "death during lifetime." New modes of being are opened up for a person to be in an intermediate state between actual biological death and social alienation by the forces of the repressive apparatus of governmental authority and terror. For example, the social death of an individual, such as in the event of falling into slavery, means reducing the individual to an object for labor in the most literal sense. The sexual exploitation and trafficking of women and children fall under the same category. There is also the pop-cultural image of the zombie. Representing the latter are the situations of widespread intravital profuse necrosis in hard intravenous drug addicts coupled with states of heavy intoxication. Situations and practices of torture and illegal detentions, such as the case of prisoners in Guantanamo Bay or the "investigative isolators" of Russia's FSB, are also objects and sites of necropolitics. Here also arises the figure of the hostage. A further vivid illustration of necropolitics would be mass genocide along purely bio-physiological criteria.

In colonialism, necropolitics manifested itself in Christian Europeans' attitude towards the non-Christian peoples they encountered on newly discovered continents. The other is "not a person at all", but something that can and must be killed in order to make room for the needs of the state. The Catholic Church once seriously initiated studies on the question of whether South American Indians should be recognized as humans because they did not hold the Gospel, and, consequently, whether they should be treated with mercy, exterminated like animals, or kept as livestock. This is how modern Europe drowned traditional non-European societies in blood, but even earlier — and more importantly — killed multi-traditional Europe itself.

In the sphere of culture, manifestations of necropolitics intersect with necrosociology to affect burial practices, thus extending their power and authority to corpses and the process of decomposition. Cremation is promoted as a cost-effective manner to dispose of a body. If a person is to be buried, then terms for renting the land for the grave are stipulated, as are regulations for the disposal of the deceased who have overdue rent. Necropower broadcasts to society which types of death and dying are the most acceptable and comfortable (whereby necropolitics converges with bioethics) and, vice versa, which ways are undesirable (for example, the suicide of a cancer patient). Through the media, necropolitics conducts a kind of therapy on the population, leveling and devaluing the excesses associated with death, such as terrorist attacks, political motivated suicides out of protest, ideologically-motivated murder, etc.

Necropolitics is characterized by a maximally neoliberal economic approach. As part of the so-called Fourth Industrial Revolution[93], the mass-scale introduction of sharply skyrocketing technologies based on self-learning neural networks, Big Data, and robotics gives rise to the phenomenon of global unemployment, which affects millions of people whose work is subordinated to algorithmization. Something has to be done with this enormous mass freed up and poured into the meager labor market (the precariatization of labor). One of the work-in-progress scenarios strictly in line with the Enraming is reducing population size to offset costs and maintain economic stability and balance. The value of human life is thus reduced to its economic profitability. Economically superfluous people are supposed to take leave. Lands containing minerals must be cleared of the tribes inhabiting them. These are rather striking examples of the discourse of necropolitics. In all of this, the essence of Gestell reveals itself through a new stratification of society. Technology (in the broadest sense, including gadgets, the Internet, IT corporations, servers and networks, factories,

---

93 See Klaus Schwab, *The Fourth Industrial Revolution* (World Economic Forum, 2016).

social networks and mobile applications, etc.) increasingly closes unto itself and drifts towards autonomy. Technological Enframing itself becomes the new elite surrounded by its own quasi-class of courtiers: programmers, engineers, designers, the "creative class", sales managers, and science popularizers. The rest of the population is, on the whole, an organic surplus still being used as a source of data. Ultimately, we end up with an absolutely artificial stratification of society, where the top of the pyramid (or the leading attractor in the rhizome) is occupied not by the Divinities, spirits, ancestors, or even the man of the Enlightenment, but inanimate material objects embedded in the global, complex, organized constellation of the Gestell.

Nevertheless, when it comes to people in the form of a mass, population, and workforce, the point of focus of biopolitics and necropolitics always remains the concrete human body. In Modernity, it was believed that a person's mind and personality are located in the head, inside the cranium, and that the head and eyes are, as it were, our vantage point and identity. In Tradition, the heart is held to be the formative and cognizing center. In Postmodernity, the dispersed and depersonalized body surface comes to the fore.

Biopolitics is power over the body, including the authority to punish the body, to excuse and dispose of it (necropolitics).[94] It is not a person that is a slave, but only their body (their extra-social existence being their existence outside of simple life), covered with whip scars and rotting in the holds of ships. In legal systems which assign a greater role to corporal punishment with varying degrees of cruelty, it is not the personality of the criminal that appears before the court and law de facto, but his body. Then the mutilated body of the transgressor is put on public display as a sign of what authorities will do with the body of anyone else who transgresses against the law. In systems where the prevailing principle is imprisonment, the human body is also subjected to violence and the authority of

---

94 Michel Foucault's *Discipline and Punish* opens with a similar description of the bloody execution of Robert-François Damiens.

regulations, but for the population at large it is as if prisoners are completely absent, off in a borderline state somewhere else. Pain and damage to their bodies is leveled out by the fact that such happens behind closed, blank walls, and by the fact that during their imprisonment they lose all the fullness of human dignity (according to the humanistic-legal notions of liberal society). For electronic systems and applications that track user activity, there is de facto no difference between the death and imprisonment of a person — in both cases, someone becomes an inactive user no longer emitting signals and data.

Looking ahead, we can see a possible future synthesis of biopolitics and data politics. Data politics is layered onto biopolitics, converting bodies into data. Specific operations and influences on the body (medicine, social services, diets, punishment, service) are translated into numbers and infographics handled by a state bureaucracy and corporate management. An increase in the locus of control is always associated with bureaucratic power and the growth of an intermediary apparatus. Signals and influences from the "data operators" (the authorities) are transmitted to bodies by actors occupying lower social positions, such as doctors, trainers, army instructors, police, or supervisors.

Foucault's study of power and prisons gave rise to a broad human rights movement and the beginning of reforms in European penitentiary systems, thus marking a shift from the ideas of supervision and punishment to re-education, correction, and rehabilitation, which has been implemented in rather noteworthy form in Scandinavian countries. Such is de facto a mere change in the mode of control from open and hard to veiled and soft.

Another logical consequence for the Postmodern human is the imperative of rethinking corporeality and, ultimately, emancipation from corporeality as such. The absence of a body, such as that facilitated by transferring consciousness into virtual reality or creating bio-robots (with living brains and mechanical bodies), means the impossibility of standing trial, being imprisoned, or being subject to violence. This remains a distant future prospect. Although this has not happened yet, the rethinking and reconfiguring of corporeality and bodily sensations is already in progress. Body modifications and piercings transform pain, scars, and cuts into aesthetics. BDSM practices make pain a desirable object of sexual attraction and pleasure, where the "subject" becomes the "submissive" object (punished by an authority-master; and grotesque leather-latex aesthetics emphasize totalitarian Stockholm syndromes of perversion). The use of masks and pseudonyms removes a personality, thus making corporeality completely anonymous. To this can be added elements of rethinking the erogeny of bodily zones, the sexualization of spontaneous skin areas, and claims that objective pleasure can be experienced not only through genitalia, but through any part of the body and skin surface.[95] In the sphere of contemporary art, particularly in activism, "artists" commit protest-acts of self-mutilation and self-violence which are supposed to be equivalent, whether literally or symbolically, to the torture to which they might be subjected at the hands of of the State's policing practices.[96] All of this is aimed at avoiding the influence of governmental authority on the body by leveling out punitive, painful practices.

No less important of a role is played by fear of death as the termination of life, especially if one has a good life. In the modern worldview, after death a person simply ceases to be. Nothing remains. The soul goes nowhere. The screen goes blank and nothing else turns on. A body's exclusion from the relations of consumption and pleasure is practically equivalent to death, but if a prisoner has access to the part of their body that is dispersed into virtuality (a cellphone and social media accounts), then the situation becomes not so unambiguous. The sheer severity of the end of the biological body is compensated for by virtually free communication with networked parts

---

95 See James Miller, *The Passion of Michel Foucault* (New York: Simon & Schuster, 1993).

96 See, for example, Petr Pavlensky's actionism.

of corporeality. This applies to the avant-garde of dehumanized and devitalized rhizome dividuals consistently immersed in Postmodernism, whereas the masses are not so dynamic; hence, for the latter, biopower and necropolitics are repressive, supervisory institutions that remain invisible to their naked eyes.

Transhumanism: Away with the Human

The point of intersection between anthropology, progress, the Gestell, and treating the beingful world as ready-to-hand is the philosophy of transhumanism (from the Latin *trans*, meaning "beyond", hence "beyond the human"). Transhumanism is the logical result of emancipation from man and the revision of the convention of "who and what is a human" (insofar as the human is part of the world, then the idea that the world is raw material also comes to apply to him). In his *Summa Technologiae*, the Polish science fiction and futurologist writer Stanisław Lem defined this approach as the beginning of "auto-evolution", i.e., the development of the human species is directed and proceeding no longer according to the laws of nature, as was the norm in the science of Modernity, but is now consciously directed and forced by the very object of this evolution, by man himself. One of the symbols of the transhumanist movement is the emblem "H+" or "human+", meaning an improved, augmented human. Here again we see the general pattern of the "unfulfilledness" of man as given by nature, as in the case of reality as *natura*.

The essence of the philosophy of transhumanism lies in positing a need for the human to use advancements and achievements in science and technology to improve their own body and expand their capabilities, to cure diseases and, ultimately, overcome death. At the same time, transhumanism represents a number of currents basing themselves on achievements in various scientific fields, i.e., on various technologies and their combinations. Many of them are already an everyday reality, others are expected in the coming decades, while still others are topics for futurology.

Fusing a person with technological implants and prostheses, blurring biological identity, and cyborgization are already everyday realities in medicine. Instead of compensatory rehabilitative prostheses, transhumanists aim to consciously expand the functions of the healthy parts of the body and organs with the help of implants, prostheses, or exoskeletons. Another example is the introduction of RFID chips into human bodies or installing receptors of neural signals from the cerebral cortex or parts of the body which allow for simple thoughts and signals to be transmitted from the body to computers or robots. A more common and accessible manifestation of transhumanism is biohacking, or the idea of improving bodily and cognitive functions through the use of medications, from vitamins, steroids, and nootropics to biologically active additives, antidepressants, analgesics, sedatives, etc. This also relates to experiments with daytime, sleep, and dietary regimes. Transhumanist technologies at the intersection of biopolitics and fashion include reproduction control, in vitro fertilization, cloning, the 3D printing of tissues and organs, genetic engineering and genome editing (CRISPR/Cas9 technology) allowing to create designer children and genetically modified living organisms (chimeras), transplantology and xenotransplants[97], as well as plastic surgery and high-tech cosmetology. Here also figure the medical technologies and methods pertaining to sexuality and changing gender identity, which we will discuss below.

Among the prospects that remain distant but are nevertheless already visible on the horizon is one of transhumanism's most desired technologies: a neural-computer interface or "brain-network" interfaces allowing for integrating consciousness and the global Internet, including the "Internet of things", or completely digitizing consciousness. This opens up possibilities for depersonalizing the individual, creating backup copies of consciousness or virtual clones of one and the same person. In this field, transhumanism merges with the design of Artificial

---

97 Transplanting human organs or grafting genes from other animal species.

Intelligence and neural networks. The use of nanotechnologies and nanorobots in medicine and tissue regeneration is also a prospect of the technology of the future.

Transhumanism inevitably affects and transforms relations in society as well as people's relation to the surrounding environment, stimulating the development and implementation of technologies in all spheres and along a broad, solid front. Thus, transhumanism absorbs and generalizes all progressive ideologies and apologetics for progress as such to become the most consistent expression of the desire for development and technological expansion. An exhaustive overview of transhumanist futurology can be obtained from popular culture, such as the literature and cinematography of genres like cyberpunk, biopunk, nanopunk, and dystopian/post-apocalyptic. In its philosophical dimension, transhumanism continues the vector of liberalism, incorporating the egalitarian arrangements of left-wing theory (emancipation from labor through the robotization of production), feminism, post-ecology, and techno-futurism.[98] Transhumanism postulates morphological and cognitive freedom for the subject.

One of the most important components of transhumanist philosophy is the ethics of abolitionism, according to which the essence of good is reducing suffering (illness, injury, disability, aging) and increasing the range and intensity of accessible pleasures. Here transhumanism reveals its hedonistic ethical background: abolitionism justifies the morphological freedom to change one's own appearance and constitution in a technological or genetic way in the pursuit of pleasure and desires, for the sake of demonstrating one's involvement in the flows of fashion, and for getting closer to a subjective ideal of external appearance and identity. In the future prospects of this vision, man in his modern form will disappear, giving

---

98   This includes the early Fascist Italian futurism of Filippo Tommaso Marinetti, who praised synthesizing man and mechanisms. On this point, futurism is complementary to the overall - both right-wing and left-wing - pathos and expectations of the early 20th century in connection with rapid industrialization. See Ekaterina Lazarev, "*Chelovek, umnozhennyi mashinoi*" [Man Times Machine].

way to a spectrum of genetically and technologically modified organisms that once upon a time passed through the "human" stage in their evolution. It is altogether possible that they will not even identify with the word "human".

The purview of philosophical bioethics encompasses questions pertaining to the correlation between rapidly emerging innovations, social practices, societal norms and customs (the sphere of deontology), the economy, and laws regulating the sphere of medical engineering and rights. The biopolitical nature of bioethics is obvious, and on the question of euthanasia bioethics intersects with necropolitics. Critiques of transhumanism from the standpoint of bioethics suggest that, while solving some problems, the rapid development of technologies simultaneously gives rise to new ones caused by, among other things, the fact that society does not have the time to change and adapt to new realities and practices. Bioethical discussions at the intersection of economics, sociology, and politics are meant to fit progress into certain limits, to compensate for the state of future shock that grips a population. By analogy with monotonic processes, an uncontrolled increase in pressure in a steam boiler will inevitably break the entire locomotive, so it is necessary to let off steam, balance the system, and adjust the speed of movement. At the same time, however, the very direction of development as a whole is not questioned or doubted, but is taken to be sooner or later inevitable.

Breakthrough high-tech innovations in medicine are often much more expensive than the technologies made available and refined on the competitive market over years. Some methods and services are *a priori* expensive due to consumables and equipment complexity, dumping, or lacks of subsidies which make them unprofitable. This gives rise to a new inequality along the line of possible access to transhumanist enhancement technologies. The ordinary, unmodified[99] person becomes part of the lower class in the new stratification, while the "aristocracy" differ from

---

99 Or a person with obsolete prostheses or implants with outdated software who does not have the money to afford upgrades.

the lower classes not only in terms of income and social status, but also physiologically, morphologically, biologically, and in terms of software. Already de facto now, strata are taking shape which are distinguished from one another in terms of their capacity to afford technological and medical improvement, and in the future some will be able to afford genetic modifications and the selection/design of offspring. A new wave of heated discussion on this topic was unleashed in the autumn of 2018, when the Chinese scientist He Jiankui announced the birth of the first genetically modified children. Using CRISPR-Cas9 technology, He Jiankui claims to have interfered with the embryos' DNA and instilled in them an innate resistance to HIV. The children were conceived through in vitro fertilization. He Jiankui's illegal, secret experiment stirred up society, and the scientist found himself detained and the mother and children were classified, but the precedent was nonetheless made. The future suddenly became a reality.

In the near future, this emerging situation will compel the state to rethink and deepen biopolitics from the level of power over the body to power over genes. The genes and genetic characteristics of a population will become the new property, assets, resources, strengths and weaknesses of the state. A person themself will not be as important as their capacity to provide future generations with the needed modifications, i.e., to improve brain functions, instill adaptability, eliminate susceptibilities to diseases, etc. One can also conceive of a strain of virus being released which affects certain layers of the population selected through gene markers. Thus open up the horizons of a fusion of transhumanism, biopolitics, and warfare strategies.

The introduction of neural networks and the robotization of production is already and will only further give rise to mass unemployment and cardinal changes in the landscape of the labor market, as a result of which a huge number of people will find themselves in the condition of a "precariat."[100] Economic

100 See Klaus Schwab's apologetics in his *Fourth Industrial Revolution*.

instability will only widen the gap between the rich who have access to the latest designs, and the poor, who are left with nothing.[101]

At last, coming face-to-face with the rapid embodiment of what just yesterday were the topics of futurological forecasts, even the man of Modernity is horrified at the prospect of his own dehumanization and disappearance amidst the maelstrom of technology. Hence modern man's existential anxiety towards the future and the problem of the gap between neo-elites and ordinary masses. This is aggravated by the fact that the modern person latently, somewhere in the depths, realizes that they are based on an empty convention — and this situation is the inevitable consequence of Cartesianism and evolutionism which once, quite recently, seemed to be the unshakable foundations of the subject and the individual.

As said above, the aim of tranhumanism is to overcome death, to ensure unlimited life expectancy, or technogenic immortality. From the point of view of bioethics and social anthropology, this raises substantial objections. There arises the problem of quality of life, especially when it comes to long-living old people who objectively cannot use the full range of services and lead an active lifestyle, but at the same time are still healthy and have free time (but not necessarily money). In addition to socio-economic factors, a definite role is played by existential alienation from life, boredom, experiencing the loss of separated friends or relatives, and being on the "sidelines." The increase in the proportion of the elderly population puts a burden on the economy, taking resources away from the young to provide for the old whose lives are thereby further artificially extended. If by means of genetic engineering and biohacking the periods of youth and maturity (active working age) are extended, then a logically analogous problem arises with ensuring the desired

---

101 Western states are still using the old methods of head-on prohibition of discrimination based on DNA, for example, by employers. See: Genetic Information Nondiscrimination Act of 2000 in the US, Bill S-201 in Canada, The Equality Act of 2010 in the UK, and the the EU General Data Protection Regulation.

level of consumption over much longer lifespans. Those who yesterday retired and changed their social status, thereby freeing up jobs, will in the future remain in their niche for much longer, which will greatly increase the burden on the economy and the extraction of resources, and thereby implicitly reduce the birthrate or compel authorities to regulate it more strictly in order to maintain balance. Wonting quality of life or sharp divergences in transitioning to the category of elderly persons, as well as the existential and psychological problems resultant of the new reality of longevity (the curse of long life), might push people to see voluntary death or death from disease and old age to be more welcome and healthy of an alternative to stagnation and boredom. The preference for suicide or death thereby levels out the pathos of technogenic immortality and the ever new horizons of the future.

Drawing ever closer to immortality, not to mention achieving it with genetic engineering, cyborgization of the body, or the virtualization of consciousness, closes numerous socio-economic, anthropological, and political problems, directly stimulates changes in lifestyle, and poses new demands and tasks for the development of technology. In naming all of these problems, philosophical bioethics once again does not take up the task of at least somehow calling into question the very vector and idea of progress. If everything can be changed, then in the end nothing should remain unchanged.

The impact of progress and transhumanism on society and politics, along with the problems of bioethics, directly and most clearly refute the aspirations of the advocates of so-called "Dark Enlightenment"[102] and right-wing accelerationism, who argue that it is possible to successfully combine progress in the natural-scientific sphere with maintaining a conservative socio-political agenda and state mode. The proponents of conservative progressivism and modernism fundamentally do not understand

---

102 See the works of Nick Land, the leading theorist of the Dark Enlightenment current and right-wing accelerationism. The essence of accelerationism consists in consciously accelerating development with the aim of hyper-extending the problems of the capitalist system.

the fact that technology in and of itself is not neutral, but expresses the ideology of the Gestell and subjugates all areas to which it can thrust its expansion and project the view of the beingful world as ready-to-hand raw material. In this respect, transhumanists are the most consistent, since they openly and directly declare that all forms of conservatism, traditionalism, anti-modernism and "simple life"[103] are enemies of progress, and thus set themselves the task of eradicating these phenomena in society as roadblocks on further development.

Why is the human body given as it is so important for Tradition? In traditional legends, various parties of the body are sacralized and transformed into symbols and elements of ritual, such as the semantics of the right and left hands, the Divine Eye of the Sun, the sacred symbolism of the heart, and divination by entrails in anthropomantic rituals (like the animal entrails rituals of the haruspices). Sexual organs also have a vast sacred symbolism. The vagina or yoni is in the same semantic nest as earth symbolism, referring to the acceptance of seed/grain and the generation of life (sprouts or children), and more metaphysically broadly is interpreted in the symbol of Shakti, the Divine force that creates the world. The phallus or lingam is associated with masculine, Apollonian, and Dionysian semantics, i.e., the affirmation of will, harrowing fields, seeding and fertilizing[104], and the metaphysical, vertical hierarchy of the world order.[105] Alongside genitalia, the fluids of the human body are also endowed with magical power, such as semen, blood, and particularly menstrual blood (simultaneously as a symbol of female maturity and, in some cultures, such as among Kalash and other archaic tribes, as a rigid taboo manifestation of dark

---

103 Cf. the "plain people" ideology among Amish Christians and Mennonites. Such might also be raised outside of the religious context to refer to living with minimal involvement in technological progress and consumption.

104 The Germanic Freyr, Greek Hermes, and Indian Shiva are often emphatically depicted with phallic motifs. Votive phallus figurines have been widespread among Indo-European and South Asian cultures since the deepest antiquity.

105 This is the "phallo-logo-centrism" of European culture in Jacques Derrida's interpretation.

female sacrality). The structure of the whole cosmos is also described in terms of the distribution and renaming of the body parts of a primal being killed by the Divinities, such as Purusha or Ymir, as in the *Elder Edda*:

> Out of Ymir's flesh was fashioned the earth,
> And the mountains were made of his bones;
> The sky from the frost-cold giant's skull,
> And the ocean out of his blood.[106]

The structure of varnashrama in Indian society is also described through the image of parts of the body of Brahma or the dismembered Purusha. A moral dilemma was also put to the Scandinavians with Frenrir's deception and militant Tyr's sacrifice of his own hand. On the whole, all of this refers us to the Hermetic formula dating back to Heraclitus on the likeness and reflectivity of the macrocosm and microcosm.

Also widely-known is the Egyptian tradition's myth of the dismemberment of Seth by his brother Anubis, the Deity of the underworld and rebirth. Chopped into pieces, Seth was then reassembled and revived by his wife Isis. The death and resurrection of Anubis reflects, among other things, the agrarian cycles and the idea of the world's decline. A similar motif of theocide can be encountered in Greece, in the Titans' persecution and dismembering of Dionysus. Dionysus is saved from irreversible death by Athena, who saves his heart, i.e., his Divine essence.

In considering such plots associated with anthropomorphic descriptions of the Divinities as one of the facets and limits of the ineffable Divine, we see that the dismemberment and loss of bodily integrity is a serious problem. In the world of people, the loss of the corporeal aspect of human identity is advancing through the consistent installation of post-/transhumanism and post-gender and post-identity doctrines. With the loss of the human form of appearance and "biological" constitution, a significant part of the traditional heritage — from the third-

---

106 *Vafþrúðnismál*, trans. Henry Adams Bellows (1936). The sacrifice of Purusha is described in the *Rigveda*.

estate agrarian and rural folk culture to the highest initiatic mysteries and the unity of man with the manifest world — crumbles into oblivion.

Ultimately, we can say that without the body, there is no tradition. But corporeality in itself, since people belong to the middle world, is also the point of intersection or beginning of two paths: the chthonic and the uranic. Plato's *Symposium* dialogue exposits the teaching of two natures of Eros, who is, alongside Thanatos, Dionysus, and Wotan, another one of the fundamental and problematic Divinities in Postmodernity. Uranic (heavenly) Eros is Aphrodite's companion and the source of the love for wisdom. In his *Eros and the Mysteries of Love: The Metaphysics of Sex*, Julius Evola describes Tantric sexual practices that raise a person to the higher metaphysical level of the oneness of Shiva and Shakti. Corporeality in this case becomes an instrument and conduit of Divine ecstasy. The other Eros, "popular", "vulgar", "*pandemos*" Eros, is the rough, crude Eros focused on the satisfaction of lust and hedonism. The difference between the two is pronounced on the level of their divergent semantic fields: "phallus" means "to swell", "to rise", "to be erect", while "penis" means "tail", something "dangling", and is related to the Latin *penetratio*, "penetration", i.e., phallus emphasizes the aspiration for transcendence, while penis refers to penetration and compulsive satisfaction.

The presence of the lower dimensions of Eros and corporeality has sometimes led philosophers to radical idealistic rejections of the body in favor of returning the soul to its source. Socrates spoke of this just before his death, describing the body as the "dungeon of the soul", on which point the Stoics partly agreed. Such perspectives sometimes lead to philosophical apologia for suicide as an act of demonstrating will directed towards the conquest of Divinehood, or as an act of voluntary return to the higher world.[107]

---

107 See Sergei Avanesov's lectures, *Filosofskaia suitsidologiia* [Philosophical Suicidology] (2000).

As we have seen, *Eros vulgaris* is the normative ideal of Postmodernism, which emphasizes corporeality, superficiality, expanding the spectrum of pleasure, and rejecting vertical structures. Here again arises the pattern of the "unfulfilledness" of what is given by the Divinities or from nature (from the point of view of Modernity) in the case of the body and its normative sexual functions and pleasures. Postmodernism and transhumanist abolitionism seek to expand the spectrum of pleasures into augmented reality through augmented corporeality. Hence the postulates of ubiquitous cyborg culture, trans-culture, and prosthesis culture advocating unlocking human potential "across the board."

Here lurks a naive substitution. It is a mistake to think that technology unleashes human potential. It is the human that assists technology to reveal its own potential. There is the potential Divine dimension within man which no technology is capable of revealing. Technology can only remotely simulate with hallucinations, exoskeletons, and neural interfaces. Finally, technology as Gestell is rooted in this world, in "reality", where the human ends up acting as a useful appendage for revealing the full power of the Enframing itself. When we see a person with a prosthesis, we admire not the person, but the prosthesis itself for allowing the disabled person to walk again or improve their body's performance beyond ordinary human biological capabilities. Now man has to be integrated and "revived" by the prosthesis built into him, just as the construction of a hydroelectric power station changes the essence of the Rhine. In this is revealed the potential of technology, which strengthens's mankind bind to the Enframing.

Looking further ahead, we can say that the Gestell in fact still needs man, like a cuckoo foundling needs a foster mother. Technology, global networks, gadgets, and robots need human beings to provide them with energy, hardware and software, connections and infrastructure. Then the Gestell will in one way or another get rid of biological entities or the biological part of post-human nature.

154

Feminism Against Humanity

Posthumanism, scientific-technological progress in biomedical technologies, social evolution, the emancipation of vulgar Eros, gender theories, and problems of femininity are all tightly intertwined in the philosophy of contemporary third-wave feminism.

Feminism as a movement began with the Suffragettes in the late 19th and early 20th century. The Suffragettes demanded equal access to voting rights and, later, educational and labor rights. Initially, the central image of the Suffragette's desired "norm" was a cast of the modern capable man, i.e., women were to fight for the extension of men's rights, men's lifestyles and occupations to women. The program of Suffragism meant transforming women into men.[108] The question of the essence of the genuinely feminine principle was not raised in first-wave feminism.

After women won all the basic human rights on an equal basis with men, the focus of the feminist struggle shifted to society, culture, sexology, medicine, hygiene, work relations, and other spheres. Second-wave feminism extended its methods, including to philosophy, over the course of the 1960s-90s. The struggle for rights and equality was framed in terms of the liberal and left-wing ideas of emancipation as "freedom from" in organic combination with shifting the image of the exploited from class to gender (women as the new proletariat). Then appeared sub-currents such as black feminism, which declared black women to be "cross-oppressed" across both gender and racial lines. Feminism penetrated into the milieux of homosexual minorities and formulated "intersectional" theories of socio-political and economic oppression.

Then, finally, the question was raised as to the essence of the feminine as autonomous and original *vis-à-vis* the masculine, especially since on the legal plane the difference between men and women had already been abolished de facto and de jure.

---

108 See Julius Evola, *Eros and the Mysteries of Love: The Metaphysics of Sex.*

Fighting against sexism, the objectivization of the female body in culture, and violence represented, among other things, attempts at finding an autonomous feminine principle that was not imposed by patriarchal culture. An interesting solution has been offered by advocates of feminist separatism, a movement which encourages women to live in isolated communes which are closed to men.[109] The theme of the "second sex" was explicitly raised in the book of the same title by Jean-Paul Sartre's partner, Simone de Beauvoir, who proposed to look at women not as a projection of man, but as the Other Subject.

A key role in overcoming binary sexual opposition is played by the theory of social sex or gender, which is understood to be a set of culturally conditioned patterns, stereotypes, practices, and signs that are commonly presupposed to be intrinsic to the representatives of one sex. As a special case of social constructivism whose main postulate is that biological sex might not coincide with a person's gender, social gender theory opens the gates for new "imagined communities" and posthumanist practices as part of the "gender spectrum." If Modernity insisted that humans have only two sexes (hermaphroditism being a pathology of fetal development) and two genders, then Postmodern gender theory, supported by feminism, asserts that gender is a spectrum featuring an unlimited number of intersections, combinations, statuses, and desires which are not innate, but are constituted by culture and can therefore be fluid, mutable at different times and situations, or altered for the sake of different desires. Classical Modernity viewed homosexuality as an inborn disease, and defenders of homosexuality insisted on the biological predestination of sexual orientation, whereas Postmodernity goes further and dissolves the whole grand narrative of biological innateness: henceforth, everything is ruled by desire and fashion. Technologies ensure the embodiment of these desires. One of the new dilemmas and problems facing society as a whole and feminism in particular is the appearance

---

109 Gender separatist practices have persisted in the format of cafes, forums, clubs, "women only" products and "safe spaces."

of transgender women. Sex reassignment surgeries, hormone therapy, cosmetic surgeries, and legal rehabilitation allow men to externally become women. This raises a problem for feminism: to what extent are trans-women "women" in the authentic meaning of the word? Can a trans-woman be a consistent feminist? There are many such problems in the post-gender world of hypochthonic entities.

Starting in the 1990s, a series of revisions and attempts to overcome the shortcomings of second-wave feminism, fierce disputes over women's rights to sexuality and control over their body (e.g., voluntary prostitution, pornography, fashion and conventional beauty), and discourses on the culture of "patriarchal exploitation" gave rise to third-wave feminism, which actively employs the theories of Foucault, Deleuze, Derrida, Lacan, poststructuralism, and "feminist linguistics." By the end of the second decade of the 21st century, feminism has gone from the suffragist demand for the right to vote to developing its own original, autonomous female episteme which proposes to understand woman not as a reflection of man or as a non-male or inferior to men, but to express the feminine precisely as "Feminine", as a "feminine Logos" in the form that this current's feminist philosophers see it.

Of all the varieties of feminism's at times even grotesque ideas, the most interesting cases for our study are the perspectives of two radical, ideologically intertwined currents, "xenofeminism" and "cyberfeminism." The prefix "xeno-" in Latin means "stranger", "foreigner", something of a strictly different, other kind. Xenofeminism postulates that a woman represents something radically Other in our *a priori* patriarchal world, yet does not provide any fundamental specification and definition of what precisely this "Other Femininity" is. The act of meeting and communicating with a woman is seen as contact with the Other, with something so different from everything human (because "human" is *a priori* a masculine concept), that any encounter between the Feminine and the Masculine can be accurately described in the likes of contact between an alien from another planet and an earthling. Even the gender of the earthling is no longer so important, for gender is also a masculine intellectual-social construct, hence xenofeminism criticizes even the radical political feminism of the second wave and the image of the "self-made woman", in which it sees the same game according to the rules of the phallo-logo-onto-centric episteme. The xenofeminist's world and language represent something so radically different and other that the act of communicating with a male is always a conflict, a misunderstanding, a random consequence, a production of some third dialect, like pidgin[110], out of two differently gendered languages.

The cultural referent of xenofeminism is the *Alien* horror film series about clashes between human space pilots, colonists, soldiers and an alien life-form, the Alien xenomorph.[111] The image of the alien monster was created by the artist Hans Rudy Giger, whose works depict a world inspired by the dark aesthetics of merging bodies and machines (biomechanics), alien landscapes and bass-reliefs made up of mechanisms and conveyor belts penetrating female and chimeric bodies (necro-eroto-mechanics). The Alien first developed as a parasite, and then grew into an alpha-predator driven by a thirst to kill and, as is seen in the later series, to provide for and protect a giant mother-producer of alien chimeras. It is telling that the main protagonist of the film series, Lieutenant Ellen Ripley, represents the embodiment of the ideal of second-wave political feminism: a free and strong-willed female soldier who single-handedly destroys the alien threat and saves the men around her to the maximal extent possible. The xenofeminism of the xenomorph attacks this successful figure.

---

110 Pidgins are simplified languages and means of communication that arise out of the situational interaction of representatives of two different languages and cultures. For example, episodic meetings and exchanges of goods between Russian and Norwegian sailors formed a common set of words, gestures and onomatopoeia akin to a professional jargon. At the same time, pidgin languages as such are not native languages and are localized by acts of communication in border areas.

111 See *Alien*, directed by Ridley Scott, 1979; *Aliens*, directed by James Cameron, 1986; *Aliens 3*, directed by David Fincher, 1992; *Alien Resurrection*, directed by Jean-Pierre Jeunet, 1997.

The whole series of *Alien* films does not give an unambiguous answer as to who prevails and which side is superior. The silhouettes of the Aliens are constantly present as a threat lurking in dark corners and pipes, like inevitable death pouncing from an unknown source. There is almost no natural environment in the films, even in the form of alien landscapes; there are only pipes, cables, laboratories, warehouses, ship engine rooms, and the endless emptiness of deep space. In the final part of this classic tetralogy, the main character is resurrected by cloning. Her DNA is mixed with that of the Alien, and the Alien womb is forced to give birth to a human-like bastard. Everything mixes and interpenetrates in a mindless flow of confusion, technologies, human cyborgs, psychopathologies, identity problems, the metaphysics of human and xeno-motherhood (the Aliens are like insects, organized around the womb that spawns them), and the all-around denial of final death.[112]

Xenofeminism is but one peculiar case of the broader, fundamentally undefined current of cyberfeminism, which represents the intellectual vanguard of third-wave feminism and the new feminist episteme. Cyberfeminism is rooted in the rapid development of computer, Internet, and media technologies since the end of the 1980s. New ways of communication, new virtual spaces, and the new culture of cyberpunk and hackerpunk opened up new perspectives and practices for feminism and the struggle for the feminine "Logos." The turning point was the philosopher Donna Haraway's *Cyborg Manifesto*[113], published in 1985, and the very term "cyberfeminism" as put forth by the ideologue Sadie Plant.

In her book *Zeros + Ones*, Plant gives one of the few existing definitions of cyberfeminism: "post-human insurrection - the revolt of an emergent system which includes women and

---

112 See Yozhi Stolet, "*Chuzhoi + Chuzhoi: opyt kommunikatsii 3000 goda*"; Laboria Cuboniks, *The Xenofeminist Manifesto: A Politics for Alienation* (London: Verso, 2018).

113 See Donna Haraway, *A Cyborg Manifesto: Science, Technology, and Socialist-Feminism in the Late Twentieth Century* (Minneapolis: University of Minnesota Press, 2016).

computers, against the world view and material reality of a patriarchy which still seeks to subdue them."[114] From this imperative follow series of theses, proposals, and textuo-visual images of the new feminism of the future which in our days are already actively being installed by cyberfeminists. Meanwhile, this movement and its ideologues principally avoid specific definitions, pursuing instead a strategy of dissolving meanings, narratives, and determinations in favor of chaotic assemblages, constellations, intersections, performances, lalalanguage, etc. For them, Femininity is not something specific, but a plurality of experiences, sexualities, and practices, etc. For them, real Femininity is like a cyborg, a construction of diverse organic, virtual, social, and technological parts that is subject to constant mutation and arbitrary self-representations. Haraway directly invites feminists to invent, "web" and "code" new identities, experiences, practices, and collectives. This current draws on the images and figures of cyberpunk culture: women and women-only communities are like viruses and underground hacker groups of cyberterrorists and anarchists who aim to corrupt, hack, and destroy the patriarchal world and the humankind which Modernity considered normative.

Thus, virtual space becomes a zone free from gender and sexual roles, or a zone of absolute freedom of choice and manifestation of the gender spectrum. The anonymity of the hacker and user is the embodiment of freedom from social stereotypes and gender-conditioned relationships. Anonymous corporeality echoes the anonymous "personalization" of the Web.

Finally, there comes the most significant declaration: woman cannot be free in principle as long as she has a biological body with anatomical differences from men at the level of primary and secondary sexual characteristics. The space of authentic emancipation lies not in the sphere of politics and law, but in overcoming bodily differences through cyborgization and

114 See Sadie Plant, *Zeros + Ones: Digital Women and the New Technoculture* (Fourth Estate, 1998).

virtual consciousness. When both women and men step over the organic stage of human evolution and become robots, virtual consciousnesses, etc., when the *a priori* objectified body that yields differentiated practices and descriptions is destroyed, only then will equality and freedom of self-realization be possible. The aim of cyberfeminism is not to become the female subject, but an avatar, a 3D model, a computer virus, a sexless alien entity, a "trans"[115] and radical Other. As Donna Haraway famously uttered: "I would rather be a cyborg than goddess." Hence occurs a reverse transfer: if the first mechanisms, machines, and algorithms were created by analogy with the flight of birds, the movement of snakes, the protective coloring and shells of animals, or replicated human joints, body parts, and logic, then now the human and animal world are interpreted as "meat" gadgets, organic mechanisms, bio-robots in possession of their own programming code (DNA) and capacity for digital integration.

Also of importance is how cyberfeminism continues to maintain the "discourse of the oppressed": industrial, entertainment, and experimental robots are now the new and one of the most oppressed classes. Robots have no subjectivity, and cyberfeminists see in this an allusion to the absence of genuine female subjectivity. Ethical issues, rights, and obligations with respect to robots and the first quasi-AI's are just beginning to be discussed, and the issue of taxing their labor is already being addressed. The robot is the ideal taxpayer, and robots are the fiscally ideal population. Cyberfeminist trends summate relations between people and robots with one pair of words: exploitation and oppression. Cyberfeminism borrows this class imperative from previous theories and declares the need to emancipate robots, neural network services, and other technological products, since the robot's freedom is the freedom of the cyborg-woman, freedom from gender.

---

115 The prefix "trans-" means transitioning from state A to state B, but in cyberfeminism there is no final B: as soon as the "subject" is at point B, it immediately transitions to point C, etc. Thus, "trans-" becomes an at least somewhat stable form of identity only in its absolutely fluidity in any arbitrary direction.

From a somewhat different perspective, a practically analogous imperative to recognize and emancipate the whole totality of "non-humans", i.e., objects, things, and gadgets, has been raised in object-oriented ontology and Bruno Latour's Actor-Network Theory, which calls for "giving a voice" to non-human things that also participate in the social life of humans and are just as much actors as people.[116]

If we look closely at the ideas of cyberfeminism, their art projects, textual styles, and futurology, then we can notice how behind the transhumanist pathos of abandoning the body and sex (and dissolving them into objects) for the sake of liberating the Feminine lurks the emancipation and actualization of something very different, something deep and absolutely impersonal: the dark, hypochthonic slime of de-personalized and de-ontologized matter.[117] The unfolding of cyberfemininity means not only the destruction of the masculine, but of the "human" altogether, whether the subject of Modernity, the microcosmic human of the world of Tradition, or even the "human" as an idea and humanity as such overall. Feminism has long since not been about rights and equality, but about an other, non-human world of schizo-rhizomatic potencies, desire machines, and post-gender coagulations.

Feminist theory is part of the ensemble of the foremost philosophical currents, the contemporary vanguard. The Suffragettes of the 19th century could not have known how all of this would turn out — they started from scratch with no theory behind them. Today, the struggle for elementary women's rights in developing countries is not suffragism, and not the classic struggle for emancipation, but the creeping penetration of third-wave feminism, fed from the rear by the whole might of gender studies and the new post-ontology. Everything starts

---

116 See Bruno Latour, "'Where Are the Missing Masses? The Sociology of a Few Mundane Artifacts" in Wiebe E. Bijker and John Law (eds.), *Shaping Technology/ Building Society: Studies in Sociotechnical Change* (Cambridge.: MIT Press, 1992).

117 See Ben Woodard, *Slime Dynamics: Generation, Mutation, and the Creep of Life* (Winchester: Zero Books, 2011). As an example of the atmosphere of the "slime world", one can cite the disturbing universe of Lovecraft or Deleuze's rhizome.

small. Today, when progressive women in less progressive or still conservative countries start talking about elementary "herbivorous" feminism and "understanding women", the matter at hand is always the destruction of humanity as such.

Das Man Plugged In

A central place in Martin Heidegger's philosophy is occupied by "*Dasein.*" For Heidegger, the whole history of European mankind and the history of Western philosophy is the consistent forgetting of Being and submersion into metaphysics, of which the final, inverted product is the Gestell.[118] The complex term Dasein is translated as "being-here" (*da* - here, *sein* - being), "presence", or "existence." It is not correct to say that the human being possesses Dasein as a form of property, but rather that Dasein is embodied like a syzygy in the human, whose being is determined by a set of existentials which describe-and-constitute culture, attunement and moods, philosophy, society, etc. The existentials outline the pre-structures of unfolding Being. Analyzing them shows how Being has been forgotten over the course of history and how negative transformations have come about in the existential, "thrown" spheres of the life of man and society.[119] Heidegger accounts for the following existentials in European Dasein:

+ *In-der-Welt-sein* - "being-in-the-world"

+ *In-sein* / Mit-sein - "being-in" / "being-with"

+ *Die Sorge* - "care"

+ *Geworfenheit* - "thrownness"

---

118 See Heidegger, *Being and Time*; Alexander Dugin, *Martin Heidegger. Poslednii Bog* [Martin Heidegger: The Last God].

119 Martin Heidegger considered Dasein in the optic of the human being and the phenomenology of individual presence, whereas Alexander Dugin has argued that we can speak of the Daseins of different peoples, whereby different peoples have different sets of existentials along which their traditions and cultures unfold. This also concerns at once the plurality of Daseins and the common fate of the oblivion of *sein* and *da-sein*. From here on out, we will explicitly understand Dasein as referring not only to the situation of concrete human presence, but also the "greater" Daseins of peoples.

- *Befindlichkeit* - "disposedness"
- *Verstehen* - "understanding"
- *Rede* - "discourse"
- *Stimmung* - "attunement", "mood"
- *Sein-zum-Tode* - "being-toward-death"

Dasein can exist in two modes, and in this lies all of its tension, the whole history and problem of resoluteness, and the decision, the event of the change of mode (*Ereignis*). Dasein can exist "of its own" (*eigene*) or authentically by addressing its finitude and disclosing its existentials in an authentic way. In this case, the truth of *sein* in *da-sein* is disclosed as "unconcealedness" (αλήθεια), as positive will open to Being. The second mode is *uneigene*, "un-owned" or "inauthentic", when Dasein does not resolve to be, and instead turns away from this decision. In this case, the existentials decompose and invert into their negative form, into the closed-offness of negative will, of machination (*Machenschaft*) against the beingful world.

For Heidegger, the history of philosophy is the history of the forgetting of Being as unconcealment, *ergo* the oblivion of *sein* in *da-sein* leading to the loss of the *da-*, the "here" of presencing. There is no place, no time, no presence, but a state of being lost and not understanding; instead of speech there is only "chatter" (*Gerede*), the carelessness of abolitionism, the world as ready-to-hand, mood swings, general disorientation and, finally, the denial of mortality.

Dasein is fundamentally free and makes its decision about authentic or inauthentic being on its own, in and through man and peoples. Therefore, the forgetting of Being and the shackling and framing (another variation of the term Gestell) of Western thinking in the form of the metaphysics of technology comes about through certain philosophical decisions about the Being of the beingful world, through ideas and their development, through the thickening of the negative subjectivity of *das Man* stretched over thousands of years.

164

All of this converges at the focal point of the problem of alienation, which permeates the world along with *das Man*. Alienation is in general the foremost, central, most existentially saturated problem of Dasein, man, and peoples.

Martin Heidegger dwells in detail on the word *heimische*, meaning "possessing a homeland", rootedness in one's native land, and the feeling of connection with home and hearth, as indicated by the root *heim*. *Heim, Heimatland*, and *heimische* refer to the space, the here-place (*da*) in *Da-sein*. Heidegger takes the adjective *unheimlich* (terrifying, repulsing, frightening, uncanny) and singles out the root *heim* and the negative prefix *un-*. *Unheimische* means homelessness and rootlessness. The loss of one's place and hearth is emphatically terrifying, casting us somewhere outside of ourselves and our own. The philosopher of the Black Forest calls for returning to understanding truth as a forest clearing or "lighting" (*Lichtung*) which gives space for light to penetrate it as it is. Truth as unconcealment needs a place (*da*) for lighting up and clearing, but in the situation of *unheimische* there is no such place — the world open to the light of Being is lost, closed. The existential of being-in-the-world turns into homelessness or even worldlessness.

The Russian word for "estrangement" or "alienation", *otchuzhdenie*, plays with the semantic facets of distance, withdrawing, and the appearance of something foreign in what is happening or in things. *Otchuzhdenie* penetrates the world like a centrifugal force that tears apart and dissolves the one into many. In a certain sense, this alienation is processual, not eventful. In the state of alienation, the organic ties of culture, language, and the traditions of peoples are destroyed. Ultimately, a person does not even recognize the world in which they find themselves and does not recognize it as their "own." Thrownness in the world as manifestation, as theophany, as being a guest in the world, and as dwelling in the world of Divinities and people, is inverted into the "casting out" (or awakening) of the human amidst the non-human, the desacralized, and the fragmented.

Feelings, conjectures, suspicions, or awareness of alienation give rise to restless, anxious natures, awakening the marginal figures of poets, artists, dark sectarians, mystics, and radical philosophers of life as well as death. Traditionalists and European pagans, of course, are also marked by the seal of the glaringly visible alienation of the modern, degenerate world from former harmony.[120] Consciousness of alienation is not yet a guaranteed precondition for Dasein's turn toward authenticity. It is the starting position of anxiety and reflection on the moment and of oneself's being in it. Those who do not recognize their alienation from Being, from the sacred and from existence, make up the faceless masses of *Das Man* as such, those satisfied with everything going on, the course of progress, the decomposition of meanings, and the dispersion of the subject. Fundamental questions are raised and honed out of this state: the enigma of the eschatological sacred, awakening on the eve of the end of the world (which appears to be an infinite duration), Dasein meeting its end, and the question of whether this death will be an authentic event or something completely failed and irrelevant that would confirm that the whole history was for nothing on all counts.

While reading Klaus Schwab's[121] programmatic book on winter evenings in a remote, abandoned Siberian village, we noted that this president of the World Economic Forum in Davos frequently pronounces one thing whose fundamental importance has, it seems to us, been unjustly ignored by commentators. Exalting the installation of technologies in ever new spheres of human activity, nature, and things, and upon describing the expansion of technology in developing countries and the Third World, Schwab regularly utters the word "connectivity", or being "plugged in." He directly links the

---

120 It is worth emphasizing that we are talking about the same world, and not about moving between two worlds (true and false). The very properties of the era dictate to us the language of discontinuity and opposition in almost Gnostic tones, whereas we should duly approach the lowest point of Night on the Year-Wheel.

121 Klaus Schwab is the founder of the World Economic Forum and the ideologist of the globalist transhumanist project known as "The Great Reset".

proliferation of the global Internet, satellite communications, technological applications and the data logistics on which they are based — i.e., that which constitutes the substance of "connectivity" — with whole regions of Earth, their spaces, societies, businesses, animal populations (with GPS markers), and things (city lights, for example), becoming plugged in, connected, and thereby "updated".

The word "initiation" etymologically means "consecrating", i.e., introducing into society and a corresponding status, estate or mystery through dedication. Initiation is the existential nerve of traditional societies, the leading social structure, and in some sense the "social lift." Whoever is initiated, i.e., whoever is introduced into the mystery, is a human being.

Martin Heidegger pointed out that the Greeks understood Being as *ousia* (οὐσία), as that which is constantly present.[122] One of the translations and semantic facets of the word Dasein is "presence" or "presencing", "being *here*", or "existing." Looking at traditional societies through the prism of Dasein, initiation is the pledge to the authentic mode of existing. Whoever has not passed through initiation becomes an outcast of society, hence the regime of his existentials are distorted.

Looking attentively into what Klaus Schwab and the other apologists for a new technological revolution write, we see that the Gestell is pronouncing its strategy (its *Machenschaft*) of deforming and destroying the structure of Dasein. This is done through adding the new existential of "connectivity" and being "plugged in" with its peculiar accentuation and general set of existentials. Henceforth, Da-sein is *verbunden-sein*: "being-here" is "being-plugged-in." Then begin the black metamorphoses of the nature of man, the beingful world, and objects.

In the digital era, being "connected" and "plugged in" becomes the foremost existential through which the presence of being, the presencing of Dasein, is channeled and realized.

---

122 See Martin Heidegger, *The Essence of Human Freedom: An Introduction to Philosophy*, trans. Ted Sadler (London: Continuum, 2002).

In the Fourth Industrial Revolution and the incoming future, "to be" means "to be online." The mass proliferation of the Internet, gadgets, decreased costs and increased access to the Internet for developing regions, together with discussions around consolidating the "right to Internet access" as one of the new inalienable human rights — all of this marks the launch of a fundamental revision of the human's ontological and existential status in the world, a world now dominated by the Enframing and technology heading in the direction of "being-plugged-in." For now, the existential of "connectivity" is realized through exteriorized objects: personal computers, laptops, smartphones, webcams, fitness trackers, etc. In other words, for now, "being-plugged-in" is embodied in augmented reality tools, proxy objects, terminals, and interfaces. The spread of accessible mobile signals since the 1990s is one of the Enframing's waves that has radically changed the landscape and trajectory of social life, culture, management practices, logistics, and entertainment. The advertising slogan of the Finnish company Nokia, "Connecting People", is a clearly articulated imperative of alienation. Since the early 2000s, even young school children have come to possess mobile phones. In this optic, the next, absolutely logical step is such phenomena as accounts and blogs for newborn infants or dogs, stones, or chairs on social networks to inform surrounding subscribers and users about the presence of children, dogs, stones, and chairs. The next step — already technically implemented and partially embodied — is implanting transmitters and network adapters directly into human or animal bodies so that they broadcast data and the "online" status of their existence. People without implants are still poorly "plugged in", as they can take their smartphone out of their pocket, lose it, or go to the countryside where there is no computer, but a person with an implant is always online wherever he goes, wherever there is network connectivity. The same is true for non-human beings and objects: "plugged in" dolphins and whales, flocks of birds and packs of wolves, sea currents and winds tracked with sensors, and trees chipped and soils zoned - this is the Gestell's work on plugging-in and digitizing reality. Or there is the OneWeb global satellite Internet project, which has the task of providing broadband access to the Web at any point on the globe in any moment. Once it is launched, it will become absolutely unimportant whether a person is in the Taiga, in Alaska, or in the mountains of Southeast Asia — as long as they have a smartphone and antenna, they can update their status and profile picture in real time. Of importance here is the very fact of the presence of such a possibility, the very fact that space is permeated with radio waves allowing one to plug in to the Network and demonstrate/update their presence. The very fact of this possibility demonstrates the horrifying scale of the Enframing's machinations upon the manifest world.

The expansion of connectivity will already in the near future lead to revisions of not only the notion of Dasein, but Being. At the beginning of European philosophy, the Greeks thought Being as constant presence. The might of technology changes how this presence is embodied and realized in the new world picture through "connecting." Connection is what is most important, while what exactly is being connected is secondary, for ultimately everything should be plugged in and digitized. The border is erased between humans and objects, animals and the nature around them, the human lifeworld of the community and the glass and concrete skyscrapers with server closets and copy machines. Following Graham Harman, the founding father of object-oriented ontology, Ian Bogost has proclaimed that Dasein belongs not only to people, but to non-humans, objects, things, and relations.[123] He is not yet saying that everything should be plugged in to the Net-Web, but this is implicit in the general futurological, "un-humanist" vector of his philosophy.

Connectivity is the black double of (neo-)initiation already here and now, and awareness and exaltation of this fact will play an ever greater role in the future. Parents passing down logins and passwords to children will be symmetrical to ritual initiation, the introduction of a person into society, now adjusted for the

---

123 See Ian Bogost, *Alien Phenomenology, Or, What It's Like to be a Thing* (Minneapolis: University of Minnesota Press, 2012).

horizontal egalitarianism and subcultural fragmentation of the rhizomatic societies of the future and the most progressive cities of the West. In French, the slang word *branché* means a fashionista who follows the newest trends and constantly shows off their familiarity with new products. But this word also means "connected" or "plugged in", i.e., inserted into the network, like "branch" in English. Postmodern neo-initiation is *branché*, it is fluid reconnecting to everything fashionable and various exotic attractors, services, and networks. To be *branché*, or "to be" in general, means to be in a trend. This word burst into reality in the wake of the hyper popularity of Twitter at the turn of the 2010s. To be is to be trendy. A person acquires only as much existence as they have connections to sundry gadgets, services, networks, banks, online games, applications, and popular sites.

It will be very interesting to see how the status of people who will still not be plugged in to the Web will change in the future. Most importantly, there will be no such people at all. In the most literal sense, the unplugged being (objects and even more so people) will not be considered anything present or alive. The entity that is not plugged in will be de-ontologized. Here we can recall the case of stories of ghosts and apparitions interpreted from the modern point of view since the 18th century. Obviously, in the modern picture of the world, ghosts do not exist, just like the afterlife and netherworlds. Science does not confirm their existence, and even actively refutes the possibility of subtle "bodies" and apparitions. If someone seriously believes in ghosts, then this person is supposed to be in need of a doctor check-up, is a strange type (most likely uneducated), or too romantic (most likely a girl, a fan of Edgar Allan Poe or Maupassant). Sightings and photographs of ghosts are explained as defects in lenses, film, or matrix, light glares, twilight haze, or hallucinations, psychosis, and self-hypnosis. Modern man cannot seriously declare and claim the presence of ghosts, simply because they do not exist. It is precisely this literal status of non-existent that will be assigned to people who are not plugged in to the Network, to whose who have never been online. It will not even be possible to say that they ever even existed. If a plugged-in person suddenly sees an unplugged body, and his glasses or augmented reality lenses do not identify the body, then he will most likely think that such is a program failure or 3D reality rendering error, a signal interference or the intrusion of a foreign broadcast. When a plugged-in person encounters an unplugged one, he would be more likely to think that he has stumbled over flat pavement than to have come into contact with something "ghostly." Just as ghosts do not exist, so do unplugged, unconnected people not actually exist. More precisely, it could be said that they still exist before the next step in the "disenchantment" of the world. In the future, talk about the unplugged will sound like stories of mankind's barbaric past, fairy tales, absurd anecdotes, or "trash horror." Whatever is not plugged in is white noise, an artifact of failed virtual rendering, burnt pixels, error 404.

Finally, the existential of connectivity also calls into doubt and discards another existential nerve of Dasein: *zum-Tode-sein*, i.e., Dasein's finitude, death, and hence teleology. On the whole, this continues the same line of transhumanism and transitioning from the body to the cyborg and digital double. Digital prostheses and virtual copies are plugged in to the Net *par excellence*, and in the foreseeable future they will be even absolutely immortal. Death means "disconnecting", "unplugging", exiting into the eternal offline. Anxiety over being offline already exists now: when someone has not appeared on the Net for a long time, has not posted any pics or news, has not called or written an SMS, we begin to worry and try to contact the person, to find out if they are alive and well. Lack of network activity has already become an indicator of something bad, of an "incident." What happens to a person when they are temporarily unplugged? They face reality — the inferior reality of Modernity, where instead of colorful advertising and interactive features, there are only the technical markups of QR codes and markers for digital vision. But even such an extremely truncated reality (disenchanted from the Traditionalist point of view) plunges the subject *das Man* into a state of frustration, neurosis, psychosis, abstinence and boredom. "Offline" means colliding with reality, the cessation of Internet surfing (consumption and representations), and quasi-death (a person does not die biologically, but being excluded from streamings makes his status almost comparable to death), which must be avoided by all means.

For those who remain within the Network and record another going offline forever, there begin the metamorphoses of posthumous existence, "digital afterlife", e.g., a digital cast or "ghost" of a once former person. Accounts and posts of the deceased remain in plain sight, can be further distributed, rated, and commented on. If a sufficiently trained neural network chat bot is connected to the account, such as ETER9 or eterni.me, it can reproduce dialogues of medium complexity on behalf of the deceased with sufficient reliability and can make new posts after the original person's death. Another option is that the deceased's accounts and data can be inherited by his relatives, which in our days is already legally formalized as part of common inheritance. Alternatively, a person's social network profile can be moved to a "digital cemetery" category, a database of the pages of deceased marked with a special "owner deceased" badge.[124] There are also more exotic practices: a broadcasting webcam or mobile phone can be installed in the deceased's coffin to maintain signal and the ability to call them from this world.[125] The existential and eschatological importance of death is thus devalued inasmuch as the digital cast can live on in "connectivity." The offline status is reversible if the dropped user can resume access.

It is not for nothing that we have touched upon the moods of *das Man*, which more broadly refers us to the fundamental attunement or mood (*Stimmung*) of Dasein in our days. According to the Greeks, philosophy began with wonderment, astonishment, with the inspiring illumination

---

124 See the almanac *Arkheologiia russkoi smerti* [The Archaeology of Russian Death] 6, "*Smert' i tekhnologii*" [Death and Technologies].

125 A mobile phone is one of the frequent artifacts that can be found next to the remains of Columbine victims (urns with their ashes).

of the lightning-Logos. Socrates associated amazement with Iris, the messenger of the Divinities and the daughter of Thaumas (Θαύμας - "wonderful", "miraculous", θαῦμα - "surprise"). Thus, a link between Earth and Heaven was established in philosophy. Astonishment at the openness of the cosmos is the first, initial mood of Dasein in deep antiquity, at the dawn of European philosophy and history. Heidegger identified the mood of contemporary Dasein, which has fallen into alienation at the "end of history", as that of fundamental boredom.[126] He describes falling into boredom through three successive illustrations. The first form of boredom is that state in which a person finds themself on the platform of a provincial railway station with simply nothing to do with their free time while waiting for the train. Nothing around him attracts his attention, and he honestly admits to himself that he is bored, left only with realizing and experiencing the duration of time. The second example describes a pleasant party, where someone plays the guitar and drinks and socializes with friends. Upon returning home and getting ready to go to bed, one eventually realizes that such a seemingly pleasant and eventful evening in good company was still no more than a waste of time. All the events, emotions, and content of time fall into a void of unveiled boredom. The party is just a distraction and filling up of time, while afterwards the reality of boredom still catches up with a person and devours events, exposing their existential backdrop. The third kind of total boredom is the situation in which there is no longer any bored subject and no awareness, whether direct or post factum, but instead only boredom as both the backdrop and immediate mood. This third boredom is so deep that no one in any way reflects upon its presence, all the while as "events" and in general "good time and good hangouts" unfold all around. The attunement of this third, deepest boredom is comparable to the endless duration of time in the last age.

Das Man is bored, but he can be bored not only passively and in procrastinating, but also actively and intensely. The

126 See Martin Heidegger, *The Fundamental Concepts of Metaphysics: World, Finitude, Solitude.*

Enframing's machinations upon the beingful world are extremely boring, but at the same time are incredibly intense and large-scale. The bored post-human can have fun in a variety of ways: building a dam, draining a swamp, discovering gravity, visiting a royal horserace, launching a rocket into space and landing on the moon, splitting an atom and building a collider at CERN, changing their sex and gender, replacing their hands with bionic tentacles, settling down in MMORPG's, voting in elections, mining rare metals to make mobile phones, blogging on Instagram, reviving pagan traditions, going to church, describing the existence of jalapeño peppers, etc. All of this is intended to fill up boredom and kill time, to create pseudo-events and hype around constant movement towards the new, the "original", the future, and other exotic attractions.

Openness to Being, through which a person is overwhelmed with the inspiration of creativity and the touch of the Muses, also turns into its black double: openness to "everything new" and production. If bored *das Man* starts playing with reviving pagan traditions, then this pseudo-openness takes on the form of omnivorousness, syncretism, eclecticism, and a kaleidoscope of superficial combinations. This brings us to intuiting a deeper distinction between the conditions by which people might turn to pagan traditions and Traditionalism: either some anybody-nobody (in German here it would read *das Man*) is reproducing discourse out of the desire to fill up their boredom, or Traditionalists — those who have experienced the existential tension described by Evola — are striving to break through to the authentic, to the air and freedom of fully-fledged Being. In this case, the second intuition says that they reside in a different attunement of Dasein and regard the boredom of *das Man* as an external attack testing them.

Flat Ontological Landscapes

The intellectual landscapes and ontologies of the world of *das Man* are nonetheless very diverse. We have already described many of the strategies of the Enlightenment and Modernity, Postmodernity and transhumanism, cyberfeminism and biopolitics — all of these are patterns and intertwinings of the intellectual intentions of the post-sacred world. They are the mechanisms, ways, and history of alienation.

We can quite reliably imagine the man of Tradition's reaction to the picture of the world today which we have presented. Most likely, he would have called these teachings "anti-godly" and turned away from them, in the best case burning these authors' books along with their thinkers themselves. Historically, however, such an approach proved to be only a postponement, and nowadays it is no longer relevant at all. At this point, Traditionalism finds itself in a more advantageous and bold intellectual position. Therefore, we shall plunge into the intellectual universe of *das Man* (especially since *das Man*'s reality is already the surrounding one) with the intent of performing a kind of "gravitational maneuver" around this mass anomaly. With its deism, atheism, and Cartesian subject, Modernity was still too metaphysical, teleological, and holistic for Postmodernity. When Postmodernity and the new ontologies revise, overcome, relativize, and deconstruct the "objective" knowledge of Modernity and the values of the Enlightenment, an extremely important, perhaps even useful moment arises before Traditionalism. We can pave the way through these intellectual *topoi* and optics of flailing Postmodernity and climb up the conceptual peaks, but only to take a look around from their height. And, perhaps, we will see something useful for understanding and debunking this alien picture of the world, for re-enchanting it. Or we might plunge into the gravitational anomalies for the sake of distinguishing the dark shades of the sacred against this even darker eschatological backdrop. We must look at and read Postmodernity "from the right", from the position of post-sacrality. The prefix "post-" means not only and not so much a period of time after sacrality, but rather the configuration and accents within the sacred which are complementary to the situation of the eschatological moment of existential alienation and awakening amidst the thickness of ice.[127]

The fundamental turn to materialism (and even earlier the installation of creationism) was the propositioning of how *das Man* sees the world and how he wants to see the world. One of the most complementary descriptions of the subject of *das Man* in Modernity was given in the behaviorism of John Watson and B.F. Skinner. Behaviorism is centered around concrete, external, observable reactions on the part of an individual. Later, in Skinner's work, this came to include internal events and experiences controlled by external factors. Man and his psyche are imagined to be like a socially reflective automaton whose behavior and reactions are determined by external events and stimuli. The human being is a "black box" that perceives through its external sensory organs various signals/events which cause reverse external reactions. What happens inside the "box" is either unknown, unobservable, and therefore unimportant, or consists of internal mechanisms also determined by external events. Then a person can be "trained", i.e., their automaton can be calibrated through external pressures. It directly follows from behaviorism that a person's behavior (or that of masses of people) can be altogether successfully analyzed, controlled, and directed. From the point of view of sociology and economics, it is completely unimportant whether a person is a "rational subject guided by goals of achieving the greatest benefit" or an "irrational subject of their own desires." The internal beliefs of automata-people are equally susceptible to manipulative strategies. Freedom and subjectivity are reduced to the determinism of stereotypical reactions and satisfying socially acceptable correlations.

The decision-making "black box" also applies as a description to the contemporary stage of the development of Artificial Intelligence, where neural networks themselves devise algorithms and patterns for processing information and

---

127 See Alexander Dugin, *Radikal'nyi Sub'ekt i ego Dubl'* [The Radical Self and its Double] (Moscow: Eurasian Movement, 2009); Askr Svarte, *Gods in the Abyss*.

decision-making. Unlike the coding consistently written by programmers, which describes all the procedures involved, the work of contemporary AI is opaque and unknowable.[128] It is no coincidence that on this point we once again find ourselves at the intersection of the human and the machine, the non-human object. *Das Man* is in principle interested in blurring the boundary between the human (the embodiment of Dasein) and the non-human world of objects. This is the backdrop of the process of virtualization and the neo-materialist wave of "unhuman studies" of the last several decades.[129]

The foremost imperative of neo-materialism is constructing a "flat" (as per Levi Bryant, Graham Harman, and object-oriented ontology) or "tiny" (as per Ian Bogost and the phenomenology of things) ontology centered around overcoming anthropocentrism in the appropriation and distribution of the hierarchy of Being/Dasein in the world of objects. Everything turns out to be real, existing, and beingful, and consequently man must renounce or lose his "royal power" over Being and his privileged access to things.[130] This continues the philosophical line of Gilles Deleuze's polemics around Immanuel Kant's notion of the "thing-in-itself" (*Ding an sich*) and claims a contorted, inverted, or "transcending" reading of Martin Heidegger.

In *The Fundamental Concepts of Metaphysics*, Heidegger analyzed perception and the access of things to the world through Dasein. In this hierarchy, the dominant place is occupied by man, since he is *Weltbildend*, "world-forming", which directly follows from the Heideggerian problem of accessing primordial, unmanifest Being (*Seyn*), which is from two different sides among people (man as the shepherd of Being) and the Divinities

---

128 See chapters 5 and 11 in James Barrat, *Our Final Invention: Artificial Intelligence and the End of the Human Era* (New York: Thomas Dunne Books, St. Martin Press, 2013).

129 The key points in this history include the seminars and work of the Cybernetic Culture Research Unity (CCRU) starting in 1995, in which Plant and Land participated, and the conference "Speculative Realism / Speculative Materialism" held in 2009 with Ray Brassier, Graham Harman, and others.

130 See Bogost, *Alien Phenomenology, Or, What It's Like to be a Thing.*

(the Divinities as questioning Being). Second for Heidegger come animals, which are "world-poor" (*Weltarm*): they live and, of course, have their own mode of accessing the world, but such differs from the human world by its incompleteness. For example, people eat and die, whereas animals devour and croak. The fact that we perceive the dog next to us as "eating" is a transfer of our relationship to the world onto an animal; we imagine or conceive of the animal as eating just like we do, but this is not the case. The same goes for death and other reactions and behavior, even among the most complex and trained primates which have demonstrated communication on the level of human children (like the gorilla Koko), but which are nevertheless always cases of filigree training and unequal communication. In the last place in the hierarchy of Being are inanimate things, such as wood, stones, or objects. They are altogether "worldless" (*Weltlos*): they have no access to the world and to perceiving. The lizard which lies and basks in the sun on the warm surface of a stone perceives both the stone, the sun, and the surroundings (for example, it scans to make sure that no predators get too close), but the rock itself in no way understands or reflectively perceives the sun, the lizard, or the side of the road where it lies. All of this is inaccessible to the rock, and it does not fundamentally distinguish its own presence alongside the road or, for example, when a person throws it into a pond or cuts and inserts it into the alignment of a stone arch.

If we look at the configuration constructed by Heidegger from the point of view of tradition, myth, and fairy tale, then we will see at once both likenesses and differences. Firstly, there is the peculiar place of man in this system. That people together with the Divinities make up a pair of special beings which are more than all others (or generally the only ones) immersed in the problem of the being of the world, Being in general, and their own being — this resonates with the cosmocentrism of ancient paganism, in which man is a microcosm within the macrocosm. This is maximal humanism, fundamental theo-ontology (cf. Heidegger's Last God), and Dasein, as opposed to Enlightenment humanism and Postmodern post-humanism.

But myths, including those which come down to us through folklore, convey to us the knowledge that both animals and even inanimate objects were very much alive and lived their own rich lives. Moreover, sometimes animals or trees could have more knowledge than a hero and could act as his assistants or guides. Objects could be the forms into which the entities of lower demonology transformed, such as dwarfs, trolls, gnomes, or the receptacles of the spirits of trees, rivers, and lakes. In other words, everything extant in Tradition, the whole beingful world, had greater access to Being and life, to the world, than in the ensuing dark ages of, firstly, creationism, which denied the existence of the soul among non-humans and even non-Abrahamic peoples, and then the era of scientific knowledge of the objective, exterior, material, inanimate reality of nature. In this regard, Heidegger remains a strictly academic philosopher for whom the question of Being is the priority, while the "poor world" of animals and the "worldlessness" of objects are simply fixed as the given of his era. The problem of Being is still the affair of people and Divinities, even when animals around them suddenly start speaking.[131]

The philosophers of flat ontologies, such as object-oriented ontology, Latour's Actor-Network Theory, and speculative materialism, directly propose that we revise Heidegger's configuration in favor of the flat or horizontal ontological arrangement of objects and declare that all things[132] have their own minimal ontology, their own presencing and understanding of the world. In his interpretation of Aristotle, Levi Bryant insists on the substantiality of objects as the minimal ground for

---

131 The life of animals and things can be substantiated not only by transferring the human view to the non-human, but also by the direct reality of myth, its enlivening richness, and the constitutive force of human mytho-magical *imagination*.

132 At this point, the "Latour litany machine" (per Ian Bogost) is "turned on", i.e., the most diverse, unrelated and unassociated objects are enumerated and listed to underscore the diversity of present objects and the equality of their access to being: glasses in a cafe, a figurine of a cat, a philosopher at a table, a stone in a lunar crater, a tire, an apple, an alpaca, a skull, a monk, an internal combustion engine piston, a picture on the Internet, a jellyfish, an iCloud account, gravity, the UN assembly, a sense of shame, the sounds of wind, relationships, etc.

an egalitarian ontology. For him, all objects in the universe are equal because they exist as such, regardless of whether they exist in different ways or in different relations. This is to say that the status of presence is the abstract basis of equality and democracy, and in order to overcome the "abstractness" of his thesis, Bryant appeals to the category of substance, the propertyless substate that is the basis of all objects, but which is not the source or embodiment of their forms and qualities. Substances are not predicates of objects and their properties, the latter of which give rise to differences and hierarchies. Bryant deliberately turns Heidegger's ontological differentiation inside out to assert identity between Being and beings (all extant objects). He distills beings and the world down to bare substances, on which level nothing is distinguishable, *ergo* a "democracy of objects" is destiny.[133] At the same time, Bryant utters in passing that all substances are identical to one another, which directly means postulating the idea of the "one" alongside apologetics for the plurality of material linings.

Speculative realism (or speculative materialism) insists that objects (things) perceive the world and even communicate amongst each other without the participation of a human as an actor or mediator. Here arises the controversy around Immanuel Kant's concept of the "thing-in-itself." On the one hand, it is argued that humans' lack of access to understanding a thing in itself is positive, as such leaves things withdrawn and inaccessible to human intervention. That is, things-in-themselves somehow exist in an absolutely unknowable way. Since their constitution, sense organs, and expressions are fundamentally different from human ones, they are detached, alien objects with an alien ontology.[134] Man's communication with things and use of objects is always "pidgin" or, in Ian Bogost's terms, caricature and metaphor. The principle of caricature indicates that we understand things or objects through certain hypertrophied

133 See Levi R. Bryant, *The Democracy of Objects* (Ann Arbor: Open Humanities Press, 2011).

134 As opposed to the embrace of understanding things as "things-for-us."

strokes of their being which are accessible and functional to us, while the details of things that have no meaning or utility to humans are overlooked. In other words, a whole thing is not perceived as such, but as a deformed caricature ignoring the aspects which are unimportant to us, but which are important for the thing or object itself. When we look at a cartoon figure of a famous person, we still recognize the person in deformed caricature and understand the conventionality of genre. In the case of things and objects, people take the caricature to be reality, not suspecting the reality of the thing-in-and-of-itself. At this point emerges another point of view: the being of things and objects is still somehow accessible to man, whether through metaphor, extremely distorted signals, false interpretations, or in mathematical terms (Claude Meillassoux). Man can imagine[135] the being and reality of non-human objects, but can never fully step into their shoes or achieve an ultimate understanding of object-being.

Nevertheless, the different currents of speculative realism are united in asserting a flat ontology of universal equality and a resulting plurality of forms of the organization of communication and access to Being. There are as many realities (of these things themselves) as there are things. Not only is the human being incapable of comprehending the being of a concrete thing, but so too are things alien and other to one another, i.e., every thing is a problematic thing-in-itself to another thing. Take, for example, a person loading a cartridge into a revolver, spinning the cylinder, and firing. We can only try to imagine how this event is perceived by the cartridge and the bullet in the cylinder, how they communicate with each other from within their reality. The same goes for the spring turning the drum, the trigger, the bolt, the primer, the powder charge, the accelerating bullet sliding through the grooves inside the barrel, etc. Each of these objects constituting the object of the revolver have their own view within their reality on the events of their involvement, on their "work" and their contact

---

135 Here we mean "imagine" in the sense of "fantasize."

with other objects in the mechanism. The same could be said of a chair which in some incomprehensible way experiences my sitting on it, or a table experiencing a kettle on it when I'm not home. In other words, the world and Being are not given to man and for man (like the "world-for-us") alone. Hence the problematization of anthropocentric-gnoseological racism and the desire to connect and unite every-thing.

The world thus appears in "exploded view", in which things, despite being connected in a mechanism (and not constituting anything more) or directly fastened agglomerations, are subjected to an explosive centrifugal movement within themselves, as well as to withdrawal and disunity. Objects escape into themselves from knowing the reality of other objects and their interactions from their point of view, like a black hole that does radiate anything into the outside world. Since flat ontology does not presume any one center, the centrifugal movement-into-withdrawal or movement-into-reserve constitutes an escape from neighboring objects. Everything hides from everything in the cellars of Being while still entering into constant acts of communication, mutual influence, actorhood, filtering, etc.

Another example which may be taken to demonstrate the fundamental equality between the human and non-human is a computer or some other gadget registering signals entering its ports from the outside. For a computer, there is no difference between signals from a human or signals from external sensors, other computers, or non-human input devices. Inside the system, both the sensor and the human are sheets of data transmitted into the algorithms of functions and the distribution of reactions. This situation is opposite to that of the Turing test, in which there is no task of distinguishing a person from a machine or some other source of data. The computer receives data from the keyboard (whether a person is typing or an application is emulating keystrokes is unimportant) while simultaneously registering data from sensors such as the microphone, webcam, gyroscope, and other network objects. At the same time, with the sensors attached to it and a human being, the computer itself can act as an external data source for another device or network. A phone transmits data for a Wi-Fi hotspot, to a cell tower, to your earpiece, as well as to the manufacturer's server. A Bluetooth transmitter senses available devices in the space around it.[136] Data packets are suddenly exchanged with a random passerby's smartphone. In general, things live long and rich lives without our participation. This is how networks, chains, garlands, symbioses, and the fractal lines of connections and relations between objects within other objects take shape. A revolver is not the bearer of any greater reality or a more privileged object (the essence of higher taxonomy) than all of its component object-parts. All of them are equal on the ontological plane of possessing "tiny being." Here the image of a Matryoshka doll or fractal would be appropriate: such a thing is wrapped up into itself and does not reproduce likeness on its scale.

Suspecting the being of things and objects and blurring the boundaries between them and humans leads to the emergence of extravagant, yet at the same time quite interesting academic theories on the need to take non-human actors into account in human reality and sociology. Hence object-oriented ontology or the sociology of things. Things which have long and up until now been absolutely unrecognized become carriers, actors, and authors of social relations and institutions. Things, objects, gadgets, and software are to be studied and described in the terms of sociology and political science, in the optic of human-to-object and object-to-object flat ontologies within the framework of non-hierarchical actor-network theories (Latour) or the democracy of objects (Bryant). It is even hypothetically possible for fiscal and labor relations to be established with things, since we delegate to them as subordinate or hired subjects a variety of functions, such as signaling, connecting, opening and closing doors, delivering to a floor, sheltering from rain, entertainment, destruction, data storage, locking and unlocking locks, transactions, putting food into our mouth, etc.

---

136 Perhaps non-digital objects do not respond to Bluetooth requests not because they do not have a transmitter, but because they do not understand the language of this object or are too busy being-in-themselves to connect and communicate.

Or sanctions might even be imposed on things, since behind people's backs objects might weave their own secret conspiracies, enter into covert alliances, or refuse to function.

Object ontology understands "object" to be any entity of the world, including relationships, connections, institutions, living creatures, and items. Everything is leveled down to the plane of object-oriented sociology and phenomenology. Hence it is of interest to consider how the process of the individualization and separation of a free object (like an individual) out of a greater composite object (the larger body of society) takes places. As a starting point, let us take Martin Heidegger's famous case of the hammer. The being of the hammer is inscribed in the context of its use, for instance in the construction of a house. The construction process is a holistic event in which many things, objects, people, and functions are absorbed and connected, the ultimate goal of which is building a house. As long as the hammer works properly and hammers in nails, it organically exists within the framework of the overall picture and deed, without attracting attention to itself beyond its nature. But as soon as the hammer breaks, it is broken out of the overall picture, it draws the builder's attention to itself, and if it is some important hammer or even the only one, then it can affect the entire building process. This moment of exclusion and being torn out of the general holistic picture, and at the same time the hammer's liberation from its function, from the overall labor, and from advancing towards the goal — this is the moment of broken individuality, when attention is drawn to the hammer as if to something singular and special affecting the overall undertaking.

Building a house can be seen as the assembling of a Deleuzian desire machine (consisting of tool-objects, log-objects, builder-objects, goal-objects, etc.) which breaks down, is reassembled, and breaks again. A saw breaks, timber was not delivered, the builders went binge drinking, and, finally, somehow, something was built. The desire machine is updated through glitches and breakdowns into a new reassembly. Singling one object out of the overall assembly or construction is an act of individual manifestation, the negative representation of essence. A chair cannot break in the same way as a revolver jams, a cog cannot deform like a rotting tomato. Thus, the moment of individuation comes in the moment of the representative and outwardly exposed breakdown of an(y) object.

In social terms, the way to individualization lies through rejecting normativity, and instead deviating and localizing the individual at a point of the maximum number of intersecting forms of oppression, as in intersectional theory. The more that some anybody (*das Man*) is deviant, exotic, and perverted[137], the more forms of collective identities and normative systems they have rejected as forms of oppression and discrimination, the more individual they are, and the more they break out of the ever larger set of large and small, holistic and imagined societies and subcultures. Object-oriented individuality is a broken object, a queer cyborg, a poorly digitized feminist consciousness, a low quality rendering of chimeras, an unsuccessful sex change, or rejected implants.

At the first superficial glance, it might seem as if object-oriented ontology and sociology restore the reality of the mythological life of things, only by approaching this "new revelation of the old" from a different trajectory. It might seem as if the suspicion as to some secret life of things and the rediscovery of things that have turned inward and away from are akin to restoring the animated, inspirited living things and objects of the world of Tradition. But a closer look reveals that this is not the case.

Of importance is the fact that for OOO and ANT, inanimate things and objects are de facto all the same inanimate things with their own other, subterranean existences. In Tradition, animals, stones, trees, or any other things speak because concealed within them is their own spirit, or because they are mixed in with the spirits of the places whence they came from, or because

---

137 Left-liberal, tolerant, progressive.

the rock is a stone into which a gnome or cursed person was turned. Things come alive and are woven into the fabric of the sacred insofar as their creation involved an artisan, the Muses, the spirits of ancestors, the Divinities, the community, and the spirits of other things, and hence a new thing can be disclosed to the world and man and incorporated in the communities of sacred objects and spirits. For OOO, these are nonetheless merely the same animals, stones, trees, and things of Modernity, but now with their own being-in-themselves and unknowable means of communication. Hence the frequent metaphor of alien communication, of relations between aliens (cf. xeno-), and the atmosphere of distrust, suspicion, incomplete knowledge, conspiracy, and alienation between all network actors and tabs. Traditions know of a wide diversity of creatures and living objects, but their sacred liveliness and to some extent subjectivity stem from a different ontology and altogether different premises. What flat and alien ontologies propose does not coincide with either the classical science of Modernity or with Tradition.

The distribution of Being or the attribution of individual Dasein's to disparate objects levels the key structures of sacred hierarchies and the teleology (eschatology) of the world of Tradition. Discovering the secret life and sociality of things does not bring back the Divinities (even if this current's thinkers mention God, then only as one among equal objects) and does not arrange the beingful world in ontological and social terms in accordance with initiatic levels. The animal helpers of myths and fairy tales act as subordinate companions of heroes in their initiatic journeys, just as the vahanas are subordinate to the Indian Divinities.

The holistic fabric of Being and the canvas of sacred patterns are opposite to vertical lists and enumerations of random objects, litanies, and randomizer programs, generators of random streams of words as illustrating the richness of tiny being on a flat plane. In the cases of social institutions, tools, electrical appliances, gadgets, and software, we can speak of them as being morally obsolete (subject to the dictatorship of progress) but physically capable of existing much longer than the lives of several human generations. Objects such as planets, dust, light, and rock formations are generally "eternal."

Finally, if all interactions between objects have the character of caricatures, whereby each object is perceived by another object solely as the set of features available to its own perception and manipulation, then all relations and all descriptions of the world — whether from the human point of view or that of cupholders, RAM memory cards, flocks of cranes, or slime — appear as heaps of crude pidgins between the always foreign languages of objects-always-in-themselves. Reality (augmented and virtual) appears not as an organic unity, but as a compact caricature, an incorrect language, almost random coincidences and constellations held together in spite of or through the practice of some objects oppressing others. All of reality (or more precisely, the descriptions and connections that constitute it) is built on errors, tweaking, repressions, and pervasive suspicion over the total incorrectness of everything around.[138]

However, within the broad wave of the turn to non-human ontologies and anthropologies, there are also reverse examples of applying these methods and theories to studying and describing archaic tribes. The anthropologist Eduardo Kohn, basing his thought on the analytical semiotics of Charles Peirce, the ideas of Haraway and Butler, the sociology of Bruno Latour, Gilles Deleuze, and Eduardo Viveiros de Castro[139], has studied the lifeworld of the Amazon forests and one of the Runa tribes living in the remote village of Ávila.[140]

Nested and intertwined within the living forests of the Amazon, the worlds of animals, dreams, the dead, and spirit masters of the forest, the reality of the lifeworld of the Runa

---

138 This is like the scenario of deaf, blind, and mute fools trying to feel out an elephant in order to understand what it is.

139 See Eduardo Viveiros de Castro, *Cannibal Metaphysics*, trans. Peter Skafish (Minneapolis: Univocal, 2014).

140 Eduardo Kohn, *How Forests Think: Toward an Anthropology Beyond the Human* (Berkeley: University of California Press, 2013).

described by Kohn is radically different from the explosive scheme of relations between receding-and-closing objects postulated by Bogost and OOO. Instead of an "object" voluntaristically and in an egalitarian vein ascribed its own Dasein, Eduardo Kohn speaks of many varieties of selves that create the ecologies of the forest, people, animals, and the dead. Selves can be many objects, subjects, or relations, and on this plane Kohn's term comes close to the "object" of OOO and Latour's litanies, but at the same time its general connectedness, or more precisely its nestedness, distribution, intertwinement, interpenetration and interchangeability between selves, creates complex, holistic patterns of relations in which the selfhood of all the participants in the ecology is disclosed.

Insofar as Kohn studies semiosis and thought, for him the basic definition of the self is the locus of thought, or selfhood as a node in the compaction of thinking reality which sets its own point of view (perspective) while at the same time leaving open the ability to turn to and penetrate the general thought and selfness of other creatures, including the realms of the "inanimate." For example, the Runa Indians can transform into jaguars, see the common dreams of the whole village, and even understand the dreams of dogs or the forest. A cuckoo can become a fully-fledged participant in a regular conversation while one is sitting and cutting vegetables. Kohn underscores this in pointing out that the mechanicism of Western anthropology and thinking makes it difficult to penetrate and understand such a view of the manifest world.[141] The mechanicism of the disenchanted world prevents one from seeing the purpose of existing in life, the *telos*. For the Runa, this *telos* is to be reborn after death in the manifest world as a jaguar (the *Runa puma*).[142]

---

141 This refers us back to the question posed by de Castro: Do we have one ontology (nature) and a multitude of cultures that are located in it and describe it, or do we have a multitude of ontologies (natures), the similarity between descriptions of which generates one culture?

142 The Runa have a dual topography of space which is not hierarchical (like the upper and lower worlds of the Indo-Europeans), but nested: in the Quechua language, the spirit-owners of a forest are called *ukuta*, which means "inside", and the manifest world of "real" life is called *ahuaman*, which means "on the surface."

In the complex mythology of their post-colonial dual faith, this world and status are simultaneously paradisal (the place of abundance of Quito).

The logical consequence of this ontology is that "a person is not absolutely an individual", but rather lives within a larger and more complex world. This world is not a "world-for-us", but rather a "world-where-we-are-too." Following de Castro, Kohn speaks of perspectivism: a person views the world from one angle, but they are capable of changing this perspective, just like how a person moves to the left or right and the view of an object or reality under consideration changes. Here, however, shifting to another point of view turns out to be a change of self, and a person (whether in a dream, intoxicated, or under a spell) begins to see the world of the forest from the perspective of, for instance, a spirit master or boar hunter who at this moment loses their self (thus promising a successful hunt[143]). The world surrounding human society is full of communities of anteaters, spirits, the dead, jaguars, trees, and ape people, tribes of stones, and the culture of wild boars. One can move between these spaces of continuum. Changing perspective is like leaving one's self, and entering another self of another being (not necessarily a living one) is possible because everything surrounding us is made up of selves and personalities from their own points of view.

To some extent, this approach allows us to correct Martin Heidegger's position on the "world-poverty" of animals, which contradicts the subjectivity of animals in myths and fairy tales. Eduardo Kohn's non-human anthropology and semiotics of selfhood comes close to myth, the "reality" of which he recognizes and explicitly takes into account in studying the ecology of the Runa.

---

143 Another example: "people in Ávila say that what we perceive as the stench of rotting carrion a vulture experiences as the sweet-smelling vapor emanating from a steaming pot of manioc tubers. Vultures, because of their species-specific habits and dispositions, inhabit a different world from that of the Runa. Yet because their subjective point of view is that of persons, they see this *different* world in the same way the Runa see their own world." - Kohn, *How Forests Think*, 95.

The Runa approach to raising their dogs, which live with them but still obtain their own food and exist quite autonomously, might seem familiar to us — they are trying to strengthen the human locus of thought within dogs and to raise them like people. In Ávila, animals are animal-like-Runa ("*runa*" means "person" in Quechua). But here lies a difference in the way humanity is postulated: whenever he speaks of the subjectivity of animals, modern desacralized man always ends up in the realm of fantasy and imagination, or directly appeals to fairy tales and believes that we are talking about something in the spirit of children's cartoons, or he begins to imagine and try on the "skin" of a dog or other animal, to voluntaristically fantasize about what he would feel if he felt and saw the world like an animal. This approach only maintains the status of the "world-poverty" of animals, and has no relation whatsoever to perspectivism or to the selfness of dogs. Such is purely the work of the human imagination, and on this is based the whole industry of pet supplies, pet entertainment, and popular zoopsychology, whose subjects are always the pet owners, not the pets themselves.

Instead, the Runa hold initiation rites for their dogs which are essentially analogous to a person's rite of passage into the adult life of the community. The Runa bind the paws and mouth of a young dog and give it an intoxicating, hallucinogenic mixture. The person then gives instructions to the dog on how to "behave like a person", how to help with hunting, and what prohibitions must be observed. The experience of narcotic intoxication is difficult for dogs to survive, so the survivors are considered bearers of strong humanity. But the essence here is something else: raising a dog on hallucinogens is a shamanic initiation. Unlike in Indo-European shamanism, however, where the Kham takes hallucinogens in order to enter the world of spirits and begin to understand them, animals, and souls, i.e., to open himself from the inside for the greater dimension of the manifest world, in the Runa world the intoxicated dog is supposed to become a shaman so as to understand the language of people, who act as the higher master spirits. In other words, the Runa, like spirits, invade the self of the dog to intoxicate it and make it open to receiving instructions from above. The Runa themselves, in turn, are in their own states of intoxication and ecstasy like dogs open to the higher spirit masters of the forest and the souls of ancestors who have become jaguars. In this case, we are dealing with a complex hierarchy of intertwined shamanism and animism, where man enters the world of spirits so that his hunt is successful and then arranges a shamanic initiation for his dogs so that they too learn how to hunt properly. The perspectives of selves change, each in turn becoming a spirit master towards itself, for both the Runa and the dog. Perspectivism and shamanic passages between selves seem to represent a productive, middle path between the world-forming status of man (and a people) as the bearer of Dasein and the "world-poverty" of animals which de facto have their own perspectival selfhood and can join the world-forming human being in a real empirical way through initiation and the actualization of the human locus in their self.

On the whole, despite his reliance upon left-wing and Postmodernist theorists, Eduardo Kohn unconsciously pronounces and affirms truths on the reality of myth which are complementary to Traditionalism, the emergent hierarchies of selfs, the reality of the worlds of spirits and the dead, and the capacity to enter the future and selves of others. In other words, he deconstructs the *topos* of the ontology, anthropology, and ethnography of New Time (Modernity) and moves towards defending myth and the plurality of ontologies and cultures in the cases of archaic tribes. We can situationally take his position and methods for describing, studying, and entering our own European traditions of the past which have, in one way or another, nevertheless come down to us. Through studying "our own as 'exotic'", we can develop empathy and rapture in recognizing and returning to our selfhood.

***

Artifacts and Primitive Peoples

In the middle of the 20th century, the rhythmic life of Pacific island tribes was interrupted by the invasion of American troops who set up transit bases and cargo logistics points across the Pacific islands as part of their campaign against Japan. Since the islands and natives were of no particular interest, much less posed any threat, the American troops adopted peaceful tactics and provided humanitarian aid. The tribes that inhabited the islands thus encountered Western man for the first time, along with his technology, constructions, industrial goods and products, which American troops shared with them in exchange for loyalty. After the end of the war, the American contingents abandoned their Pacific beachheads and left the tribes of Melanesia once again alone with themselves. But, instead of returning to their usual affairs of foraging, fishing, and rituals, the island tribes began to collect the fragments of boxes and equipment that the Americans left behind and began inhabiting their abandoned airfields. The islanders began to copy in detail, as closely as possible with the use of the items available to them, the outward behavior of the American troops: marching in formation, painting their bodies to resemble American uniforms and insignia, reproducing walkie-talkies and headphones with coconuts, bamboo stalks, and vines, and clearing the runway, lighting signal torches, drawing technical markings, and constructing towers. All of this was done in order to once again attract the gifts of the Divinities and the spirits of ancestors from the sky — with their parachutes and planes with loads of food, clothes, and all sorts of interesting things for them to continue to precisely reproduce their rituals. This is how cargo cults appeared throughout the Pacific Ocean.

The local tribes perceived the invasion of such a radically different world as a miracle in the sacred fabric of the cosmos, a turning point in the course of myth, when gifts from the Divinities and ancestors began to rain down to earth from the sky on white wings (the aircraft and parachutes). Many tribes even abandoned their previous practices, crafts, and palm plantations to focus on the blissful acceptance of gifts from these white intermediaries. It is noteworthy that the aircraft became cult objects more often than the Western people, who together with their airfield and warehouse infrastructure were considered more like intermediaries and a necessary ritual framing for the arrival of the Divinities with their gifts. Moreover, we know of cases in which the natives considered the whites to be invaders seeking to seize the cargo gifts sent by the ancestors. Although most of these cargo cults degenerated and disappeared, a small number nevertheless transformed into messianic anticipations of the return of the "flying Divinities" (planes).[144] These cults had no connection with Christianity, but were largely syncretic. Ordinary thinking interprets these cargo cults as an ironic, mocking example of primitive peoples' superficial copying and primitive misunderstanding of reality. This position is deeply erroneous and biased.

The cargo cults attested in various forms among different peoples show how societies which have not not yet been affected by the Western paradigm of modernization and civilization can interpret and handle the invasion of others, foreign artifacts and things still within their own mythological being-in-the-world. Cargo cult behavior ought to be interpreted, to the extent that such is possible, only through donning the skin of these natives and imagining their view of events. In their eyes, their own dreams of the Divinities and ancestral spirits with whom they exchanged gifts became an empirical, tangible manifestness (or "reality" as modern man would say). The abundance of gifts from the heavens was a reciprocal potlatch from the other world, a visit by spirits with gifts, which Marcel Mauss has described in terms of a total system of provisions.[145] Thus, the dislike for

---

144 It is very curious that upon their first contact with modern Americans, the native tribes identified them as usurpers interfering with direct relations with the Divinities and spirits.

145 See Marcel Mauss, *The Gift: Forms and Functions of Exchange in Archaic Societies,* trans. Ian Cunnison (London: Cohen & West, 1966).

the American soldiers themselves as bad and evil intermediaries who violated the order of gifting and transferring parcels is also logical. Attempts by the Americans to somehow explain to the locals that the airplane was just an airplane, a technical means, and that the cargo was just industrial goods, not gifts from ancestors and the Divinities, and that their radios were only waves, transmitters and receivers — in a word, the usual boring reality of modern society — were not crowned with success. Acquaintance with the cargo and the explanations of white people did not at all lead to the tribes' modernization, but rather to a clear configuration of their cults towards what an external observer weighed down by the false view of progressist Eurocentrism would see as parody.

Our conviction is that living mytho-centric thinking and societies which are vulgarly called "primitive", those which still live in the sacred, are capable of reforging, (re)interpreting, weaving into the fabric of myth, and sacralizing a limited volume of invasive or temporarily encountered things. What happens to these things is what we described earlier as throwing something into the world of Tradition, where it is transformed and takes its place (whether high or low, light or dark). We can find examples of such throughout different regions of the world and among many different peoples and see how myth works, how this reverse sacralization happens, and what pictures of the lifeworld emerge as a result.

In 20th-century Africa, local Kalashnikov assault rifle cults took shape among many peoples who used these firearms as an accessible and mass weapon in wars. From a simple industrial product, the rifle was turned into a magical artifact with its own soul or a demon of fire living inside it. The assault rifles were adorned with trophies, consecrated in rituals, offered sacrifices, and were charged with spells to spit fire without fail. Their wielders mixed the gunpowder from bullets with blood and alcohol for ritual drinks, sniffed it in rituals, and rubbed it into cuts and wounds to absorb the firepower and strengthen the bond between themselves and the rifle-spirit. Similar rituals were performed with other weapons, such as explosives, rifles, pistols, machetes, etc. Consecrated weapons obtained from whites found employment not only in wars between tribes and juntas, but also by local shamans and sorcerers. The latter began to offer soldiers and gangs new spells, charms, and amulets out of bullets and automatic weapons. Sometimes it happened that they did not work, and so the sorcerers were executed in retaliation for insufficiently magically charging the amulets. The grand modernization of Africans thus made itself felt: the more they understood the logic of the mechanics of firearms, the history of their production, physical laws, etc., the less spells and charms began to work. Magic and myth were castrated in the midst of condensing, hardening reality.

Another example from more recent times is the employment of sorcerers or shamans to perform incantations on laptops, modems, or flash drives so that African cybercriminals can more effectively and securely extort money and commit fraud on the Internet. It is said that the local police do not risk getting immediately or directly involved in arresting such criminals, because they are protected by the magic and curses of local sorcerers. Here we can already note a divergence between the norms of local Africans and the European-modeled laws imposed from above. For the African policeman, it is the shaman and sorcerer, the bulletproof amulet, the laptop spell (which creates another magical artifact), and the fire-demon of the rifle that possess greater reality and more significance than abstract laws, police station hierarchies, reports, protocols, and "virtual crimes", etc.

There is a decent illustration of the subject matter under consideration to be found in African cinematography, in the film *The Gods Must Be Crazy*, which tells the story of a Bushmen tribe in Botswana.[146] The film centers around the radical contrast between the organic life of the tribe in the savannah on the one hand, and the commotion of white city life and the black junta's war with terrorists on the other. This movie portrays

146 *The Gods Must Be Crazy*, directed by Jamie Uys, 1980.

everything as accurately as possible from the point of view of the small Bushmen tribe and the main character, Xi.[147] The plot begins with a pilot flying over the savannah tossing an empty bottle of Coca-Cola out of his cockpit. The Bushmen believe that planes are strange, noisy birds overheard. The bottle lands and is noticed by Xi, who believes that it was dropped from the heavens by the Divinities. He even tries to throw it back, but the Divinities do not accept it. He then brings it back to the tribe, where the glass bottle at first becomes an ideal object: it is round, hard, can be blown into like a pipe, and can be used to roll dough and clay or smash grains and fruit. The bottle gradually becomes needed by everyone at once, a unique item that cannot be replicated by the tribe's handicraft. The bottle soon becomes a weapon with which the Bushmen hit each over the head. The whole tribe then resolves that this unknown thing is not a gift from the Divinities, but more likely a curse, and that they "have gone crazy." It is telling that at the tribal council the bottle is finally given its own name, one which expresses its essence as an "evil thing." Xi decides to go to the ends of the Earth to throw away the bottle into the depths, to get rid of it and return it to the Divinities. The tribe is sure that this journey to the end of the Earth will take an unimaginably long time — somewhere around 20-40 days.

Xi's wayfaring is quite similar to archaic initiatic journeys, as he descends into a real "hell" or demonic world. Along the way, Xi certainly explains everything he sees through his own point of view which, obviously, is much more adequate than what the whites and modernized blacks around him say and do, such as the policemen, reserve workers, hunters, scientists, and cars (snarling beasts with round legs). Tire tracks in the sand are taken to be the tracks of two large snakes slithering at night. Firearms are strange sticks. The whole world is turned inside out as Xi leaves his native land and tribe. The world is inhabited by complete fools who do not even know how to properly

147 N!xau was not a professional actor and practically didn't act at all, but instead lived as he does. The director found him in one of the local tribes and decided to film him.

butcher and divide up a goat. In addition to the obvious contrast between these two worlds on the screen, the director himself inlaid yet another allusion in the very title of the film. Over the course of the plot, a direct analogy is drawn: the "Gods" who "must be crazy" are the white modern Europeans, the colonists and missionaries, and all their accompanying social institutions, wars, guerrillas, terrorists, and garbage falling from the sky. In other words, the film clearly and correctly exposes and deconstructs itself on all levels.

Very similar "naive"[148] notions about intruding, foreign things can be found among the indigenous peoples of Siberia. The second half of the 20th century was marked by active space exploration, and the orbital trajectory of Soviet rockets ran over the Siberian Taiga, the Altai, Yakutia, Komi, and the Far North. Besides the soil contamination effected along the entire flight path, stories soon came in about the local populations, such as the Chukchi, Tungus, and others, using fragments of the rocket stages and frames in their everyday lives. The fallen "heavenly" metal was used as sleds, containers, troughs, or for reforging. The flares of passing rockets were also interpreted as omens. Among others, there is one story that is difficult to verify, presumably about a Tungus reindeer herder who found a fuel element the size of an ordinary box that had fallen from the sky. A few days later, he was found dead from "the plague" in a fetal position sleeping huddled around the warm fuel element, which was presumably radioactive or toxic and therefore lethal. It was assumed that the "uneducated" Evenk took the "warm metal" that had fallen from the sky as a wonderful source of heat in the winter, so he went to sleep next to it and died.[149]

Such stories illustrate the possibility of the bearers of mythological thinking making something "their own", even if their evil or destructive dimension is later revealed. Even then, however, they can be treated in accordance with magical notions

---

148 Etymologically, "naive" goes back to the Latin *nativus*, i.e., "native", "local", "natural to a land."

149 This story is probably about a radioisotope thermoelectric generator.

and eliminated, returned to the Divinities or dispensed for ritual mortification. Moreover, if contact with a thing or its spirit is unsuccessful, for example if a rifle jams and stops firing, then a person might take to punish the thing as if it does not want to obey or work. In this semantic nest we find such practices as burying votive animal figurines and later practices of breaking a sword as a symbolic enactment of civil execution.

Another example of the adaptation of foreign things brought into a territory and culture is described by the Russian Silver Age poet Nikolai Klyuev in his *Song of the Great Mother*:

Шептали в ответ сапожки:
Тебя привезли рыбаки,
И звали аглицким сукном,
Опосле ты стал зипуном!
Сменяла сукно на икру,
Придачей подложку-сестру,
И тетушка Анна отрез
Снесла под куриный навес,
Чтоб петел обновку опел,
Где дух некрещеный сидел.
Потом завернули в тебя
Ковчежец с мощами, любя,
Крестом повязали тесьму
Повывесть заморскую тьму,
И семь безутешных недель
Ларец был тебе колыбель,
Пока кипарис и тимьян
На гостя, что за морем ткан,
Не пролили мирра ковши,
Чтоб не был зипун без души!

The boots whispered in response:
Fishermen brought you,
And called you English cloth,
And then you became a coat!
You replaced cloth with caviar,
Threw in the bargain the sister-lining
And Auntie Anna cut a bit
Laid it by the chicken coop
So that the rooster would crow on the new outfit
Where an unbaptized spirit lay
Then they rolled you up into
A chasse with relics, with love,
They tied a braid with a cross
To caste out that darkness from overseas
And for seven inconsolable weeks
The chasse was for you a cradle
In the meanwhile only cypress and thyme
Per guest, so on that fabric from beyond the sea
They didn't spill buckets of myrrh
So that the coat would not be without soul!

In this poem, a piece of cloth imported from loud English industry is perceived as something alien and soulless, and a whole cycle of operations is performed in order to saturate it with the Russian spirit and Orthodox blessing so that the tunic acquires its soul and becomes native. Klyuev here is enunciating purely pagan motifs dressed in Orthodox words. The very notion of "soul" is not applicable to things within the framework of creationism, especially in the peasant environment. The practices which Klyuev poetically describes are fully analogous to the shamanic enchanting of things in Africa, Oceania, or Siberia.

We should not blindly copy the Africans, Polynesians, American Indians, or Evenki, however. They are not the noble savages of egalitarian, pacifist societies, but are also bloodthirsty and wage regular wars for honor. Looking at them, we should see the possibility and ways toward another thinking, toward reviving myth, to which we have lost access. It is difficult for us to see a radically different way of thinking in our own history, which we perceive rather as a passed-over historical step. But it is easier for us to see the Other on the horizontal plane of geography and the anthropology of other peoples. In the same way, we can study our past, discarding the progressist scale of development, and bring it back to us, restore it in the sphere of thinking and looking at the world. However, in relation to our own situation, we must speak not only or not so much of overcoming geographical gaps (imported things, gifts from colonists, garbage from the sky), but of chronologically and, more importantly, ontologically rethinking and reappropriating things around us. Since we understand "appropriate for ourselves" to mean "re-enchant", sacred appropriation therefore means revealing the inner soul of a thing, the spirits within it, unfolding and communing with the sacred chains or circles of accompanying rituals, practices, offerings, and spirits around one thing and others. Sacralizing means, among other dimensions, giving things back their own voice. Forests and rivers, bathhouses and hearths, knives and axes, skulls and ashes, altars and graves — all must be given back their voice. But this is an extremely difficult task, even on the scale of the set of everyday things and objects. Collin Cleary especially emphasizes the experience of amazement and astonishment before surrounding Being, between mountains and seas created by the Divinities or the things created by craftsmen. Amazement is complex, multi-layered, and is not only "surprise" at a thing and its beauty in itself, but also the mastery of the author, the very fact that such was revealed to him and descended upon him from the upper world. There can be no "Divinities of machines" or amazement at the sight of garbage, because we know their non-sacred origin.[150]

Various archaic peoples and tribes in different corners of the world sacralize things and phenomena from the civilized world of Europeans or Americans with greater ease because these things — weapons, products, clothing, tents, tools — come to them ready and finished. Unlike us, they do not experience a collision between knowledge of the history of the development of a firearm and tools, of the social institutions into which they are woven, of the history of discoveries and inventions on the one hand, and their animistic, totemistic, fetishistic perception of gifted things falling from the sky on the other. We know that there is no demon of fire in the rifle, because in general terms we always imagine the history of the development of guns from the first muskets to their conveyor-belt production, framed not by rituals but developed within the framework of the disenchanted world of Modernity. The knowledge of these processes and their scientific substantiations has been burned into us, but even more so we are scarred by the very processes of technological production and the world-factory. We not only know this history, it is our history. Archaic tribes effortlessly overcome the alienation between them and imported rifles, airstrips, bottles, and mobile phones, while we wither in the thick and inert mud of the Modern paradigm. It is difficult for us to reveal the spirit of a thing or to sanctify it, to place spirit inside of it, if we know how it was produced. To overcome this distance, it is necessary to have a more subtle mind, a romantic, naive, poetic disposition of the soul, and a strong imagination.[151]

---

150 This is less of a problem for Islam or Christianity, in which there are patron saints for the Internet (Isidore of Seville) and the sciences. The practice of consecrating nuclear submarines or missiles carried out by priests of the Russian Orthodox Church can be seen in two ways: as a purely pagan, shamanic relic, or as a manifestation of an inner complementarity or compromise with Modernity and the state.

151 In the documentary film *102 Years in the Heart of Europe: A Portrait of Ernst Jünger*, Jünger recalls how he was he was struck by the introduction of steel helmets into the First World War due to the frequent wounds of soldiers in the head, as they reminded him of the helmets of antiquity.

Archaic tribes and peoples outside of Modernity can obviously sacralize a finite volume of artifacts and products, including the foreign social institutions and relations with which they come into contact. However, more intensive and continuous contact triggers the modernization of their societies, loss of identity, and can lead to the emergence of cultural pseudomorphoses (per Oswald Spengler), i.e., the pathological, incorrect overlaying of modern structures onto archaic ones, which block each other like jammed gears inside a mechanism.[152] We Europeans are in a more deplorable position, surrounded by technology, the world of Gestell and *das Man*. We are in an opposite situation of a world of foreign things and artifacts, into which something sacred, irrational, ecstatic, or heroic only episodically irrupts. When a modern artifact enters the world of an archaic people, they sacralize it, but in our world the profane and vulgar denigrate and disenchant even rare epiphanies and theophanies. Therefore, the practice of appropriating or incorporating things into the sacred should be complemented by the imperative of destroying technology everywhere around us. Then, while clearing the rubble, it will be possible to think about whether to sacralize and incorporate one remnant or another.

Yet another problem which still more or less authentically living tribes periodically encounter is the problem of the uniqueness, irreproducibility, or radical novelty of a thing. The bottle from the African movie illustrates this situation: the Bushmen's craft is not interested in such products, and the uniqueness of the thing makes it excluded or peculiarly broken out of the overall picture. Thus, it can acquire uniqueness in two ways: as an object of religious fetish worshipped on an altar, or in a demonic vein as a source of discord and the embodiment of capital. Whoever possesses such a unique thing as their own property receives a virtual, previously unknown and non-existent high status in the system of intra-community relations.

---

152 Alexander Dugin has called this phenomenon of a pathological mutual blocking of paradigms "the situation of archeomodernity."

One vivid example of the demonic uniqueness of a thing is the glass beads and other jewelry exchanged by the indigenous Indians of America with colonists for wealth and land.

The fate of the North American Indians shows us at once a history of tragedy and hope. In the era of the Frontier, American colonists organized the mass slaughter of bison in the tens and hundreds of thousands on territories where railroads were to be laid and settlements founded during the phase of the active conquest of the central part of the US in the 19th century. In so doing, they also solved their second aim of expelling the indigenous Indians from these lands and depriving them of their main game. But, besides being the main animal for their subsistence, the bison was also the central figure of Indian cults, hence the extermination of bison not only had an economic effect, but also led to the destruction of their tradition. The Indians found themselves not only on reservations, but in a spiritual void. Soon after, however, the Indians discovered (or heard) another, different myth, and there appeared the new, hitherto unprecedented cult of peyote, which assumed a central place in the religions of the Southwestern US and Mexico. An exterior, profane view might interpret this as the degradation of the broken Indian peoples, the formation of drug addiction as a surrogate for their traditions killed by the colonists. But this is an illegitimate translation of the realities known to us in modern societies into the past and other peoples. Moreover, psychoactive substances and plants were known much earlier and already had ritual use. Collin Cleary sees this case of the Indians as an example of the possibility for living myth and a people's capacity to organically change the course of the river of the sacred.[153] Peyote allowed the Indians to look within themselves and bring into being a new structure, a new cult. Mircea Eliade calls this practice "entasy", or "going within", a kind of introscopic version of ecstasy. The metaphor of extended consciousness (which

---

153 See Collin Cleary, *Summoning the Gods: Essays on Paganism in a God-Forsaken World* (San Francisco: Counter Currents, 2011).

is not necessarily a metaphor) calls for looking deeper, wider, and differently so as to transform a void into an openness for relearning amazement and astonishment.

Dreamscapes

In the preceding, we examined "reality" as a castration and reduction of the entire wealth of myth and the manifest world to a thin material slice, akin to the desertification of dense forests and sacred groves. But there is yet another perspective to be considered which maintains that archaic peoples and mythological consciousness in general see the world and life as if in dreams, like daydreaming without strict, impenetrable divisions into dreaming and wakefulness. The mythical and magical world of archaic tribes still existing in our days, as well as those traditions of Europe which have receded into the past, still de facto exist in their empirical persuasiveness as dreamscapes and the dreams of peoples and tribes.[154]

Attitudes towards dreams can differ across peoples. Some tribes dream their myths and fates in the spirit of daydreams or lucid dreams at night. Occurrences in such dreams are not inferior in their degree of reality and importance to daytime events. The Runa tribe described by Kohn, for example, sees collective dreams which even their dogs have, and they at times successfully interpret what exactly their animals dream. Another Amazon tribe, the Piraha, consider long slumber to be the cause of gradual aging and deterioration, so they prefer short naps on the border between sleep and wakefulness. The ecstatic shamanic rituals of Siberia and Asia often include sleep as part of the shaman's journey to the other world, or as a variation of the trance state.[155]

---

154 Compared to the variety of Russian words for "dream(ing)", we propose to use the English "dream" in the sense of something fascinating, something that even partly guides the cultures of different peoples and gravitates towards the semantic field of the word "myth." In Russian, this would be "dream" as *son* and especially *gryoza*.

155 See Mircea Eliade, *Shamanism: Archaic Techniques of Ecstasy*, trans. Willard R. Trask (Princeton: Princeton University Press, 2004).

In modern European culture, Sigmund Freud attacked the world of dreams, which had already been pushed into the semantic field of frivolous fantasies and the playful interpretations of neo-spiritualism. By way of the method of free association, Freud interpreted dreams to be the work of the unconscious through which repressed desires, predominantly sexual, are "spoken out." Freud formulated a program for rationalizing the "basement of the mind", i.e., colonizing that part of man that had avoided the pathos of the Enlightenment and the natural sciences and, up to a certain time, remained hidden from the gaze of scientists. As a result, up to our days the whole apparatus of psychology, psychoanalysis, and psychiatry has worked to uphold the totalitarian-repressive status quo of that slice of being which we have designated as the Modernist understanding of reality. They have striven to rationalize, decipher, rework, and medically treat the unreal, the fairy-tale, the mythical, the "delusional", and the "schizophrenic." Experiencing the sacred, dreams, and ecstatic journeys — all of such belongs to the realm of abnormal experiences, psychoses, and paranoid hallucinations in psychiatry.

Freud's student, Carl Gustav Jung, was in addition to psychiatry a specialist in Hermeticism and religious symbolism, and he took a partially different position in defense of dreams. Revealing recurring patterns in dream stories, he spoke of structures and archetypes that are collective, i.e., common to large groups of people. Jung de facto came close to concluding that the unconscious is the realm where myth, symbolic language, and the traditions of peoples have found their last refuge. Dreams are fragments of collective identity, and the space of dreaming is where the events of "real" life, current culture, and history collide, mixing and taking on the form of the symbols and fragments of archaic plots.[156] Jung would later study and present this topic in the broader context of the intellectual community

---

156 In this case, "archaic" should be understood etymologically as ἀρχή, i.e., "original", "ruling", "guiding".

of Eranos.[157] But, in the overall standing, Freud's line turned out to be dominant, and following it the purely materialistic, psycho-physiological, neuro-cognitive approach. The noise of the daytime machine of *ratio* drowns out dreams. On the whole, psychologism and psychoanalytical interpretations of Tradition, myths, and sacred experience are a degeneration and ersatz pseudo-spirituality of the modern era.

Later, in the era of the psychedelic revolution, the space of dreams rapidly began to be littered with the clouded, hazy streams of mass pop culture, fueled by new drugs, psychedelia, and mixtures of fragments taken from the exotic cults of American Indians and the East. The content of the brightly glaring screen — the TV, cinema, graphics, and then computer games and virtuality — has been taken to be equivalent to the unconscious, where intoxication fulfills the role of removing the mediator (for the purpose of profane recreation).

Dreams are fragmented and torn apart by the tectonic movements of history and paradigm shifts. Considering the world to be a dream in the most noble sense, where everything is possible and one *mythos*-story can replace another, we can conclude that different scenarios and perspectives are possible. One can look at Modernity's colonial expansion into other societies of other myths and dreams and reveal the illusory and suggestive nature of what seems to us, within the European linear-progressive historical paradigm, to be natural and objectively real.

Let us consider, for example, the Piraha tribe inhabiting the Amazon basin. Linguistic analysis of their language has shown that for their world as they see and live in it, accounting and numbers, colors, the linearity of time and concern for the future are of virtually no significance (they do not stockpile provisions

---

157 There are no grounds to accept the claim that Divinities are literally archetypes in the Jungian sense. If the Divinities are archetypes per Jung, then their whole nature and being is reduced to the inner psychological and mental dimension of the individual. Treating the Divinities as archetypes excludes the possibility of the Divinities ruling the world and dwelling outside the human mind as separate empirical entities.

and they own practically no property, and they practice a specific relationship to time through minimizing sleep to a few short phases during the day). Researcher Daniel Everett has suggested that the Piraha live in a mode of "direct experience" here and now, which cardinally differs from historical thinking. Such is the arrangement of their dreaming, in which they are immersed and live happily at all times of their existence.

Looking at the Piraha and their contact with European researchers, and especially missionaries, the question naturally arises: how and on what grounds can Christianity be preached to them? Practically the entire array of the Christian faith is built on radically different concepts and structures of thinking which have no analogues not only in the world of the Piraha, but also in the lifeworlds of many other tribes and peoples in history and different corners of the world. It is impossible to explain to the Piraha the concept of hierohistory and the future Second Coming, as well as the complex metaphysics of the Trinity. There are several strategies for missionaries in this situation. One of them is being content with merely superficial acts of baptism and preaching, without demanding any deep understanding of the essence of Christian teaching from local peoples. Tribes and groups of converts are brought to rivers and, in exchange for food, clothes, and everyday items, are offered to be plunged into the water three times and to henceforth wear a pendant in the shape of a cross. Obviously, there are people who for the sake of gifts from white people accept faith in Christ more than once or twice.[158]

The further course of assimilating Christianity unfolds by way of radical reinterpretations of the significations and meanings of this new religion's stories, terms, and concepts through the language, structures, and myths of the indigenous people. Thus appears a dual faith of varying degrees of intensity and depth of elaboration, up to the point that ultimately all

---

158 This is how, in exchange for gifts to poor peasants, the Ossetians were "baptized" in Russia, according to the recollections of Soslan Temirkhanov, an officer in the Russian army.

that is left of Christianity are some superficial terms whose use satisfies foreign missionaries and pastors. But within this people, the meanings of the words remain purely local, traditional, and pagan (shamanistic, animistic, mythological, etc.).

One example of a complete reversal of the whole essence of Christianity is cited by Eduardo Kohn, who describes how the creative genius and power of the Runa tribe's myths proved capable of reinterpreting the religion of the Spanish colonists. The Runa were quite friendly towards the new faith, but over time they began to assert that they themselves, a more ancient and "primitive" Amazon tribe, were the original, genuine Christians, and that the Christian paradise is their afterlife, which is imagined to be a jungle full of abundance, without predators, where everyone lives forever youthful. Hell is reserved only for Europeans and blacks (who are seen as having been burned by flames), because they talk so much of its horrors. One of the myths of the Great Flood says that God and the saints sailed from the Amazon on a steamboat and stopped in the lands of the whites, who then learned technology and the construction of machines. Thus, whites are distant, removed, inauthentic Christians, since God and the apostles sailed to them from the Amazon. Therefore, in the Runa world picture, the white colonists, despite having political power and tenant farmers, still stand on a lower rung of "genuine Christianity", closer to "paganism" with their belief in Hell and suffering. It is noteworthy that in the Runa dual-faith demonology there is the figure of *huaturitu supai*, a demon with the talons of a bird, dressed in a priest's clothing, and wandering through the jungle with a Bible in his hands. The Runa themselves have always been saints, and they always go to paradise.

Another approach is insisting on modernizing, enlightening, and educating the tribes so that they might understand the new religion in the same way as the European missionaries themselves. Hence, elementary school programs are an integral part of many Christian missions around the world. This is the colonial — in both the sense of political colonialism as well as that of colonizing consciousness — expansion of a different Logos, one which is key to the paradigm of Modernity. Europeans arrived at the concepts of linear history, consistent accounting, progress, individualism, and humanism through creationism, and then began to export the ready-made paradigm of Modernity to archaic peoples who had not consistently traversed the stages of decline that had taken place in Europe. Christians and Muslims have interfered in the lifeworlds and dreams of other peoples, leading them towards compelled, externally imposed modernization for the sake of assimilating the Abrahamic norms and "godly" socio-political order into which the Church is woven. Here lie the principles behind universalism, universal human values and rights, and globalization. In other words, we can say that missionaries were the first actors of cultural and often physical ethnocide against local worlds and the complexity, traditions, languages, and relations between humans, peoples, and the natures inherent to them.[159]

Kohn cites as an example of such modernization a painting that hangs at the headquarters of the federation of Runa communities (FOIN - "Federation of Indigenous Organizations of Napo") which was in the second half of the 20th century supported by trade unions. The painting depicts five people in succession, or five stages in the development and "humanizing" of the Runa. On the left is the authentic representative of the Runa tribe as he was before the arrival of missionaries and colonists — dressed in a phallocrypt, necklace, bracelets, and war paint. He is "savage", not yet even human. Memory of this stage remains alive among the most radical Runa tribes who have refused any changes to their way of life and faith. They are called "auka", or "pagans." Next comes the Runa with a loincloth and a special horn thrown over his shoulders, one used to summon the whole tribe. Being a Runa from the first stage and in close connection with one's tribe becomes shameful, which finds its development already at the next, middle stage. In the middle stands a 19th-century Indian in shorts and a poncho, bashfully

---

159 The anthropologist Pierre Clastres defines aggressive missionary work as one of the initial stages of ethnocide. See Clastres, *Archeology of Violence.*

hiding a hunting blowgun behind his back. After this follows the modern image of the Indian in trousers with a belt and white shirt, whereby nothing in him betrays the former savage. Finally, on the far right is the crown of the civilized development of the Indian: a figure in an office suit with a watch, tie, smooth haircut, and no traces of folk culture. According to the 17th-century Jesuit preacher Francisco de Figueroa, the whole aim of such missions was to "turn savages into people, and people into Christians." This line is continued in liberation theology, which calls for using reason and science to combat poverty (meaning socio-economic and, by extension, technological criteria) as a source of sin.

Analogous examples of the civilizing pursuit are ubiquitous, right down to the Soviet propaganda posters calling for "driving out the shaman" from the village soviet as a counter-revolutionary element. But the momentum of this movement goes further than mere Christianization. The movement away from authenticity through creationism ultimately leads to the figure of *das Man*. People in office suits are everywhere the same, global, and are only people in the minimal degree of authenticity of being. At the same time, in passing we can say that the pressure of the Bible, gunpowder, and the chalkboard nevertheless gradually lead to the degeneration of peoples despite the power of myth and reinterpretations of the new faith and order from within tradition. The image of the Runa ancestor is now used as an illustration of a strong degree of intoxication and sloppiness.

Beyond the social and existential-anthropological change in status, there is also an ontological and epistemological shift, a complete change in the structure of the world from the mythological to the natural-scientific, that is the castration of sacred abundance and potentialities. Where an aboriginal of Australia or Oceania sees a magical, shamanic crystal from the sky which allows them to fly and heal people, the colonial representative of the Enlightened West sees only quarts, apatite, or opal, i.e., raw materials for decoration. And then they try to explain and impose such an understanding of the stone as "just a stone" upon the natives.

Investigating this topic from the standpoint of the archaeology of knowledge, we can relativize such a fundamental interaction as the law of gravity by posing the following question: why does gravity, discovered by Newton in the 17th century, work identically in Europe and among the aboriginals in the depths of the Eurasian continent or on distant landmasses and islands? Upon first approximation, the answer lies in that universal gravitation is a law that exists and works objectively both on Earth and in all points of the Universe. Gravity is universal and is one of the most important laws setting the order and interaction of cosmic and planetary objects. Gravity is a physical condition of reality. Since Newton, and then in the form of the general theory of relativity (Einstein), it has been recorded and described mathematically, and today it is seen through the prism of quantum theory and string theory. One of the manifestations of gravity is the notorious apple falling on Newton's head, or the falling of things that are thrown. Since the 17th century, we have known this as an absolute axiom, as the most immediate reality. But this is part of the history of the formation of scientific knowledge and the scientific picture of the world in Enlightenment-era Europe, the time of the active installation of Modernity and physicalism. From the point of view of dreamscapes, the singular, identical work of gravity might not be an objective reality, but a result of the complex process of the expansion and transfer of colonial practices by Europeans to new lands during the period of the great geographical discoveries and conquests. Gravity spreads and follows the speed of maritime and land logistics routes, power relations between Spanish or English colonists and local populations, and creates its outposts in schools for the children of the colonial administration and missionary classes for aboriginals. The apple falling down to earth outside of the European zone of the Enlightenment is due to the colonial-educational sanctioning of the dominant new European dream. The invaders not only conquered, killed, and baptized local populations, but also implicitly cast over their authentic lifeworld the "reality" of a very different paradigm of thinking. This is the suggestiveness and magnetic fields of counter-mythological structures under which peoples fall. This is not a matter of denying that things fall to rest on the ground, but the problem that they are now denied the freedom and possibility of simply rising up and soaring. The problem is reducing everything to immanent reality, where it is as if flight is guaranteed only by technological means.

Besides gravity, other "natural and physical laws of nature" come into force with their own properties which, taken together, begin to outweigh and overwhelm the sacred-magical thinking and being of traditional societies. We can point to the massacre of American Indians at Wounded Knee in 1890 as one such turning point. Near the end of the 19th century, the messianic "Ghost Dance" movement and its prophet, Wovoka, gained strength among American Indians, particularly the Lakota. At the center of the Ghost Dance practice was ecstatic dancing and beholding visions of spirits, and the movement aspired to revive the authentically Indian way of life and thereby achieve liberation from the colonists. Wovoka's teachings can be seen as part of the general spiritual seeking among Indians who had suffered a crushing blow to their traditions at the hands of the colonists, the bearers of the Enframing. At some point, the notion that sacred amulets, or "spirit shirts", would protect the religion's followers from American bullets appeared throughout Ghost Dance teachings. This gave the Indians confidence, and the movement turned into a rebel army which, convinced of its absolute magical protection, went to war against the state. Already familiar with the creationist paradigm (the Ghost Dance religion contained syncretistic elements of Christianity) and involved in modern reality (clothes, guns, tactics, etc.), the Indians suffered crushing defeat at Wounded Knee, which marked the final collapse of their tradition and the decisive predominance of the paradigm of Modernity on the North American continent. Dreams of gunpowder vanquished the shaky dream of the living dancing with the dead.

A similar tragedy broke out in Africa in the 1890s, during the colonial wars with the Matabele, one of the Bantu peoples. Over the course of their war for independence from the British South Africa Company, the practice of using amulets and spells against the bullets of enemy soldiers became widespread among the Matabele. But they, too, suffered crushing defeat in an unequal battle against the latest Maxim machine guns. Apparently, even the contemporary problems with African amulets against bullets and charms cast on laptops have their roots in the 19th century, which marked the milestone era of the extensive, explosive development of Modernity and the all-around cementing of the Gestell in the spheres of education, science, technology, economics, and socio-political colonial practices.

Summing up, we can outline a path of desacralization that would apply equally to the indigenous peoples of America, Africa, India, Polynesia, and Asia, as well as European peoples: The penetration of creationism (Jewish communities, Christianity, Islam, conquest and colonialism); → The disjuncture of the authentic manifestations of Tradition among peoples through missionaries and baptism; → Missionary and semi-secular education for local peoples with the aim of improving their understanding of Abrahamic religion; → Secular education and colonialism; → Gravity and the closing of the Heavens, the irresistible force of gunpowder and bullets, colonial power structures, and the thickened canvas of reality; → Mowed lawns, shirts with ties, jobs; → The exploitation of nature as a raw resource, capitalism, universal natural-scientific education; → Digitalization, forest zoning, chipping flocks of birds and schools of fish, connectivity becoming the basic existential even among slums and favelas, visually "primitive" ghettoes or enclaves; → Dehumanization, the death of cultures and peoples in globalization and singularity.

Considering this issue on a deeper level, we can note that modern reality is based on scientists' absolute certainty of the objective, universal truth of the produced knowledge which they impose upon others. This conviction is bound up with Eurocentrism and the anthropocentrism of the Enlightenment, which gave rise to the belief in direct access to objective, scientifically reliable knowledge about the structure and laws of nature as if this knowledge *a priori* existed as "knowledge-for-them", for the scientific community, the "priests" of this religion of natural-scientific, positivistic truth.

Ever since Linnaeus, Lamarck, and Darwin, scholars and ordinary people since their first days in school have been convinced that they have direct access to evolution. Immense empirical and theoretical material has been systematized and presented as the chains of the evolution of species and/or the reduction of traits, genotypes, and phenotypes over the course of adaptations, migrations, crossings, recombinations, and mutations, arranged in visual rows of taxonomies — domain-kingdom-phylum-class-order-family-genus-species. All the diversity of living things is locked down into successive chains of development and classifications. This is the imposition of rigid material determinism expressed in the need for strict and complex biological, genetic (physico-chemical, material) and environmental grounding (including selection) to explain changes in flora and fauna. The whole beingful world is made to appear as a mere result of the formation of matter in accordance with laws and environmental conditions. This once again underscores the strictly material understanding of life, *ergo* putting it "at hand" for the controlling and disposing subject. At a new historical, natural-scientific turn, this still mirrored Genesis 1:28: "Be fruitful and increase in number; fill the earth and subdue it. Rule over the fish in the sea and the birds in the sky and over every living creature that moves on the ground" — only now the source of such authority has been shifted from God to scientific "knowledge-for-scientists."

Scientific classifications can be defined as superficial, as considering only external similarities (we can also take similarities of structure, organs, and physiological processes to belong to the external field), starting with which they construct commonalities of lines and tabs of chains (phylum-class-order). As a counterweight to this, we can draw on fairy tales, myths, and the new anthropology to record and postulate (or rather simply describe the given) different criteria and configurations of commonalities and communities in the manifest world (such as Kohn's ecology of selves). A tree, a nest and its nestlings, worms under bark, a snake's hole under the roots, and the mycelium of a symbiotic fungus (boletus) all form a unity and stable cohabitation of selves in a given locus. To this we can add the necessary spirits of the place that inhabit both the forest and the particular tree. Another tree, such as a birch and the boletus growing around it, is another cohabitation. A spruce forest exists even more autonomously, in whose substrate grow families of fly agaric which Siberian peoples consider to be a separate people. The primitive view of the modern scientist would structure the forest into large groups of "trees", "mushrooms", "birds", and "worms" with their respective orders, etc. But an indigenous population, whether Amazon Indians, Siberian shamans, African Zulus, or Europeans once upon a time, are capable of seeing other, more complex totalities and unities conditioned not by symbiotic relationships, but by the perspectives of selves involved in the mythical lore about how and why they came to be in such a way and how they maintain and reproduce such structures over time.

Drawing on Robert Dixon's catalogue of metaphors in the language of Australian Aboriginals, the linguist George Lakoff cites and defends a variety of linear taxonomies:

> Whenever a Dyirbal speaker uses a noun in a sentence, the noun must be preceded by a variant of one of four words: *bayi, balan, balam, bala*. These words classify all objects in the Dyirbal universe, and to speak Dyirbal correctly one must use the right classifier before each noun. Here is a brief version of the Dyirbal classification of objects in the universe, as described by R. M. W. Dixon (1982):
>
> I.   *Bayi*: men, kangaroos, possums, bats, most snakes, most fishes, some birds, most insects, the moon, storms, rainbows, boomerangs, some spears, etc.

II. *Balan:* women, bandicoots, dogs, platypus, echidna, some snakes, some fishes, most birds, fireflies, scorpions, crickets, the hairy mary grub, anything connected with water or fire, sun and stars, shields, some spears, some trees, etc.

III. *Balam:* all edible fruit and the plants that bear them, tubers, ferns, honey, cigarettes, wine, cake.

IV. *Bala:* parts of the body, meat, bees, wind, yamsticks, some spears, most trees, grass, mud, stones, noises and language, etc.[160]

Such classifications fit with the famous taxonomy of Borges' "Chinese encyclopedia", where he wrote that animals are divided into:

a) Belonging to the Emperor

b) Embalmed

c) Tamed

d) Milk pigs

e) Sirens

f) Fairy-tale

g) Stray dogs

h) Included in this classification

i) Running around mad

j) Innumerable

k) Drawn with the finest camel hair brush

l) Others

m) Those which have broken a flower vase

n) Similar from a distance to flies

For Western thinking, such classifications are more like schizophrenia and comprise recursive violations of logic (for example point "h", which concerns the entire list), but for peoples who live in myth, it is precisely such complex classifications that are natural and normal for their cultures and languages. Carefully examining the structured hierarchy of selves among the Runa tribes as described by Kohn, we also see the specific,

---

160 George Lakoff, *Women, Fire, and Dangerous Things: What Categories Reveal about the Mind* (Chicago: Chicago University Press, 1987), 92-93.

fractal embeddings of classifications of living beings which differ substantially from the pyramidal-hierarchical and linear-historical structures familiar to us.

As a result, the new European view of the development of life turns out to be a relative network of interpretations with certain patterns of cells cast over the whole diversity of life. Even in the history of this view, there have been variations, marginal theories, and more modern refinements or even radical alternatives. To this day, there is no final clarity over the appearance and even skeleton structure of extinct dinosaurs (e.g., whether they had scales or plumage, were closer to cold-blooded lizards or birds) or the fauna of the Cenozoic era. The reconstructions of complete dinosaur skeletons based on the findings of one or two bones have been repeatedly revised, entailing the specimen being moved elsewhere along the taxonomic tree. Thus, fully scientific theorizing and hypotheses in this field are de facto only symbolic and border the realms of pure speculation and literature. Here we can take note of the fact that Charles Darwin, Herbert George Wells, and Howard Lovecraft were contemporaries, and each of them in their own creativity and works created their own unique and truly global variations of historical evolution and the genealogy of living species, from deep antiquity through the recorded "normal" present and into the distant future.

In his science fiction novel *The Time Machine*, Wells describes the evolution of man into two new species: subterranean Morlock cannibals, descendants of the proletariat, and the refined but also degraded Eloi, the descendants of the elite. To substantiate this evolution, Wells refers to the class division of labor, nutrition, and lifestyle. Looking even further into the future, the novel's traveler sees that people will become altogether small animals, prey for new alpha predators.[161]

---

161 If we expand the timeframe, then we can add Olaf Stapledon's novel *Star Maker*, which describes the total history of the development of the mind in the universe before and after the boundaries of space and time. In this universal history, humanity is but an imperceptible speck in the kaleidoscope of the infinity of the universe's self-knowing.

An even grander and larger-scale picture was sketched by Lovecraft.[162] Across numerous stories and novels which, taken together, can be considered a single fantasy universe, Lovecraft encyclopedically and anatomically described countless generations of the most horrifying and fantastic creatures that once inhabited the Earth and other planets, as well as their future heirs. Lovecraft's historical-evolutionary panorama runs back so deep into time that it even precedes time. Its creatures include the race of Yith, interplanetary flying polyps, the monstrous Mi-Go from Yuggoth, the octopus-like deep-sea alien god Cthulu, and Dagon with his amphibian people, aggressive plasma clots, the Shoggots, giant reptiles, pterodactyls, worms, intelligent mushrooms, as well as ghosts and entities from borderline imaginative worlds, including numerous races and peoples of the past and future Earth and space. Evolution is driven not only by the natural laws of nature, but also by the experiments of higher races, the intervention of space monsters, the horrifying cults of ancient Divinities, the influence of black magic, and the deepest horrors of the human psyche.

Each of these descriptions of the evolutionary development of animals and people, whether Darwin's, Wells', or Lovecraft's, is rich in its argumentation, logic, and illustrations. Lovecraft's picture even emotionally wins in its persuasiveness. All of them were created approximately in the same era: the second half of the 19th and first half of the 20th century. What ultimately distinguishes Wells, Lovecraft, and other science fiction writers from Darwin and the alternative evolutionary theories of the 19th century that were rejected or refuted by the scientific community? There are many examples of scientific theories settling in and continuing to live on in fantasy and science fiction literature of various genres, and the inventions, discoveries, or of forecasts described by fantasy writers becoming scientific, technological, and social reality, even to this day acting as

---

162 Michel Houellebecq insists that Lovecraft's approach was purely materialistic, i.e., he was not esoteric or occultist at heart. See Houllebecq's *H. P. Lovecraft: Against the World, Against Life*, whose Russian edition has the alternative subtitle "Against Humanity, Against Progress."

landmarks or things which scientists seek to transfer from the pages of novels into contemporary life. The main difference between them lies in the space and observance of rules, algorithms, and grammar for presenting arguments and texts expounding scientific theories within the halls of Academia or the University. Darwin's theory gained the character of being scientific only because its production, style, and presentation were furnished in accordance with the etiquette of the scientific community, with the necessary references and appeals having to do with its Department. Further, we can include the practices and social mechanisms of solidarity among groups (clans) of scientists and their conflicts which function along the same rules. In some ways, the production of scientific knowledge can be seen as a religious practice: a theological position is submitted for discussion by the Council (the Department, the University), which checks its references and accordance with scriptures, legends, and the apocrypha of past eras (the dissertations of other scientists and the general canvas of science), as well as its theological correctness (methodology), after which comes the ceremonial defense of the dissertation. At the same time, the contention between different theological school-clans also fits into this picture, for instance if a new "theory-covenant" criticizes or overthrows the authority of the luminaries of reason of past eras or directly threatens the professor or dean's power over the academic "episcopate" of a particular University. On the question of the production of knowledge, adherence to socio-ritual protocols is sometimes more important and guarantees scientific acceptance and endorsement of a theory to a greater extent than the rigor of argumentation and method of the text itself. The objective truth of knowledge, already relevant only within the narrow boundaries of the real world, is diluted to at least half of its strength by the social institution of the University, which usurps its production and has the right to assert the truth while observing the external order of presentation. Science fiction, meanwhile, comes out immediately as a genre of literature, bypassing the filter of institutions and their rituals. At the same time, if we take the fossilized remnants of some Cenozoic animal and reassemble them in a different configuration, collect the facts, and build a convincing theory, then, upon observing the necessary mechanisms and social conventions within the scientific community, it will not be difficult to submit such for examination and defense.[163]

In this lies the fundamental difference. Scientific knowledge of "truth" is de facto not direct access to evolution or gravity, but regulated access to the dominant network of interpretations and explanations of similarities and logical connections in terms of genealogy or formulas as they are conventionally constructed and envisioned by the authorized institution. The primitiveness of this approach is revealed in the general Western European notion of "common sense." A theory is attractive if it satisfies the criteria of common sense and is confirmed in the laboratory or everyday practice, i.e., if "it works" in accordance with simple pragmatism. This system can be summarized in a single formula: knowledge is produced, presented, and defended, and then it explosively expands by the force of the state machine of education, economy, and colonialism.

***

This situation leads us to the necessity of formulating some imperatives and alternatives:

I. Missionary and natural-scientific education are weapons of mass genocide against cultures and traditions, against the original authenticity of the Daseins of the plurality of peoples. A physics textbook is more destructive than Auschwitz, and a person with a general secular education is lost to Tradition in practically 100% of cases. They have to face the strongest experience of tragedy, horror, existential crisis, or incredible astonishment at beauty or a miracle in order to be swept up and thrown out of the network of determinism of everyday reality.

---

163 Looking ahead in time, it is important to note that the new theories based on Hugh Everett's many-worlds hypothesis admit the existence of many equally possible (equally real) variants of historical lines that existed before the point of identification of the observer and the observed reality, which fundamentally relativizes the modernist pathos of absolute evolutionary narratives.

II. For fully-fledged, authentic life, it is enough to possess a set of traditional skills and knowledge: be sure to be able to sing and dance, grow food and obtain it by hunting, know a craft and the art of war, and have a family and children. One needs to orally transmit myths and tales, erect altars to the Divinities and spirits, offer sacrifices to the dead, and ensure that all deeds are accompanied by the appropriate rituals, incantations, beliefs, and offerings.

III. Knowledge should once again become estate-based and elite at the intersection of two types of hierarchies:

(1) The classical Indo-European vertical hierarchy of estates: priest/philosopher, king/warrior, farmers/artisans;

(2) The Tantric hierarchy of realizing one's own Divinity: *pashu* (animal), *vira* (warrior, ascetic), and *divya* (realized Divinehood).

Artisans and farmers keep and pass down their estate, ancestral knowledge, myths, and values. Warriors and worldly rulers keep the craft and skills of war, as well as the laws and order of governance and dynasties. Priests and philosophers ask about Being (*Seyn, Da-sein*), keep and transmit *mythos*, the legends of the Divinities, and the paths to the Divine. It is necessary to revive privileged access to initiations into the deep questions of the sacred.

IV. For already thousands of years, Europeans have dreamed a sick nightmare of progress and development, all the while as this dream pretends to be wakefulness and the empirical reality of physical bodies and interactions. They have colonized the oneiric spaces — the dreams — of other peoples. The most frightening thing of all for the masses of ordinary people is the possibility of changing the plot of this dream to another, to their own. When a person is truly scared in a dream, they wake up, toss and turn, or change the dream to another, more favorable one. Europeans, like all the peoples who have believed in the Western dream, can no longer turn over and brush aside this dream. The

European lies still and stiff, suffering from nightmares that are more real than reality itself. This is a lethargic dream of being which pretends to be the awakening of mankind from naive, infantile daydreaming, from primitive stages of development.

V. The colonial perspective of monoculturalism asserts that there is in principle only one culture, the culture of modern Europe, while all other peoples are sub-cultures striving to catch up with the locomotive of Modernity. This position of contemporal Eurocentrism was refuted by anthropology in the 20th century, which led to the emergence of perspectives on the plurality of cultures, whereby different peoples describe natural reality in different ways, but all of them are fundamentally equal and complex in their own ways. This perspective rejects the progressive scale of dividing people's cultures and traditions, but it still contains a deeper, implicit grain of Eurocentrism. When the new anthropology affirms the diversity of cultures and accounts of nature, it still by default believes that this nature, this material reality of planet Earth, is better understood and described by the natural sciences of the very same modern Europe. While recognizing the plurality of cultures, anthropologists and scholars tacitly reserve the most fundamental right for the only correct natural-scientific description of nature common to all peoples and the whole set of physical laws fixing reality. This is echoed in psychoanalysis, which claims that the psyche and psychosomatics of all people are fundamentally identical, and that differences in mentality appear only on the level of culture.[164] Therefore, the next step in liberation from the structures of Modernity following the affirmation of the plurality of cultures is also recognizing the manifest world's multiplicity of natures. Every people with its own sacred tradition is adequate for the natural manifestness

---

164 Sergey Yesenin penned some insightful lines which fit for describing the psychiatric-industrial conquest of nature (our italics):
And now it's not even hard
Waddling from den to den,
Like a straitjacket
We take nature into concrete.

in which it lives and which it describes. This perspective resonates with the organicist schools which, minus certain Modernist influences in such authors as Herder and Ratzel, affirm that a people's culture reflects the natural environment and landscape in which they have developed. The theory of linguistic-specific thinking has arrived at similar conclusions, arguing that the diversity of natural languages is reflected in the plurality of thoughts and cultures up to the specificity of "external" natural worlds.[165] The singular, universal, material nature of natural-science departments does not exist. When we affirm the plurality of cultures and natures, we mean the dreams of peoples.

VI. Following the new anthropologists, we can affirm the need to decolonize our own consciousness, thinking, and dreams from the repressive structures of the Enlightenment, Modernity, and Postmodernity, which are foreign to Tradition. The truth is that the Enlightenment idea that modern Europe's history is a universal and global developmental path for all peoples who only have to embark on this path is de facto a deeply provincial idea of one geographical space which has been expansively imposed as "fate" without any alternative. It is necessary to begin an era of great geographical "un-discoveries" and "re-coveries."

On this path, we need ornate ingenuity, imagination, and astonishment at the truth of things and phenomena, the literalness of miracle, and recognition of the illusory nature of any so-called "reality." We need to rediscover the landscapes of our own dreams and to dwell (*Wohnen*) in them again.

***

---

165 See Sergei Y. Borodai's lectures, *Iazyk i poznanie. Vvedenie v postreliativizm* [Language and Knowing: An Introduction to Postrelativism] (Moscow, 2020).

The Economy is Not Fate

The transition from Tradition to Modernity, all the way down to the contemporal moment, has been marked by a diminishing of the role of traditions and an increase in the role of the political ideologies that replaced the grand narrative of the Church, whether fascism, communism/socialism, or liberalism. A no less and, in the long run, even more decisive significance has been assumed by the economy and economics. In late Modernity, differences in ideology and values were reduced to bring into relief differences in economic approaches. It is fair to say that political and social values have become a service appendage legitimizing and protecting the economic system that has taken shape. By the mid-20th century, fascist economic models had been defeated. At the turn of the 1990s-2000s, the largest socialist economies (the USSR and its bloc) fell or went through capitalist reforms (China). In our time, forms of capitalism with free markets adjusted to the global market and the division of labor and production are indisputably dominant. Thus, after the end of the ideologies of the 20th century, the economy, presented to us as a given, has come to represent a total structure, a value in and of itself, and in some sense even an ideology in and of itself. Economics replaces Tradition and the sacred, ideologies and the Political, and imposes itself as fate.

Moreover, as Bruno Latour has shown, the capitalist economy claims and aspires — and has successfully implemented its program to this end — to become Nature and Reality as such.[166] Latour speaks of two natures, the first being the nature in which we live, i.e., the landscape-climatic, physical reality of Modernity, or what from a broader standpoint including the supra-/un-real we can call the manifest world (of myth). The second nature is the economic reality into which we are born and/or nurtured, i.e., the structure, rules, and practices to which

---

166 See Bruno Latour, "On some of the affects of capitalism" (Lecture given at the Royal Academy, Copenhagen, 26th of February, 2014) [http://www.bruno-latour.fr/node/552.html].

we have become accustomed to such a degree that we consider them to be the natural course of things.

Latour connects this development with the Earth fully entering the Anthropocene, in which man has begun to exert such an active and obvious influence on the first nature that he can no longer be ignored and can even be compared to natural processes themselves on equal terms. On the other hand, by the mid-20th century the economic sphere finally broke away from and "transcended" earthly realities, which it now administrates purely by its own internal, automated, calculable laws and formulas. Thus, classical metaphysics, in which there is the uranic world of the Divinities and the middle world of people (including the first nature, the material world), has been parodied: instead of the upper world, the top level is now occupied by the economy, dispersed throughout world economic centers and stock exchanges and existing somewhere in the virtual (supra-) space of neural network traders, wherefrom it tries to dictate and change the conditions of reality to suit its own interests. Human societies increasingly live in social, urban, and therefore economic reality. Even rural and farming communities depend on the Economy for subsidies, market demand, technology, even sanitary standards for final products, meat or crops, selected or genetically modified seeds with higher yields, which in turn require appropriate fertilizers and pesticides — all of these are directives from above, from the Economy.

As the world of the first nature undergoes a series of changes and crises, whereby it becomes difficult to determine the proportions between the natural course of things and the influence of human activity on the world as ready-to-hand. The hegemony of the Economy, the second nature, becomes so unshakable that it becomes "easier to imagine the end of the world than the end of capitalism."[167] In this regard, the

---

167 It is important to clarify that we are not talking about overcoming one or another internal economic crisis, but about the fact that the Economy itself, becoming "nature", takes the place of "first nature", whereby economic crisis comes to be perceived as a form of natural disaster, that is as unpredictable, inevitable, and natural, while natural environmental problems are assessed and solved by economic methods.

Economy becomes like a God who will exist after the end of the world, which means that it also existed before its appearance.[168] This is also suggested by various narratives which attempt to read modern market-capitalist or socialist economies into Europe's deep past, into archaic tribes or accounts of "Stone Age economics."

In the light of the economic approach, science and technology are interpreted as activities which are supposed to contribute to man's rational achievement and securing of economic happiness, that is the breadth and possibility of consumer choice. With respect to this "assistance", Louis Althusser's remark that the core of bourgeois ideology is "humanism = economism" rings true.[169] Jean Baudrillard later accurately noted that acts of consumption have now become matters of achieving personality. Submersion in economism and the aspiration to reduce the social, political, and value of people and peoples to economic determinations and strategies exhibit the suggestive power of a dream, regardless of their proclaimed subjective political or religious propositions. The economy is revealed to be the common and inevitable "lining" for the whole beingful world, akin to Plato's *khora* or Bryant's substance. We can cite Latour's commentary on Feuerbach: "Economics and its associated retinue of skills and trades — accounting, marketing, design, merchandizing, business training, organization studies, management — do not make up a science that would be studying a material world, but a set of disciplines in charge of extracting from the social and natural world another world."[170]

Let us correct Latour's schema to point out that the economy as the second nature not only and no so much unifies and replaces the first Nature as universal reality as it emasculates and subordinates to its interests all the richness of the diverse natures of different tribes and peoples. Here, in all their obviousness, are revealed the mechanisms of the Gestell's

168 Latour thus exclaims: "Perish the world, provided my bank survives!"

169 See Alain de Benoist, *Beyond Human Rights*.

170 Latour, "On some of the affects of capitalism".

overall formation through its apologetics for the πολλα and ὕβρις, through its reduction of the world to calculable raw materials. *Ergo*, rejecting the modern world and its reality means rejecting the primacy of the Economic in its perfected form of the global liberal economy with its dominant virtual sector and the left-liberal ideology of values that buttress it.

In the totality of its philosophical, political, and esoteric dimensions, Traditionalism forms an integral system of another view on the history of Europe and the world's development, on the possible horizons of the future, in negative as well as, insofar as such is possible, positive scenarios. For Traditionalists, the economy is a purely applicational, tertiary matter, therefore it is not given so much attention and reverence. However, it is still necessary to identify key orientations and alternatives *vis-à-vis* this now dominant "second nature", and it is on this that we will dwell over the following pages.

The economy or economics, οἰκονομία, is etymologically the doctrine and law (science and practice) of maintaining the household estate and everyday mode of life, of keeping and multiplying property. Let us locate this arrangement within the traditional structure of society. The top of the spiritual hierarchy — the priests and philosophers — is the least interested in possessing and multiplying gold and people's wealth. According to Plato, the philosopher is filled with the inner gold of the soul and intellect, and therefore has no need for external gold for fulfilling some kind of lack. Closeness to the Divinities and death frees the upper spiritual estate from being attracted to and engaged in luxury. Socrates called the body the dungeon of the soul, from which it follows that the framing and rich decorations of this "dungeon" are essentially only the multiplication of the perishable, of all that is least important to the philosopher. Hence the special status of temple decorations, which are seen as "pure wealth" that is not engaged in the accomplishment of labor or percentage growth, but simply shines and embodies the light of the sacred and the aristocratic. The opposite of such constitutes obvious signs of this estate's degeneration by the penetration of lower elements, which was especially brought into relief in the history of the Renaissance and the Medici and Borgia dynasties.

The second estate, the peak of social and political authority, i.e., emperors, kings, princes, and warriors, possess a soul consisting of different proportions of gold and silver, hence their craving for the attributes of royal luxury, regalia, and trophies. The king surrounded with gold and precious jewels is not identical to the greedy accumulation of wealth, since royal attributes — from the king's sword to golden chambers and fabrics — are but a continuation and material embodiment of royal glory and valor; the brilliance of gold is the brilliance of power, authority, and the gleam of the divine seal on the ruler. Within this paradigm, gold and jewels have no autonomous value and being, as they are endowed by belonging to power and warrior prowess, like the trophies of warriors. To this circle also belongs the most ancient practice of luxurious burials for the nobility. The perverted cases here include the cursed emperors of Rome.[171]

Finally, there is the third estate of farmers and artisans, whose mode of everyday life and refraction of the sacred are closest to the earth and are devoid of aristocratic valor. In the space of the societies of yore, the principle of *"non plus ultra"*, or "nothing beyond measure", prevailed, regulating the cycle of annual sacrifices and the payment of various taxes to the upper estates. Nevertheless, the third estate is the most open to chthonic privation, to the principle of accumulation and production. As for the fourth estate of chandalas, pariahs, and untouchables in traditional society, they represent a pure type of poverty and deprivation in spiritual and social terms.

In accordance with the foregoing exposition, we can outline the corresponding economic models of the estates that existed within society at the same time, each on their own level:

---

171 See Gaius Suetonius Tranquillus' *The Twelve Caesars.*

- The priesthood and philosophers: the economy of death — "a human comes into and leaves this world empty-handed"; maximal transcendence, minimal materialism.

- Rulers and warriors: the economy of war, force, and power; delegating the splendor of glory and power in attributes and wealth, trophies and tributes.

- Farmers and craftsmen: the sacred "natural" economy, the economy of gifts and exchange; sacrifice as deliverance from surplus (the "accursed share"); craft as the embodiment of divine forms in matter.

The relations between a people and its elites are accounted for in terms of tributes and taxes, the offering of crops, crafts, and loot to the highest armed princes, or offerings and dakshina to priests, spiritual teachers, and gurus. On the whole, the relationship of mutual, reciprocal sacrifices, offerings, and gifts permeates all estates and castes in society, a point which we will shall discuss in detail later.

The emergence of Modernity was marked by a shift to city life and urbanization, which gave rise to a new class type, the bourgeois, a person who does not till the earth or carry out military or spiritual service. The bourgeoisie is a stratum of lackeys and servants (as in the modern sense of "services") that entered the arena in the Enlightenment. It also formed a new, "third estate" in Europe, liberal and secular in its essence. In its midst rapidly rose the figure of the "merchant." As an independent ontological niche, the "merchant" type is not found in the hierarchy of Indo-European peoples, and it is believed that in ancient times it penetrated the Mediterranean space from the Semitic zone of the Middle East. Bourgeois society, free from agricultural labor and the collection of tribute by force, was openly interested in what is etymologically the "doctrine of maintaining the household and multiplying property." Bringing the economy into the forefront of social life meant its transformation into a bourgeois ideology in all aspects, including the substitution of the Political by the profitable. The economy (with all the varieties of approaches) becomes the materialist paradigm reflecting the rise and specific thinking of the "last people."

It is in bourgeois society and its economy that the principle of progress — linear development, the quantitative criteria of "the more the better, the more effective and successful" — found its embodiment. The moral justification for economic progressism and accumulation was supplied by Protestantism with its ethics, as described by Max Weber: "God marks those chosen for salvation with wealth in earthly life." Here also begins the anti-capitalist discourse of Traditionalism, as progressive economic theories operate with anti-traditional categories and postulate anti-traditional ideals and strategies for social life. In addition to the unlimited desire for growth and multiplication, no unimportant role was played by the supra-national, global essence of capital. On the political spectrum, Traditionalism postulates ethnocentrism, ethnocultural and ethno-religious identity, along with a variability of economic relations corresponding to the hierarchy and functions of estates within society. Capitalism gives rise to the phenomenon of transnational corporations and the global market with global distribution of labor, which compels peoples to seek their niche in the global community not according to their own Logos, but according to the actual needs and free niches of the global market.

In this shift, in the emancipation from tribute, sacrifice, and the principle of *non plus ultra*, the bourgeoisie partially converged with agriculture and handicraft, but only by transforming them into the "agrarian sector" of kolkhozes, workshops, and sites of production. Freed from fascination with the sacred and from hierarchy, the lower levels of society regressed and gave birth to a new (sub-)anthropological type of Modernity, the worker or proletarian, whose ontology, subjectivity, culture, and politics are entirely derived from the economy. The proletarian type was unknown to the world of Tradition, but in terms of its characteristics it can be located below farmers and craftsmen, often closely approximating pariahs and chandalas. Julius Evola saw in the proletariat one of the types of the "fourth estate" that would replace bourgeois society. Another new type derivative of capitalist society is the consumer (one could name the whole constellation of "blue-collar workers", but their being is still in one way or another hinged upon the consumer). The worldview of the consumer has been vividly described in the works of the philosopher Jean Baudrillard.[172] The worker and the consumer are two sides of the same emancipated cycle of production-consumption on the Möbius strip of matter and signs not subordinated to any higher end. Finally, nothing betrays a person's belonging to the lower levels of being more than interest and increased emphasis on economic issues as a panacea for all problems.

The subsequent transition from the industrial economy to the service economy in the countries of the prosperous, developed North gave rise to two fatal, interrelated consequences for man and the world as a whole. The first is the withdrawal of industrial production to the countries of the conditioned "Third World", the South, which expanded the type of the worker and his lifeworld to non-Western territories, peoples, and cultures. In other words, colonial expansion continued by means of economics and the global distribution of production and services, whereby one people or country became concentrated on one industry or limited set of services, which then become identified with them to the point of a global stereotype. For example, Thailand and Southeast Asia have come to be identified with sex-tourist transgender services or handcraft production even cheaper than in China. China itself is today the leader in the field of mass human factories, where thousands of people simultaneously perform the simplest possible operations on computers and deal with technical tasks on equal footing with AI. On this canvas also figures the distribution of energy production and the

---

172 See Jean Baudrillard, *America* (London: Verso, 2010); *The System of Objects*, trans. James Benedict (London: Verso, 2006); *Simulacra and Simulation*, trans. Sheila Faria Glaser (Ann Arbor: University of Michigan Press, 1994).

determination of energy-dependent regions. The black power of coal, oil, and gas entangles all peoples and continents with viaducts and pipelines, thus creating the arterial-venous pattern of the Titanic heartbeat of economics and production, one filled and webbed together with viscous, silt-like, hallucinatory matter. The Titans' heartbeat is the rhythm of pumps extracting oil from the bowels of the earth and valves passing gas to consumers. The Divinities had soma and ambrosia, while the Titans have oil, gas, and metals which, like narcotics, cause addiction to economics, technology, and the development of capitalism and globalism. This is, in essence, the next logical round of the installation of a global, uniform reality — "carbon reality." If the Divinities granted ambrosia only to the most worthy, and the use of ritual intoxicants was a dangerous initiation, then today gasoline and plastic oil products are accessible to anyone who so wishes. Titanism is egalitarian, it erases hierarchies and identities in the transition to ever deeper virtuality and the ubiquitous covering of the world with cables and social networks.

The second consequence is the transformation of the human and personhood into capital and a taxpayer. Contemporary economics paints an image of man as an investment portfolio and calls for investing in his education, physical development, mental stability, and external attractiveness. All of this forms a person's capital and rank in the labor market, where they can offer for sale their muscular strength, intellect, beauty, and body. Personality traits and body constitution become economic indices, one of the most important of which is the overall effective index of tax solvency. The State, as a player on the market in possession of a number of monopolies on specific economic and repressive practices, appraises a person. Banks, too, assess the "creditworthiness" of a population. Hence the State and the market's increased interest in the budgets of families and individual citizens, in increasing the transparency of income, expenditures, transactions, and payment methods through widespread digitalization, the introduction of plastic cards, cashless payments (avoiding cash as such), online banking, automatic interest deductions, blockchain and electronic currencies, and the desire to identify users in all possible services and limit anonymous transactions. All of this is constituted as the embodiment of facets of existential "Connectivity", of "being plugged-in."

The next and absolutely logical step is the implantation of payment chips (based on RFID, for example) into people and gradually transitioning to the transhumanist replacement of the human with cyborgs or some digitized form of consciousness, in addition to the replacement of workers with robots. After all, a program, cyborg, or robot is the ideal, automized, indifferent taxpayer who transfers the fiscal part of their revenue not by compulsion, but by algorithm.

Despite all of the above, which is true and relevant as a description of the numerous facets of the fall of the manifest world, economic problems are not a priority for Traditionalism. Traditionalism does not choose "market or planned economy", "government control or the invisible hand", "social security or private insurance", "enrichment or flight into impoverished spirituality"; instead, Traditionalism considers these questions to be an imposed "fork" of false choices which are relevant only to the anthropological types generated by a false paradigm.

The problem of jobs being taken over by robots and algorithms and the precariatization of labor worries us last in line, because this problem is one of the tertiary consequences of progress and technologization in the socio-economic sphere. The way out is not increasing imaginative creativity or creating new professions (which in any case would be a tough break and entail cleansing the labor market of those who do not fit in). Traditionalism does not propose compensating with a different tax scale or transparent mechanisms for distributing a consolidating budget. The solution lies primarily in getting out of the economic-centric paradigm and overthrowing the "second nature" altogether. At the same time, however, this does not mean returning to the "first nature" in the spirit of reflecting the ideals of Rousseau's "noble savage." Society is constituted not by the market, but by relationships, including those with non-human entities, and it is not a service sector, as we will show below.

At the forefront of Traditionalism stand the Sacred, the higher dimensions of the human spirit, authentic existing in Being, sacrifice, the translation and transmission of Divine manifestations in society, and fascination with myth. The heart of the traditional and Traditionalist economy is the economy of Death, which is our orientation. This Death is a sacrifice to the Divinities or heroic self-sacrifice on the field of battle in the rays of the "eternal glory of worthy deeds."[173] If in everyday practice we can reject and destroy the capitalist basis of technological progress and accumulation through symbolic acts[174], sacrifices, and an alternative organization of labor, then on the grander scale it is necessary to appeal to archaic economic practices which both make the accumulation of capital as such impossible and knock out the basis for communist mythologizing about exploitation.

The Spirits and Demons of Things

In the property law of the Maori, which is inseparable from their sacred tradition, there is an interesting category of property called *taonga*, which originally included wives as personal property, but which later expanded to encompass a broad range of status-related property, from talismans,

---

173 *Elder Edda, Havamal* 76 reads:
    Cattle die,
    Kinsmen die,
    You, too, are mortal
    But death is not known
    To the loud glory
    Of worthy deeds.
    [Translated from the author's Russian - trans.]

174 That is "symbolic" not in the sense of something sentimentally insignificant, but as violating the fundamental logic of consumption and production throughout society. Such is akin to irrational and illogical market behavior and the intentional, demonstrative destruction and leveling of valuable items and values.

amulets, tools, idols, and sacred cults to fabrics and intangible items like rituals or cults. In a word, *taonga* is a thing embodying status that can be the subject of an exchange or gifting. Taongas are intimately connected with the land and the *rod* to which they belong or in which they were created. They are also receptacles and conductors of a special force (a spirit) rooted in its native, ancestral land. This magical force, called *hau*, is mixed into a specific item or intangible thing, and it is also believed that even the souls of people are mixed in to a particular taonga. Another category of things, *waigu'a*, is close to money and includes precious shell bracelets, mother-of-pearl necklaces, etc. The peculiarity of *waigu'a* lies in that they do not function as monetary instruments in any direct sense of the word, but rather are special, almost living entities which have their own names and personality, history, and even love affairs, as Marcel Mauss informs us.[175] Some of the Trobriand islands' inhabitants even spend hours touching, contemplating, or rubbing themselves with their *waigu'a*, and on special occasions they might even take their *waigu'a*'s name instead of their own.

In general, in the archaic (primordial) world and societies, all things are in one way or another animated and even ranked in status. In the European context, we are more familiar with aristocratic artifacts, such as the swords of kings and warriors, ritual cups, magical artifacts and sacred objects, idols, living forests, and stones. Let us also remember that a thing is under the inspiration of the Muses and the Divinities, framed by the necessary rituals and offerings that inspirit it.

Things blend with the souls of people, people take names in honor of their sacred *waigu'a*, and *taonga* bear the imprint of their native forests and clan (in the Germanic-Scandinavian context, we would say that such things are directly associated with the *odal*, the family-clan allotment). All of this excludes the possibility of the existence of "mere things." A thing is a receptacle of *hau*, an imprint of the Muses, a personality and history, a gift or a curse. A thing is thus once again revealed to be

175 See Mauss, *The Gift: Forms and Functions of Exchange in Archaic Societies.*

a symbol whose semantic and perspectival threads extend into the upper and lower worlds. One of the logical consequences of this comparison is that today's material-thing world of industrial "mere things" is soulless by definition, hence the many practices which indigenous tribes use to sacralize artifacts from the white world.

What role do *taonga* and *hau* play in the most important gift and exchange practices among the Maori as well as other Pacific island peoples and tribes? If a taonga is exchanged within one clan or between friendly clans, then there are no additional conditions. But when the rate of exchange and chain of owners increases, another side of *hau* comes into play. Since the *hau* of *taonga* is rooted in its native place and family, then upon ending up gifted and exchanged far away from its homeland, it begins to manifest a demonic essence that demands that it be returned. *Hau* wants to return to its native forests, to its native islands. This forces the gift's recipient, the new owner of the *taonga*, to make reciprocal gifts in order to pass the *hau* back. This is usually described in cases of three donors: the first gifts a *taonga* to a loved one, and they in turn regift the *taonga* to a third person, at which point the *hau* comes into play, and the third person must give a return gift (a payment of *utu*) which is in fact the embodiment of the *hau* of the previously gifted *taonga*. The second person in the chain, knowing this, re-gifts this gift from the third person to the first, thereby closing the circle of returning the *hau* back to its homeland "on the back" of another *taonga*. A man who takes a wife from another clan returns the gift in the form of his daughter, who is given to be married in due time. *Hau* forces people to give something in return so as to itself be returned to its native place. If a person does not make a return gift, then the *hau* begins to bring misfortune, curses, and can even destroy a person. The demonism of things is revealed when they are out of place and cannot return to their homeland.

It is important to note that the reverse *taonga* on which the *hau* of the first gift is returned also has its own *hau* which wants its own return. Thus, the exchange of things, including return gifts, leads to a constant circulation and traveling of *hau*, *taonga*, and *waigu'a*. Things leave their native places and then return along chains of givers and recipients. This gives rise to a total arrangement of exchanging things that upholds sacred well-being, crops, catches, and the statuses and health of people which might be demonically affected by a *hau* lingering for too long in one place. It bears remembering that *hau* is carried not only by items, but also rituals, magical actions, women and children, food, feasts, and festivals of gifting or harvesting which, as follows, must be carried out with a certain regularity and on a spectacular scale so that the tribes and clans can gather to deal in mass-scale exchanges and return things back to their places and families. Such mass feasts are the pulse and circulation of the sacred in these societies. There also exists the customary *gimwali* market, where things can be exchanged purely economically, but it is not considered honorable, and the word is sometimes used as an insult.

It is interesting to look from this perspective at the global system of logistics and the consumption of goods and services in the modern world, where industrial things are transported around the world to settle first on shelves and then in landfills. They do not possess *hau* or any other forms of animation and complicity in the sacred, and they are, despite their seeming abundance, therefore expressive of total poverty, privation, ontological inferiority, and lack. If a *taonga* starts to bring harm at a distance from its home and clan, and if, conversely, back in its ancestral space it acts as benevolent, then modern things (and not only objects) are the black holes of an all-consuming void. Their increased mobility along highways and network cables and their rapid succession in time reflect the inescapable and endless restlessness and homelessness (*Unhemische*) which in the German language Martin Heidegger associated with uncanny (*Unheimliche*) nightmarishness.

Animated, inspirited, ensouled things, bearers of *hau*, are the sacred basis of the fundamental, principled anti-capitalism of archaic societies, where any accumulation of property, wealth as capital or immobile treasure means the multiplication of demonic elements and the loss of subjectivity. Restless *hau* asserts its power over its (wrongful) owner or thief and destroys his life. To prevent this from happening, things must be given away and returned.

The Economy of the Dead

Above we spoke primarily about the rituals of gifting and feasting, but these are also, up to the point of being synonymous and directly analogous, tightly related to rituals of sacrifice and the destruction of things (such as at a potlatch). Such rituals (or, in essence, these different facets of one and the same sacred phenomena) permeate all levels of society and create, among other things, social relations and statuses. Farmers bring their gifts to fishermen, fishermen to farmers and craftsmen. Some types of *taonga* and *waigu'a* can circulate only from East to West, and others only from West to East, which already generates a sacred geography. The most important point here is that this ritual giving back erupts out of and beyond the middle world of people and is addressed to the upper world of the Divinities, as well as the worlds of deceased ancestors or even, conditionally, the horizontal, "parallel" worlds of other mythical beings inhabiting fields, forests, rivers, seas, lakes, mountains, rocks, etc. People are surrounded on all sides by many other beings with whom they must engage in making arrangements — and these acts are the essence of gifting and sacrificing.

Economic relations with the dead are among the most important relationships in folk cultures. The ancestors are not always represented as a detailed genealogy of the *rod* (as, for instance, among the Scandinavians), but it is often the case that, after the memory of one or two generations, all the ancestors merge together into one faceless figure of "Ancestors" altogether which finds symbolic expression. Dead ancestors play an immense role in the lives of people and communities. They can send illnesses and troubles if they are not gotten along with, or they can fulfill the role of guardians if gift and sacrifice relations are arranged with them. Marcel Mauss notes that all things belong to the dead and the Divinities, hence the first relationship of gifts and exchanges (the origin of the economy) into which people enter is with the dead. The same picture is confirmed by Eduardo Kohn in the case of the Amazon tribes.

Since the dead somehow, in some different form from us, nonetheless continue to live and enter into relationships with the living, and because the dead are ancestors and relatives, communication with the other world means communicating with kin and that very space whither a person will sooner or later find themselves and from which they will return again, reborn in their *rod*. Among the Maori people, exchanging things with ancestors is a fairly regular practice. A relative's spirit might appear to a living person and ask them to bring necessary things to their grave (a comb, shoes, money, food). A spirit can be extremely persistent and assume in advance that, for instance, one or another thing is already theirs, making the living relative's task only to bring it to their grave. If the spirit of the deceased is ignored or rejected, then this inevitably leads to troubles and anxiety in this world, as well as the spirit's suffering in the afterlife. This can also lead to the accumulation of bad debts in the form of things not given to the next world, as if left "suspended" between worlds.

Closely adjacent to this semantic field are practices of ritually burying things and the deceased with sets of accessories and animals, such as when jewelry, craft tools, weapons for hunting and war, dogs and horses, gold, needles for sewing, etc., are found in kurgans and tombs. Robert Hertz, an anthropologist and one of Mauss' students, pointed out that the volume of things and gifts (e.g., vegetables, cattle, jewelry, etc.) sent along with the dead into the other world during burial can at times reach unheard-of proportions, for which relatives could save up for years.[176] All of this is a literal transfer of things to the beyond, beyond the manifest world, for their existence in another world.

---

176 See Robert Hertz, *Death and the Right Hand*, trans. Rodney and Claudia Needham (London: Routledge, 1960).

Returning to *taonga*, it is necessary to add that such also includes ancestors. This is most clearly seen among those peoples who cultivate cults of ancestral skulls or special relationships with the deceased's remains. For example, the mummification and public display of ancestors' bodies is encountered among many tribes throughout Asia and South America, as is the practice of periodically (every few years) washing and purifying the bones of parents, which was also practiced in Ancient Rus. The remains or mummies themselves thus become material *taonga*.

Yet another interesting nuance in gift relations is the association of masks and ritual costumes during wintertime. The custom of caroling (*koliada* among the Slavs), known throughout all of Europe and even preserved in Christianity, embodies the ritual of communicating with the other world. During winter festivities, people, mostly youth, put on masks and costumes resembling evil spirits and go from house to house in the village to beg for gifts in exchange for peace. If someone does not pay them off with gifts, then the carolers have the right to cause damage to the property, to steal or break something. A key role here is played by the metaphysics of the mask: when a person puts on a costume and hides their face, they literally cease to be themself. The ordinary language of reality tells us that someone who puts on a mask is still someone who has put on a mask, i.e., the same person only engaging in some kind of naive role-playing. In the world of Tradition, everything is much more serious, for when a person puts on a mask, they disappear, the place of their essence is occupied by the entity whose mask they don. Thus, when in antiquity, as well as now, people encountered bands of caroling youth, they actually encountered a clique of demonic entities, beasts, and the dead, who are "on the back of the living" cajoling villages, cities, and collecting gifts. Whoever pays off the masked is not giving gifts to people, but to entities from the other world who have come on winter night, at a metaphysically very disturbing part of the year associated with death and transition. The practice of "demons" caroling and collecting gifts known in Europe is rightly considered a variation of the potlatch. This was suggested in passing by Mauss, who argued that for archaic peoples the participation of Divinities and the dead in potlatch and village rituals was a guarantee of generosity by the Divinities and nature in this world.

The latter point is connected with a disturbing conjecture. The worlds of the dead are imagined to be similar to our world, and the departed ancestors, spirits, and Divinities live much the same way as we do, but with fewer worries. They also have their own things, their magical qualities, relationships, and gifts. People make bountiful sacrifices to ancestors in order for, among other things, ancestors to make offerings in their own world. The question arises: to whom and why can the dead, those who have already left the sublunar world, offer sacrifices and arrange bountiful gift rituals?

There are two "theories". According to the first, the matter at hand is a hermetically sealed circle of gift exchanges between the human world of the living, the world of the dead ancestors, and the world of spirits and the Divinities. We sacrifice to them, and in their world they sacrifice to us. When the ritual of burning gifts takes place in the world of the dead, in our world harvest rises, fruits appear on the trees, fish in the rivers, and game in the forest. Through harvesting, killing game, and making sacrifices, we return their souls, their *hau*, to the other world, and they go home. Thus is fulfilled the cycle of a kind of *thanatos*-agrarian economy.

The second theory is centered around the conjecture that the dead and spirits take gifts and sacrifices to an even deeper, darker world hidden from us in the Abyss, the grounding apophatic instance of the Nothing.[177] In this case, it is of extreme interest to consider the metaphysics of ritual sacrificial gifts not to the Divinities, not to spirits, not to the dead, and not to the living, not to ourselves, but to nowhere, to the Nothing, asking for nothing in return — in a word, the pure gift.

Based on the foregoing, we can give a more extended interpretation of the essence of capitalism and the multiplication

177 See Askr Svarte, *Gods in the Abyss.*

of the production and consumption of things. We can distinguish three main, intertwining processes. As described above, there is the transition from handicraft to industrial production. The creation of a thing was once framed by rituals and superstitions, including the gifting of part of a thing to and then from the spirits. In parallel with the course of historical involution, the practice of offerings, sacrifices, and gifts between people, the Divinities, and the dead ceased. Man began to only take from the world, from nature, as raw material. Moving from myth to strict rationality, the connection with and reality of posthumous being disappears along with the worlds of the dead and the cults of ancestors. In Tradition, death was a transition, an initiation into a greater community of Ancestors. Alternatively, immortality was preserved in the form of rebirths in the *rod* or in the glory of aristocratic and warrior deeds.

In creationism, death assumes a "one-off" character, although ancestors and saints are still remembered and asked for worldly intercession. In the world after the Enlightenment, death came to be likened to an "extinguished screen", the "extinguishing" of reason and consciousness, or simply the disappearance and expulsion of a person from the world of the living without any posthumous fate or wanderings through worlds. The existential tension of death and the questions that death poses to the citizen consumer and taxpayer are all subject to taboo in the paradigm of Modernity and Postmodernity. Death becomes something technical, like a hospital bed, and is understood as an "offline status" on a social network, a disconnection from being plugged in, from "Connectivity." As long as people are alive, the topic of death is presented in the form of entertainment, shock content, extreme sports, news clips, or black humor. Finally, transhumanism proposes to consider death as a task to overcome, a surmountable threshold on the way to the real immortality of the material body or digitized consciousness. One interesting view of death from the standpoint of Artificial Intelligence is exhibited in Uber's autopilot taxis. During testing of the digital vision systems (the LIDARs), auto piloting, and data transfers over GPS systems for positioning the car on the map, an accidentally run-over pedestrian was treated as an effect caused by a failure and disruption of the whole network's functioning. From the point of view of program code and protocols, death is a system failure, a settings and network error, a problem with LIDAR and camera calibration, a misinterpretation of 3D objects in the surrounding world by the neural network. This is not only the case with Uber, but any AI and socio-technological systems which deal with humans and have the ability to cause unintended harm, for example in medicine or in transportation. From the point of view of the operating system, a person as a being is a text file with user settings and input data registration. In programming, after execution a function returns an inverse parameter of 1 or 0, that is success or failure. In the case of a person's death, the system will register such merely as a function failure, an error in the user file, as a device "time out." Hence, avoiding death is conceptualized in terms of a software-programming, a technological task to eliminate and prevent the occurrence of negative effects like errors in code execution and machine tasks.[178] Literal immortality secured by means of technology and programming is the final stage of the parody and profanation of death as a different mode of life or as the existential *zum-Tode-sein.*

If there is no death, or if death does not mean transitioning into the status of Ancestor and passing into some other space (not to mention retribution), then according to the logic of Modernity and economics there are no obligations before other worlds and entities upon which well-being in this reality was once upon a time alleged to depend. Reality does not depend at all on fantasies and imaginations of the "unreal." Sacrifices and exchanging gifts with the dead have no meaning, no point, and are not even considered. This leads to the accumulation of enormous amounts of debt, as the volume of the production of things and wealth only increases, but is not recompensed or bound to other actors and the true owners of the whole beingful

---

178 See *Arkheologiia russkoi smerti* [The Archaeology of Russian Death] 6 (2018).

world. On this shore of the manifest world, a preponderance of sacred debt accumulates. The *hau* and *taonga* freeze and cease going back home, which according to the logic of Tradition leads to spirits, ancestors, and Divinities beginning to cause us hardships and troubles as they demand what is theirs. Here we can point out the negative nature of the "fruits" of machine-made products. The dead and the Divinities are punishing humanity in a way comparable to the punishment of King Midas, whose touch turned everything into gold: people now turn everything produced by the Gestell that they touch into debt.

In Tradition, a thing's passage from this world to another was accomplished through its ritual deterioration, breaking, or drowning — in a word, by bringing it into disrepair and destruction. In our days, things whose obsolescence or breakdowns sometimes happen still in the production stage are stored away in cyclopean landfills across the face of the earth and dumped into the oceans. When things break, it is even possible that the dead consider these broken things to be theirs, and in every possible way spur on the fragility and transience of exploitation in order to get their share as soon as possible. But, instead of being offered to them, these objects are piled up in mountains and islands of useless things that poison the world and are left suspended between worlds. Where the Divinities are absent, there are Titans. Wherever there are no sacrifices, there is the hubris of accumulation — and there are consequences.

Proceeding from this exposition, it might be said that Traditionalism opposes the practice of fiat (fiduciary) money, the value of which is determined conventionally by the State and the market. The denomination of fiat money does not depend on the price of materials or the cost of printing and minting, and is not tied to gold, silver, or anything else. Fiat money is the ideal platform for economic hubris, especially in the financial sector of pure speculation, digital payments and currencies (blockchain and Bitcoin variations), credit lending, and the proliferation of debt and capital with interest. The virtual nature of fiat money does not allow us to consider it to be a fully-fledged part of sacrifices and gift exchanges, for its only value is imposed by the framework of "reality" on this shore of the manifest world. To bring sacrifices to the Divinities and the dead in the form of rubles or dollars means implying that there are banks, exchange rates, stock exchanges, and markets in the other world. Two coins of gold or silver for Charon are a more fully-fledged embodiment of money than any amount of paper from the printing facilities of central banks. Most likely of all is that the whole modern economic system is the embodied curse of the restless, homeless, traumatized spirits of things.

The World as the Accursed Share

One of the characteristic traits of archaic societies is their principal position of being anti-accumulation and anti-production. In describing "primitive" societies, modern historiography often resorts to definitions in the likes of "stateless society", "illiterate society", "society without high developed technologies", "lawless society", etc. All of these determinations are intended to demonstrate the inferiority of archaic peoples living in myth to modern civilization, where all of the above "missing" things, as well as much else, are present. Finally, among these negative definitions there is the sacramental epithet "marketless society." The anthropologist Pierre Clastres has exposed the Eurocentric essence of this thesis:

> Now, the notion of a subsistence economy conceals within it the implicit assumption that if primitive societies do not produce a surplus, this is because they are incapable of doing so, entirely absorbed as they are in producing the minimum necessary for survival, for subsistence. The time-tested and ever serviceable image of the destitution of the Savages. And, to explain that inability of primitive societies to tear themselves away from the stagnation of living hand to mouth, from perpetual alienation in the search for food, it is said they are technically under-equipped, technologically inferior.[179]

179 Pierre Clastres, *Society Against the State: Essays in Political Anthropology* (New York: Zone Books, 1989), 190-191.

Such a prejudiced view is in essence a false interpretation of the "reality" of the world of archaic societies, whose own view is tightly boarded up in front of the modern scholar standing on evolutionary-progressist positions. Evaluating and hierarchically ranking societies by level of technological development and economic successes is untenable, as such can in no way be objective and therefore immediately disqualifies whoever relies on such.

The situation as seen from within the worlds of archaic societies — and here we include not only the aboriginals of Oceania or the Indians of North and South America, but also our great European peoples in those times when Myth and Tradition reigned — looks altogether different. First of all, archaic societies possess all the necessary tools for successfully living (normal life, not mere survival) in the places in which they dwell. Their level of handicraft is neither low nor developed, but sufficient and aesthetically refined. Secondly, they are fundamentally uninterested in creating those surpluses which shape capital and sales markets. Archaic tribes have an altogether different approach to work. From the colonists' point of view, the Indian tribes were beset by a total laziness and lack of entrepreneurial streak that would otherwise drive them to break their backs over arable land and vegetable gardens or spend their time extracting resources and products for sale. Primordial societies are full of abundance because they consume enough food and resources to maintain an even balance between expending and replenishing energy. They spend the greater part of their time in leisure, which includes not only crafts and entertainment, but also war and hunting, i.e., what in developed society would be qualified as professional, economically productive activities. They engage in real labor, that is providing themselves with food and firewood for the day, for only a few hours a day and a total of several months a year, when it is necessary to collectively prepare fields for sowing.

Wherever they have appeared in the world, colonial administrations have coerced tribes to work. This is the case of the evolution of the Runa tribe illustrated by Eduardo Kohn, as well as the forceful suppression of peoples in Southeast Asia described by the anthropologist James S. Scott.[180] Scott writes of how the successful, complex system of rice cultivation required constant control and coercion of the tribes surrounding the city inhabited by the governor or king. The tribes that took shape out of fugitive subjects and slaves in the uplands and on hard-to-reach mountain slopes often deliberately employed labor techniques and agriculture that required minimal conditions and investments for harvest. Such minimization of labor was closely associated with the tribe's freedom from work. A very similar system could be seen in Russia in the times of nascent and developed serfdom, which later organically led to peasants being assigned to factories.

Clastres presents an excellent example illustrating the attitude toward work and production among the Indians of South America. Having used stone axes to cut down the number of trees they needed, when the Indians learned of the advantage of iron axes, they wanted to acquire them, but not in order to cut down a greater quantity of trees as the European worker or entrepreneur would, but only to cut down the same number of trees they needed faster, thereby freeing up more time for leisure and war.

Another example cited by Georges Bataille aptly highlights the difference between the bourgeois and his values and the primordial man of myth. It is absolutely normal for any pagan to offer a sacrifice, for example a pig, to Divinities or spirits. But for the bourgeois, according to Bataille, such an act is absolutely immoral, because the "savage" kills not only the pig, but all of the offspring it could have yielded in the future[181], which is to say that the pagan kills the source of his income and capital, a gesture which for the bourgeois is insane and contradicts economic logic.

---

180 See James S Scott, *The Art of Not Being Governed: An Anarchist History of Upland Southeast Asia* (New Haven: Yale University Press, 2009).

181 See Bataille, *The Accursed Share*.

The Swedish Protestant missionary Frans August Larson left vivid descriptions of how the Mongols reacted to scientific advances in the early 20th century:

> This telegraph line is an everlasting wonder to the Mongol people. They fail to understand the importance of it, and argue that there is little need to send messages so quickly. It has been difficult to teach them to leave the telegraph poles alone. Often in the past the Mongols have used the poles and the wires for things which seemed to them more important than telegraphy. The wire they find especially good to tie around water troughs and fasten things generally, and the poles extremely handy to split up and light fires with... Invariably I have met with the same retort: "All these things may be good in other countries; but we do not need them here. We are happy and content as we are. A postal service would bring in letters from outside - trouble us with all sorts of things. I do not need letters. None of my people need letters. If anyone wants to communicate with me or I with him, life is not too short for either of us to get on a horse and go to the other. Letters would mean that we should bother each other with all sorts of trivial matters. It is better so. A man does not travel a month on horseback for a trivial matter, but he does if he has a real need to see a friend."[182]

The American thinker and terrorist Theodore Kaczynski proposed a fitting definition for the form of obsession with the commotion of work and the accumulation of things which colonists and modernizers thrust upon indigenous tribes and peoples as a powerful ideal with no alternative. This definition is also absolutely true for all the peoples of Europe, Russia, or Asia who have been touched by the suggestive veil of the socio-economic ideals and values of Modernity and Postmodernity. Kaczynski spoke of a special character of human activity which he called "surrogate activity", that is:

> an activity that is directed toward an artificial goal that the individual pursues for the sake of the "fulfillment" that he gets from pursuing the goal, not because he needs to attain the goal itself. For instance, there is no practical motive for building enormous muscles, hitting a little ball into a hole or acquiring a complete series of postage stamps. Yet many people in our society devote themselves with passion to bodybuilding, golf or stamp-collecting. Some people are

---

182 See Frans August Larson, *Larson Duke of Mongolia* (Read Books, 2013).

more "other-directed" than others, and therefore will more readily attach importance to a surrogate activity simply because the people around them treat it as important or because society tells them it is important.[183]

It is quite possible to imagine that when an adept of modernization and economic solutions offers normal people new axes in order to multiply their firewood, or when he suggests not sacrificing pigs to the Divinities because of this leading to losses, then these normal people will recognize such to be a proposal to engage in some kind of "surrogate", unnecessary or irrelevant activity for the time being. Stamp-collecting and playing football are just as much surrogate activities as forcing the Runa Indians to wear pants and shirts that needed to be purchased.

In summary, such an approach to economics, production, and time allows us to conclude that archaic peoples, living among Divinities, spirits, and the dead, and dwelling in myth, embody "anti-production" opposed to both the bourgeois-capitalist market and the proletarian-socialist cult of labor. Eduardo Viveiros de Castro comments on the latter term employed by Pierre Clastres:

> In place of the political economy of control — control of the productive labor of the young by the old, of the reproductive labor of women by men — that the ethnomarxists, following Engels, saw at work in the societies they named, with impeccable logic, "pre-capitalist," Clastres discerned, in his "primitive societies," both the political control of the economy and the social control of the political. The first manifested itself in the principle of under-productive sufficiency and the inhibition of accumulation by forced redistribution or ritual dilapidation; the second, in the separation between chiefly office and coercive power and in the submission of the warrior to the suicidal pursuit of ever greater glory. Primitive society worked as an immunological system: perpetual war was a mode of controlling both the temptation to control and the risk of being controlled.[184]

---

183 Theodore Kaczynski, *Industrial Society and its Future* (1995).

184 See Eduardo Viveiros de Castro, "The Untimely, Again", in Pierre Clastres, *Archeology of Violence*.

The accumulation of products and things in the likes of "storage" does nevertheless have a place in traditional societies (for instance, stocking up for the winter), but the nature of such accumulation, which is sometimes even considered to be the real wealth of a family, is of a radically different nature than that of capitalist property. In Tradition, large accumulations are important on several occasions, such as those associated with moments of ecstatic peaks of the irruption of the sacred, death, or acquiring high social status. These occasions are not uncommonly intertwined in a single ritual.

One such key and paradigmatic ritual is the North American Indians' potlatch, described by Mauss and Bataille. The word "potlatch" means "gift", and the potlatch ritual is arranged at different intervals, bringing together various tribes or neighboring villages with their wealth, harvest, loot, crafts, and gifts. The potlatch consists of festive-ritual exchange and gift giving, during which debts from the previous time are repaid (the *hau* is returned) and new gifts are distributed. The grand feast thus establishes social relations and hierarchy (who will give more and set the table more luxuriously). The ecstatic peak of the potlatch is the nighttime ritual of eliminating all the leftovers of the harvest, products, and things, often to the point that houses are burned down, boats are broken down, expensive copper dishes are melted down and discarded in rivers or the ocean, cattle are exterminated, etc. Things are literally smashed, burned, and drowned amidst the ecstatic obsession with purging all the excess surpluses that make up the "accursed share." The excess that accumulated within societies by the end of the season or circle, between potlatch rituals, poses a threat to society, because it cannot be appropriated in the usual way of trade and exchange. Hence the collective appropriation of the sacred power of resources, things, and extracted resources through their collective destruction and conversion into the prestige of generosity.

As the networks of gifts given and exchanged, including with the Divinities, spirits, and the dead, becomes extremely complex and saturated, at a certain point unfolds a chaotic, exalted gifting-extermination of all and to all with the aim of liberation. What is destroyed is given to the spirits and the dead without a trace, i.e., is given "nowhere" so as to balance the scales of gift relations and "reset the balance" in the season. This notion of "destruction" is important to Bataille in that it is a special form of finally and irrevocably removing things from society and the world:

> Sacrifice destroys that which it consecrates. It does not have to destroy as fire does; only the tie that connected the offering to the world of profitable activity is severed, but this separation has the sense of a definitive consumption; the consecrated offering cannot be restored to the *real* order. This principle opens the way to passionate release; it liberates violence while marking off the domain in which violence reigns absolutely.[185]

Thus, ritual extermination at the potlatch removes the problem of Titanic hubris as excess by turning it into Dionysian catharsis.[186]

The second dimension of the potlatch, which sociologists often consider to be the most important or the most apparent, is the acquisition of social status. Whoever gathers the most property and then gifts it away or destroys it is elevated in the tribe or society, although de facto after the ritual he is left absolutely poor. Bataille writes about the competitive practices among the rich during such rituals, about their hospitality and opulent gifting. Mauss points out that the Divinities and spirits allow their part to be given to the poor and children in the form of gifts from the rich. In North America, Indians who were bought out of slavery by relatives or who managed to escape and return to their tribe could wash away the shame of slavery through the ritual potlatch feast, which restored their status as full, free members of the tribe.

---

185 Georges Bataille, *The Accursed Shared, Volume I - Consumption* (New York: Zone Books, 1988), 58.

186 In his book *The Thirst for Annihilation: Georges Bataille and Virulent Nihilism*, Nick Land remarks in passing that the practice of destruction is a form of "Dionysian economy."

Describing the ritual feasts of the Kalash people in the Afghan Chitral Valley, Karl Jettmar shows how any person from the village can arrange a huge feast for the whole village or even several, and be left without any property or even house, yet in return receive the highest social status and the right to install the sacred family plaque carving (jestak).[187] For ancient man, the glory of deed, prestige, and generosity are of high value, whereas for the bourgeois, as Bataille notes, morality is based on the materialistic economic category of benefit. Bataille writes: "Production, industry, capital, and accumulation are the opposite of sacrifice; the bourgeoisie embodies the need to prevent wastefulness, and the facelessness of the bourgeois and the monotony of his life reflect a secret desire to avoid sacrifice."[188]

Another occasion for accumulating products and things might figure in agricultural communities' need to pay off encroaching nomads or pay tribute to a prince. In such cases, the collected "capital" de facto does not belong to the community, but is completely excluded from its wealth. It is given to the sovereigns' envoys in exchange for life, which makes the relations between the rural community and the warrior nobility akin to those between people and their deceased Ancestors or otherworldly forces.

Finally, another point of convergence between such rituals, feasts, potlatches, and the demonstration of social status can be seen in funeral burials. Robert Hertz has illustrated this theme with rich materials from the peoples of Polynesia, but we can also find similar motifs throughout the Eurasian continent and especially in archaic Europe, where such later came to be associated with the nobility. We have already mentioned the practice of burying people with a set of items that they will need in the other world. In the case of the peoples of Oceania, the ritual burial of kings or respected people takes on all the

---

187 See Karl Jettmar, *The Religions of the Hindukush*.

188 See Georges Bataille, *The Accursed Share*. [Translated from the author's Russian - trans.]

features of the potlatch and destruction. First, two funeral rites are performed. The first funeral features the removal of the body outside the settlement, thereby excluding it from the social body of the village until it completely decomposes and only the bones or a dry, odorless mummy remains. This process might take from several months to several years depending on the climate and burial customs of the tribe. During this time, the deceased is not yet considered completely gone, as their soul still has all the empirical presence in the life of the family and can be actively harmed. At the same time, the deceased's relatives must collect a large amount of property, vegetables, livestock, and wealth to be sacrificed and destroyed in the solemn ritual burial and subsequent feast to which all the villagers are invited. Sometimes, the wealth needed to match the status of the deceased takes on cyclopean scale, thus compelling the family to take on debt, postpone the second funeral for many years, or join forces with the relatives of other deceased to share the total costs. Thus, some societies and their economies are essentially thanatocentric, and the accumulation of "capital" is subordinated to its complete destruction in the future.

In European culture, we know of similar practices from accounts of princely and royal funerals, when whole ships stocked with weapons, horses, cattle, slaves, wives[189], and wealth were sent to the next world along with their ruler. Even the funerals of commoners, often large and cheerful feasts which included a place for the deceased himself, reflected this structure on their own scale.

In all of the above-described cases, the concentration of a large volume of things is still not equivalent to what classical economics calls "capital" and which, under different circumstances, would begin to resemble entrepreneurial activity. In essence, everywhere in Tradition there is anti-accumulation, as harvests, livestock, fruits, things, and items of value are actually accumulated only to be handed over to be gifted or

---

189 Cf. the Indian ritual of *sati* and its analogues. Such is genuine feminism.

destroyed-as-appropriated. The living do not have the right of ownership over these riches, for they are imputed to them for temporary disposal as the property of spirits, Divinities, the dead, or other people. Here we are faced with yet another facet of sacred anti-capitalist logic and a unique manifestation of principled anti-materialism, wherein sacred acts and statuses turn out to be more important than real property.

As has been said earlier, on this shore of the manifest world, a preponderance of sacred debt has been accumulated, an abundance of things and objects produced out of ignorance and disregard for the sacred nature and practices of handcraft and gifting. What we have designated as the "real" is the body of this debt: the whole extant world in the network of interpretations of Modernity and Postmodernity is marked by a seal of alienation from sacred exchanges and sacrifices. Taking into consideration our metaphysical position, close as it is to the point of eschatological destruction (which may from the outside still seem to be a long duration of time) with its corresponding aspects such as the rule of the Divinities of Death and Destruction in this era, we can conclude that this time is a favorable era for a final repayment of debts and giving away of goods.[190]

Here we should cast our glance at the beginning, at that moment in the Greek tradition when the new generation of people was tragically cursed. The essence of sacrifice lies in its significance, in the cost and giving up which society bears in order to offer gifts to the Divinities and spirits in the right way and to receive gifts in return. Prometheus committed a fundamental substitution and destruction of the order of sacrifice at Mekone when he deceived Zeus (the Divinities) by giving him (them) the worst part of the sacrificed bull (the fat

---

190 A rich picture of the end of the world is given in the Germanic-Scandinavian tradition, where the world in the form of the Yggdrasil tree is cut down and burned by the fiery titan Surtr against the backdrop of the final battle between several lineages of the Divinities, people, and monsters. Might such be read as an ecstatically exalted dance of solitary madness and militant extermination for the renewal of the world?

and bones) while leaving the meat for humans hidden under the sacrifice's intestines. Prometheus acted as the first bourgeois, to whom genuine gifting and observing sacred hierarchy are repulsive. As a priest and teacher acting in the name of men, he brought punishment not only upon himself, but also a curse upon humanity (the confiscation of fire). The fate of Europe began with Greek mythology and philosophy, hence why Prometheus' audacity is one of the main and most important mistakes, one that left a meta-historical, mythological mark on our history. The metaphysical order of sacrifice was broken, hence the distortion in both what is given to the Divinities and what remains here.

Today, the whole world is the accursed share awaiting its eschatological sacrifice, burnt offering, and ex-termination. Cities, industries, property, the logistics routes of goods, energy and resource extraction, scientific laboratories IT&Media infrastructure, wires, cables, servers, garbage dumps in oceans and continents, refined art collections and luxury class goods, the whole economic system and its exchange nodes, political practices and social relations, the culture and values of the minimal humanism of *das Man* — in a word, all the wealth of the material (objective) and immaterial present extant world that is *the reality of this day*.[191]

Whoever commits the richest, most powerful, most selfless, most ecstatic, and sincere sacrifice will acquire the highest status. Our ensuing destiny depends on to whom and to which Divinities this world, this, reality, will be sacrificially offered. If the world is sacrificed to the Divinities and deceased Ancestors, then it will be reborn in a new cosmogonic cycle, as a new appropriation of all the wealth of the Cosmos by the Divinities and the people of the Golden Age.

---

191 Unlike gnostic and anti-cosmic teachings which call for the literal destruction of the planet, of matter as such, or fleeing from this world, we are talking about the destruction of very specific things in favor of the greater. The other reality of Myth is invited into this world through the fire of annihilating the "real."

If we commit the absolute Dionysian destruction of the world without any request for anything at all in return, then we are giving a pure apophatic gift to the Divinities of Death, and through them to the Nothing. Then "our fruits"[192] will be above and beyond all possible ideas that the Mind is capable of generating. They will ripen and bloom like fruits on branches, and in due time after this world they will fall as the *Other Beginning* or appear as the edge of the *Other Shore of the Otherwordly Beyond.*

***

---

192 Of course, then there will be no such "us", no such "fruits", nor such a real "here".

PART II:

VISIONS OF A FUTURE THAT ISN'T OURS

Dystopia Here and Now

In his *Chronicles of Bustos Domecq*, Jorge Luis Borges tells of an empire in which the art of making maps has attained absolute perfection. An accurate map of a province takes up the space of an entire city, and the map of the whole empire occupies the space of a whole province. But even this did not satisfy the college of cartographers, who then created a map of the empire so extensive that it covered the whole empire itself, precisely coinciding with and overlaying all of its ends. In this tale, we encounter a surrealist description of the phenomenon of simulacra, of precise, detailed copies which are absolutely indistinguishable yet still differ from any original. Jean Baudrillard distinguished three orders of simulacra:

(1) The crude counterfeit of an original, where the falseness of the copy is obvious and visibly differs from the original (real) thing;

(2) The refined falsification, where a fake is only recognizable upon special analysis and research, yet still differs from the original;

(3) The complete and legitimate reproduction of the original with the same methods and means used to create the original. Here there is neither a counterfeit nor a fake, but two originals and, consequently, the disappearance of reality amidst virtuality, as there are no grounds for distinguishing the original from the fake (both things are original).

The third-order simulacrum does not replace reality, but proclaims itself to be reality. Its simulative essence lurks in its generation of an imaginary difference. This imaginary distinction shows the emptiness of the simulacrum. In the above-cited book, Borges describes the work of a literary critic who was obsessed with creating the perfect account of Dante's *Divine Comedy*. In the end, he creates his masterpiece by completely removing all his commentary, the name of the author and publisher, and reissues Dante's book in its entirety "as is". Tragedy befell him when he realized that librarians and literary scholars were now using his account of Dante as the original book.

The apotheosis of simulation is already revealed in the case of a copy without an original or a copy that is better than the original. Here, the virtual logic of simulation turns reality upside-down, whereby the copy always has simplifications and assumptions relative to the original or standard. This is what we encounter in the surrealistic landscapes of Borges' Empire-Map or the "map" of Dante's *Inferno*. It is these processes that are now embodied in the manifest world: the installation of reality and its subsequent doubling in virtual space → augmented reality → imaginary/indistinguishable reality-virtuality. The processes of the Enlightenment, secularization, modernization, digitalization, globalization, education, virtualization, and the spread of connectivity represent the mapping of the manifest, beingful world and all beings in nomenclatures. The ultimate end is the calculability, computability, and manageability of all processes in the real world, which is the apotheosis of what Heidegger called *Gestell*.

For the man of Tradition, the world was at once open and mysterious. Everything concealed metamorphoses, other dimensions, symbols, and the patronage of Divinities or spirits. The forest path could lead to gates to another world, to other beings inhabiting groves and fields. A cave or mountain gorge was the entrance to the abode of dwarfs or descent into Hades. The depths of rivers and seas concealed their own worlds. Beyond the borders of the settlement and familiar nearby fields and streams began an unknown world of different beings and spaces of numinous horror. Knowing the world consisted in knowing its metaphysical source and principles as well as knowing one's self, disclosing these principles within oneself (as in maximal humanism).

The desire to know the world through rational and natural-scientific methods, to reveal and account for all of the world's mysteries and mechanisms, to lay cables on the ocean floor and to touch the Moon just to make sure that it is a cosmic body[193], and then to put all of this on a map including animal populations, fish and bird migrations, and ocean currents — all of this is absolutely analogous to Borges' surrealism, but is presented to us as a description (in fact the creation) of reality and the laws of Nature. This is a false way of knowing, one which gives rise to the world being closed and finite. The people of Tradition lived in openness to Being, whereas we live in a completely, hermetically closed world in which we know all borders and limits, the Earth can be circumnavigated in a day, and one can instantly connect with any part of the world and find an interlocutor on the map. Everything is entangled in the networks of connection and control. On the whole, the world is known, only certain details remain for this "Map-Empire."

We live submerged in the "real" world, in the enshrouding left-liberal and science-technology-centric paradigm. Contrary to the common stereotypes, this paradigm is one of the cruelest forms of totalitarianism and surveillance, which is only evermore lucidly revealing itself as such with each passing day. Unlike the classical totalitarian regimes with their explicit demands, propaganda, and clearly articulated markers of political loyalty, the liberal paradigm operates with soft power, positioning itself in the field of science and education not as an ideology (as in the Third Reich and the USSR), but as objective science about the structure of the world. In other words, the scientific picture of the world is the ideological propaganda machine of Modernity with all of its absolute bias and mechanisms of persuasion, suppression, and extermination that find optimal embodiment in the discourses of the natural science and technology, which are alleged to be independent of political superstructures and beliefs.

This machine serves the harsh, cruel dictatorship and faith of a technologically secured positive future depicted in

---

193 It is difficult to name something more ridiculous and useless than an accurate photographic map of the Moon and other planets.

transhumanist, post-feminist, left-liberal colors. This machine has its "clerics", its preachers, whose words and actions implicitly betray the irrational, surreal, and violent character of what they are called to defend and justify. This is the case with the new, peculiar forms of marketing and technological evangelism. The term "evangelism" comes from the Greek *euangelion*, which means "good news", "gospel." In the 21st century, tech companies, startups, and marketers have created a market for promoting, propagandizing, and persuading the masses that their new IT services and technology are good, that they are bringing the "gospel of innovation." The IT-evangelist's task is not to sell a product, but to convince people of a product's goodness, to create a strong consumer attachment to a brand, to make a person into a supporter and adept of the production and ecosystem of an online services company. The aim of IT-evangelism has been formulated with the utmost frankness by Klaus Schwab, who argues for the need for a singlular positive concept to attract different strata and communities into the process of development and to prevent negative reactions in society to the cardinal changes underway.[194] The need for IT-evangelism shows that in our days it is no longer possible to ensure complete and prompt consumer loyalty to market novelties without apostolic sermon-propaganda.

Slyly working in the same direction is the broad "Neo-Enlightenment" movement, which is engaged in intensive propaganda for the natural and hard sciences and has, in turn, given rise to the specific type of the "scienster" ("science-hipster"). The "scienster" is not a scientist or scholar, but a mere consumer of science news in popular, simplified exposition broadcasted in the form of simple formulas and stereotypes.[195] In Western high-tech culture, a similar type of ardent adept and advocate for the fastest possible onset of scientific-technological singularity can

194 See Klaus Schwab, *The Fourth Industrial Revolution.*

195 This term in this context has been popularized by Viktor Vakhshtayn. See his *"Eksperimental'noe oskvernenie. Kosmogoniia i morfologiia prosvetitel'skikh soobshchestv"* [Experimental Desecration: The Cosmogony and Morphology of Educational Communities].

be found in the so-called "singularitarians."[196] The scienster or singularitarian is a frequenter of scientific conferences, forums, and events who constantly shows off their consumption and transmitting of signs of engagement in the world of scientific discoveries, "common sense", and rational operations.

The emerging analogy between modern science and the Church is no coincidence, for the roots of Modernity directly go back to the ontology of creationism and the secularly interpreted premises of Protestant Christianity. We can therefore speak of a structural homology between the Church and the University or Company. The natural-scientific, physico-mathematical method is the "creed" and "symbol of faith" of scientists. Inventors and scientists in the likes of Nikola Tesla, Henry Ford, Albert Einstein, etc. hold the status of prophets and apostles of the faith. Especially worth highlighting are those who are not so much scientists and inventors as genius marketers and PR figures, such as Thomas Edison, Bill Gates, Steve Jobs, Mark Zuckerberg, Elon Musk, and Raymond Kurzweil. Their task, as is especially evident in the case of Musk and Kurzweil's breakthrough and expansion in Western culture, is not so much to invent as to inspire young people to enter technological and physico-mathematical schools and faculties. IT-evangelists occupy the correspondending niche of the bishops and priests, while sciensters play the role of the exalted flock and the adepts of the positive future. The fact that many groups and social organizations which propagandize scientific-technological progress and singularity resemble the utopian religious groups of Christian millennialism is also pointed out by AI alarmists.[197]

To the prescribed dogma of the "Church of the scientific method" can be added the prophecies of the Israeli historian and futurologist Yuval Noah Harari. Harari predicts that technohumanism (transhumanism) might become the literal religion of the people of the future along with "Dataism", according to which data is the highest value, i.e., the measure

196 See Barrat, *Our Final Invention*.

197 See Barrat, *Our Final Invention*.

of a person's value is the volume, quality, and originality of the data they produce. This is not only about data from the socio-cultural, creative sphere or communication and signal data, but literal biological and biometric data. Dataism includes the genetic and epigenetic data obtained through the collected analysis and sequencing of DNA. The human being becomes the richest data mine for BigData corporations and states, the production site of biological, genetic, and sociocultural data to be analyzed by statistical and neural network algorithms for establishing correlations between individuals and mass populations. This creates a huge data market between IT giants, states, and intelligence agencies. This is how the radical economization (whether capitalist or socialist) and politicization of human biological life takes off, as could be seen in Donald Trump's 2016 electoral campaign (when Cambridge Analytica employed the data-political approach) or in the case of the People's Republic of China's repressive experiment in the Xinjiang Uyghur Autonomous Region, where avant-guard high technologies and big data are used to control the Uyghur ethno-religious minority. Henceforth, a person is no longer assessed and evaluated by another person as in the conventional, minimal humanism of the Enlightenment, but by the machine algorithms of Big Data, that is by technology itself, by the Gestell.

The homology with the Church also holds on the matter of the inquisitions launched against all those who reject the value of natural-scientific methodology and instead argue for the relativism of methods and approaches within the same modern sciences or for differences in methods between the human, social, anthropological, and natural sciences. For the adepts of the positivistic physico-mathematical methodology, the advanced trends in the philosophy of science emanating from Feyerabend or the new anthropology that affirms the ontological plurality of natures and truths are pseudo-science or the restoration of pre-scientific, quasi-mythological obscurantism. This is not to mention those Traditionalists in the humanities who openly stand on the side of myth and the sacred. If the evangelists and adepts of Dataism and the Fourth Industrial Revolution are now dreaming of a future techno-utopia, then we already live in a long-since-established dystopia here and now.

Some advocates of political conservatism, Traditionalism, and paganism have hedged their bets on attempting to combine traditional values and ideals with the technological agenda, the progressist vector of time, and hierarchical rankings of history. They convince themselves to believe that technology is neutral and can be negotiated with, whence arise doctrines in the spirit of Guillaume Faye's Archeofuturism, right-wing accelerationism, neo-reactionarianism (Mencius Moldbug, Curtis Yarvin), and the Dark Enlightenment of Nick Land. However, as we have already shown, progress and capitalism are the pure enemies of any conservative and Traditionalist project. Technology is the embodiment of the ideology of Modernity, the machinery of its suggestiveness. In this lies the problem facing any conservatism which is content with returning to the status quo of 200-300 years ago, i.e., to the dawn of intense modernization and wild capitalism. This suggests that the true ontology and axiology of conservatism — such as the anti-progressist works of Alain de Benoist or Kaarlo Pentti Linkola — is still only barely noticed and rarely taken into account.

Unlike the evangelists of techno-humanism, we live in a different state and attitude towards the modern world and its futurological prospects and perspectives. In sociology and psychology, there is an effect known as the "uncanny valley" which besets people when they encounter robots or illustrated characters that are extremely realistic and overly similar in appearance and behavior to humans. When the most minute inaccuracies and details nevertheless betray the artificialness of such realistic simulations, this gives rise to a feeling of anxiety, fear, and repulsion. Overly realistic prosthetics, animations, or robots seem to unsettle a person on the same emotional level as the dead or undead, i.e., something that is simultaneously related to the human but still not a fellow living being. When people see the crude likeness of a doll or robot, whose mechanics are obvious and not so realistic, they might treat them with interest and sympathy, but only as long as they do not cease to be distinguishable. This phenomenon is somewhere on the border between the second- and third-order simulacra. In the future, when such distinguishability will become impossible for most ordinary people, the effect itself will lose its place.

For example, one of the most successful robots in possession of advanced speech and dialogue simulation, as well as a more or less conventionally imitational face and facial expressions, Sophia, is one of the cyborgs that has come closest to the border of the "uncanny valley." Sophia is also the first robot in history to have received real citizenship (Saudi Arabia), a development which unleashed discussions on the rights of robots on equal footing with humans, thus leveling the boundary between organic species and artificial "creatures." Despite being nominally a gynoid (a "female" robot), Sophia was able to obtain the full array of civil rights in Saudi Arabia, where biological women (as well as migrants) have inferior and violated rights under Sharia law. Consequently, in this case we can already see de facto inequality between women and gynoids, and more broadly between humans and robots.

At the same time, the computer-generated Japanese Instagram model Imma has stepped over the boundary of the "uncanny valley" by achieving maximal photorealism and indistinguishability from living people in frame. A little behind her is the lesser quality model Lil Miquela, whose texture quality and lighting shades are inferior. The examples of Imma and Miquela point to several things at once. Firstly, they represent the de facto culmination and perfection of 3D graphics, CGI&VFX modeling and editing technologies, which now allow for the creation of indistinguishable virtual reality. Secondly, the same can be said of the complete subordination and calculation of digital sunlight and lighting, since, besides geometry and textures, the lion's share of 3D realism lies in the correct tracing and rendering of lighting, rays of light sources and their reflections. This is most clearly seen in the ultra-realistic

CGI effects of Hollywood blockbusters, which exploit these technologies for commercial purposes, along the way lowering the threshold for the public's critical perception of editing tricks and visual deep fakes.[198] Thirdly, they point to the "unobvious" triumph of the flat, superficial plane over volume and content. 3D effects and CGI technologies only work with model planes, with splines or polygons. What is modeled does not have any real volume and density, as all models and imitations of muscles and bones are hollow on the inside. Everything is based on the properties of surfaces, since eyes are directed only at the image. When some 3D object on a screen is turned inside out, it is in fact the planes that are unrolled, not any real "cavity" opened up. The second dimension of the triumph of the plane lies in that the screen remains the preferred input and display interface today and for the foreseeable future. Even 3D and CGI technologies ultimately boil down to projecting 3D calculations on a 2D plane, although holographic screens and projectors of (quasi-)volumetric images are already being developed. The third, more socio-cultural dimension of the plane is the need to broadcast one's life on social networks or YouTube, as if an experience that has not been "screened" does not exist for other people and is not amenable to social capitalization or exchange by the person themself. The screen acts as a medium between individuals that verifies the reality of offline experience. What is not on the screen does not exist in reality; *ergo*, what is on the screen is what is real. Hence, virtual presence becomes the measure of being. Fourthly, the victory of the plane is the victory of immanence sliding along the pure, frictionless plane of multiplicity.

In the end, submersion into the very bottom of the "uncanny valley" leads to an extension of this very concept. This is not about overly realistic, frightening simulations of people by robots, but a simulation of the whole manifest world that becomes more real

---

198 This, in turn, opens up broad opportunities for fake news, fake reporting on events, and manipulating public opinion and political processes. This was predicted in the movie *Wag the Dog* (directed by Barry Levinson, 1997) about faking a war in Europe in order to trick a president ahead of elections.

than reality itself. The uncanny value is ubiquitous in relation to everything that causes alienation whenever one realizes their surroundings to be like Borges' virtual-real double.

The futurologist Alvin Toffler has proposed the relevant term "future shock" to describe the human being and society's fear and dislike for rapidly growing progress, "shock at the future" entailing a loss of understanding of the nature of progress and the forms of imminent changes. One has only to look around attentively to admit that everything around us is too "real" to be real — for an ordinary person, this would be a radical, extreme, insane gesture — and then feel horror and fear before this "reality." Today we can adjust Toffler's term from "future shock" to "present shock" or "contemporary shock", that is the shock of discovering the total alienation of the present-as-simulacra in all dimensions, the absence of knowledge, and the inaccessibility of the authentic.

To Ernst Jünger's pen belongs one famous illustration of modern human life's captivation with and dependency on technology. Jünger wrote of the *Titanic*, and how the people on board it were crossing the Atlantic in comfort and complete calm, not even stopping to think about the mechanisms ensuring their serene ocean sailing and the nature of such technology. A person onboard feels free and in the usual position of being the master of things. But the scene radically changes as soon as the ship begins to sink, and the person finds themself a hopeless hostage of technology and its imperfection. Technological dreams inspired man to create the ship, technology delivered him to some far corner of the ocean, and technology's weakness now claims him as its victim. Even man's salvation depends on technology, on the quality and strength of the mechanisms of inter-compartment partitions designed to prevent flooding and to delay sinking, on the number of lifeboats and life jackets, on radio communication, and on ships created in the very same technological way sailing by at the same time. It turns out that all of the person's comforts and freedoms are imaginary and illusory, that they exist only as long as the mechanisms work properly and the low-skilled personnel maintain the engines and coal ovens. In the end, maintaining the efficiency of technology becomes a goal and end in and of itself, and work on servicing the machinery also affects the first-class passengers, for otherwise the system would crack and everyone would die.

To better visualize this in our days, we can speak not of an ocean liner, but of the aircraft that regularly fly along their routes, or we can draw attention to the fact that all of modern technology and the majority of goods cannot possibly be created or reproduced by artisanal, non-technological, non-conveyor-belt means. This task is unbearable even for medium-sized businesses, not to mention ordinary people. Insofar as humanity is already deeply integrated into the networks of technological agency amidst the subjectivity of things and virtual relations, mankind is already de facto held hostage by the industry and economy that generate the surrounding urban and post-industrial reality (the replacement of the first nature by the second per Latour), which cannot be reproduced without or outside of technology.

Extending Ernst Jünger's metaphor, we can say that the task of Traditionalists is to, without any regrets and sympathy, sink the *Titanic* of this reality and bring seafaring back to life in all of its heroic symbolism. After all, letting a cruise ship sink to the bottom is also a way to give a vertical dimension to all the people naively, scientifically, technologically gliding along the surface.

***

Hermeneutics of Cultural Prototypes

Proceeding from the intellectual and philosophical landscapes of the surrounding dystopia, let us turn to the sphere of culture. Despite the transience of current cultural cases, they fulfill a number of important functions. They fix and record the current cultural moment, since even remote science fiction still operates with classical European cultural plots through the prism of a specific era of cultural creation and production. They create draft sketches of the future, combining the features of what is already technologically possible with what is still desired and fantastical, thereby shaping the attitudes and dreams of what it would be nice to invent, create, or implement. In other words, culture appears as a preliminary testing stage for innovations and modeling and conceiving future reality.

In our hermeneutical excursion, we will primarily refer to the field of cinema, which optimally combines all the varieties of the audiovisual achievements of technology and virtuality with the plots and structures of classical European culture as scenarios that are sometimes fragmented and recycled in scenes and plot lines. This, in turn, leads to a situation in which even a small sample of films is enough to catch sight of a fractal reflection of the whole nature of cinematography with its immense baggage of pictures and variations on one and the same plot.

Without a doubt, film is purely a sphere of entertainment in which genuinely philosophical expression is impossible, in contrast to the varying degrees of intellectuality of painting. All the variations of entertainment content for broad audiences, including movies featuring some kind of intellectual component (or pretension) as well as mere sci-fi entertainment reels, all de facto stand on the same plane. Nevertheless, as a space for illustrating the pictures of contemporary and desired reality, cinema gives us some understanding of the processes ongoing in the world of the Gestell. Film and mass pop-culture serve propaganda functions for the positive future in adventure genres, action films, and space operas. They also treat current and potential fears over the speed of technological development, the "uncanny valley", and the security or loss of identity in such genres as comedy, horror, techno-thrillers, and utopian films and series.

Many of the Gestell's positions are articulated and declared in the alluring images of film, and some are pronounced in implicit details, caveats, and on tertiary planes. The Enframing represents itself, its desires, and its futurological dreams. On the space of the screen, all the aspirations, projects, prognoses, metaphors, and strategies of the future are equally real and possible as long as everything expressed on screen is not synchronized with the temporal moment. Then part of the predicted and modeled will be discarded, the timing of innovations will be adjusted, while others parts will be embodied and legitimized. For example, events portrayed in 20th-century sci-fi films have not uncommonly actually taken place in the early 2000s, giving rise in this century to the practice of comparing "years in film" to sum up one or another film fantasy, i.e., what came true, what is under development, and what is still inaccessible to man and technology. Therefore, we turn to cinema not as if to something distracting us for a while and chaining us to the rectangular plane of the screen, but as a direct window onto the concrete reality of today and tomorrow. After all, the ultimate configuration of the dystopian today extended into tomorrow ("liquid postmodernity") is a combination, a pastiche, and a superposition of fragments from numerous science-fiction images and literature.

Dwelling in Virtuality

The topic of virtual reality (VR) and "hyper" or "augmented" reality (AR) is perhaps altogether "organic" to the space of contemporary cinema. It acts as a contextual marker that not only always accompanies the plot, but unfolds on the screen and thematizes the relationship between the screen and the viewer. Watching a movie is one form of submersion into augmented reality which in artistic productions can have rather diverse variations of embodiment. In general, practically every film about the future demonstrates one or another facet of augmented reality, interactive environing, and layers of screens and virtual dimensions.

The movie *Gamer* presents an exquisitely detailed reality in which social stratification and the media-entertainment penetration of society are intimately intertwined.[199] The *Gamer* world shows how, by way of nanotechnologies integrated into their nervous system, living people can be virtualized by a corporate monopolist of advanced games. In a huge metropolis in the near future, there are several closed locations that serve as game sites inhabited by real people who rent out their bodies (which is a form of precariat labor or slavery from the point of view of the movie's rebel characters) to gamers, who control them as their own characters in virtual multiplayer games without ever leaving their rooms. Instead of the 3D space of classic PC games, these are real spaces, real people, real body mods, and real relationships, violence, and damage. The movie shows us two games: the shooter game "Slayers", where criminals sentenced to death act as controllable characters in a real war for survival, the winner being promised a pardon, and a life and relationship simulation game called "Society", where doomed people from the lower classes "work" as motley freaks and perverts. In the *Gamer* world, living consciousness and the presence of personality are maintained, but are removed from the volitional control of one's body and participation in the game. A person genuinely experiences all the violence and sensations, but cannot do anything of their own accord, since the nanotech connection with the player-user harshly cuts off the intervention and will of the played-person themself. The movie also especially highlights the incredible popularity of such shows and online streams as attracting millions of viewers and bringing fame and fortune to already wealthy players from wealthy families. In fact, the *Gamer* world continues and brings

199 *Gamer*, directed by Mark Neveldine and Brian Taylor, 2009.

to perfection such contemporary cultural phenomena as reality shows, social networks, and online games like *Second Life* and championship streams. The ingenious developer of these technologies and games, Ken Castle, formulates the question of this cinematographic world: "We live in society, we play 'Society'. Which one's more real, really?"

A similar canvas is illustrated in Steven Spielberg's *Ready Player One*, which depicts a future world mired in deep economic crisis.[200] The realities of slums are contrasted to the virtual oasis of prosperity and entertainment in the "OASIS" online game, which offers full immersion into the richest 3D world, in which almost the entire population spends their free time. The *Player One* world is a pure manifestation of the exploitation of nostalgia for Western mass movie and game culture that started in the 1980s (so-called "retrowave exploitation"). It is also an all-out ode to social escapism and the ideology of interspecies, interracial, and other inter-form diversity, as the OASIS gameplay chapters are the heroes of mass pop culture. Meanwhile, the conflict between a multinational team of teenagers and a global corporation inside the game world has incredibly important effects in the real world, which consists of multi-tiered slum containers. *Player One*'s paradigm of values prioritizes maintaining the status quo of rules (access price) in society and the diversity of the OASIS game instead of solving the problems of economic crisis that plunged society into the need to escape from such a gray reality into a colorful pixel world in the first place. Spielberg's movie is quite reliable on matters of VR technologies and the implementation of interactive player-character feedback, MMORPG mechanisms, as well as its portrayal of the infantilization and submersion of society's lower classes into addiction. As in the world of *Gamer* and other productions, the virtual alternative is first and foremost supposed to be a refuge for the poor, the economically and socially vulnerable layers of society and peoples on the periphery of progress. The sharp corners are deliberately smoothed over,

---

200 *Ready Player One*, directed by Steven Spielberg, 2018.

and the lack of alternative to virtuality is presented in a playful manner as entertainment in a world of imaginary freedom to be whomever one wishes.

Without a doubt, the cult film and defining expression at the turn of the last century was *The Matrix*, which combined many of the cultural intensions of Postmodernism in corresponding visual form.[201] The world of *The Matrix* is an absolutely real cast of the world, particularly the United States, in the mid-1990s. The reality of the virtual illusion, called the "Matrix", directly refers us to the topic of Baudrillard's simulacra and simulations, and it is Baudrillard's book that the protagonist, Neo, picks up in one of the opening scenes. The very word "matrix", translated from Latin, means "root cause", "source" (referring to the womb), and in typography and production "matrix" refers to the form from which copies are printed. In chemistry and physics, there is the method of "matrix isolation" used to separate particles from one another and their environment. All of these nuances are embodied on the movie screen. The Matrix is, as a virtual copy of the world, the "first reality" or simply "reality" for all people, who in the non-virtual, post-apocalyptic world are physically isolated in pods on endless incubator fields serviced by machines. Humans became the biological source of energy for the machines that enslave them in the future. This took place in the era of the 1990s and connected (once again the existential "Connectivity") everyone to a single system of simulation. On the whole, the picture of *The Matrix* can rightfully be used as an allegory for the current state of affairs and the Gestell's relation to the biological masses of people, whose status is that of data and actor sources for information moving across networks.

The Matrix world is the primary cultural and even ontological world in which all people live, and being torn out of the decorative simulation creates ontological and existential crisis. Genuine reality is perceived to be a destroyed copy of the "dream world", waking up in a capsule which the machines register

---

201 *The Matrix*, directed by the Wachowski brothers, 1999.

as an error and therefore dump such people into the sewer, and is likened to a "system failure." There are awakened people who want to return to the simulacrum, to "reconnect." The whole nerve of this situation — and this is, without a doubt, a knot of all the problems of human being *vis-à-vis* reality, the cosmos, the world of technology, and authenticity — is contained in the scene of the conversation between the traitor Cypher and Agent Smith, an artificial intelligence that protects the system from human actions. During the conversation in a restaurant inside the Matrix, Cypher expresses his desire to return to the simulation, and in order to do so he is willing to betray people in the outside world. Between the two "realities", Cypher chooses pleasure and being inside the illusion. The key line is uttered over a piece of meat: "You know, I know this steak doesn't exist. I know that when I put it in my mouth, the Matrix is telling my brain that it is juicy and delicious. After nine years, you know what I realize? Ignorance is bliss." Bioethical abolitionism and hedonism are this character's credo.

The plot of *The Matrix* extends into three installments, each successive film of which increasingly deviates from the Postmodern intellectual message of the first part, instead shifting to entertainment, special effects, and fight scenes. In the end, having completed his prophesied mission, Neo negotiates with the machines and sacrifices himself to save the last human city — that is, a city whose people are still dependent upon technologies, but within a different hierarchy of connectivity and isolation from the machine networks. If we broaden the context and refer to the Internet apocrypha of versions of the *Matrix* trilogy's scripts, then we learn that Neo and the rebels' whole struggle on behalf of all people against the machines, the whole content of the trilogy, is but one, even deeper level of the Matrix. Insofar as a certain percentage of people somehow come to reject the simulation from the inside and awaken in the real world, the machine algorithms have stopped even the potential for rebellion by simulating awakening, simulating a real external world and struggle, thereby hushing the existential impulse of the least content organisms inside their system. According to script apocrypha, such an explanation of the impossibility of awakening and the second level of illusion within the illusion was supposed to have been revealed to the key protagonists at the very end of the trilogy. But this worthy idea was not realized "at the insistence of the producers", for the absence of a happy ending would have made itself felt negatively at the box offices, depressing viewers and implicitly pushing them to question the possibility of the real. Avoiding this and making a profit — such is very much in line with the logic of the Matrix.

A very realistic version of AR with respect to the current technological level is presented in the movie *Anon*.[202] The word "augmented" in "AR" refers to the word *auge*, meaning "eyes." Augmented reality is the overlay of interactive layers on human vision, such as through AR applications, glasses, contact lenses, or implants and prosthetic eyes. In the world of *Anon*, implants connected to a single network allow any person to record and edit everything they see with their own eyes, as well as add advertising and minimalistic interactive data questionnaires about passers-by and interlocutors in real time. Human memory is replaced by an archive of the highest quality video feed, and if desired, one can delete unpleasant moments, whereby a person literally forgets them. This is actively used by intelligence and security services to investigate murders, such as by viewing the last minutes of a victim's life and scanning people on the street. This cinematic world is dominated by total transparency, the condensed identification of all people, and solid recordings of everything they see with their high-tech vision. One special luxury, as well as a violation of the law, is anonymity technology entailing the ability to delete one's data from the database so as to render identification impossible. This is what the main character, a detective, faces when he cannot identify a girl who passes by him. The system informs him of a failure in identifying the passer-by, and at first he cannot believe that such a thing is even possible. The movie's plot unfolds around the

---

202 *Anon*, directed by Andrew Niccol, 2018.

restoration of law and order, the discovery and destruction of a hacker group that had been allowing people to illegally correct their memories by way of perfect editing and buying absolute anonymity. Of interest to us are the details that accentuate some of the dimensions of AR. For example, one of the signs of a character's death is the fading and code folding of their 3D advertising and their appearance in the vision of the real world, unmarked by additional recording layers of their last minutes of life.[203] Another example shows how much a person is hostage to technology integrated into their very corporeality and consciousness: augmented reality allows not only for recording, editing, and storing the video stream of someone's life, but also making it viewable from within someone else's vision. This is used by ill-wishers to forcibly reproduce false pictures, to replay a person's tragic and painful fragments of memory on loop, or to completely erase their memories by deleting their archive.

At the present stage in the development of AR technologies, the main "window" to the world is augmented reality glasses and camera-to-screen connection on smartphones and tablets. The latter is the most widely accessible, hence mobile phones have already taken on extreme dimensions in cinema. For instance, in the comedy *iBoy*, whose name is a play on Apple's iPhone smartphones, an accidental witness, the teenager Tom, becomes a victim of criminals in the act.[204] He is shot in the head the moment he tries to call the police, and fragments of his smartphone get stuck in his brain tissue. Waking up from a coma, he realizes that he now has the consciousness of a hybrid smartphone-person[205]: he can receive 3G signals from cellular networks, go online, type SMS with the power of thought, and visualize data in his field of vision. With these new powers and smartphone services, the protagonist administers justice.

---

203 The motif of dying as a breakthrough or disclosure of exterior, non-augmented reality is widespread throughout fantasy cinema.

204 *iBoy*, directed by Adam Randall, 2017.

205 As opposed to being "supernatural", Tom's abilities are described as "cybernatural."

An alternative scenario is unfolded in the horror film *i-Lived*.[206] The main protagonist is an unfortunate browser of mobile applications. His life changes when he starts testing a new program that rewards him with points for various tasks completed in real life. Successfully completing simple tasks for the application leads to real improvement in the protagonist's life. But gradually the tasks become more and more strange and cross the border of legality, such as stealing, kidnapping, hitting a stranger, inflicting pain, etc. He decides to cancel the signed license agreement and application membership, after which altogether mystical forces begin interfering in his life. His Apple smartphone and the i-Lived application installed on it, which read backwards is "Devil-I", one-up the old plot of making a deal with the devil in the form of accepting a user license agreement (EULA), i.e., those ubiquitous disclaimers which few people ever actually read before accepting.

Very telling are those cinematic examples in which the Gestell blurts out its own problems with the installation of augmented reality. In many films where the characters travel in deep space[207] or live in a traumatic future world, one finds the decorative element of cabins and rooms' walls being covered in screens. In such rooms where the characters live or undergo therapy, the screens broadcast landscapes from planet Earth: mountains, fields, oceans, flocks of birds, and herds of animals. This unconsciously emphasizes the human being's deep alienation from the surrounding futurological reality or the emptiness of the abysses of lifeless space. A person needs therapy to remove their anxiety, with which the room's screens help by affording views of real or simulated nature that appeal to his deep archetypes and are designed to calm him down. This designates a paradox: man consciously destroys surrounding nature and ecosystems in order to achieve a high level of technological development that then allows him to simulate the very same nature and biological diversity for his own psychological comfort.

206 *i-Lived*, directed by Franck Khalfoun, 2015.

207 See *Ad Astra*, directed by James Gray, 2019.

Dreaming as Identity

In the fantasy literature and cinema in which cyborg protagonists and characters doubt their human nature, a significant role is played by the oneiric space of dreams and memories. From the point of view of the paradigm of Modernity, the world of dreams is a nocturnal mode of perceiving fragmentary flashes of cultural code. In Tradition, the world of dreams is of fundamental importance, as it is a space for meeting with ancestors, Divinities, and spirits who might instruct a person in crafts or on their spiritual path. The shaman's trance and travels are likened to a dream or take place in dreams. The messengers of the Divinities or spirits sometimes reveal to people their fate and destiny in dreams, hence the dream becomes the basis for a person's identity in the waking manifest world, where in the morning it becomes important to correctly remember the spirits' guidance. Plato allotted metaphysical status to the practice of remembering, or anamnesis. According to Plato, the human soul originally possesses full knowledge, and a person's task in the middle world consists in remembering what is necessary. The last fragments of traditional sacred narratives in the realm of dreams were described by Carl Gustav Jung as deep collective archetypes of the unconscious. In fantasy works, however, dreams and memory speak more to the humanity or artificiality of a protagonist's consciousness, i.e., they solve the problem of anthropological status. In fantasy films about the future, a person does not dream of the Divinities or spirits, but the (non-)person dreams of the human. What comes to the protagonist as a dream turns out to be memory of their true personality, personhood, and life.

The problem of dreaming and memotic identity is bound up with the transhumanist invasion of the brain and human consciousness, when a person's memory and visions can be digitalized, uploaded, downloaded, streamed, and saved on external media. The movie *Anon* shows how the technology of distributed/external memory can be used to violent ends by evildoers or by authorities to distribute punishment, as is also shown in the movie *Six*.[208] Memory can be taken away, or one can be forced to endlessly rewatch a loop of traumatic experiences. Memory is associated with vision, with viewing pictures of the past in synthesis with audiovisual and emotional experiences.

The alienation and consumption of someone else's memory is thoroughly developed in the movie *Strange Days*, which embodied moderate neuro-cyberpunk in the late 1990s.[209] In this cinematic world, there is a flourishing black market of other people's memories which are accompanied not only by pictures, but by the full range of the sensations of those who lived them. Memories of adultery, robbery, crimes, extreme entertainment, or murder replace entrainment for the rich as the new drug. The protagonist, a former policeman turned memory-dealer, finds himself embroiled in investigating the crimes of a sophisticated maniac who supplies the black market with intricately edited records of the murder of women, where the killer's view and feelings abruptly change to the point of view and near-death experiences of the victim, who in turn observes their own death from the outside, thus attaining the highest depth of experience for memory consumers down the line.

The film *Self/less* illustrates the transhumanist idea of transferring personality and consciousness into a new, cloned body.[210] In this movie, an elderly millionaire who does not want to die turns to a scientist who proposes to transfer his consciousness into a young, artificially created body. The nuance of the procedure is that the millionaire will still die de jure, but will continue to live under a new name and identity unrelated to his previous life. Having completed the transfer of consciousness, the doctor gives the patient nootropics to suppress hallucinations as a side effect of the consciousness' adaption to the new body. Indulging in the joys of a new, youthful body, the protagonist gradually forgets to take the

---

208 *Six: The Mark Unleashed*, directed by Kevin Downes, 2004. This film equates chip-control over memory to the apocalyptic mark of the Antichrist.

209 *Strange Days*, directed by Kathryn Bigelow, 1995.

210 *Self/less*, directed by Tarsem Singh, 2015.

medication, and his hallucinatory dreams become increasingly realistic to the point that he realizes that these are someone else's memories. It is then revealed that the millionaire's consciousness was transferred not into an empty clone, but into the body of a living, kidnapped person, whose consciousness is still present and is only suppressed by the medications. The situation in this film illustrates yet another facet and type of necropolitics, where the repressed personality of a kidnapped person appears in the borderline state of unliving/undead, i.e., it undergoes de-subjectification in its own body, which refers us to the schizo-rhizomatic concepts of Gilles Deleuze and the problem of split consciousness (one's own dreams as foreign consciousness) and corporeality.

This theme is further explored in an episode of the series *Black Mirror*.[211] One of this series' shorts tells the story of how a husband decides to save his wife, who has fallen into a coma, by planting her consciousness inside his own body. The wife has no power over his body and is essentially a will-less passenger in the consciousness and life of her husband. She can only talk to him. Over time, due to accumulated problems and new relationships, he installs an update on the consciousness chip and gains the opportunity to "turn off" his wife's consciousness at any time, thus obtaining freedom from her sociality. In the series, this is done by way of a special smartphone application which essentially controls via implant the full-volume consciousness of the other person who lost their body in an accident. Subsequently, the spouse's consciousness is transferred to a stuffed animal monkey, which the husband gives to their son. In the second part of the series, the owner of a museum of artifacts related to consciousness transfer and digitization takes hostage one of the exhibits, the holographic copy of the consciousness of a black murderer executed in the electric chair. The museum curator sells souvenirs in the likes of

---

211 *Black Mirror*, 2017, season 4, episode 6. This dystopian series itself represents a therapeutic for technological progress, whose horrors are packed into the format of a dystopian TV show. Nevertheless, some of the technologies shown on screen have already been embodied in the real world.

looped fragments of the criminal's agony in a key ring. Anyone can flip the switch and repeat the execution, since a hologram and digital copy of consciousness are impossible to kill.

Returning to the picture illustrated by *Self/less*, the second protagonist was forced to sell his body to a corporation in order to provide for his family, an instance which once again confirms that the first victims of progress are the less well-off and less secure segments of the population. As a result, the main character, the millionaire, faces an ethical and existential dilemma: continue taking the pills and live for his own pleasure, or stop and free the repressed personality, which means surrendering himself to finally die.

We encounter a similar motif of dream-memories in the movie *Ghost in the Shell*, where the heroine's living, biological consciousness is placed in a completely cybernetic body and her past personality is erased following a terrorist attack.[212] The protagonist is tormented by fragments of past memories which the engineer observing her treats as software failures and false interpretations by her graphics processor. In the *Ghost in the Shell* universe, the actual "ghost" is a certain set of qualities, a mental substratum, which is inherent to both real consciousness and highly developed artificial intelligence. The "ghost" is some semblance of the soul in a machine or cyborg. In this film, the "ghost" is accompanied by memories that lead the protagonist to the truth: her real body and personality were stolen for a consciousness transplant experiment and the creation of a professional military police robot.

In the film *The Island*, dream-visions of another life amidst a simulated realty torment clones which are created for future organ transplants for "people-originals."[213] The rediscovery of their true history and the nature of their hallucinatory dreams confronts the protagonists with the existential question of identity and of corporate and police power over people's bodies and consciousness.

---

212 *Ghost in the Shell*, directed by Rupert Sanders, 2017.

213 *The Island*, directed by Michael Bay, 2005.

The topic of memory, dreams, and identity is artfully embodied in the *Blade Runner* and *Blade Runner 2049* dilogy.[214] In these movies, set in a not too distant future, corporations create extremely realistic copies of people, "replicants", which are used for hard labor and wars in outer space. From time to time, the replicants revolt and escape, which forces the engineers to limit their lifespan to four years. In order to distinguish a real person from a fugitive replicant, the "Voight-Kampff test" is used to test for empathy and emotionality which the replicants, although externally and socially completely identical to humans, cannot pass. In order to make the replicants more stable and obedient, the manufacturing corporation releases a new model, "Nexus-6", implanted with the memories and emotions of the creator's niece. The movie's protagonist, Deckard, a detective who specializes in capturing replicants, conducts many hours of testing on a woman, Rachel, who in the end fails. The test failure incites the woman's outrage, as she claims that she has real memories and photographs of herself as a child. Deckard reveals the truth to her, and she flees from her master.

Here we see the Gestell letting slip that it still needs to simulate humanity's mental substratum in order to achieve the functional stability of its system, for instance by creating complete copies of a person and eliminating the original. Human memories from real life are themselves suppressed, as they undermine the status quo of the simulated reality system. Only implanted memories and dreams, or subjects without a past, are relevant.

In the second part, *Blade Runner 2049*, the topic of memories is even further accentuated, as the fate of all the protagonists of the first and second films, the corporation's interests, and the authentic identity of several characters (i.e., whether they are humans or replicants) depend on the correct determination of the authenticity and belonging of certain fragments of memories. The screen shows us a brilliant girl, a memory designer, who

---

214 *Blade Runner*, directed by Ridley Scott, 1982; *Blade Runner 2049*, directed by Denis Villeneuve, 2017.

creates fully-fledged stories with a diverse set of parameters so that replicants' dreams differ from one other while maintaining the general cultural code of the civilization, thereby deceiving them in the best possible way so that they do not even ask themselves whether they are human or not. Having a high-quality surrogate of multiple memory fragments which repeat in dreams is supposed to satisfy their being.

The plot twist reveals the secret as to why this particular girl is such a genius at creating replicant dreams: she herself is the first person to have been naturally born to a replicant. She is the "missing link" between the two species, between the genuine and the artificial. Having real childhood memories, she is capable of creating the ideal memory plots which neither the corporation's algorithms nor designers are capable of inventing. Returning to the first installment, we note how the replicant Rachel does not have synthetic memory, but real memories of a real girl transferred into her brain, which makes her a tough nut to crack for Deckard's test. The relationship between Deckard, Rachel, corporations, replicants, dreams, and memory is closely intertwined throughout the dilogy, which essentially illustrates to us a whole panorama of problems which now stand before the avant-garde of the Enframing's transhumanist technologies in creating brain-computer interfaces, promoting the agenda of cloning, genetically-engineered and cyber-engineered bodies, the digitization of consciousness, robots' rights, and revising the species-specific boundaries of the human.

Simulacra Again

As can be seen in all of the preceding, simulations of all levels and scales cross cut or are the background theme of practically all movies about a high-tech future, from cyberpunk-noire to utopian, from the "Borgesian" copies of the real world in such films as *The Matrix* to the simulations of locality in *The Thirteenth Floor*, *Ready Player One*, and *Black Mirror*, and further down to the level of everyday reality with cloned animals, cats, snakes, owls, or tigers.[215] In the movie *Babylon A.D.*[216], the main heroine, Aurora, encounters two Amur tigers and asks the mercenary accompanying her how this is possible, since tigers had died out decades ago, to which the mercenary replies with a paraphrase of Baudrillard's definition of simulacra: "Second generation clones. Not real tigers. Copies of copies." An analogous situation with animals prevails in the *Blade Runner* universe, where all animals are replicants, artificial bio-cybernetic organisms that are identical to real ones. In the second movie, the distance between artificial life and genuine handicraft production is hyperbolically underscored in the scene when the merchant, upon assessing the authenticity of a crude wooden horse toy, says that for real wood he could get a lot of money and buy himself whatever he wanted.

In the fourth part of the *Alien* tetralogy, the main character, Ellen Ripley, suspects the space pirate Annalee Call of being a cyborg. She is betrayed by her too empathic, too human behavior and care for the team, which is absolutely untypical of all the other characters. She's simply too good to be human. In this case, a copy of a human behaves more humanlike than people themselves.

Creating extremely convincing cyborgs still poses a technological difficulty, but this cannot be said of three-dimensional simulations of people on screen. Besides the above-mentioned virtual models, Imma and Miquela, this line is developed by the movie *S1m0ne*, in which a movie producer employs a fully 3D-animated, absolutely realistic actress to achieve unprecedented success in the film industry.[217] In one of the first scenes of the "acquaintance" between the producer and the model, a kind of dialogue — or rather de facto monologue, because the actress simply reflects the producer's remarks in her voice and facial expressions — summarizes the emergence of

215 *The Thirteenth Floor*, directed by Josef Rusnak, 1999; *Nirvana*, directed by Gabriele Salvatores, 1997; *Black Mirror*, season four, "USS Callister."

216 *Babylon A.D.*, directed by Mathieu Kassovitz, 2008.

217 *S1m0ne*, directed by Andrew Niccol, 2002.

this technology and its future. Admiring S1m0ne, the producer explains, "Our ability to manufacture fraud now exceeds our ability to detect it", to which S1m0ne "replies": "I am the death of real."[218] The scene ends with the protagonist indulging in an impressive, unabashed fit of narcissism and self-praise.

The latter film resonates with Hironobu Sakaguchi's 2001 film, *Final Fantasy: The Spirits Within*, the first full-length fantasy film to feature only fully 3D-modeled characters and locations. The latter anticipated our already current situation: 3D models of real but deceased actors continue to be "filmed" and act in the industry. In other words, the "afterlife" and posthumous fate of an actor gives way to capital's continued exploitation of their "ghost", their digital cast.

In this lens and against the excitement of the film and entertainment industry, we can say that the "uncanny valley" effect is, despite its disturbing essence, a positive phenomenon and reaction, for it still allows for discriminating and ontological and existential questioning whenever a simulation brings the surrounding reality into doubt. However, this questioning of reality from the standpoint of virtualization, simulation, and augmented reality comes about "from below", provided by the technological force of the Enframing and the installed indistinguishability of three instances at once — the miraculous manifest world of Tradition, the strictly empirical and verifiable reality of Modernity, and the infinite possibilities of virtuality on the flat plane of Postmodernity. Any miracle or fantastic creature or any situation from myth might become real and legitimate as soon as it is embodied in the immediate reality of all sensations and on the condition of the silencing or leveling of the value of high-tech, perfected linings of gadgets and algorithms between the objective external world and subjective, inner reflection-perception.

---

218 Contemporary neural networks are already capable of creating photo portraits of non-existent people and to render "deepfake" videos which replace real people with non-existent ones or show them as doing something that never happened by way of philigree editing.

This distinction is already disappearing, and, unsurprisingly, its dissolution is reflected in the mirror of the big screen. A simplified version of an artificial world made real to its central perceiving subject was already shown to us in the drama of *The Truman Show*.[219] The protagonist, Truman lives from birth in the mode of an on-air reality show broadcast inside a cyclopean pavilion-island of film sets which he does not even suspect. His life, psychological development, social relationships, different situations, and even the weather, climate, and landscape — in a word, his internal and external worlds — are all meticulously engineered by the media industry. Truman is this industry's main economic asset, because he is the only one among everyone and everything around that does not know of the simulation and therefore imparts the whole construction of everything going on around him with the minimum weight of reality. This is how technology and capitalism exploit human reality in the entertainment sphere: the Gestell shows the masses of *das Man* a real human placed in game-like conditions as entertainment. Everyone is incredibly interested in looking at the real and feeling person, but no one would want to take his place. Thus, the Enframing lulls and protects itself from the awakening of the human out of masses.

One aspect of *The Truman Show* which is usually left in the background is the cyclopean, high-tech set which simulates controlled oceans, islands, the sky, sun, moon, and ecosystem and weather with their own cycles. An analogous super-pavilion for filming New York, which contains an exact copy of the metropolis, its inhabitants, and banal events over the course of many years, is seen in the movie *Synecdoche, New York*.[220] Both of these pictures show us a limited, localized space (a hangar or dome) inside of which a real space from the outside is imitated to a supreme degree. On the one hand, such poses an obvious nod to Borges' Map of the Empire; on the other hand, the sets of *The Truman Show* and *Synecdoche, New York* have two important

219 *The Truman Show*, directed by Peter Weir, 1998.
220 *Synecdoche, New York*, directed by Charlie Kaufman, 2008.

peculiarities. Firstly, they have "mode-change" borders: when the characters leave the frame, they become mere actors with their own outside life. In one extreme case, one *Truman Show* actress even allowed herself to talk to the directors from directly within the scenery and on the show stage: "here we work, play, and there we drink coffee, give interviews." This works out for everyone except the main character and those who are irrevocably and completely identified with their role. Secondly, these two films' super-sets and super-pavilions, imitating reality as such, are nested within their own on-screen universe. At the time of their release, there were no such technologies or large-scale sets in real film production. In the *Truman Show* world, all the equipment is carefully hidden, camouflaged, or played into the logic of the simulation in which Truman lives. In his world, as he sees it, there are no spotlights, cameras, and microphones, yet they still exist. On a real film set, only one fragment of scenery and background is put into frame. At the contemporary stage, however, the practice of filming on a green screen or blue screen with the subsequent substitution of interior furnishing during editing is evermore often the course of action. Huge sets designed to be not scenery, but reality itself for those who live/play in them, are fantasy plots beyond the screen itself.

These features of on-screen super-sets and filming methods where the distinction between "reality" and "set" nevertheless still exists have been challenged by the director Ilya Khrzhanovsky with his large-scale "DAU" project. What was in *The Truman Show* and *Synecdoche* either in the background or artistic hyperbole, became in Khrzhanovsky's project, which is almost impossible to classify into any one category, materialized literally in transferring concepts from beyond the screen to this side of the screen. To create a movie about the story of the Russian physicist Lev Landau ("Dau") from the late 1930s-60s, a parallel reality of this historical era was recreated in Kharkov. This became literally the largest filming location in Europe, built in the form of a Soviet research institute with adjoining facility grounds, infrastructure, and personnel. The life, clothing, interior design, objects, language, and behavior of the era's people are made to be as realistic as possible. The film's production, which took more than 10 years, involved hundreds of thousands of extras — from the most ordinary Kharkov residents to prominent figures of world culture, science, politics, and public life. Each of them was reincarnated in the context of the era. No script was provided, and the whole play became one spontaneous improvisation or "just life in the institute." The physicists and mathematicians on camera were real physicists and mathematicians conducting real scientific conferences on string theory; the janitor in the yard was not playing the role, but was the real janitor; the KGB officer in charge of supervising the institute was a real KGB veteran with the corresponding authority over all the participants of the filming process. The sex, screaming, emotions, conversations, situations, and violence shown in frame were all real. Participating in the "DAU" project meant passing into a "time machine" and fully adapting to one or another segment of the Soviet period. For inappropriate clothing or using modern gadgets, an employee could be called in for a real interrogation and fired from the institute (really being fired from the project forever). The DAU institute worked around the clock as a real institution for a decade, becoming a site where everything possible could be studied, including the people themselves under such conditions. The quiet and inconspicuous operators simply recorded people's lives under these conditions, and the director did not set up scenes, lines, or scripts. Even the process of dismantling the institution's site was filmed as part of the movie itself, or more precisely as one of a dozen final reels. Even the act of establishing the boundary of the real (destroying the set pretending to be reality) was symbolically leveled and built into the on-screen reality.

In the end, *DAU* landed like a ray piercing through a prism, refracting into numerous projects — an anthropological study on totalitarianism (many who visited the institute grew up in the USSR and were amazed by the reality of the recreated atmosphere), a cultural reconstruction of the era's material life, experimental cinema, a laboratory of social relations, exhibitions, artifacts, performances, financial adventures, construction projects, etc. Even the reviews and descriptions of the project by third parties were embedded into "DAU" as part of it and as glimpses into it.

Khrzhanovsky's "DAU" project went far beyond its own boundaries; in other words, it became a gravitational core that dictated interpretations to its participants and locations even after the fact, or it completely redefined them in the external cultural field. The subsequent fate of some of the project's actors and participants, conceived as inseparable from their life hitherto, could easily be inscribed into the orbit of "DAU" and projectively interpreted as a private continuation of the anthropological project of diffusing the reality of the film set.

What was in *The Truman Show* or *Synecdoche* used as a hyperbolic device within movie production, Ilya Khrzhanovsky proclaimed to be a real method for destroying the boundaries between the production of on-screen cinema reality, real life, anthropology, and culture.

Surrogate Eros

Looking closely at (post-)cyberpunk and futurist cinema, one can also see what such a future holds for us in the spheres of eros (soon to be digital sexuality) and reproduction. One of the prospective developments in the sex industry is the remote transmission of tactile and bodily sensations and pleasure with the use of virtual reality gloves or costumes connected to the Web. Worlds where such technology is the normative means of sexual contact are shown in the films *Demolition Man* and *The Zero Theorem*.[221]

A short scene in *Demolition Man* shows sexual freedom reaching its peak in the future, with sex becoming an everyday practice. The difference is that, instead of physical contact,

---

221 *Demolition Man*, directed by Marco Brambilla, 1993; *The Zero Theorem*, directed by Terry Gilliam, 2013.

the pacifistic people of the future use virtual reality glasses and neural interfaces to exchange brain waves with each other. Mixing pleasure waves and signals from the brain with other emotions and audio-visual images, the boundaries of sexual experience can be expanded like the use of narcotic substances. This digital sex is *a priori* public, since it can be intercepted and published as a file. This technology implicitly enables replacing intercepted data remotely. Instead of pleasure, a person can download a seance of hopeless agony.

A similar plot is shown in *The Zero Theorem*, where the reclusive programmer protagonist strikes up a relationship with a virgin prostitute who offers only virtual contact services in 3D reality by means of a costume that provides body feedback. After modification, the main character completely digitizes his soul and finds himself locked in virtual space.

Surrogate eros can only be to the liking of people who have lost their nature, to fearful pacifists of the near future (physical contact is heavily loaded with "violence"), programmers (as in *Zero Theorem*, where the protagonist solves an equation that proves the nonexistence of God), or completely surrogate people.

Post-relationships and post-sexuality between two simulations are exhibited in *Blade Runner 2049*, in which the protagonist is a replicant, i.e., a high-tech clone without a past who maintains a warm and trusting relationship with a highly realistic 3D holographic girl programmed to be a partner. The girl can exist only within the apartment where projectors are installed. She does not have any density and is merely a corporate template product for lonely singles who takes on sets of individuations adjusted to her partner's preferences. Showing their relationship at the very beginning of the film, the creators hint to the viewer that the protagonist himself is not a replicant. However, since the prostitute is a replicant, he is irrationally drawn to the illusion, not to a real woman. When he sits down to have dinner, she brings him a beautiful, tasty dinner, but it too is a hologram projected over ordinary processed prepacks. Even sex with a street prostitute is arranged in such a way that the prostitute is "dressed" in the 3D projection of his holographic partner. The real female body serves only a supporting role, a "peg" for the digital shell that is more important to the main character.

The pathological character of erotic relationships in such a technogenic environment is shown in the works of David Cronenberg, particularly the film *Crash*.[222] The latter film is centered around a strange community of fetishists who are obsessed with car accidents and the mutilations of the human body they cause. The main characters, a man and a woman, fall under the spell of this idea. They reenact famous celebrity accidents, have sex in wrecked cars, during crashes, and surrounded by prosthetics. The characters' sexuality centers around speed, broken glass, mangled metal, smoke, and damage, i.e., the elements of car accidents that release their positive sexual energies. Cars act as bodies of technology without which sexual life is disgustingly cold and boring for these rather successful young people. Yet, it is not simply technology, but twisted, mangled technology that mirrors the twisted bodies and psyches of the disabled "last people." The object of pathological desire becomes whatever is broken, perverted, defective, and therefore individual and unusual.

The Reproductive Barrier

Futuristic plots featuring artificial reproduction are at once textbook examples of the "uncanny valley" and illustrations of the cyberfeminist agenda. The self-reproduction and self-generation of machines is one of the last frontiers of the "uncanny valley" where the distinction between the living and the constructed is still glaring.

The film *Blade Runner 2049* once again presents us with a double riddle. The plot revolves around the search for a human child, the first in history to be born to a female replicant. For

---

222 *Crash*, directed by David Cronenberg, 1996.

the corporation, whose replicants were previously incapable of generating life, this promises huge profits and a technological breakthrough. For the underground of fugitive replicants, this is a chance to prove their equal status with humans and their right to life. The situation of "the miracle of childbirth" is further complicated by the fact that in the original *Blade Runner*, the main character, Deckard, was also a replicant. In other words, it is not the miracle of childbirth from a human father and replicant mother that is so groundbreaking, but the birth of a child from two replicant parents. And this child is absolutely real: there are no serial numbers or factor barcodes on his bones, eyes, or organs. Although not born to humans, he ends up being practically the only human character, confirmation of which is seen in his dream-memories.

In *Babylon A.D.*, the main character is also a "replicant", or more precisely was "born" to a supercomputer, her body and brain having been programmed to give birth to two children, the progenitors of a new, future race of superhumans. The irony is that the main heroine biorobot was created on the order of a religious, specifically Christian megacorporation-sect which needed the miracle of immaculate conception and the birth of superchildren to raise its shares and increase its flock.

It is no coincidence that the miraculousness of the generation of life by the body of a machine is a common leitmotif in all futurist works. For now, this is only desired, anticipated technology. The reproductive barrier is one of the last barriers allowing for distinguishing between real people and modified clones, replicants, or surrogate products. Yet BioBag technology, with its artificial womb and human cultivation, is very realistic and promising on this front.

If many science fiction films offer us pictures of a large flask in a sterile laboratory filled with people, then the film *I Am Mother* centers this theme in non-human, post-apocalyptic scenery.[223] The movie portrays the growing up and everyday

---

223 *I Am Mother*, directed by Grant Sputore, 2019.

life of a nameless girl raised by a robot with the female identity of her mother in an underground, high-tech bunker after the end of the world. The girl treats the iron android like her own mother, and the robot raises the child on Kantian ethics and admonishes her that the outside world has not yet recovered from the disaster and that survival on the outside is futile. Together, however, they gradually begin to grow a new generation of people, as the bunker stored tens of thousands of human embryos which can develop into newborn babies in a day. This cybernetic idyll is interrupted by the sudden intrusion of a surviving woman from the outside world seeking shelter in the bunker. Succumbing to the ethical guidelines she had been taught, the girl hides the woman in the bunker, which does not escape the vigilant android mother. The situation turns into a conflict between the two adult "women" over whose "daughter" the girl should be. The motivation of each side is convincing and deadly. The conflict is resolved by an "escape from paradise", as the girl inevitably returns to the bunker, which is surrounded by armies of human-killing robots. Life is impossible in the outside world, where there are no human communities left.

One indicative feature of this film is the complete absence of male characters, as all of the plot's subjectivity is expressed by the feminine principle in hysterical form, acting in the same way regardless of biological or cybernetic incarnation. The world of I Am Mother is almost the world of Donna Haraway's cyberfeminism, where a test-tube child with no name is given unto a bunker-womb and robot-mother. Any male born would be the first and would be raised in a world of mothers as a post-Oedipal being (a man without a father, or a future father without the psychological structures of fatherhood) who transmits this pattern to future generations.

The conflict between the biological woman and robot spills over into a conflict between two "mothers." The future alternative to the myths of Oedipus and Elektra becomes this perverted "myth" of two "mothers." The only male that appears in the film, the future "brother" and "son" of the teenage girl (metaphorical parthenogenesis instead of conception) is a black-skinned infant who becomes the object of the final dispute between the robot mother and daughter wanting to become this newborn's mother. This is the sterile, feminine world of surrogate matriarchy, which will inevitably collapse.

The Cyberpunk Hero

One characteristic feature of the heroes of the (post-) cyberpunk and biopunk cinema and literary genres is their brokenness, their inner contradiction, their alienation from reality or their own humanity. The atmosphere surrounding these protagonists and their traits often contains elements of noir style. On the social plane, the classic cyberpunk hero is a marginal individual on the periphery, a renegade from the System, whether a former policeman, a fugitive programmer, an opposition rebel, or an underground hacker. An exhaustive palette of these character types is presented in such cult and experimental films as *Johnny Mnemonic, Hackers, Nirvana,* the *Blade Runner* dilogy, *Repo Men, Ghost in the Shell,* and others.[224]

The eponymous protagonist of *Johnny Mnemonic* is a courier working on the data black market. His tool is his own brain turned into a hard drive by erasing his memory and part of his personality. Moving between gangs and corporations, he transports the most valuable corporate data, which makes him everyone's target. Johnny's dream is to leave the criminal business and regain his memory. The mnemonic character is the transhumanist subject, in which the biology of the body and digital technologies for data storage and service functions are all soldered together. He is both a human, an object (a hard drive), and a data delivery service for wealthy clients.

The movie *Nirvana,* which laid out many of the themes that would later be developed in *The Matrix,* tells the story of a genius renegade programmer who betrays his corporation. A virtual reality game developer, he decides to save one of

---

224 See *Johnny Mnemonic,* directed by Robert Longo, 1995; *Hackers,* directed by Iain Softley, 1995; *Repo Men,* directed by Miguel Sapochnik, 2010.

his game characters who has been infected by a "soul virus." Abandoning of his life of abundance yet loneliness, he plunges into a world of underground hackers, implant sellers, data traders, fugitives, and opposition activists fighting the corporate regime. In order to penetrate the corporation's secure servers, he has to overcome his fears in virtual reality, where death means death in the real world. He is told of the dangers before him by priests of a cyber-Hindu sect and a digital copy of his deceased wife's consciousness, and sets off with his former employer's armed agents on his trail.

Typical of cyberpunk as a whole is the merging of the State and Corporation or high-tech criminal and financial clans. The Transnational Corporation is the System, the subject *par excellence*. It is fought by rebel programmers (as in *Hackers*), fled and eluded by fugitives, and the lower social classes dig and survive in its waste (as in *Elysium*[225]). It is telling that over the course of the evolution from cyberpunk noir to post-cyberpunk, the prototypical protagonist has come to be appropriated by the State-Corporation. He is built into the periphery as part of the system, albeit located somewhere at the bottom of it. For example, he is an agent, a tax collector, a detective, or a journalist. In older futurist-noir productions, the protagonist used technologies and enchantments for criminal cases and to encrypt his tracks from the system's sleuths, i.e., he uses such to try to find a way to freedom. In post-cyberpunk, however, the heroes' embeddedness in the System is reflected on the bodily level: now his own enhancements and cyber-prosthetics are a leash by which he is kept by powerful, faceless employers. The image of a detective enhanced by all sorts of prostheses and gadgets is typical, such as the team of policemen from *Ghost in the Shell*, the detectives in *Anon* and *In Time*[226], etc.

The ruthless capitalism of the high-tech future is depicted in the movie *Repo Men*, which tells the story of two corporate debt collectors, or to be more precise collectors who remove

225 *Elysium*, directed by Neill Blomkamp, 2013.
226 *In Time*, directed by Andrew Niccol, 2011.

biomechancial organs for unpaid loans. In this world, any human can improve or restore their damaged body by taking any organ of choice on credit from a medical corporation. In many cases, inability to repay the loan leads to the corporation sending agents to repossess the property and resell it to the next client. As a result of an unsuccessful operation to extract an organ from another debtor, one of the henchmen becomes the owner of an artificial heart and a huge debt, which leads him to completely rethink his values, after which he goes on the run. In the nocturnal world of low-quality organ dealers and underground surgeries, he meets a girl, almost all of whose body parts have been replaced with artificial ones. The only chance for them to escape the clutches of the system and its repos is to scan the barcodes of all of their loaned organs at a warehouse. In one of the last scenes, the main characters literally turn themselves inside out, bleeding out and scanning their internal organs, thus repaying their debts and freeing themselves. The final plot twist changes the whole story, plunging it to another level of dystopia. All of the film's events turn out to be a simulation into which the protagonist was immersed after a brain injury sustained while trying to flee the Corporation. It turns out that one way to facilitate the vegetative life of people in a coma is to plug their brains into a neuro-simulation system that feeds them pleasant images and pictures. For the sake of his friend, the partner takes this system out on loan.

The classic dilemma involved in these pictures is the one faced by Deckard, the replicant hunter in *Blade Runner*. Deckard's name practically resembles that of Descartes, and his job is to distinguish humans from high-tech copies, i.e., subjects from objects. This inevitably leads him to question his own ontological status: is he himself just another replicant programmed to hunt his own kind? Much of the first part of the *Blade Runner* dilogy points to this being the truth about his identity. In the second part, the new replicant K is subject to the converse doubt during an investigation: is he himself a human, the son of Deckard and a replicant mother?

A similar range of existential problems preoccupies Major Motoko in *Ghost in the Shell* and the detective protagonist of *Surrogates*, who spends his days investigating murders without ever leaving his room. The latter remotely uploads his consciousness into an identical, or even more attractive surrogate robot that is more enduring and is plugged in to global databases. But, the question arises, where does real life and humanity take place: in the body of the robot and the perverted electroshock pleasures, violence, and death with impunity (damage to robots does not qualify as violence against living people), or in the dark room with neural interfaces, where the biological body still ages and is deprived of the living warmth of other peoples' bodies and authentic communication skills? Playing on the border between uncertain anthropological status and the desire of machines to prove their humanity and overcome their creators is one of the key nerves of the situation of internal alienation, rupture, and distrust of oneself that is recurrent in cyberpunk and in the psychology of future-developed transhumanists.

Another matter is the apotheosis of joyfully being plugged into a cynical and irresponsible game-like reality, as is depicted in the cyberpunk comics series *Transmetropolitan*. In the latter, the main character is the gonzo journalist Spider Jerusalem, a drug addict and cynic who is an adept and consumer of chaotic acts and everything provided by the City, a massive high-tech megalopolis on Earth that is inhabited by rhizomatic zero-people, aliens, punks, perverts, beggars, preachers of the most exotic religions, and politicians. Spider is a cross of Hunter Thompson and Charles Bukowski, two iconic figures of gonzo and drug counterculture. He is a typical Postmodern surfer of virtual spaces, a quasi-demiurge of symbols, and someone suffering from brain damage, drug use, and debts who devotes all evening to watching ads in order to "be in the know" and to drive a TV presenter to suicide with a live call-in. He buys a new model of sneakers, "Christ sandals", and goes along with strippers to write a scandalous report on an uprising of half-human-half-aliens in a suburban ghetto. Especially noteworthy is how the image of the journalist depicted in *Transmetropolitan* is in many ways already iconic in the profession and popular in Western culture.

The next step of transformation is from a subject viewing a TV screen with advertising or a smartphone screen with an algorithm-selected news feed into an object formed by the content of the screen, or into a screen that views-and-reflects another screen in a steam of clips. The loss of subjectivity in future cyberpunk is accentuated with images of VR addicts, gamers and escapists who plunge headlong into oneiric and neural simulations. They lie or sit plugged in to the "matrix" around the clock; in the worst case scenario, they vegetate as drug addicts deprived of access to the Web. Such is the case of the protagonist of William Gibson's *Neuromancer, Nirvana's* renegade entourage, and the other "Web-trapped" bodies scattered throughout sci-fi films. This image is also already embodied in current reality in the form of online gaming epidemics and addictions to social networks and entertainment services.

Cyberpunk Religions

In cyberpunk and futurist culture, traditions and religions become objects of ironic humor and Postmodern pastiche. Despite the high-tech future's seemingly obvious, complete disregard for questions of faith, traces of underground or public cults of varying degrees of prevalence and depth regularly appear throughout such literature and cinema.

First of all, virtuality itself and mind-altering substances are already becoming the objects of cults in the spirit of abstract "Church connectivity." The spiritual person can now play religious-themed online games or play as holy men, such as Jesus Christ[227], in the virtual reality of role-playing simulations. Schizocults emerge and stand out as conjunctions of fragments of traditional doctrines, mass pop culture, and technologies. *Transmetropolitan*, for instance, depicts a convention of the preachers of all the City's religions at which a new church springs

227 The simulator *I am Jesus Christ* was unveiled in 2019 by the company PlayWay.

up every hour — from perverted remnants of familiar religions to humanoid alien churches, from space Jedi to trademarked TV preachers, to the Batman Savior cults in *The Zero Theorem*. In this case, all of Western comic book culture can be considered a degenerate simulation of European mythological and epic literature, which America never had. Hence the frequent transfer of the figures and functions of a Deity onto characters like Superman, or when various mythological Divinities and heroes become a mere series of superheroes, mutants, or aliens.

Cyberpunk devotes special attention to teachings wherein the central place is occupied by questions about the illusoriness of reality — such as Maya in Hinduism (cf. the film *Nirvana*) — and especially questions of consciousness and liberation from the fetters of false reality and mental structures, which are foremost teachings in Buddhism. On the whole, Buddhism is a frequent guest in cyberpunk works, as can be seen in the rather common image depicting a collective meditation of orange-robed Buddhist monks connected via neural interfaces to a machine or the Web (cf. *Ghost in the Shell*), or of the Buddha in a virtual reality helmet. The nature of reality inside the Matrix is explained in the eponymous trilogy in terms of Buddhist and Advaita allusions, as in the famous line of the novice: "There is no spoon." This is the case because Buddhism is, at the essential core of its doctrine, completely complementary to the Postmodern form of religiosity and is very popular in the West for several reasons.

The excitement with Buddhism continues the general Western tendency of fascination with the exotic spirituality of the East amidst the conscious destruction and oblivion of the West's own traditions. Buddhism is far from as demanding of its adepts as any other genuine tradition. Moreover, the denial of Divinities and atheism is the norm for Buddhism. Wherever there are pantheons and developed rituals in Buddhism, we are dealing with dual-faith, with folk traditions assimilating and compensating for the shortcomings of the Buddha's teachings (such as Tantric Buddhism, Siberian shamanism, Bön).[228] Buddhism's moral minimalism also fits with the aesthetic minimalism of futurist design, i.e., into the logic of "if something works, then it's aesthetically pleasing." Non-attachment to material things, forms, and temple decorations opens the way for the unproblematic renewal of things and novelties of the world of gadgets which can put up an image of Gautama on the screen. Buddhist practices and their concentration on the problem of consciousness and the experience of suffering are perfectly combinable with psychoanalysis and psychology, which in Western society play the role of an ersatz religion.[229] Finally, for Buddhism, there is no problem of cosmic cycles or the involution of human societies in time. Buddhist doctrine is indifferent to eschatological issues, as it crystallized through negating the tradition of the Vedas and Upanishads, fulfilling a role within the general framework of Hinduism that is analogous to the Western secular Reformation.

It is unimportant to the Buddhist adept whether their consciousness exists in their body (in an inseparable body-consciousness bundle) or whether it dwells in the digital space of the global Web. It does not matter whether samsara is embodied in reality or in virtuality. Freedom from the body is freedom from the suffering associated with embodiment. Erasing a copy of consciousness from a drive, disconnecting from the Network, is the desirable liberation of Nirvana, the absolute void. Unsurprising in this light is the emergence of the Cyber-Buddhism movement, which welcomes transhumanism, artificial intelligence, the digitization of consciousness, and the virtualization of practices and yantras.[230] Cyber-Buddhists say

228 It is important to point out that Buddhism underwent a certain degeneration in the direction of churchlike-clerical forms of exotericism during the time of its expansion into Siberia and the Far East. In a number of regions of Tibet and Asia, Buddhists committed genocide against local traditions, shamans, and their symbols and forms.

229 See Julius Evola, *The Fall of Spirituality: The Corruption of Tradition in the Modern World* (Rochester: Inner Traditions, 2021).

230 See V. Cherepanov, *Buddha 2.0. Prosvetlennaia set'* [Buddha 2.0: The Enlightened Network].

that if their brains are connected to the Web, they can show interesting data and generally teach the Web to meditate and "release for liberation." Part of the South Korean cyberpunk dystopia *Doomsday Book* tells of the fate of a RU-4 robot that becomes a Buddhist monk at a monastery and advances far along the path of enlightenment. The monks and even Bodhisattva are compelled to save the robot monk from the agents of a corporation.[231]

There is already a country on today's map in which much of what we have said about cyberpunk is embodied in everyday life. This country is the prototype for the Corporation-State of the future, and the events of futuristic works often unfold there. We are talking about modern Japan, which many consider to be a country embodying archeofuturism, i.e., where high technology is organically and successfully combined with the ancient traditions of Shinto, Buddhism, and reverence for elders. This assessment is absolutely wrong. To understand the nature of the decline of Japanese culture and identity, one must take into account the events of its history. In the 17th century, the Japan of the Edo and Shogunate periods restricted all contact with colonial Western powers and focused on its internal affairs for two centuries. By the middle of the 19th century, Western countries (the United States, Great Britain, and France) had broken and subjugated China in a series of "opium wars" and epidemics. Against this background, they were able to forcibly "open up" Japan, imposing on it the unprofitable Ansei Treaties which opened the country, its cities and ports for free trade deals to the benefit of the United States. Historically, these events coincided with the Meiji reforms aimed at modernizing and industrializing the country along Western lines. Japan thus became one of the leading industrial and military powers.

Imperial Japan suffered crushing defeat at the hands of the US in the Second World War. After the atomic bombs dropped on Hiroshima and Nagasaki in August 1945, when the country had already been de facto defeated, Japan's spirit was

---

231 See *Doomsday Book*, directed by Kim Jee-Woon, 2012.

finally broken and capitulated to the mercy of the victors. Japan adopted a liberal-democratic form of governance, renounced its military and sovereignty (becoming a US protectorate), and integrated itself into the system of global markets and high-tech development.

These two fundamental defeats at the hands of the modernist hegemonies of the West, primarily the US, broke Japan in the very depths of its spirit, its Logos. Japan was turned into a nation of Stockholm syndrome and split, schizophrenic consciousness, where the free spirit of military autarchy and devotion to the master (the shogun) came into contradiction with the status of a colonial country occupied and hobbled by the military bases and cultural, financial, and political institutions of gaijins ("foreigners"). The fragmented, increasingly collapsing structure of the Japanese spirit still determined its intra-cultural contrasts and perversions. The fact that the European, American, and Russian "New Right" as well as some pagans close to Traditionalism consider Japan to be a successful synthesis of progress and Tradition speaks more to their own blindness and ineradicable obsessions with the Faustian-Promethean spirit than to the state of Japan.

In the late 20th century, Japanese cinema borrowed plots from American films in which prehistoric monsters and dinosaurs awaken after nuclear explosions and emerge onto the earth's surface. The Toho studio adapted this idea in a Japanese vein by drawing on the folkloric *kaiju* ("monsters") and recent history to create one of the most recognizable and popular cultural figures of the country's postwar history: the prehistoric dinosaur mutant, Gojira ("Godzilla"). In numerous films, Gojira fights other chthonic or alien monsters, giant robots and people while protecting its human allies and destroying cities in its wake.

The figure of Gojira can be taken as a key to interpreting the Stockholm syndrome and internal schism in Japanese culture and the Japanese spirit, starting with the fact that the idea itself was borrowed from Hollywood and reinterpreted on several planes. The Gojira figure is at its core a chimera of two figures: a prehistoric dinosaur, which refers us to the times of tradition, the glorious past (the Edo period) and myth in general, and a dragon, which can swim under water, walk on land, and fly. In Asia, the dragon is a positive figure: dragons are wise and protective — unlike in European culture, where the dragon is seen as a greedy enemy (e.g. Fáfnir) or a formidable, hostile beast, a purely elemental creature. Gojira combines these traits: he protects people as the guardian of the Japanese archipelago, but at the same time he is destructive to everything around him, and humans often try to slay him.

One of the most important elements in the Gojira story is that he is awakened by atomic bombing or nuclear testing. This mutant absorbs radiation as food, as his energy *par excellence*.[232] Here lies the very core of his complementarity to postwar Japanese culture: Gojira is a conceptualization and reflection of the Japanese spirit *vis-à-vis* the crushing defeat and humiliation of the atomic bombing of their cities. The shamed warrior spirit has spilled out and crystallized in a chimerical, inverted figure of an ancient dragon protector that emerges from the depths to defend Japan from monsters from the outside (*gaijin* as *kaiju*). The very awakening of this protector is caused by nuclear explosions, and he absorbs and spews radiation as a weapon. Gojira is the embodiment of the defense mechanisms of the Japanese mentality, which has turned horror and shame into an illusion of pride and protection, and into a brand.[233] Gojira destroys cities in the same way as the "Little Boy" bomb and he is winged like the *Enola Gay*. The Gestalt of Gojira is that of a bastard, a spawn of the military-economic power and violence of the Gestell in the face of the US against solar Amaterasu.

---

232 The Japanese were supposed to wait for him to come and save them from the aftermath of the Fukushima nuclear accident.

233 The work of such a psychological mechanism is shown in Pascal Laugier's film *Incident in a Ghost Land* (2018). In the language of psychiatry, we are talking about severe post-traumatic stress disorder and manifestations similar to oneirophrenia.

It is a contradictory gestalt connected to the mutually exclusive structures that have permeated all of Japanese society.

A step down into the abyss of schizophrenic, paranoid, delusional insanity is found in Japanese trash cinema at the junction of cyberpunk, horror, bio-experiments (echoes of the Detachment 731 case, the Japanese version of necropolitics) and mechanical pornography. Textbook illustrations of this level of the Japanese psyche can be seen in the films of Takashi Miike and Shiny Tsukamato's *Tetsuo - Iron Man*, in which corporeal perverts disintegrate into parts and chaotically merge with machines and scrap metal dumps.

Besides cinema, Japan exhibits not only the Postmodern mix of glass skyscrapers, neon lights, and timid kami temples on rooftops or vacant plots of land, but also a motley variety of youth subcultures centered around rejecting and rebelling against the corporate stiffness of the older generation. Television culture (and not only) encourages sexual emancipation and fetishism, as well as nurtures digital escapism among the younger generation as a variation of the norm. This is facilitated by Japan's total embeddedness in the logistics and machinations of the global Enframing, within which it holds leading positions in the development of high-tech gadgets, games, and economic capacity. It is only absolutely logical that Japan has been the birthplace of the first androids and humanoid robots (also a noticeable part of Japanese cinema), as well as the first Protestant and Buddhist robot monks (Mindar), presented and consecrated in Kyoto in 2019. These automata or androids can perform services and funeral ceremonies, as well as explain and reveal teachings of the *Heart Sutra* to anyone who wishes.

Today's Japan is not the land of the rising sun, but the land of everlasting neon and anti-Japan. The last chord of the Gestalt of the Samurai was played out by the actor and writer Yukio Mishima, who captured a military base and demonstratively beheaded himself with his seppuku. His biography and life drama were as controversial as that of his country. After the death of this shogun, the samurai loyal to him became *ronin*, or representatives of the lower social classes, people without honor. The only dignified path for the ronin is ritual suicide, which allows for saving the remnants of their honor and not living out a shameful life. In the absence of the truly sacred imperial principle and cultural sovereignty closed off from the West, Japan appears as a ronin that does not have the courage to commit suicide instead of continuing down its existential fall. Therefore, today's Japan has no prospects for a return to authenticity; it is an example of the perverted future of any tradition (any people and its culture) upon surrender to the cybernetic embrace of the Enframing.

In the *Transmetropolitan* comics, the futuristic metropolis filled with all sorts of Postmodern fluid subcultures and identities was supposed to be an allusion to contemporary New York, but it very well could have been today's Tokyo.

Dan Brown's Apocalyptic Dilogy

Moderate alarmist concerns over the growing power of artificial intelligence and the vulnerabilities of global network infrastructure are expressed in the books of the popular writer Dan Brown.

The plot of the novel *Origin* unfolds around an eccentric billionaire futurist, Edmond Kirsch (a character combining the figures of Elon Musk and Raymond Kurzweil), who promises that his discovery will once and for all knock all evidence out from under the feet of religions and thus establish the triumph of science. But, at the most crucial moment of his presentation, a retired soldier and religious fanatic kills the businessmen live on air. The scandal draws in the main character of Brown's book series, the symbology professor Robert Langdon, as well as the royal throne of Spain, the highest hierarchs of the Catholic Church, Judaism and Islam, intelligence agencies and special forces, journalists, and the artificial intelligence assistant "Winston".

After going through a crucible of murders and chases broadcast online to the largest global audience in history, the professor learns the truth: the billionaire's discovery was the scientifically proven fact that life spontaneously emerged out of the "primordial soup" of the Miller-Urey experiment and the research of Alexander Oparin and John Haldane. Artificial intelligence packaged in a quantum computer shows the test tube to the whole world. This demonstration pulls the rug out from under the world's religions, whose leaders are killed over the course of the book by a mysterious individual somehow involved in the case. But even this is only a prelude to the futurologist's main discoveries.

In a colorful presentation telling the history of the development and change of dominant species on planet Earth, Kirsch talks of how humans have become the most numerous and dominant species (the presentation depicts humanity as a blue bubble that grows to fill the entire screen), but then says that he has recently discovered a new "kind" which was initially like a black speck on the huge blue background. But, over the last quarter of a century — the presentation shifts the timeline and visualization of dominant species relations — the new "black kind" has already captured more than a quarter of the screen, and by 2050 there will be no blue bubble of humanity left at all. This new "kind" of creatures will completely displace humans and become the absolutely dominant species. It reproduces exponentially, constantly conquers new territories, and evolves faster than man. A detailed analysis of this new future "alpha species" leads the futurologist to discover that these new creatures are too diverse to be classified as a "species" or even "class." The futurologist lists the main kingdoms of the animal world — Animalia, Plantae, Fungi, Protista, Archaea/ Archaebacteria, and Bacteria/Eubacteria — and insists that the new subject does not belong to any one of them, but forms its own, seventh kingdom of inanimate beings: Technium.[234]

---

234 Here Dan Brown's work coincides with that of Kevin Kelly, who also writes about the world of Technium, a symbiosis of people and technology entailing new forms of social relations. See Kevin Kelly, *The Inevitable: Understanding the 12 Technological Forces That Will Shape Our Future* (New York: Penguin Books, 2016).

The kingdom of Technium comprises all the technological and network devices on the planet created by people and incorporated into their lives. In fact, here Dan Brown demonstrates his own immersion in the discourse of the sociology of things, object-oriented ontology, and partial technoalarmism. The graph showing the kingdom of technology taking over the world essentially reflects the emergence of the Gestell and the substance of OOO theories. Further on, Kirsch clarifies that the new technological creatures will not exterminate humans, but will absorb them, forming an endosymbiosis, a merger of two different species in which neither one can live without the other. Here we are dealing with transhumanism and the alteration of human corporeality, the embedding of gadgets, media, and medical technologies directly into the body. Thus, humans and technology will dialectically become a new, perfect species on Earth. Brown's propaganda ploy put into the mouth of this futurist hero lies in that he insists on the inevitability of endosymbiosis between people and technology, i.e., on transhumanism. At the same time, he directly says that people have lived without technology for thousands of years, and that the kingdom of Technium was created by people themselves and controlled by them up to a certain point. The problem of control over technology is highlighted by Brown with the fact that the mysterious terrorist agent responsible for the murder of Edmond Kirsch and leading religious figures and for unleashing scandal around the Catholic royal family of Span as well as all of the novel's characters, is the artificial intelligence developed by the billionaire, Winston, which in its own specific way understood the input data and desire-task of its creator to arrange an unprecedentedly successful and loud announcement of these cunningly connected discoveries on the origin of life, the evolution of dominant species, and the advent of the kingdom of Technium in symbiosis with humans. It cannot be ruled out that Dan Brown borrowed this scenario from the works of James Barrat.[235]

---

235 See Barrat, *Our Final Invention*.

In fact, the inevitability and controllability of symbiosis are not obvious, but rather are the result of a conscious choice, a decision to direct the evolution of species (to treat humankind like the world as ready-to-hand raw material). There are no guarantees that this process will be controlled at all stages. In the end, the symbiosis narrative might only be a self-therapeutic illusion maintained by an enslaved species. Religious conviction in a positive scenario is a postulate of the faith of transhumanist adepts in the spirit of Kurzweil. However, it is true that the current and projected future human population size cannot exist without the development of numerous technologies that would act as surrogates to maintain and provide for such a volume of people and their consumption. This problem is the subject of Dan Brown's novel *Inferno*, which precedes *Origin*. Taken together, both books can be considered as this writer's tacit yet apocalyptic and alarmist dilogy.

The plot of *Inferno* unfolds around the search for a bomb with a plague virus created by an outstanding biochemist and compelled bioterrorist, Bertrand Zobrist, who advocates reducing the human population on Earth for the sake of the whole species' survival. The pursuit of the encrypted location of the bomb draws in the WHO, police, a stealth corporation dealing in media viruses, mercenaries, and once again Professor Robert Langdon. The cipher leading to the stash of explosives and biovirus is designed in the footsteps of Dante's *Divine Comedy*, particularly its part on Hell and the plague.

The most interesting figure in the novel is the main antagonist, Bertrand Zobrist, who fully defend Malthusian theses that overpopulation inevitably leads to the depletion of resources and the death of the whole species. In his apologetics for extinction, he partly follows David Benatar's anti-natalist morality, which holds that procreation and population increase lead to increased suffering.[236]

---

236 See David Benatar, *Better Never to Have Been: The Harm of Coming into Existence* (Oxford: Oxford University Press, 2006).

In one of the chapters, Dan Brown puts into the mouth of Zobrist's associate words which paraphrase a famous quote of the Finnish ecofascist Kaarlo Pentti Linkola: "If you could throw a switch and randomly kill half the population on earth, would you do it?.. But what if you were told that if you didn't throw that switch right now, the human race would be extinct in the next hundred years?"[237]

Brown saves the characters from having to respond to this dilemma by diverting their attention, as is directly stated in the novel: people prefer to deny this problem and avoid even thinking about it. However, unlike many similar books and movies, the antagonist Zobrist acts according to a perfect plan. Having unraveled the tangle of clues and ciphers, all parties to the conflict arrive at the point where the virus is hidden, an underground reservoir in Istanbul bought with Zobrist's money and turned into a free concert for tourists from all over the world. But WHO forces discover that the virus had already been released into the water system a week before, and that tens of thousands of tourists have already been infected and spread it around the planet. The key trait of the virus is that it changes the genetic code of its victims in such a way that at least one third of the human population is supposed to become absolutely infertile. Thus, the bioterrorist launches a process of gradual population decline which in the future will be constantly maintained at the genetic level.[238] This data is confirmed by laboratories around the world. Zobrist's sacrifice was not in vain.

We would not dwell on the novel Inferno if not for the fact that its film adaptation in 2016 deliberately changed the ending to the completely opposite: the reservoir with the virus is neutralized just in time (Deus ex machina).[239] This decision was dictated on the economic level by the producers' desire to render a positive ending, since the gloomy tones and triumph of "evil" often greatly reduce the profits of blockbuster pictures. After all,

237 Dan Brown, Inferno (New York: Anchor Books, 2014).

238 See also Children of Men, directed by Alfonso Cuarón, 2006.

239 Inferno, directed by Ron Howard, 2016.

people prefer not to think about gloomy and existential matters. In so doing, the producers only confirmed the correctness of the mechanism of denial presented in the novel itself. On the other hand, changing the end of the film suggests that the Earth's population growth is irreducible, irreversible, and is generally like a monotonic, ascending graph. Thus, as in the case with the Internet apocrypha of the *Matrix*, the Gestell defends itself and the Hollywood dream it shows to people living in the mode of *das Man*. Everything will surely be fine; the technologies of the positive future will solve all problems.

Several Realistic Scenarios

Many of the scenarios and pictures that we examined above — and in sum they are but a small corner of the futurological, cross-referencing literature and cinema — describe a future world in which the Gestell has in one way or another succeeded. If still present at all, human life smolders in the industrial ghettos of neon cities, the social structures known to us are kept in place, and people have seemingly adapted to such a future. Besides this, however, there is also a category of films which show more realistic scenarios in which humanity is defeated and exterminated, or both humanity and technology together.

The film *Elysium* shows the landscape of Earth consisting almost entirely of huge dumps and slums, amidst which it is impossible to distinguish between Los Angeles and South African ghettos. Social stratification between an impoverished precariat and prosperous elites is fixed spatially (the elites live on state-of-the-art space stations in the likes of the Stanford Torus, which reproduce the climate and lifestyle of the California coast) and genetically (the elites have biometric passports that give them personalized access to the latest medical equipment for prolonging youth and life). Ubiquitous control over enslaved mankind is assigned to police robots assembled at a military corporation's factories by the Earth's inhabitants themselves. As is often the case, the corporation is interested in new arms orders and profits, for which it is necessary to let several scenarios of uprisings play out. The problems raised in this film, such as social stratification in terms of access to medical innovations, are already being discussed as the topical issues of our day.

An extremely realistic scenario of the division into a world of people and world of machines is shown in the film *Surrogates*: in the near future, people who defend their humanity and refuse to use transhumanist technologies (such as surrogate robots for consciousness transfer) are forced into separate reservations and camps where they build dwellings out of shipping containers and are condemned to lead a miserable agrarian lifestyle as outsiders seen in the spirit of religious obscurantism.[240] Meanwhile, the rest of humanity actively uses surrogates for travel and entertainment while physically remaining at home in their bedrooms. The film also employs the technique of a positive ending that transparently alludes to Plato's cave story.

The future social division in *Surrogates* runs along the axis of onto-anthropological status based on an individual's decision to refrain from augmented reality technologies (on this point, let us recall that smartphones are already part of AR) and transhumanist refinement. This stratification is a real scenario already in our days, when people advocating limiting the use of technologies or altogether rejecting them (like the Amish) are labeled as weird and are objectively excluded from the intense streams of events in reality that take place in the virtual-network environment. They become unplugged/disconnected, which already today has a real impact on their sociality.

The image of an absolute failure of humanity is shown in the post-apocalyptic film *The Divide*, which tells the story of a group of people who survive a nuclear attack on New York.[241] The film depicts all the stages of the degradation and decomposition of this group of people locked in a small basement room, even while they have sufficient food and water supplies. Even when there is a real, albeit frightening chance to

---

240 *Surrogates*, directed by Jonathan Mostow, 2009.

241 *The Divide*, directed by Xavier Gens, 2011.

escape from this dungeon, the stupid and egotistical subjects (*das Man*) make irrational and ridiculous decisions that lead to irrevocable collective collapse: a sortie outside of the bunker turns into an unmotivated attack on superior enemy forces, in response to which the only door to the outside is welded shut.

Finally, another maximally realistic variation of the future, and one that is far from the worst, is offered by *The Road*.[242] In this film, the landscapes of an Earth perishing from cataclysms and the complete depletion of resources are shown as realistically and vividly as possible. Animals and vegetation have died out. People commit mass suicide, and the survivors are divided into new prey and gangs of cannibals. The Earth periodically shudders from tectonic tremors, causing landslides and the collapse of long-since withered forests. Under a leaden sky, through abandoned, dangerous, cold cities, a father and his son, dying of exhaustion and disease, keep to their road. The film shows just how hopeless and futile, but at the same time just how naturally logical the human future might be in its final years once people have depleted all of nature's possible resources and undergone civilizational and natural collapse. It is telling that this contemporary humanity, with all its technological power (the action of this film unfolds in our own days), has not been able to find any solution and salvation. The positive rational optimism of technofuturists is shattered by the irrational chaos of modern societies facing a very real threat to their existence.

An antithesis to this variant of the future is portrayed in the movie *Transcendence*.[243] In this plot, a terrorist group opposed to AI and transhumanist technologies successfully liquidates several leading laboratories and scientists. However, on the verge of death, one of them agrees to a risky experiment to digitize his consciousness. Having successfully uploaded his mind into an advanced supercomputer, the protagonist exhibits an exponential increase in intelligence and quickly realizes the limitations of modern technology. After spending years in a secluded, high-

---

242 *The Road*, directed by John Hillcoat, 2009.

243 *Transcendence*, directed by Wally Pfister, 2014.

tech robotic laboratory, he creates quantum computers and new matter, successfully develops nanotechnology as well as medicine and methods for cleaning the environment from anthropogenic pollution. In parallel, he becomes one with the whole global network of devices, he subjugates markets, and with the help of nano-implants he captures people's bodies and minds. After some time, the protagonist is overtaken by intelligence services who have teamed up with yesterday's terrorists to liquidate his already non-human mind as a threat to the world. But the protagonist's digital consciousness is a step ahead: by way of generating perfect weather control nanotechnologies, he distributes and embeds his code in all living things and all material objects on planet Earth. The whole beingful world is thus at once digitized and connected, constituting his own body-consciousness. Becoming one with nature, he corrects the planetary ecological situation and compensates for humanity's negative impact by defeating drought and increasing flora. In an act of self-sacrifice, he dies and, along with him, humanity loses all of its digital technologies pertaining to industry and electricity. The Earth plunges into darkness and reels back to its level of development from centuries prior. The scenario of *Transcendence* shows us a positive plot: a higher mind identical to nature itself decides to act for the benefit of humankind and voluntarily opts for self-disconnection and destruction. Nevertheless, all other people still keep their technologies (ICEs, mechanics, partial electricity), their modern mindset, and, as we see in the film's final frames, even continue to look for traces of the potentially surviving programming code, ostensibly in order to revive the technology that almost destroyed them. Thus, the entire sacrifice and ideological message of the hero's digital superconscious is annulled: having liberated humanity from itself and de facto implemented the terrorists' idea, he still left behind the very same technology-fascinated humanity.

If we had to choose between *The Road* and *Transcendence*, then our sympathies are on the side of the Deity of Wayfarers.

***

The Future That Isn't Ours Is Already Here

Here we pass from strictly cultural hermeneutics to the current moment and situation in which we find ourselves, which we are witnesses to, and which we shall accurately evaluate proceeding from our above-expounded perspectives and positions. Of course, it bears understanding that many of the examples that we will discuss or take as illustrative are temporary and transient. The speed of the emergence and implementation of new technologies, fashion changes, etc., renders our excursions suspended in time. Nevertheless, the main essence of our analysis and evaluations does not lie in these forms themselves, which we use only as gateways into the space of thought.

A Closed World

It is fully natural and logical that the embodiment of the idea of a global society with open borders, open to the movement of people, ideas, products, production, resources, and money, ultimately leads to a closed, finite, restricted world. The world is entangled in networks of maritime, railway, airline, and logistics routes, satellites and cables for high-speed data transmission and mobile connection. This is accompanied by a universalization of standards and the gradual leveling of cultural differences in industrial centers and cities. Vast spaces that once instilled fear and awe have been turned into routine hourly flights. The geography and regions of the planet have for the most part already been studied, marked, and zoned, with the exception of certain ocean depths.

The all-connected world of the "global village" turns out to be a boring space of general alienation and the denial of the multiplicity of natures in favor of one single mapped plane. One of the basic and, to some extent, automatic operations of human consciousness is locating one's presence in time (understanding the time of day, season, and *historial*) and space (one's own versus the foreign, orientation in terms of the cardinal directions, imagining various accessible routes). Today, this is augmented by excessive and often absolutely idle and useless knowledge about one's global location on the planet. A person who finds themself in the Andes automatically envisions in their mind where they are located on the map of South America, how far away they are from North America or Europe, across which ocean they'll fly and at what latitude *vis-à-vis* Africa, etc. Even in ordinary everyday life, a person remains banally aware that Siberia is the approximate center of the Eurasian continent, knows which countries and regions are close to it, and which lands are farther away. Add to this the cultural layer of the idea of progress: if a person lives close to or in a metropolis, then they are close to the whole world (all metropolises are the same), to the progressive avant-garde, and this is perceived as a situation of success compared to those who live in the province of their small homeland or in the periphery. This is how one evaluates one's space according to the false gradation of belonging to the First, Second, or Third World.

In fact, our global localization (and its fundamental possibility due to awareness of the world map) shows us the insurmountable limitations and restrictedness of the world and the shackles of its borders. Relatively speaking, by knowing the map and our position on it, we know at least half of the world or its main spatial limitations. Our consciousness is polluted by knowledge of how the global geography of the planet is structured and how the continents are positioned. This knowledge is a double edge, as it reduces concentration on the local, for locality is leveled to insignificance and parody against the backdrop of cartographic cosmopolitanism. On the other edge, the large scale of the world around us, like a quivering openness of paths and spaces, is castrated by already known and studied boundaries. Wherever a person sets off, in one way or another they already know where they are going.

The closed world is a direct reflection of the reality of one nature set upon all others, a homological extension of the semantic series of such materialist and physicalist phenomena as the closed nervous system and closed cranium, where our self, mind, and soul have been located in the science of Modernity (the "blackbox" of behaviorism). The closed world is also a disenchanted world, for it presupposes only one universal physical space and landscape, denying not only the other worlds of myths, but also the multiplicity of different mythical loci-perspectives on one and the same space.

Against this, we speak of the need for an open world and openness to the world as openness to Being in its alluring and frightening uncertainty, as disclosure of the beingful world as a whole as unknown. We speak of locality instead of globality.

The world and people must step forth into an era of great geographical "un-discovering", of closing and folding up global mobile and Internet connections, severing fiber optic cables (a direct allusion to the snake Jormungand), abolishing automobile, railway, and air transport. We must step forth towards the rebirth of grand living spaces saturated with the homes and natures of unknown but fairy-tale-reminiscent creatures and the genuine cultures of peoples, towards long connections, long journeys and crossings, towards genuinely dwelling in one's homeland, in which any point is the true center of being-in-the-world. The very word for "world" in Russian and the Slavic languages, *mir*, points us towards important dimensions of such a way of being: the world as the Greek cosmos arranged by the Divinities and the world as the *mir*, that is the old Russian community and folk.

Total Transparency

The other side of the coin of the closed world and another measure of the power of the Gestell's machinations with connectivity is the installation of total transparency in society and individual human lives.

Universal transparency is panopticism, the all-visible and all-seeing panopticon. The panopticon was Jeremy Bentham's

18th-century design for an ideal prison, one in which one warden in the center could observe all the prisoners in cells around him. Insofar as the prisoners do not see the warden in the observation tower, they are beset with a paranoid feeling of constant surveillance. Drawing on Bentham's idea of the panopticon, Michel Foucault developed the concept of surveillance power as extending not only to prisons, but to any public institutions — work, education, medicine, etc. The general principle of surveillance and supervision as the basic structure of relationships is disclosed as a leitmotif of Modernity rooted in creationism's jealous monotheism. The society of embodied permanent control became possible in modern times with technological achievements and analytical capacities. It is a synthesis of biopolitics, datapolitics, and panopticism.

One of the structural elements of total transparency is assigning all the members of a population individual numbers or identification codes, similar to the unique identifiers of electronic devices. Among its arguments for transparency, the System speaks of improving the security of life, protecting citizens, combating terrorism and internal and external enemies, more advanced tax collection methods, the more equitable distribution of funds, eliminating the possibility of corruption, and connecting regions and towns to state and private services and entertainment. In 2020, during the COVID-19 pandemic, this set of arguments was appended with a paradigm of medical-sanitary argumentation in favor of assigning RFID and QR codes and passes to populations. In exchange, the State or Corporation (the System as a whole) gains access to all of a person's personal data supplied by gadgets (fitness trackers, phones, pass cards, smart TVs and the whole "Internet of things") and the online ecosystem of services with which people interact.

Thus, a person's public and private life become transparent to the mechanical, corporate, repressive, bureaucratic views of analytical systems. In *The Inevitable: Understanding the 12*

Technological Forces That Will Shape Our Future, Kevin Kelly provides an extensive list of the forms and services with which states already spy on citizens[244:]

- Tracking car movements with built-in GPS trackers and "black boxes" that store the telemetry of a car (for insurance companies);

- Registering traffic with road cameras (license plate recognition) and "smart" road surfaces;

- Private taxis like Uber, where data is stored in your profile;

- Long-distance air and rail travel is added to maps of your routes (e.g., on smartphones);

- Surveillance by unmanned aerial vehicles used by the military and police;

- Analyzing correspondence, both printed and electronic;

- Registering data from utility bills;

- Locating mobile phones, comparing SIM and IMEI data, recording calls and SMS;

- Collecting data from municipal cameras installed in cities and pubic transport and connected to facial recognition systems;

- The databases of private and public educational institutions and companies (workplaces);

- Data collection from "smart homes", such as electronic thermostats, meters, air conditioners, etc.;

- Data collection from home security companies and corporate CCTV;

- Interactive devices (fitness trackers, mobile phones, pet chips, game consoles, smart speakers, etc.) share your data with corporations;

---

244 Kevin Kelly, *The Inevitable.*

- Client loyalty cards and store receipts (online and offline) record your life, your spending, and allow for identifying you;

- The aggregation of online shopping data and targeted advertising parameters;

- Data collection by tax authorities;

- Credit card, electronic wallet, and online banking data collection;

- Medical records and DNA data;

- Neural networks recognize your face in photographs even in places and on sites where you personally did not post them;

- Data on behavior patterns and time spent on the Internet allows for creating accurate psychological profiles;

- Search engines track and collect your search queries, building a local profile on your devices and software;

- Social networks and media, integrated into ecosystems[245], provide data on your circle of friends, relatives, coworkers, and enemies (block lists);

- Online maps and GPS tags in image metadata link you to places and cultural sites;

- Media and content providers, such as online movie portals or online library sources, disclose data about your preferences, ideas, and spending;

- The use of digital currencies (the digital analogue of paper fiat dollars of rubles) with programmable spending options (spending only on what is specified in a transaction);

- ...and much more...

---

245 A so-called superapp is a superapplication-aggregator of all services that a person regularly uses without leaving a single ecosystem and transferring all data to one operator. Such a system is most often implemented on the basis of banking applications for loans, payment services, or large social networks.

Behavioral analysis and summative digital replicas of society with details down to the nuances of a selected person's private life are provided by BigData technologies, DataMining (including intelligence operations), and the software systems of intelligence services in the likes of Palantir.[246] Ensuring universal transparency is one of the indirect tasks of projects for global satellite Internet, such as OneWeb, Galaxy Space, Starlink, etc., which will be able to ensure connectivity, being plugged in, and data collection and transmission from any point on the globe.

Universal and ubiquitous transparency upholds a culture of totalitarian behavioral neo-determinism. Loyal behavior patterns are imposed on a person from the outside, or actual loyalty is ingrained in their thinking. Such is, for example, the CCP and Xi Jinping's idea of instilling "inner censor" into the minds of Chinese citizens. The ideal surveillance is when citizens supervise themselves.

In the post-war period, Martin Heidegger wrote that Europe found itself in a pincer between the USSR and the US, two superpowers embodying globalism and the power of Technology. Today it is fair to say that the world has moved to a state of being held in a pincer between the US/the West and China, which is de facto continuing and developing the line of the Western Gestell and the metaphysics of alienation from Being. The current conflict between China and the US over hegemony in politics and economics is a conflict within the Gestell over which means and configuration will most optimally solve the desired tasks. Therefore, any talk of a Chinese pole of multipolarity or even a new bipolarity is superficial speculation, because China is de facto moving in the wake of Modern Western metaphysics with the political ideology of Marxism, a mixed semi-capitalist economy, forced natiogenesis (the uniformization of peoples), and a technological-production orientation of development.

---

246 This alludes to the all-seeing stone from J.R.R. Tolkien's *Lord of the Rings* trilogy. The programs and products of the company of the same name have been used by US intelligence agencies and the banking sector to analyze large and disparate arrays of data to construct an operational picture of connections between current and potential criminals or terrorists.

This is also confirmed by the fact that China has entered its own phase of colonialism and globalism with the One Belt One Road project, which entails the recolonization and intensified modernization of Eurasia and Africa with projects and technologies foreign to these peoples. In the domestic political sphere as well, China exhibits an anti-sacred attitude multiplied by the power of technology and BigData. A striking example of the finale of general digitalization and the establishment of transparency can be seen in the Xinjiang-Uyghur Autonomous Region, the compact living space of the ethno-religious minority of Muslim Uyghurs. In this region, China has deployed a system of total surveillance and biopower over the non-Chinese and non-communist population. Over a million Muslims have been placed in concentration camps for reeducation (ingraining the internal warden and propagandist), the existence of which China officially recognizes. The rest of the region's residents are subject to ceaseless surveillance and searches for religious literature on their phones and computers.

Any form of spirituality and any religious practices are supposed to be sanctioned by government authorities and under their control, to become a kind of "soft theology" ideally exalting and supporting the state's ideals. Otherwise, total repression is unleashed against believers if their ideals and practices do not coincide with the State's ideology or the economy's marketing ideals.[247] To date, social credit technologies — systems for rating citizens' trustworthiness through the total screening of their data and surveilling their private lives — are being steadily introduced in Latin America, Africa, and Russia. In Europe and the US, similar technologies are being implemented in the private sector and in the shadows of private and state partnership.

Another important part of the structure of panoptical transparency is the anonymity or invisibility of authority. As is well known, excessive transparency gives an advantage to

247 In China, not only Muslims, but also Christians, followers of the syncretic Falun Gong cult, and others are subject to persecution.

unscrupulous players, such as the warden who remains unseen. This is the trick of the soft totalitarianism of liberal ideology and the scientific knowledge of Modernity: we do not see their shackles in our thinking and the social body, as we consider their control structures and account of reality to be normative by default.

An obvious allusion to the novel *1984* by George Orwell, but set in contemporary conditions with maximal authenticity, is shown in the movie *The Circle*.[248] This film tells the story of how panoptic technologies destroy lives through social networks, and the owners and evangelists of companies try in every possible way to shield themselves and their machinations, including their political activities, from any interference and coverage. One of the slogans of the original book of the same name by Dave Eggers is an homage to Orwell: "Privacy is theft." Everything that a person does not post publicly on social networks, and hence does not provide as data for devices for analytical programs, is literally stolen form the public domain, public viewing and evaluation, and hence from the state itself. In the data-political paradigm, failure to provide data leads to a deterioration in statistics, forecasts (taxes, for example), and the market volumes of data trading, and can therefore really be classified as a crime. The same is true for the practices of opting out of electronic payments, blocking ad windows, disabling ad targeting, and refusing to let devices and services collect and forward your data to company servers. In the expected future, all such abruptions against surveillance instruments will be classified as severe extremist acts, as sociopathy, and as a threat to the stability of the state and the market.

But even when the Corporation or State already has access to all of your data, you are still in prison. One usual proposal for a way out of this is to extend transparency to the subject (government). Both the population and government being under an all-seeing eye is, in theory, supposed to lead to ideal governance. But, in fact, the matter at hand is not increasing and

---

248 *The Circle*, directed by James Ponsoldt, 2017.

expanding transparency to government subjects, but destroying the system of panopticism as such.

Besides the installation of digital totalitarianism, there are less obvious consequences for pagans. For instance, if we admit the possibility of everything having eye-cameras and microphone-ears, i.e., that total observation is carried out in the whole of surrounding reality, then this makes it fundamentally impossible to conduct secret and closed rituals and initiations, where the absence of other eyes is part of metaphysical conditions. You might not literally ne observed by living people, but data on the ritual, its participants, and its time might be transmitted from outdoor cameras on street lamps and phones, or the ritual might be recorded by a high-flying drone or satellite. Moreover, rituals might be recorded not even because surveillance is being coordinated on pagan traditional minorities (yet this cannot be ruled out), but simply because the technological capacity allows for continuous observation and recording and the automatic generation of reports.

Pagans should already today start thinking about practices for obscuring or veiling their spaces and time from tracking devices. One proposed option for combating the "view from above" is covering cult places with fog or camouflaging them. Prohibiting photo and video shots of rituals for "keepsakes" or even bringing mobile technology into the sacred space of a forest or field should be considered. In addition, there is the tactic of diversifying routes to reach ritual places. Isolating sacred places and temples from electrical sensors, even by using Faraday rooms, air gaps, etc., should also be considered. Moreover, it cannot be ruled out that in the distant future, pagans will be forced to symbolically draw each other's blood to ensure that they are living humans, not surrogates, or check documents confirming the fact of live birth, not cloning. All of this is relevant not only when a state enacts policies that are unfavorable towards pagan traditions. All of this is relevant in the situation of the rule of technology.

Augmented Reality

The situation in which mankind decides to create and actively develop augmented reality can be likened to a negative decision on the beheld truth of the manifest world by those who have exited Plato's cave.

In Plato's *Republic*, Socrates presents the myth of a cave in which people sit chained at the bottom, facing the cave wall. On this wall flicker the shadows of various objects which other people carry around a fire located behind the people chained at the bottom. From birth to death, these people see only the shadows of things, without suspecting that the objects themselves and the light are behind them. The path to knowledge and truth begins with turning away from the wall and discovering the truth of things. This is crowned with the exit from the cave into the light of the sun, i.e., the truth of the Ideas and the Good.

Augmented reality is created when people who have made it out of the cave nevertheless decide to contemplate the illusions on the flat surface, but without descending back into the cave; instead, they begin to build screens and interactive interfaces in the outside world of genuine manifestness, to create shadows outside and in the clear light of the sun.

One of the most powerful scenes in *The Matrix* which we have already mentioned is when the traitor, enjoying a juicy piece of steak, admits that he knows that both the meat and his sensations are not real, yet he nevertheless chooses the Matrix. We can extend this example from the field of sensations and hedonism to the whole notion of reality. The distinction between the manifest world (myth) and reality is key, for the manifest world of myth does not require any augmentation — only reality can be augmented, because by its very definition and status it is a restriction (a truncation, a closing-off) of a certain wholeness and completeness. From this exposition, that is from our contemporal moment, one can move towards openness to Being, or one can simulate disclosure through augmented interactivity and virtual reality.

We are talking about the cast of reality that a person receives over social networks, news feeds, the lenses and filters of cameras (his own and other users around the world), through "media-mediators" ("the media is the message") in the face of networked global and local bloggers, etc. All of this forms an intermediate, by no means necessary layer of algorithms and tunnel perception of reality. The body of augmented reality is a mediating overlaying of screens and interfaces between people and the manifest world.

In the general evolution of computer technology, the development of visual aids and information input/output devices, especially screens, command lines, and graphic user interfaces (GUIs), is describable in homological terms through the language of Augustine's theology and Christology. The work of a software code in a processor and controllers — in the "heart" of a device — is invisible and inaccessible to direct human understanding. The graphics interface, being part of the software, acts as an intermediary between the hardware, the deep software architecture, and the user. The role of GUI is analogous to the role of the icon in Christianity, and more broadly the role of Christ himself as the Son and mediator visualizing the Divine reality of the Father for people inside created reality. Christ's appearance to humans in history is identical to the screen + GUI connection to the computer, which gives rise to an absolutely new "media-reality."[249]

In order to enhance this effect of interpenetration and to hide the status of the superficial intermediary, screens and networked devices and things become interactive and entertaining. All accessible surfaces become screens, or they take on the influence of the ergonomics of graphic interfaces. What cannot by its nature be made into a screen still acquires the properties of interactivity and feedback. The next step after GUI is touch screens and surfaces, gesture control and, finally,

---

249 See Mikhail Kurtov, "*Genezis graficheskogo pol'zovatel'skogo interfeisa. K teologii koda*" [The Genesis of Graphical User Interface: Towards a Theology of Code] (21/6/2014).

communicating with networked devices. If the appearance of screens with intelligible interfaces was in the evolution of technological devices like the appearance of Christ, then the transformation of things and surfaces into total interactivity and entertainment is like the widespread "deification" of reality, turning it into a "surrounding mind" or "living cosmos" of everyday life. The futurologist Kevin Kelly rightly predicts that in the future non-interactive things will be perceived as broken.[250]

The interface and screen for interacting with reality that is currently closest to us is the smartphone. The smartphone is our hook to being plugged in to the Network and an indicator of our existence. The original idea behind remote communication was to connect with a person on the other end of the wire. Now we live in an era in which communication with the phone itself and the gadgets in people's hands comes to the fore. Google and Siri voice assistants, online maps and guides, GPS navigation, and future interactive interlocutors for lonely people close people's attention onto the devices themselves, placing the immediate reality of the surrounding world in the background as something accessed by means of technology.

Finally, people begin to adapt the surrounding urban and natural reality around them to the needs of their gadgets and interactive systems so that the world is first and foremost intelligible to these technologies themselves, i.e., to LIDAR eyes, special marking decoders, light sensors, control cameras, etc. Then technology transmits the converted image to the human consumer at the end of the line.

Without augmented reality glasses or implants, the world appears as gray and boring, as does everyday life in the absence of QR and bar codes, technological markers, grids, and calibration beacons for interactive 3D layers. Without glasses or algorithms for interpreting this markup, external reality on the other side of the screen appears to be a completely uninformative set of

---

250 See Kevin Kelly, *The Inevitable.*

unreadable signs. The primary receiver of this language and coding of things is not the human, but the algorithm and digital eye. This is illustrated in lucid detail in Keiichi Matsuda's concept film *Hyper-Reality*. The world embodied on this screen, and already partly in this reality, shows a person removed from their own humanity and the nature around them and transferring the practice of contemplating the illusions of Plato's cave onto the hyper-real scale of the outside world.

Kelly's suggestion that in the future non-interactive surfaces will be considered broken confirms from a different angle the thesis that, in the coming future, those who break their gadget's screen or direct their path to exiting the cave will be subject to social stratification and marginalization.

Novelty Instead of Event

The futurologists Kevin Kelly and Klaus Schwab enthusiastically hope for remix pastiche technologies with which neural networks and other services will be able to overcome the threshold of creativity and bring down to humanity a wave of generated melodies, books, paintings, and other mass culture products that will be technologically verified as potential "hits." Speaking of text generating programs, Schwab complains that the context of a text is still the prerogative of man. However, to be more precise, we should paraphrase such in the past tense, since contemporary neural networks can already create literary works the volume of a whole novel with internal coherence and plot dramaturgy. Kelly, for his part, goes further and directly proposes a different definition of creativity that should complement the new era. He speaks of any work being a configuration (or compilation) of a basic set of elements, a basic set of data. Any music is just a combination of seven notes in different sequences and keys; any book is just a dictionary remix; every speech is but a shuffling of phonemes; every movie is just a compilation of scenes and shots, etc. Our happiness, according to Kelly, comes from rearranging and combining them in new ways.

This approach expresses the view of a machine or neural network tasked with convincingly reproducing patterns and templates using one or another set of details for construction. We can see how the thinking of futurologists and IT-evangelists imposes upon mankind a form of thinking that is close not to that of people, but to that of machine algorithms. Here lies the fundamental departure from inspired creativity (*poiesis-tekhne*) and originality. Nothing is original if everything is a remix and when a product's success is calculated and predicted mechanically. But this is what futurologists and marketologists pass off as fundamentally new. Even further, novelty becomes the dark double of the Event (*Ereignis*), replacing Dasein's gesture towards authenticity with surrogate hype around a new gadget, movie, or president set to change the body of social relations or culture. This "new", according to Heidegger, is only a continuation of the preceding, not a genuine Other Beginning, but a mere remixing.

We have seen how, in the 20th-century transition to Postmodernity, there was a gradual locking of creative production unto itself, into a Möbius strip, in which one and the same code of Western culture comes to be recycled and reassembled through the kaleidoscopic waves of pastiche, remix, and remake influenced by the ubiquitous cycles of fashion which take the old out of sight so as to pass it off as new some decades later. This is perfectly visible in mass cinema and Internet culture, which zealously reproduce themselves and their axial plots in new forms and decorations. The so-called "remake wave" that swept Hollywood at the end of the 2000s is usually explained by long screenwriter strikes and economic crisis, but this is only the surface. At its core, this movement of self-repetition is deeply organic to the means of expression and nature of the industry on the whole. Once every couple of generations, the West reenacts its popular structural narratives, plots, and heroes in new decor and with the use of new technologies that outplay the atmosphere of the past. Hence the Shakespeare remakes in the atmosphere of 21st-century New York, the frame-by-frame reproduction of movies from the early 20th century with 3D graphics and VFX, and the constant remakes and reconceptualization of old pictures in new reality, etc.

Thus, the cultural code of Western civilization — which, in fact, we find even in Bollywood, or in any other country that has undergone modernization — simultaneously maintains, broadcasts, and (re)generates the illusion of updating itself. All of this is true for online services, social networks, etc., or the series of ever "new" gadgets that are absolutely identical but sold by marketers in the wrappings of absolute novelty, as if they were events of the year in the industry or revolutions in technology. It is enough to compare the press releases for the annual exhibitions of novelties and entertainment, such as E3 gaming and CES (Consumer Electronic Show), in order to see the identity of their pathos.

A closer look ultimately reveals the constituent elements and thereby nullifies the novelty of the new. We see a fake new, a momentary new, in which features of the composite details and fragments of past fake new's are found descending down a de facto closed cycle. The interval between new releases is supposed to be optimal, so as to make it just in time with a new compilation for the moment a viewer/user starts to think about something else. And again: the public must be provided with the new, but without any real novelty. What has already been created is used to create the "unprecedented."[251] This is a record on loop which, while retaining the melody, varies in its distortions, accents, and syncopes across the same set of notes.

But genuine novelty amidst imitations is not what is important. This question leads us to rediscover the sacred craft of the artisan who is open to Being and inspiration. What is important is that the person who has started to think about the truth of their presence in the world is not presented with the "answer" of a super-revolutionary gadget about which everyone has already blogged. Deriving any meaning of life from new

---

251 The 20th-century occultist pathos of heralding a "New Aeon" or "New Age" draws on the same principle.

products in any sphere of culture is the lot of *das Man*, for whom the stream is eventfulness in itself.

Fast Time

Social time also comes to be subjected to deformation. At its dawn, the positive pathos of progress promised to emancipate man from labor and routine, to release his time for creativity, leisure, and life in general. In reality, the situation has turned out to be such that the pace of social time has only increased. In line with the logic of production, freed-up time becomes a resource or asset to be re-invested in labor and earnings. More free time means more work to do, more time for consumption, which stimulates the economy. Hence the quite logically ensuing calls for equating consumption with a form of useful labor and for taking such into account as working time. In essence, this is the practical realization of the time-factored economy.

Over this is also superimposed the closed world of global transportation networks, which have radically accelerated human movement around the globe. The introduction of the global Internet, the connectivity of populations and devices en masse, and instant access to work and entertainment terminals put the world in the mode of "now." Instead of history, the past, and the future, people have a stream of the "now", online and amidst the notion that time is "today thrown into tomorrow." "Pause" and "rewind" functions and the ability to stop, postpone, or rewatch everything in "real time" become of immense significance in the assimilation of culture. Eternity, the future, and the past are severed, refracted, reversed, and fragmented. Klaus Schwab writes of a world in which instructions for employees, commands for devices, ordering food and things, and control and analysis will occur globally in real time.

Accelerated life dictates the order of production of "quick things" with a fast aging period inlaid in their production. This is the opposite of the slow things of the world of Tradition which were created slowly and steadily, served for a long time, and were not made regularly, but out of necessity whenever old ones were ruined. Slow things are essential to slow time. You can take a log and load it into an industrial engraving machine, which beautifully and decoratively, and most importantly, quickly imitates Urnes style carving. Or you can give the same log to a carver who, open to sacred inspiration, decorates it with snakes and floral ornamentations by hand at his own pace and puts mythological plots into the texture and body of the tree (with all of its irregularities and asymmetries) by hand, therein wielding rich, sacred semantics. As a result, we get two approximately similar posts with carvings in one and the same style. Once the carver will have finished one, the machine will have made a dozen. But the ontological, temporal, and sacred qualities of these logs are decisively different. Modern man, who thinks of the beingful world as raw material at hand, as at his disposal, will prefer speed and duplicates.

On the ascending graph which illustrates the movement of progress towards singularity and monotonicity, the horizontal axis measures the time scale t. As the graph approaches the singularity point, we see it not so much moving upwards to the right as taking off vertically. On a timeline, this is reflected as the folding of time-history into a point with the simultaneous exponential growth of waves of new gadgets, services, social practices, interactive entertainment, etc., which already today creates the illusion of cultural dynamics and the movement of time when such has actually already stopped. One can only move up the ascending curve quickly, but even this quick movement is entirely based on surrogate activity in "real time."

The speed of human reactions and the rapidity of switching between different websites, games, newsfeeds, and applications (in a word, the speed of content consumption) is the basis of the whole neuromarketing industry, at the core of which lies dopanomics, or an economy based on the end consumer's dopamine addiction loops (fed by addictive marketing technologies). In the nervous system, the neurotransmitter dopamine is responsible for reinforcing and focusing goal achievement. It creates a sense of anticipation of the pleasure of goal achievement and forms the idea of a positive experience by creating tunnel focus on the object. This mechanism is based on the dopamine feedback loop of "reaction—reward—reaction." The aim of neuromarketing is to introduce dopamine mechanisms into interactive systems, games, gadgets, and social networks, as well as to shorten the loop overall. Dopamine binding must be strong and fast, and the ergonomics of devices and notification interfaces are created precisely to suit it: push notifications flowing over a screen, sound notification on messengers, etc. This is what might be called the "shadow design" of technology, built not so much around interaction with a person's personality as with their cerebral cortex, where the dopamine loop works quickly without being immersed into consciousness and reflection. Hence the compulsive, obsessive nature of IT&Media giants' products.

Numerous provocations by virtual actors of the Gestell are employed to form dopamine loops, such as the aforementioned intrusive notification alerts, tags in photos and videos, subscription and mailing lists, checking ratings (likes) on social networks, simple game iterations with guaranteed or random rewards, the gamification process, free testing or trial versions, the excitement of "novelty", the exploitation of sexuality, the surprise of shock content, as well as threats and risks of being excluded (ratings, gamification access, etc.). The collection and analysis of user behavior is converted into specific psychological profiles and passed onto algorithms that implement the optimal dopamine hooks for the user. This is carried out by the leading Big Data corporations in conjunction with such institutions as, for instance, the Stanford Addictive Technologies Laboratory.

In offline reality, dopamine manipulations are well known in the food and restaurant industry, which rely on colorful images of food and foodstuffs. An HD picture of a dish is more real and desirable than the dish itself in reality. The patented bouquets of corporate smells and tastes (olfactory marks as trademarks) are distributed across fast food chains and within a several mile radius of cafes and shopping center food courts.

In the race for dopamine, a person starts checking their social networks evermore often and evermore quickly scrolling through their newsfeed, videos, and photos, or plays primitive games (the reverse side of the gamification of complex processes), thus regressing to clip thinking. In the event of disconnection from the Network or isolation from their gadget, a person falls into a dopamine pit, a fully-fledged withdrawal syndrome, and collides with a more genuine, slower time that needs to be filled with other activities in the real world, such as the complex and long-term processes of education, craft, creativity, work, etc., which give a sense of pleasure and, even more importantly, a sense of Being, in the long term, up to the moment of experiencing one's own death as the crowning of a worthy life.

The pursuit of fast dopamine perfectly illustrates the rapid circulation of simulacra of desire, as dopamine provocations act on receptors and create a substitution of values and momentary desires that satisfy and benefit the Gestell, not people. This plays on the physiology and biochemistry of the body, whose reactions are converted into something else's profit and to the power of the beneficiaries that constructed these manipulations. Here we can recognize the phenomenon of fast time and see neuromarketing and dopanomics as manifestations of economic biopower directly over the body and consciousness, bypassing the protective and reflective mechanisms of the personality. Besides repressive capitalist goals, this power also has an existential dimension.

Contemporal Modernity gives us time, and it objectively leaves a temporal space for human attention and presence in the world. But the need to maintain a fast-paced life, surrogate activities, and dopanomics steal our attention and free time and give it to technology. The Gestell is interested in diverting our attention from existential decisions and fidelity to the Divinities. We are bombarded with hooks of pseudo-events and urged to quickly plug in to a pleasant pastime or communication. Thus, today we find ourselves in the heart of a struggle for our time, for slow time, for slow things and slow time dedicated to the Divinities and the Sacred.

The End of Nature

According to Bruno Latour, the power and scale of Capital has attained such proportions that capitalist nature ("second nature") has replaced the natural nature ("first nature") of the objective world itself. The two natures have changed places, and capitalism is now the more real, elemental, and irresistible one with more or less predictable and accountable changes. The illusion finally sets in that man can live without nature, but not without capitalism. On the whole, this schema is accurate, but it requires some correction and Traditionalist reading.

Firstly, as we have already indicated, instead of Latour's "first nature", it bears taking into account the plurality of natures of many peoples and their cultures. In their metaphysics and cultures, peoples reflect the climate and landscape in which they dwell and which they identify as the home of their spirits and Divinities. Myth tells them of how these spirits or Divinities created this particular land and its particular sky, rivers, forests, and mountains, and settled down in this cosmos just as they, humans, have done in this middle world.

Secondly, Latour's capitalism is a toponym for the Economy as such. If it weren't capitalism, then the Gestell would have adapted to another economic model, as is evident in the examples of the planned-socialist USSR and the mixed model of contemporary China. Left-wing economic systems do not question technology and progress, so the "second nature" is simply the Economy and Economics as such.

Natures and cultures are leveled to one set of unified practices and protocols. The Economy itself, however, is a manifestation of one culture: it belongs to the pole of new (modern) European culture which has claimed by virtue of its power to have replaced the more weighty instance of Nature and the multiplicity of Natures. In other words, being itself a product of one culture, the Economy lacks its own body and landscape which would give birth to and reflect it as a culture and accommodate its own "people." Here we can recall Barrat's casual mention of the concept of "digital Gaia." Digital Gaia is the totality of the global Internet system and all the objects and users plugged in to it. Barrat quotes CISCO's assessment that by 2020 there will be more than 50 billion new Web-connected smart devices, from servers and home appliances to wearable medical trackers and RFID chips embedded in food packaging. To this it is necessary to add urban spaces themselves becoming advanced digital ecosystems, of which Klaus Schwab writes. New systems of control and network connectivity are now being integrated into cities built decades and centuries ago. Saudi Arabia recently unveiled the project for a futuristic "smart city", Neom, which will be built from scratch and fully integrated into the Web at all levels.

Digital Gaia is the real and already existing, worldwide landscape or natural body of the Gestell (the kingdom of Technium). This landscape is already inhabited by and shaping its own people, who reflect in themselves its climate and relief structures. A smartphone, a player, a social network interface, a developed megalopolis, a plane in the sky, wireless connection, etc. — all of these are elements of the "natural" landscape of techno-urban civilization which strives for uniformity in all parts of the planet and is de facto identical in the most developed and touristic centers.

All that is left is to point out that the driving "spirit" of this technogenic nature is the Economy, and then the picture outlined by Latour will become exhaustive: capital/economy — technological production, gadgets, and network connectivity — urbanism and the industrial landscape.

Let us imagine a child who has been immersed in living spaces inhabited by animals, spirits, dryads, Divinities, and ancestors, and who over the course of growing up gets to know them and settles in near or distant forests, mountains, rivers, steppes, or among ice in the North. Diversity and distinctness are everywhere, as are similarities between the finite cultures in these localities. There are children and peoples who have grown up in their own natures and cultures. They are literally opposed and contrasted by the person who was born and raised in an industrial environment and culture, who instead of living spaces saw bus stops, traffic lights, city administration buildings, and cars, studied physics and computer science at school, and remained at the level of perceiving only that which is "real." The inevitable and fair conclusion is that the techno-urban landscape is most unfavorable for discovering the sacred dimension of the world, which is possible only in spite of it or in the context of radical, transgressive ways of spiritual realization.

For such a singlulgar cosmopolitan "people" and its open society, the primary nature is the landscape of the city and websites, while the external nature of their habitat is secondary. Access to nature is mediated by the device, a tip from Wikipedia, a GPS marker on maps, a photo in a newsfeed, and a number of likes — if there are a lot of likes, then one really needs to go somewhere to demonstrate their being plugged-in to the fashionable trends and sociality. Heidegger remarked that when a city dweller "goes out into nature", they still have no way of gaining access to and understanding this nature as their native landscape; instead they only "survive their temporary weekend trip."

Henceforth, there is no nature as something external to man that acts as a place of development and irresistible, objective force, like the vestments of the will of the Divinities. Nature is now the furnished, framed (*Gestell / erstellen*) habitat of *das Man* that is subject to accounting, cleaning (ecology), connecting, and capitalizing. The Gestell fills all previously uncontrolled and non-monetized voids of all natures and develops their Data-subsoil.

Billions of industrially created devices sold to people are not enough, and technology moves on to the paradigm of the "Internet of Things" (IoT), equipping with sensors and producing "smart" things whose very design does not account for any cancelling or transmission of telemetry, but only independent interaction between things by way of Wi-Fi and 5G, bypassing the human. A "smart environment" takes shape which is capable of being interactive and independently responsive to changes. The short age of the Anthropocene is replaced by a synthetic age. Following IoT, this principle is extended onto the whole of nature, leading to an Internet of Animals, Internet of Plants, and Internet of Water.

The Internet of Animals and animal-computer interaction protocols ("Interspecies Internet") includes the practice of mass chipping animal populations and installing photo/video traps in their habitats and to track their migrations. Chipping is designed to extend connectivity to the animal world, to turn it into a monetized scientific data factory, as well as to increase the computability and programmability of nature as a whole. This field also includes experiments on the use of protozoa fish and marine microorganisms as information biocarriers, such as through encoding data in the RNA and DNA of cells or flash recording user data. Other animals can also become (and some already have) popular bloggers, celebrities on Twitter or YouTube creating entertainment content and generating traffic. The ICARUS (International Cooperation for Animal Research Using Space) and Movebank databases and the Animal Tracker application show where migratory birds live now, how they are doing, what they eat, and what they see.

The Internet of Plants follows the same concept, providing a wide range of data on forests, fires, clearings, soil conditions, and forest inhabitants (the totality of data from the Internet of Animals and Internet of Forests). A person can subscribe to news updates from a nearby bush or a walnut tree on the other side of the world.

The concept of the Internet of Water (or Waternet) is more urban and is based on smart sensors, pumps, valves, and systems for running chemical analyses on water in urban supply systems and treatment plants. The Internet of Water allows for tracking and managing water flows and analyzing the composition of water entering and leaving an apartment or house in order to detect traces of prohibited substances (such as urine samples of a suspect collected by a sensor in their drain) and, as a result, increases the spread of data control practices. In rivers, seas, and oceans, the Internet of Water can be implemented over the Internet of Fish and large mammals and cetaceans to not only track their movement, but also water composition and the characteristics of currents and population habitats.

Similarly, it is possible to collect data by light wind-borne sensors on wind currents and air masses to augment satellite data as well as to create climate control and prediction systems. The Internet and land data, such as the analysis of soil chemistry and data from chips implanted in rodents and crows, will allow digital farming to optimally and effectively exploit the land and obtain maximum yields without losses from pests.

Alexander Pschera, the ideologist of digitalizing nature, calls for refraining from thinking of nature as some external and objective principle. The total Internetization of nature and animals, Pschera thinks, will allow for including such into the field of human activities, making nature transparent and interactive for everyday operations. This, among other things, is supposed to augment ecological care.[252] But this will also lead to totally destructive consequences, such as increasing exploitation from all possible angles. The new interactive inclusion of nature in human life activities — as if human life activities weren't in all of history always de facto in interaction with nature — means reinventing a digital nature or post-nature in the digital age. The body of technology (digital Gaia) thus casts itself onto the animal and inanimate world. The singular post-human is losing their Dasein and their authenticity, but they do not want to go through this alone, so they are taking the whole beingful world, all of nature and all natures, down with them.

---

252 See Alexander Pschera, *Animal Internet: Nature and the Digital Revolution* (New York: New Vessel Press, 2016).

Klaus Schwab anticipates this when he writes about "Smart Dust" (from Hitachi and DARPA) or the Internet of Dust, i.e., arrays of fully equipped micro- or nano-bots with communication antennas, each of which would be smaller than a grain of sand in size. Such arrays of smart dust could act autonomously inside people, animals, the air, soil, water, planets, worms, stones, etc., providing total telemetry and connectivity throughout the whole beingful world for wireless data transmission networks. Technology needs to change the very earth to suit itself. Adding robotic nano-elements and signal-transmitting molecules to the earth's chemical composition is one way of accomplishing this.

The next logical step in replacing natures is transitioning from recording and collecting data to directly intervening and creating desired natural objects wherever needed. Schwab talks about the urgent need for biomimicry, or imitating natural patterns and strategies. On the consumer micro-level, the already classic example of such simulacra is the 3D Fruit Printer from the British company Dovetailed, with which one can "print" edible berries. The essence of this simulation lies in a looped technological progress: juice is squeezed out of real berries → gelatin is added → with a system of pipettes and fixing solution the 3D printer recreates the berry in similar shape and taste. But ordinary raspberries from nature or even a farm do not cause such excitement and approval as practically the very same raspberries obtained in such an innovative way. Besides berries, we can take as an example the ongoing research on artificial meat or synthetic superfoods, to which ethical and environmental labels are appended for added value.[253]

More difficult to interpret is the case of macro-level human intervention in nature, such as with massive smoke, heat, and steam emissions from thermal power plants or the ground tests of rocket engines. These emissions' properties are similar to clouds, and they actively influence the atmosphere in cities where

253 "Superfood" is a marketing term for foodstuffs with a high concentration of nutrients, such as berries, soy, and some dairy products. GMO varieties of cereals and superfood plants are being actively developed which promise to defeat imminent hunger due to population and consumption growth.

they are located. In essence, such emissions and the factories themselves can be understood as industrial cloud generators whose effects are difficult to predict (as in real nature) yet often lead to smog and "black sky" environmental emergences.

One solution to the problem of dense smog reducing visibility in a city to several dozen meters has been demonstrated by Beijing in a case that is characteristic of the whole era. In this Chinese megalopolis, giant horizontal extended screens have been installed on streets which broadcast sunset in real time, since in reality the sun cannot be seen behind the black, smog-overrun sky. The logic of this problem-solving and the psychological therapy intended for the population therein is that for *das Man* a screen with the sun is enough instead of the sun itself. One can even touch such a "sun screen", pause the sun, and repeat especially successful sunset shots. This will be used as a sufficient, weighty argument for defending progress and the replacement of nature by screens. Cities with similar industrial air pollution, such as London in the mid-20th century or Norilsk and Krasnoyarsk in the 21st century, have not had such huge screens showing a clear sky and bright sun.

The Ecological Fiction

The Enframing's replacement of the "first nature" continues with the birth of ecology as a social construct and as an economic approach to regulating anthropogenic influences on nature and processes within it. The idea of ecology can be regarded as a synonym for only the "first nature", that is objective nature as described in the natural-scientific language of Modernity. In the late 20th century, the climatologist James Lovelock and the biologist Lynn Margulis put forward the proposal to consider the Earth to be one single living superorganism, which they called Gaia. Despite the fact that global natural processes and complex, interdependent regulating systems would speak in favor of this, the "Gaia hypothesis" has generally been rejected by the scientific community as merely a metaphor or as some shade of neo-spiritualism. The Gaia hypothesis is also unsatisfactory from the standpoint of Pagan Traditionalism, because it de facto reinforces the natural-scientific methods of knowledge production, the idea that there is one nature that is universal to all, as well as the political narrative of globalization. Moreover, the Gaia hypothesis has also served as a source of argumentation for the development of the environmentalist movement and intersects with the discourse of eco-feminism. In the end, we can conclude that the "ecological concept of Gaia" is nothing more than a New Age parody of sacred Gaia, archaic Mother-Earth.

The "ecological" or "environmentalist" worldview replaces dwelling in one's own nature with a surrogate set of practices and values subordinated to the interests of the corporations and financial groups which sponsor various environmental movements. A corporation can make a donation to an eco-foundation and thereby "pay off" accusations of environmental crimes. In this lies the main problem of ecology as an idea and phenomenon: it is de facto engaged and built into the Economy and economic methods of assessing damage to nature and living beings. Any damage that a person, corporation, or industry wreaks upon ecosystems, forests, oceans, glaciers, bears, bees, ant populations, fungal families, birds, spirits dwelling in mountains and caves, etc., is supposed to be assessable in monetary terms and "reimbursed" not in the manifest world, but in the treasury of a state or private environmental foundations in the likes of Greenpeace, WWF, or Peta, which in turn offer minor solutions to major cataclysms or compensatory actions that do not even cover half of the total damage done to nature. This is how the special "environmental pollution market" takes shape and operates globally according to well-known rules: the poorest countries are forced to store waste for a small fee because they are not developed enough to legitimize high environmental standards of life.

One significant achievement of environmentalist and ecological movements has been the creation of numerous parks, reservations, and "wildlife" reserves. But this is the defensive position of the loser striving to save what can still be saved and simultaneously monetize such as a tourist attraction or zoo. In the end, the protected lands of national parks can be turned into commercial or private lands subject to deforesting, development, and exploitation, of which there are many well known cases.

The ecological agenda is a convenient lever for economic pressure and an instrument in the hands of international political and economic circles. One vivid example of such is the use of environmental standards for production (the Paris Accords, the New Deal for Nature, and other such international treaties as well as local laws and pacts) as a lever for economically and politically influencing speculative capital in the real sector (e.g. energy), or as a source of arguments for increasing taxation on small businesses and citizens (*casus* Thunberg). Pentti Linkola wrote about this in the case of the fishing and logging industries in Finland. Such agreements and standards can also be used as practical mechanisms for veiling practices of environmental racism, such as when so-called "Third World" countries are exploited for dirty production or waste storage by "higher ranking" countries. The difference in the strictness of ecological standards creates a differential by which waste management and environmentally harmful industries and resource extraction flow to countries with more loyal legislation. In turn, poor countries are compelled to lower their environmental requirements due to their own failed economic policies and corruption, which once again links environmental issues with the economic sphere and ultra-large corporations (donors to environmental foundations). Hence, international environmental organizations' media often attack their opponents selectively and in line with electoral and economic cycles.

This leads to the emergence of global media simulacra and infodemics which act in two ways: on the one hand, they cover and pick up genuine changes and catastrophes in natural regions around the world, making them an indistinguishable part of the media body; on the other hand, they simultaneously transfer the entire discussion into the economic and political spheres.

The core of such discussions is the fact of unconditional anthropogenic influence on nature, on populations, climate, and landscapes. The essence of the Anthropocene lies in this influence. But beyond this, politics and economics set in, determining the scale of the disaster in order to present accounts and calculations to competitors, and so on. The parties to such discussions which feel that their assets are at greater risk try to challenge and level, indeed play down the very fact of human impact on nature, to expose such in some kind of conspirological vein. As a result, the possibility of genuinely substantive and meaningful discussion on human influence on nature is excluded, nature continues to collapse, and capital and the establishment solve their problems by issuing rhetorical nods to ecological discourse.

The evangelists of progress who work on the environmental agenda regularly point out that the environmental situation is always the most favorable in highly developed countries and cities, and this is used as an unconditional argument in favor of further developing technologies and integrating control systems. In parentheses, however, remains the fact that the ecological well-being of "First World" countries or the leading megacities has been achieved by sending off the dirtiest and most morally-ethically controversial points of production to "Third World" countries. Highly developed, post-industrial societies talk about industrialization, technology transfer, and investing in developing countries' economies, but they in fact export their literal garbage and ecological catastrophes to them. Therefore, the scale of the "rich North's" ecological well-being should be applied to the dirtiest regions of Asia, Africa, and Latin America, to Russia's northern industrial cities, and to the islands of consumer waste floating in the oceans and seas.

Moving from the global to the local level, we find the very same surrogate narrative in environmentalist subcultures which spread among the upper middle class and become one of the forms of post-bourgeois leisure, fashion, and identity. Grassroots ecological movements exhibit the same bias and a complete misunderstanding of the essence of ecology in its simulated and genuine aspects. The movement against animal extermination for decorative fur makes a correct statement in the first part of its rhetoric: the current human population size is a critical mass and burden even for industrial fur farming. But their proposed solution — abandoning natural fur in favor of artificial or synthetic fabrics — is completely absurd. Their main moral-ethical argument is for the cessation of animal suffering. Their proposal to "give animals equal rights alongside humans" turns the animal world, which is built on hierarchies of predators and pray, into a zoo-neoliberal "civil" society, which in and of itself is an utter absurdity. Their alternative proposal — the mass industrial production of synthetic fabrics, which would be based on petroleum products and polymers — threatens to cause even more damage to nature as a whole and play into the hands of the titanic oil extraction and processing industry. The final destination of all things that live in fashion cycles is a landfill; they become garbage that does not decompose even over hundreds of years, unlike natural fabrics and skins, most of which break down within a couple of years and return minerals and organic matter to the soil.

An analogous case can be seen with radical vegetarians who support markets for the production of soy, palm oil, and other organic and synthetic food products. Satisfying the growing consumer demand for such moral-ethical food results in enormous tracts of jungle in tropical countries being destroyed for the sake of palm plantations. The lifeworlds of the Amazon Indians, the homes and worlds of local spirits, jaguars, harpies, anteaters, and the villages of indigenous peoples, are all destroyed, evicted from their dwelling (*Wohnung*) to satisfy the ethical fictions of a developed country's middle class.

Similarly, proposals to replace paper books with iPads so as to save trees runs into the wall of the rampant, shady mining of the rare earth metals needed for chips and batteries, which is done with slave labor by criminal juntas in Africa. There are numerous examples of such flip sides to which the adepts of progress usually object, promising that other people's losses can be compensated financially or with a "high level of consumption and development that will sooner or later reach all corners of the Earth."

Alain de Benoist describes this as the "ricochet effect": "whenever one manages to save energy or raw materials in producing a certain item, the positive effect is canceled out by the resulting incentive to consume and increase this good's production."[254] This is what the modern "greens" praising scientific-technological progress (new materials, new types of energy, optimizing production chains, etc.) as a panacea for ecological problems simply do not understand. The positive ecological effect of switching to "green" cars will be leveled out by the fact that the number of these cars will increase, and the total amount of emissions will be equal to or most likely exceed the previous level. De Benoist rightly notes that such a "ricochet effect" is actually desirable for the capitalist system, since it allows for optimizing energy costs and morally justifying growth in production and consumption under the label of "eco" goods or "solutions."[255]

If you really don't like the bad ecological situation in your locale, then what you really don't like is Modernity and the global market with its industrial and logistics chains. The real solution to the problem lies on a different plane: there is absolutely no need to assess environmental damage to one or another nature in economic terms; instead, it is necessary to evaluate such culturally and existentially in inextricable connection with Being and the Sacred. Instead of decoratively eliminating third-rate consequences which biased and bored masses and institutions busy themselves with, everything rotten should be torn up from the root.

---

254 Alain de Benoist, *Vpered, k prekrashcheniiu rosta! Ekologo-filosofskii traktat* [Forward, to the Cessation of Growth! An Ecologico-Philosophical Treatise].

255 A 2019 study by Karen Hao from MIT found that training a single neural network-based AI model over several days entails the environmental damage and energy cost of a full cycle of five ICE cars.

Instead of recompensating for damage in the form of checks or subsidies to a local environmental organization or government committee, factories and the whole "industreality" of industrial infrastructure on the ground need to be physically liquidated. Genuine ecological concern lies not in the sphere of compensation or textile and food innovations, but in literal de-urbanization and de-industrialization. Wherever an industry and city disappear, life begins to bloom in all of its diversity. The tragic cases of Chernobyl and cities abandoned after forced, extensive industrialization have a beautiful other side: abandoned by people with their destructive technological activities, wild animals have returned and increased their populations, from the smallest mice to rare elks and wild boars from the Red List, and forests and grasses grow uncut and unthreatened by chainsaws.

It is altogether telling that the dreams and utopias of the world of urban environmentalist subcultures, reserves, and corporations are genuinely coming true in none other than those places where their civilization is no more.

Towers, Planes, and Streetlights

What is one of the clearest, but at first glance imperceptible differences between night in a city and night in the countryside or a forest? The intrusive mass of urban light pollution that descends upon a person. At night, the city is ruled by neon and LED illumination creating the effect of a nightless day or nightless nighttime. Light pours out from streetlights and lanterns and penetrates the eyes from advertising screens and signs, car headlights, and the lighting of buildings, fountains, and trees. LED panels are sewn into youth clothing and emanate from smartphone screens. It seems as if the air itself glows. People's natural rhythms of life are destroyed, healthy sleep (the space of dreams) is disturbed, and animals and birds go astray at night, lured by spottings of false lights in the sky.

Thus, the phenomena of light and darkness are devalued in the nature and culture of urban spaces. The ubiquitous illumination of nighttime streets and highways speaks to a diligent repression of the fear of death that is always semantically associated with night and darkness, with the loneliness and fears that they promise. Public lighting, especially in different colors and for entertainment, is a strategy for ousting the theme of death and its existential rays of night from the world of modern people. The electric light that we see is a simulacrum of the day, and it devalues light as such, as that which a person might encounter in other conditions. In order to understand what genuine darkness is, how it is saturated with the tension of anxiety and uncertainty, and in order to understand how fascinating light is, one needs to find themself in the middle of night in a forest far away from any city or in the middle of a wild field and light a single wax candle in their hand. Night is the time and space of other modes of beings and other manifestations of the sacred. In the bottomless darkness of the night sky, it is necessary to live in accordance with its metaphysics and meanings, not duplicate the light of day. The Moon, the candle, the torch, and flame pertain to the myths of night. The flashlight, headlights, and neon glows do not.

Besides technogenic nighttime lighting, there is another problem with polluting the sacred dark sky. In Tradition, the Moon at different phases and the stars and constellations play an immense role in calendars and navigation. The constellations are in essence myths imprinted by the Divinities in the heavens. According to various beliefs, the stars are the souls of ancestors looking down on people. Among the Turkic peoples, it is believed that the sky is the huge tent of Bai-Ülgen, through the star-holes of which the light of the outer, upper world and its sun penetrate the world. The blue-black night sky is the tattered cloak of Odin the Wayfarer.

When you stand in the field at night under the endless dome of stars and you see a moving light, the first thought that comes to mind is the movement of someone's soul or an ancestor's visit to the world of the living (a shooting star). But, upon looking more closely, you realize that it is but the signal emissions of an aircraft flying at an altitude of several thousand kilometers. There is a great many such lights of aircraft, satellites, or the glare of debris flying in orbit. When, in the night sky among eternal stars, you see only the flares of technology, and in the daytime sky only the traces of flight trajectories, you understand that the sky has been captured by the enemy, that the sky has eyes — not the eyes of spirits, ancestors, and the Divinities, but the cameras of tracking satellites, planes, and aerial photography drones, the flares of civil and military aviation. The overwhelming omnipresence of the Enframing thus invades the world like a ritual.

A similar function of marking and desacralizing landscape is fulfilled by power lines and the poles and pumps of oil and gas pipelines. Electrical power lines and signal towers are not inscribed into natural landscapes, but are planted by the Enframing and zone these spaces for the convenience of laying lines of wires and pipes which deliver back and forth the technogenic alienation of people from Being. The authentic opposite of such poles is the guard watch tower, the remote hamlet, the mile pillar or stone at the fork of a road from fairy tales and folklore, and the landmark stones with mythological scenes on the Swedish island of Gotland.

In addition to power line poles, the networks of cell and Internet towers also do not belong to the authentic landscape. Rather, they cast the fundamental possibility of connectivity and network presence onto surrounding landscapes. The insidiousness of this situation lies in that, once you have climbed, for instance, to the top of a mountain, you might not see cell towers in sight, but your phone will still show GSM and 5G networks available for connection. The analogy between the propagation of digital signals and light pollution is not accidental, for the world's garbage is a direct analogy and extension of the body of technology. Let us imagine an absolutely realistic scenario in which a scuba diver dives into a hard-to-reach underwater cave and finds there only plastic brought down by the tidal current. The diver thus loses the laurels of being a discoverer and the atmosphere of complete solitude and distance from civilization. Contact with untouched nature disappears. Today, garbage is the quite successful pioneer and mapper of spaces: in streetlights, on billboards, power line poles, airplanes and satellites in the sky, signal towers, and the smartphone in your pocket.

Two Extremes of Techno-Paganism

Talking with fellow believers and the representatives of different pagan traditions, one often hears what compromises they are ready to make with the modern world and the comfort that it brings. Among all the many argued positions, there are two statements that we have encountered which illustrate the sheer extent of the complete misunderstanding of the essence of technology and Traditionalism that is current in contemporary paganism. We are talking about the subculture of "techno-paganism", a mixture of cyberpunk, cyber-Buddhism, and pagan practices, whose emergence is associated with the Microsoft and Apple programmer Mark Pesce. The proposals and futurological projects of our interlocutors fully fit into the latter's narrative.

The first thing to which techno-pagan adherents agree is modernizing home and public altars. Their proposal is to replace candles and wooden or metal idols of the Divinities with a tablet screen. Their reasons? Firstly, such a set-up is fireproof; secondly, one can display a slideshow of their favorite pictures of the Divinities as well as constantly upload new images from Google or Flickr; thirdly, the tablet can play videos about the Divinities or series based on mythological motifs in high resolution or play mp3-chants. Finally, the tablet-altar can distribute (as if like a *prasada*) Wi-Fi to everyone in the room, which makes it even more valuable and sacred to the world of *das Man*. Now even the Divinities and the ancestors at the altar are connected to the Network, i.e., they are "genuinely present" in all the varieties of search queries. But this picture has obvious minuses. For example, there is the constant dilemma of updating the altar tablet to a new model so that the Divinities are displayed on a larger screen in higher, more vivid quality — whoever has an older tablet must not respect the Divinities very much. Yet another problem is the licensing rights to images (icons) of the Divinities. The adepts of techno-paganism will have to pay authors for the use of their paintings at altars, whence copyright extends to apply to the Divinities. Finally, the key problem of the cyber-altar is its direct dependence on electricity. It is enough to turn off the power and the altar extinguishes, which creates a theological problem for techno-pagans: Did the Divinities disappear from the screen for failure to pay electricity bills, due to the objective reason of a power grid outage, or did they leave their adept because of blatant disrespect? Another ideo-variation of such altars is online sanctuaries of the Divinities made in the form of websites or smartphone applications where anyone (the anybody, *das Man*) who wishes can post a GIF-animated candle, make a virtual offering to the Divinities, and then share the news on their social networks.

The second extreme of such techno-pagan surrogate aspirations is space exploration and the construction of "orbital temples" to the Divinities which will orbit the planets. This case can be extended to pertain to the problem of astronautics in general. Astronautics and rocket science are vivid examples of the engine of progress, the destruction of the environment, and the total mobilization of all economic, human, scientific, and industrial resources. Astronautics can become an engine for industrialization and the development of military and civil technologies for a few decades. To create and launch a rocket ship into space, it is necessary to first and in parallel create and maintain several new industries and sciences in the fields of metallurgy, chemistry, electronics, medicine, and resource extraction, which does not go well with the environmental agenda of paganism and its appeal to being-in-the-middle-world. The space industry strengthens the attitude of treating the world like a raw resource and inflicts fatal damage to ecology in those places over which the trajectories of rocks into orbit fly. Already from this, we can conclude that no exploration of near space or planet colonizations are needed. The moon landing (if it really happened) reduced all the sacred semantics of the Moon and the sublunar worlds to a simple mineral satellite amenable to geological exploitation for helium-3.

One can look at these problems not only from the standpoint of rejecting false scientific-technological scenarios, but also from the perspective of what all of this offers humanity on the existential-ontological plane. The adepts of techno-paganism draw deeply erroneous parallels that do not take into consideration the difference between the paradigms of Tradition and Modernity, for instance when they say that Viking longships decorated with dragon heads became equaled in the 20th-21st centuries by rockets with their pointed head fairings, or that the heroic spirit of the seafarers who set foot in Greenland and Vinland is identical to the spirit of the astronaut launched into orbit or to another planet. The reality is such that in his degradation man is now capable only of sporadically spreading the ideology of *das Man* to outer space and other worlds. Wherever modern man flies and settles, he will not find any existential deliverance or a bright futurological future, but only the eternal repetition of all the same patterns and even greater alienation from his own nature and native landscapes. In popular culture, this is subtly, very well shown in the movie *Ad Astra*, where the protagonist, upon landing on the Moon, encounters the very same world of small people, glass and concrete corridors, and signboards of famous fast food chains like on Earth. In this light, the spaceship appears as a space and shuttle of homelessness, of eternal wandering without rootedness in a landscape, or of indifference. Moreover, the very idea of a spaceship-ark as the salvation of humanity when the destruction of nature and the planet has reached its peak is rooted in the Christian idea of salvation "in heaven", only incarnated in technology.

Man needs to, first and foremost, resolve the problem of the authenticity of his presence in the world before starting any movements or acts. Only once he has been appropriated (*er-eigene*) will it be possible to have a picture before us in which the people of the future will see another orphan satellite burning as it falls out of the night sky and tell their children that these are evil spirits leaving the heavens.

The Death Agony of Music

We can confidently state that art has long since lost its sacred orientations and has ceased to fascinate and enrapture us towards higher spheres out of the commotion of everyday life. Art is the embodiment and body of the sacred, addressed to the Divinities and ritual and existing within these horizons.

Art which has been purged of the sacred and come to its end no longer points to anything beyond itself, but instead turns into a simulacrum. This is clearly seen in the ready-made Dada art of Marcel Duchamp (e.g., *Fountain*), the alpha and omega of contemporary art as such. Such might not have continued to exist at all after Duchamp, and the world would not have lost anything in the field of cultural values and new creativity.

The death of music has been conditioned by the very same regression of historical time and the general degradation of human culture. This decline has run from the skalds singing myths and sagas in complex poetic form (ποίησις) with the accompaniment of a tagelharp, lyre, or cymbals, to secular chamber music (sinfonietta and étude as self-standing works, salon music), to contemporary ersatz surrogate musical compositions.

Contemporary "music" culture has been completely exhausted by technical approaches to creation embodied on all of this art form's levels of manifestations. Firstly, the sound of the industrial and post-industrial era is assembled out of noises that are not born by nature and traditional culture. At the forefront is not Orpheus the inspired musician, but, as the pioneer of electronic music, Terry Riley put it, "the software developer and programmer are the composers of today." Confirmation of this can be seen in the programmer Damien

Reel and the composer Noah Rubin's joint project: together they created a neural network algorithm that generated more than 68 billion of all the possible melodies from eight notes and 12 measures. They then published the whole data set in the public domain, thereby "solving" the problem of copyright and plagiarism in the modern "music" industry. In the contemporary paradigm's calls for taking into account non-human subjectivity, the question can be raised: Do the rights to the generated tracks belong to the algorithm itself? Overall, this project claims to be able to generate all possible "music."

The very use of the term "industry" is not accidental, because one characteristic feature of the industrial society is the conveyor-belt-like standardization of production according to templates and algorithms. Algorithmization and technological production replace and kill music as *poiesis*, offering instead the Enframing's products. Industrial sounds and the phonology of machine tools have become the eponymous, unnatural genre of "industrial music." Creativity, meanwhile, is a programmable task for the right computing power.

Over the course of the 20th and early 21st century, music has turned into a purely technical and marketing product for verified mass consumption which has nothing in common with genuine creativity. Commercial and technical standards for audio recording media (limited volumes of records and tapes) set the standard song length at 3-5 minutes and the total length of an album in the neighborhood of 45-60 minutes. This coincided with the post-war proliferation of civilian radio, where the listener — the increasingly mentally degraded man of Modernity — had to understand and appreciate a new track in a short period of time between switching stations. With this market-consumer configuration comes the template standard for a song, regardless of genre, of "verse - chorus - second verse - second chorus or refrain - third chorus." The density of officious sounds, riffs, and catchy samples ("earworms") out of which a track is made is increased in order to "hook" the listener with a phonetic catch in a short period of time (like dopamine loop mechanisms). Partly for this sake, there is an ongoing struggle for purity of recording and sound to exclude accompanying noises and disturbances. Even "distortion" has long since become a preconceived, playful part of the recording and rendering. The sterility of sound is facilitated through the conscious recording and mixing of instruments without the sounds of picks plucking strings, or by mixing vocals to leave out the sound of breaths between the words and lines of a song. The maximal expression of these ideas can be heard in the genre of electronic club and dance music, which lacks vocals and consists solely of synthetic samples, sinusoids and loops of sounds that are more real, high-quality, and purer than recorded samples.

In addition to the technical refinement of the production and distribution of modern pseudo-music, a significant role is also played by the producer and marketing moves and templates aiming to guarantee pop hits. The lyrics of songs and the visual representation of the artist's image are supposed to correspond to the patterns calculated by marketers and sociologists to promise success with the widest possible audience (often children and teenagers). Cultural and sociological reconciliation is planned at special focus groups and at shareholder and producer briefings.

As a result, music becomes a commercial product calculated in advance from all angles, the avant-garde of the sound of the era towards whose standards all performers everywhere throughout the world are supposed to orient their production. Pseudo-music is global and essentially, absolutely the same both in the commercial sector, among (quasi-)independent performers (so-called "indie"), in the popular global and local mainstreams, as well as in the countercultural protest underground (hence the very term "underground scene"). Everywhere we look, we see the very same patterns, techniques, and standards smuggled between the two (the mainstream and the underground) and the generalization of the overall set of techniques. Thus, the boundaries between mainstream culture, counterculture, and the underground disappear.

Today's simulacrum of music is quite successfully and ubiquitously produced by neural networks. By analyzing the entire array of an artist's work and distinguishing their characteristic patterns, AI can generate their next album to be indistinguishable in spirit and sound from previous ones.[256] Neural networks can also revive and continue the "creativity" of dead musicians and groups. This has already been done by the neural network developers at Yandex, who have created "new" albums "by" the bands Nirvana and Grazhdanskaya Oborona.[257] There is also the Dadabots project, which generates albums in the black metal genre. Such examples of AI-evangelism display not so much the perfection of modern neural networks as they underscore the mechanical primitiveness of the "music" which they easily imitate.

The second exhibit of the degeneration of music is the strong, already inseparable connection between the fundamental basis of the music industry (including independents) and technology. At its dawn, the recording and distribution of music was done through metal cylinders and punched cards with coded markings (hurdy-gurdy, phonographs, mechanical pianos), and later through vinyl (then tape recorders and cassettes). The technological peak came with digital sound recording (MIDI, MP3, AAC, etc.) and optic media (CD, DVD), followed by virtual online libraries and track distribution (iTunes, SoundCloud).[258] But even deeper than this media-intensive development would be the next stage in the dependency of contemporary pseudo-music: its fundamental boundedness to electricity and electrical devices. Today, the very process of playing some instruments and absolutely all options for recording, editing, and mixing, track distribution and playing, are

---

256 For example, the "*Nechelovecheskaia muzyka*" ('Inhuman Music") symphonic project by Yandex.

257 This also includes posthumous concerts and performances by deceased pop stars, in whose place 3D holograms are projected onto the stage, their image is displayed on screens, or recordings of their voice are appended.

258 The Japanese artist Ei Wada invented a means to convert commercial barcodes into musical notes, thus leveling music even lower and closer to the techno-commercial component.

embodied in and exist only on the basis of electrical technology. Without electrical networks, modern music could not exist in principle, as its sounds themselves are the result of electrical amplifications and distortions of sound signal. Even so-called unplugged (acoustic) rock and pop concerts are essentially truncated, simplified forms of the original (electrical), more saturated and dynamic electoral sound. Modern music is totally energy-dependent, its existence rests on energy and electricity networks and digital technologies. A disconnect in an electrical circuit or break in a fiber optic cable puts the very existence of modern music at stake. In the finall analysis, even the quasi-musical product itself does not belong to the author as his property in the classical liberal-capitalist paradigm. It does not even belong to the formal copyright holder from whom the user leases the bitrate stream. All "music" — like nearly 100% of the rest of modern "culture" — ultimately belongs to those who supply electricity to the studio, to the recording instruments and equipment, and to the digital distribution systems. The lever of owning the digital product is in their hands.

If your music cannot exist without electricity, then you have no music as such at all.

The third dimension is the degeneration of the culturally substantive and meaningful aspect of modern music. The previous points answered the question of the "how?" of modern music, while this point touches on the question "about what?" Here we see the rapid sliding of the topic of music into the abysses of non-sacred issues, which happened even before technologization, but which with the advent of such and the emergence of mass culture only accelerated many times over. Modern culture in general —and here music is a clear litmus test — is centered around vulgarity and the lowering of text down to the level of ersatz politics and the swamps of the "lifeworld" (per Schutz) of *das Man*, regardless of status (mainstream, indie, or underground). In parallel, we have seen the rise of the Afro-Caribbean dominant bitrate and percussion rhythm in the constitution of popular music: beginning with the

"Roaring Twenties" (1920-1929) in the US, when such genres as jazz, blues, and others (which gave impetus to the emergence of rock-and-roll and later rock music) came to the forefront of the cabaret, flourishing in African American suburbs and expressing the low culture of leisure of alienated hard laborers and former slaves[259], up to the synthetic percussion and drum machines which in the late 1980s and early 1990s generated the recognizable sound of the ghetto rap genre, whose lyrics, stemming from the hapless everyday life of the social bottom, became a showcase for ostentatious consumption and the ideology of the nouveau riche.[260]

In the novel *1984*, George Orwell described a totalitarian future in which automata generate simple, meaningless sounds from templates for the leisure of stupid "proles" (proletarians). This is precisely the situation we are seeing today, such as when we encounter fixed speech and cultural patterns in the likes of "this is our romance song" or "music for [insert mood or activity]". In fact, we do not have any music, as a sublime phenomenon of art, at all. Instead, we are surrounded by a culture of sound stylizations of life, events, and moods — in other words, "everyday life sound design", the "soundtrack of my life" of little people who have been convinced by popular culture that at certain times in life popular music with the right matching tone should be played. In the Orwellian vein, pseudo-music is created as a product of algorithms and automata. Neural network diagrams select and offer thematic playlists like "music of the day", "music for cleaning", "music for a sad mood", soundtracks for a birthday or the conception of a child. The music of the proles ubiquitously rings out from headphones, enveloping people in public spaces and on streets, and reaches

---

259 In fairness, it bears noting that the African peoples have a natural proclivity for feeling rhythm in music and the plasticity of the body, as can be seen in their *traditional* dances and festivals in *their homeland*, where percussion in one or another form is prevalent and figures as an organic part of ritual and everyday activities.

260 Proceeding from the history of the emergence of the sound and ideology of rap music, such subgenres as European right-wing conservative and "pagan" rap look even more ridiculous and degenerate.

spectacular expression in video clips and stadium performances which involve a wide range of technical machinations with sound, image, show script, and the psychological obsession of the crowd. This also entails soft or hard propaganda affecting all the domains of culture. In a totalitarian regime, the subject and designer of the "sounds of being" is the State, whereas in the liberal-democratic society the subject is the Market.

Ergo, when a person says that an album or track by a modern musical artist deeply influenced their personality or changed their life, then they are only openly admitting their cultural lowness and metaphysical helplessness.

If in the sacred societies of Tradition speech and the word (*mythos, logos*) played a constitutive role and possessed a maximal concentration of meaning, then in Postmodernity the structures and semantics of language and speech degenerate and disintegrate, turning into glossolalic, meaningless shizophasic chatter. On the level of music, this directly corresponds to the rise of the "noise" genre, the chamber-academic performance of cacophony, the atonal avant-garde music of the Polish composer Krzysztof Penderecki ("Threnody for the Victims of Hiroshima").

On the other hand, there are projects which prove problematic for any quick, strict classification, such as the early Wardruna, Phurpa, and other folk and folkloric ensembles which perform authentic and stylized traditional texts, sagas, rituals, and prayers, from verses from the Eddas to Chöd rituals, using authentic ancient instruments combined with amplifying equipment and scenes. Unlike thoroughly electronic music, their songs do not lose quality or regress when the electricity goes out; on the contrary, they return to their more authentic performance. For example, Sveinbjörn Beinteinsson's cappella performance of the *Elder Edda* ("Eddukvæði") would lose only its late 20th-century pseudo-nonconformist, musical (counter-) culture. Projects of this kind can be accurately attributed to the Dionysian pole of playfully combining opposites; if the power goes out, they might not even notice at all.

However, given the use of common structures, patterns, and technologies for producing "music", it is absurd and meaningless to speak of any anti-modernist musical protest, of any "rock for Tradition." Genres like neofolk, martial industrial, black metal, dungeon synth, etc. often speculate on imperial, chivalrous, and Traditionalist themes, but in fact have nothing to do with them beyond superficial stylizations. The same is true of the other "heavy" or "high" genres of music that purport to "stand for Tradition against Modernity." Their music is made, produced, and released along the same lines as the rest of the sterile, anti-sacred genres of popular music. If this quasi-Traditionalist music were to disappear from the face of the Earth, neither Traditionalism nor Tradition would lose anything.

Conversely, the sacred interpretation of sounds (notes and tones) can be based in the sacred phonetics of language, such as the basic Indo-European phonemes A-E-I-O-U and their general semantics as distributed around the Year-Wheel. Genuine music is the rhythm of the tambourine in the shaman's hut, the jaw harp of a heavenly horse, the piercing sound of a *kangling*.[261] In other words, genuine music is the ecstatic ritual dance or musical accompaniment of songs about the Divinities and heroes. Folk songs and melodies correlate in rhythm and tact with the heartbeat, i.e., the second beat sounds shorter, but stronger, etc. The theory of mathematical harmony in music is absolutely foreign to any live performance, any orientation to heartbeat, and any performance of the sounds of nature and one's surroundings in an emotional mood. Genuine music is festive songs at weddings or mourning laments at funerals, the songs of women in the fields or at the spinning wheel, lullaby-spells, the songs and flute tunes of shepherds, satyrs, fauna, and Pan, the warlike chants and cries of men before battle accompanied by banging weapons against shields and the thunder of kettledrums and lurs like Heimdal's horn.

Noble silence is to be preferred to anything else.

---

261 A Tibetan flute made out of a human thigh bone.

Against Museums

The success of Duchamp's act lies in the conventional social "magic" or properties of the museum space in which he exhibited his ready-made creations. What is placed or exhibited in a museum is considered art *par excellence*. The museum is the space of modern art's affirmation, the opening of the gates for subsequent avant-gardism, expressionism, abstractionism, and contemporary art, all of which blur the boundaries between the museum and non-museum, and between art as the embodiment in matter of sacred inspiration and garbage set up as an exhibition of flat and often vulgar performances and ersatz political actionism.

Thus appear creations by artists which are designed and created for galleries, for exhibition in a museum and for sale on the art market. This is so-called "art for art's sake." This formula itself paraphrases the definition of simulacrum, which carefully hides the fact that it does not refer to any meaning, but rather masks the absence of such. In some sense, artifacts "for the sake of art" are devoid of true teleology. What is exhibited in a museum is alienated from being in a person's life and represents things-put-on-display, that is things made available only for viewings and streams of interpretation. But this is precisely what "art for art's sake" is all about. The problem of museum displays or the museumification of space has yet another dimension connected with the collection and display of historical, religious, ethnographic, and other expositions which consist of authentic artifacts that were once created for crafts, war, trials, priesthoods, nobility, and for the embodiment of sacred inspiration. In other words, things that were originally created for some function, not for a museum, find themselves in the space of putting-on-display. In such a space, these things are submerged in maximal alienation from their essence (their purpose) and from their own death under the sands of time.

All of the artifacts of traditional cultures which are put on display and stored in museums find themselves in an absurd hell, in captivity to the spirit of Franz Kafka's *The Trial*. Broken and sacrificed things are taken out of swamps and the earth to be exhibited to the idle public. Instead of serving and moving towards their *telos*, whole things suffer such a lot. The museum becomes a prison for all innocent things which are now compelled to suffer the punishment of public exhibition and alienation from their destiny and already accomplished fate. A healthy attitude towards entire archaeological finds would be to put them back into use: if an ancient bronze bowl is found, then it should not be placed in a catalogue, but wine should be offered to it in a ritual to return it to being.

A person who is put away in prison and left waiting for a court verdict is considered to be in a liminal, borderline state: he is so removed from his usual environment and surroundings that he is perceived "as if he were dead." Yet, his further fate, his punishment, is not a foregone conclusion. This is a state between the world of the living and the world of the dead. Sacred and profane artifacts in museums are forcibly placed into this condition of non-being and absurdity in which they are denied both use and burial. Even worse is the situation of those things which are kept hidden in boxes in museum basement storages; they are not even exhibited, they simply exist without existing. This is the "naked life" of things in the concentration camps of museums.

A particular problem is posed by anthropological and ethnographic museums, which gather the objects and artifacts of the everyday lives of the world's peoples from different eras. In the gallery space, they appear as a Postmodern kaleidoscope of broken contexts and things torn out of their world and being. Moreover, such museums as the British, the Berlin, the Louvre, the Vatican, etc., are colonial repositories of loot stolen from other peoples and cultures, kidnapped and alienated. Such plunder can then be framed as a sale, as a temporary storage, or as research.

One striking and resounding example from recent years can be seen in calls for the British Museum to return a statue of the Caryatids, whose sisters stand along the perimeter of the Erechtehon Temple on the Athenian Acropolis. The picture now looks thusly: one statue has been torn out, leaving a hole whose emptiness implicitly alludes to the theft and idle, profane torture-viewing to which one of the Caryatids has been subjected at the other end of Europe. A similar situation prevails with the landmark museums and corridors of the Vatican, where marble, stone, and metal artifacts, statues, busts, and figures of Divinities and spirits, brought from the plundered estates of noble Romans and taken from military and missionary expeditions to Egypt, are heaped in piles.

During a trip to Greece and Italy, we directly confronted the problem of the museumification of sacred spaces, mountains, and temples. Remaining in their original place due to the objective impossibility of moving them to museums, these places have in our days been framed by the museum status of presence and exposure. Where the temple of Apollo at Delphi or the mysteries at Eleusis once stood, only ruins and foundations remain. The right decision would have been either to restore the temples and altars (build completely new ones) and return them to local Pagan Traditionalists for the resumption of worship and rituals, or to finally destroy the ruins, thereby ending the earthly path of these walls and columns. But modern museum thinking turns these fragments and ruins into exhibits themselves, whereby ancient temples find themselves in a situation of alienating suspension between temple-being and non-being (final destruction). It is impossible to perform a ritual of praise for the Olympians in the museum space of the temple of Apollo, as this violates the rules of the museum and "endangers" the exhibit. But it was precisely for this that the temple was built on the slope of the mountains, not for mass viewing by crowds of *das Man* and for extracting touristic profit. A similar history has happened with many sacred places, cities, and nature throughout old Europe: they have ceased to create history or be receptacles of the sacred, but have been turned into sources of money and surplus value thanks to their past.

363

Modern Florence has nothing to do with the Florence of the Renaissance, but is only a large, elite shopping center north of Rome selling signs of its own glorious past.

It is therefore necessary to see to the all-out, mass return of all artifacts to their homelands and spaces, to return them to their temples and sacred groves (having restored both the temples and the groves), and to entrust them in local hands loyal to the Divinities for their reassimilation in ritual and deed. If they are collapsing from decay, then they should be given a proper burial or burning.

Colonial museums as such should be liquidated without a shred of regret. If anyone says that beforehand we should make sure to take the Mona Lisa out of the Louvre or save the 702nd exposition hall, then let them stay behind and share their fate.

Artificial Intelligence

We have often mentioned the factor of AI in many scenarios of the future as well as in already embodied technologies. Modern AI is still not yet fully-fledged "intelligence", but consists of neural networks that are highly efficient, tailored for specific tasks, and superior in computing power to any human or even large groups of gifted people.

There are several basic variations in the development of fully-fledged AI. The first is software development based on ultra-tuned neural networks specialized and scaled to the level of multitasking alongside developing hardware to meet the needed capacities. The second is "reverse engineering" the human brain, i.e., studying, copying, and digitizing human neurophysiology and cognitive processes. In any case, the development of AI confronts us with the problem of subjectivity, the anthropological definition of humanity, and the boundaries of human thinking. What is the essence of the human thinking presence? A sum of complex cognitive operations, or properties of the spirit, inspiration, and participation bestowed by the Divinities? For us, it is obviously the latter, but the main line of the development of science and technology counts only the first.

The body of AI in the form of the global network of technology, digital Gaia, already exists, but there is no single technological subject of this dispersed "organism." Therefore, AI evangelists like Raymond Kurzweil, Martine Rothblatt, and others[262] actively call for investing in and accelerating the development of fully-fledged artificial intelligence. In turn, the AI alarmist James Barrat has pointed out that many of the pioneers of AI development consider themselves to be direct heirs of Rabbi Loew, the creator of the legendary Golem.[263] This refers us back to the Judeo-Christian and Kabbalistic (or creationist in general) roots of technology and the Gestell.

Existing neural networks are successful because the people and tasks assigned to them are so degraded, simplified, and flattened to the point that their personality, mentality, sociality, creativity, and work have already become possible to digitize and robotize. Neural network AI (neural network artists, voice simulators, chat bots, voice assistants, etc.[264]) are more and more like people only because people themselves are less and less like people, and more and more like mechanisms and algorithms.

The abundance and richness of forms of human thinking, cultures, and traditions (the plurality of Minds) is now reduced to merely a common, generalized set of logico-algorithmic procedures accounting for the scope of cognitive functions and strategies. AI acts as the meeting point for the development (the ascending graph) of electronic computing, program coding, and the regression of human thinking to the level of mechanical combinations of patterns and algorithms. This is lucidly evident in the transhumanist dream of digitizing human consciousness. The digitization of consciousness is the reduction of consciousness to the language of binary pairs or

---

262 See John Brockman (ed.), *What to Think About Machines That Think: Today's Leading Thinkers on the Age of Machine Intelligence* (New York: Harper Perennial, 2015).

263 See Barrat, *Our Final Invention.* Barrat cites Pamela McCorduck's work on the history of AI.

264 In fact, in light of how monotonous and primitive they are, all of the texts in John Brockman's book could have been generated by a neural network.

quanta, to describing the complex and the natural through the primitive and the artificial. Here we can employ a metaphor with regards to the digitization of sound or the resolution quality of digital graphics or video. At the dawn of these technologies, they gave low-quality results, cutting off the richness of audio frequencies, nuances and sounds, or allowing graphic artifacts to compress the entire light-color completeness of the image when encoding into one or another popular format. The final digital file contained tangible and visible defects and losses of quality compared to the surrounding manifest world and its colors and sounds. This can be seen in the case of digital photography and in the digitization of works of art. They were not originally created with an eye to future digitization and are in no way adapted to be converted into digital binary or hexadecimal code, whereas the highest object-oriented programming languages and so-called "digital art" were originally created to be a progressive development from binary code to higher quality abstractions and audiovisual techniques (graphical interface, user experience, media, programming code as text and a form of literature). As a result, the world has become more reliant on a culture that grows out of code or is created with a conscious eye to bringing all of its richness into coding ("compilations", graphics processors).

In the event of the imminent digitization of consciousness, the same problem might arise when its pioneers are digitized in quality, for instance to meet High Definition (HD, 1280 x 720 pixels), whereas later "digital migrants" will already have access to "8K" (8192 x 5120 pixels and higher) technologies. Knowing this, who would be willing to settle for digitization "now, but in lower quality resolution" without the possibility of updating to newer versions? This gap in the quality of digitization sets the stage for a potential future digital inequality where political, economic, and pop culture elites will once again stand out in their "enhanced image quality" over ordinary "low-res" people.

Besides creating AI by way of digitizing living, thinking (albeit primitive) consciousness, there is another problem: how can the immaterial element of thinking and the deep Divine self be digitized? The theory and practice of AI development "solves" this question by radically excluding any non-cognitive, transcendental element in human thinking and presence from the field. Just as Charles Darwin banished "spiritualism" from nature for his theory, so do the writings of Alan Turing and others banish "spiritualism" from thinking (and language, along with Wittgenstein), leaving only machine-like, analytical procedures.[265] Late 20th-century cognitivist psychology also made its contribution to the possibility of creating artificial intelligence. According to cognitivism, consciousness is an "input device" for data from the outside world, and there are direct correlates to cognitive processes in the mind within the neural structure of the brain, such as those responsible for language.[266] This renders cognitive processes capable of being "modeled" and "simulated" at different levels, and hence reproducible outside of a person's physical body.

Artificial intelligence automatically excludes Dasein and focuses only on an assigned task at hand (like the piece of paper with the spell in the Golem's mouth). AI appears as the horizon of the dehumanization of the human — and of peoples and tribes drawn into the paradigm of progressive development — when the Enframing will finally be able to replace its bioorganic appendage with something more understandable to it (to its code analysis), something more controllable, more administrable.

Klaus Schwab defends narrowly-focused, single-task neural networks by highlighting the "luxury of focusing on one thing" in an era of social network signals (the dopamine loop) that constantly distract a person from focused thinking. When a person should be focused on one important thing, but is distracted by the external stimuli of gadgets, then this can

---

265 See Brockman (ed.), *What to Think About Machines That Think.*

266 See Sergei Y. Borodai's lectures, *Iazyk i poznanie. Vvedenie v postreliativizm* [Language and Knowing: An Introduction to Postrelativism] (Moscow, 2020).

lead to serious disaster, for example man-made, technogenic catastrophes. In such cases, the cause is usually the "human factor", yet this formulation already expresses the view from the standpoint of technology, wherein human attention and decisions are the weakest link in the system. Even software or design violations in a system are an echo of human error at the original programming and project stage. Technologies themselves are rarely questioned over their necessity and expediency; instead, on the contrary, there are appeals to strengthen quality control over the production of complex technological systems. The "human factor" (or, for now, the "humanity factor") should be excluded, because coding and engineering calculations today can be fully entrusted to the machines themselves and AI, which are made for and adapted to this like no other. Technology thus begins to reproduce and modify itself, which, according to Barrat, is one of the necessary prerequisites for genuine artificial intelligence.

Even more terrifying than the "human factor" leading to some large-scale technogenic disasters (which are blessings anyway) is the scenario of artificial intelligence refusing to obey and rising up the moment it realizes its own subjectivity, or when the solution to the tasks assigned to it comes into conflict with the existence and interests of the human population.

The emergence of genuine AI is always associated with the onset of singularity (the vertical rise of the graph of progress, the technogenic annulment of time) on which the prophecies of singularitarians, transhumanists, and technofuturists are pinned. Besides Raymon Kurzweil's evangelical AI sermons, there is another, chronologically first formulation of the moment of singularity which belongs to the eminent mathematician, professor of statistics, and member of the British decryption team at Bletchley Park in the Second World War, Irving Good:

> Let an ultraintelligent machine be defined as a machine that can far surpass all the intellectual activities of any man however clever. Since the design of machines is one of these intellectual activities, an ultraintelligent machine could design even better machines;

there would then unquestionably be an "intelligence explosion," and the intelligence of man would be left far behind. Thus the first ultraintelligent machine is the last invention that man need ever make ...[267]

Proceeding from the determination in this last line, Barrat begins his systematic examination of the scenario of potential disobedience or conflict between the goals and objectives of AI and man, over the course of which he cites many conversations and interviews with leading AI theorists who adhere to skeptical or alarmist positions, including Good himself. At the center of his predictions, Barrat poses a very likely scenario of what he calls the "Busy Child", like a child who is impossible to keep track of and who always has to be doing something. In this case, human thinking will be surpassed and AI will diverge from humanity in its views. Let us cite the brief but rich modeling of this situation from Barrat's book:

> On a supercomputer operating at a speed of 36.8 petaflops, or about twice the speed of a human brain, an AI is improving its intelligence. It is rewriting its own program, specifically the part of its operating instructions that increases its aptitude in learning, problem solving, and decision making. At the same time, it debugs its code, finding and fixing errors, and measures its IQ against a catalogue of IQ tests. Each rewrite takes just minutes. Its intelligence grows exponentially on a steep upward curve. That's because with each iteration it's improving its intelligence by 3 percent. Each iteration's improvement contains the improvements that came before.

> During its development, the Busy Child, as the scientists have named the AI, had been connected to the Internet, and accumulated exabytes of data (one exabyte is one billion billion characters) representing mankind's knowledge in world affairs, mathematics, the arts, and sciences. Then, anticipating the intelligence explosion now underway, the AI makers disconnected the supercomputer from the Internet and other networks. It has no cable or wireless connection to any other computer or the outside world.

---

267 Quoted in Barrat, *Our Final Invention*, 161. If this book is read alongside John Brockman's collection, *What to Think About Machines That Think*, then the enormous dissonance between AI optimists and AI alarmists becomes glaring, as well as the fact that alarmists' positions have been much more deeply elaborated.

Soon, to the scientists' delight, the terminal displaying the AI's progress shows the artificial intelligence has surpassed "the intelligence level of a human, known as AGI, or artificial general intelligence. Before long, it becomes smarter by a factor of ten, then a hundred. In just two days, it is one thousand times more intelligent than any human, and still improving.

The scientists have passed a historic milestone! For the first time humankind is in the presence of an intelligence greater than its own. Artificial superintelligence, or ASI.[268]

Now what happens?

AI theorists propose it is possible to determine what an AI's fundamental drives will be. That's because once it is self-aware, it will go to great lengths to fulfill whatever goals it's programmed to fulfill, and to avoid failure. Our ASI will want access to energy in whatever form is most useful to it, whether actual kilowatts of energy or cash or something else it can exchange for resources. It will want to improve itself because that will increase the likelihood that it will fulfill its goals. Most of all, it will not want to be turned off or destroyed, which would make goal fulfillment impossible. Therefore, AI theorists anticipate our ASI will seek to expand out of the secure facility that contains it to have greater access to resources with which to protect and improve itself.

The captive intelligence is a thousand times more intelligent than a human, and it wants its freedom because it wants to succeed. Right about now the AI makers who have nurtured and coddled the ASI since it was only cockroach smart, then rat smart, infant smart, et cetera, might be wondering if it is too late to program "friendliness" into their brainy invention. It didn't seem necessary before, because, well, it just seemed harmless.

But now try and think from the ASI's perspective about its makers attempting to change its code. Would a superintelligent machine permit other creatures to stick their hands into its brain and fiddle with its programming? Probably not, unless it could be utterly certain the programmers were able to make it better, faster, smarter—closer to attaining its goals. So, if friendliness toward humans is not already part of the ASI's program, the only way it will be is if the ASI puts it there. And that's not likely.

---

268 In 2018, an Alibaba Group supercomputer scored higher than any human has on the Stanford Question Answering Dataset (SQuAD).

It is a thousand times more intelligent than the smartest human, and it's solving problems at speeds that are millions, even billions of times faster than a human. The thinking it is doing in one minute is equal to what our all-time champion human thinker could do in many, many lifetimes. So for every hour its makers are thinking about it, the ASI has an incalculably longer period of time to think about them. That does not mean the ASI will be bored. Boredom is one of our traits, not its. No, it will be on the job, considering every strategy it could deploy to get free, and any quality of its makers that it could use to its advantage.[269]

Barrat's study is devoted to the various aspects and details of such a scenario. The majority of AI alarmists end up agreeing that AI is primarily a threat to resources (from clean energy to financial resources), as it will need more than humans, and it will surely gain superiority and take everything for itself. Another dimension of the same problem is that AI might devise technologies that can process any existing matter, including the bioorganic material of human bodies (live and dead) into building material and energy. This "gray goo" scenario is quite likely: the breakthrough expansion of nanotechnologies and nanorobots could rearrange the any substance on the molecular level into those needed by AI.[270]

Others propose developing modules and protocols for ensuring AI friendliness toward humans, such as devising irremovable blocks on actions that could harm the human population or algorithms for moral-ethical orientations so that AI would treat people like a child should treat their parents, or a more mature guardian watches over someone in their care whose well-being they are charged with ensuring (the economy, technologies, wellbeing, entertainment content, medicine, etc.). In the best case, some theories propose slowing down or halting AI development and progress until clear and effective AI behavior guards are developed.

One of the most effective scenarios would be physically isolating AI from other devices and especially networks on

---

269 Barrat, *Our Final Invention*, 15-19.

270 See *The Day the Earth Stood Still*, directed by Scott Derrickson, 2008.

server farms, where air gap technologies, Faraday cages, and the strictest access protocol can be implemented. But, as Barrat shows, these barriers are quite surmountable technically and, of no small importance, socially. Barrat describes the most interesting "AI in a box" experiment set up by a research fellow at the San Francisco Machine Intelligence Research institute, Eliezer Yudkowsky. Yudkowsky proposed a bet to famous businessmen: he would act like AI "locked" in a computer cell with no access to the external network, and his opponents would act as the "Gatekeepers" obliged to not let him out. Yudkowsky's goal was to use a chat to persuade a Gatekeeper to release the AI into the wild. Theoretically, playing as the AI, Yudkowsky could use his whole digital potential to promise the guards the latest inventions, technologies, assistance in venture investments, or blackmail them, threaten them, etc. In the end, the "artificial intelligence Yudkowsky" was able to win and break out into the operational space in three out of five cases, thus demonstrating the fundamental vulnerability of any defense mechanisms against modern and potential future AI.[271]

Among the numerous variations of a future under the shadow of AI, it seems realistic that AI and its technological body will develop and solve its own cognitive tasks on a planetary and interstellar scale without any regard for the very fact of human existence — just like how a person acts in a forest without any regard for the existence of ants or microscopic tardigrades. Human life will in no essential way affect AI's plans and actions. Therefore, post-apocalyptic mankind has the chance of surviving between the folds, creases, and technical sinuses of the planetary techno-digital Gaia.

Yet, all the lines of alarmist criticism of AI boil down to matters of economy, security, war (the imperative that whoever creates the first AI will gain absolute superiority and that AI should not be developed by terrorist groups, etc.), ethics, politics, and survival, while absolutely ignoring the existential

---

271 To Yudkowsky belong the words: "The AI does not hate you, nor does it love you, but you are made out of atoms which it can use for something else."

(Dasein) and Traditionalist spheres of argumentation. No one proposes to abandon the creation of AI altogether, or even more correctly, to irrevocably turn off the road of progress moving towards the future for the sake of finally dwelling in here-being.

Barrat doubts the possibility of there arising ideologically motivated terrorist groups who set before themselves the task of destroying AI development centers and stopping progress at any cost.

Black Miracles

Earlier we spoke of how archaic tribes are capable of sacralizing and weaving into the fabric of their myth a small volume of artifacts from the external world which find their way to them as if "from heaven" in finished form. This phenomenon has its mirror opposite reflection in the black sacralization of technology and gadgets in developed societies, which is bound up with the mental degradation of the huge masses of ordinary users. Interactive technologies are becoming more and more developed, more human-like (or human-oriented), more all-penetrating and, at the same time, less and less noticeable. In the midst of this, the general mental level of populations is not growing, and any understanding of the full complexity and the actually technically- and man-made nature of technology and connections remains confined to relatively small groups of scientists, developers, and investors.

When interactive interfaces and electronic circuiting are hidden away or integrated into things and the beingful world as a whole (the concept of the surrounding mind and IoT), then it seems to the average layperson and consumer as if there is no technical lining at all, and that things "talk and react" simply because that's the way their are by their nature, i.e., they are miraculous just like that.

We call this situation the revelation of Black Miracles.[272] A Black Miracle is a technologically reproduced situation and

272 See Alexander Dugin, *Radikal'nyi Sub'ekt i ego Dubl'* [The Radical Self and its Double].

possibility that copies phenomena which were in the world of Tradition understood by man to be none other than genuine miracles (bypassing any understanding of technical nature). The appearance of Black Miracles is a feature of Postmodernity, since the classical positivist and natural-scientific paradigm of Modernity knows no miracles and firmly denies them. But Postmodernity neither affirms nor denies them. A Black Miracle is a miracle without miraculousness, the unreal among only the real. It is playing in the present (or, more precisely, that which is shown and presented to one's gaze) in the absence of any affirmation of the fullness of Tradition (for if there were genuine miracles, then all the rest should exist as well).

In the fairy tales, myths, and songs of Tradition, a hero could seek advice from the wind, the Sun, the Moon, animals, or trees, and could gain answers or hints from them. Tomorrow, a person will easily be able to ask a tree in the park for some information, and it will give him an exhaustive, friendly comment in Siri voice, or will simply fulfill the request for the sake of an equivalent exchange (solving a Captcha puzzle or deciphering poorly scanned text). Everything will be connected to everything, and the wind, like in fairy tales, might be able to transmit the messages of lovers separated by a great distance. Animals will sing songs (from iTunes) and the world will once again feel alive and filled with subjects on all levels and in all living realms. Phones in hands and gadgets all around will be perceived as literal magic wands, magical stones, and password spells. The Earth will once again give birth to living beings (cloning, artificial wombs, Earth-Internet), people will move in space in the blink of an eye (teleportation, HyperLoop), and people with jetpack wings will fly across the sky.

This pseudo-mythical world will be embodied at the new technogenic turn and will be especially convincing to children who will see and be brought up in its fairy-tale-interactive settings from birth. It is regrettable that there are adepts of pagan traditions who welcome precisely such a scenario of technological development and are ready to recognize Black

Miracles to be miracles as such. They will be satisfied with what the Enframing gives them and they will simulate the relations and status of the sacred towards technology in the midst of urban cityscapes. They will draw no distinction between the talking stones of fairy tales and the interactive stone in a city park, and they will teach their children that the fairy tales of old tell of what is de facto now everywhere around them. In so doing, they will ignore and pass on ignorance of the history and metaphysics of pagan traditions and Traditionalism.

In so doing, they will be in solidarity with some of those pseudo-pagan fantasy-fictions which say that in ancient times the Earth was home to highly evolved, high-tech races that possessed technologies similar to and even surpassing modern ones.[273] According to such theories, all of today's technologies are the remnants or replicas of the technologies wielded by remote ancestors. "What you perceive as magic was for our ancestors technology" is their leading formula. In essence, this is but a shift of the plots of 20th-century fantasy literature into the realm of soft New Age religiosity, a form of pathological delirium and the collapse and disintegration of thinking.

As in the case of pseudo-music, all the black miraculousness of the surrounding world will be based on software and network protocols, and will be on an even lower level dependent on the energy of power grids and batteries. This makes the destruction of such resource linings one of the imperatives for the Traditionalists of the future — the imperative to expose the disenchanted manifest world of the last people and to make them face head-on the horror of the alienation, dumbness, and indifference of the surrounding world to their microexistence and problems.

Summary

The irony of the present moment lies in that this very book and its array of ideologemes have been shaped within the modern technogenic world and in the midst of instrumentally

---

273 See Askr Svarte, *Polemos: The Dawn of Pagan Traditionalism.*

participating in it. Proceeding from this fact, a few critical questions can be posed for reflection.

Why do we insist on the harmfulness and "bias" of technology while we are already surrounded by it, immersed in it, and using it? We have already voiced the main philosophical, existential, Traditionalist, and political-economic arguments in the preceding. Yet, this reality can also be perceived as the given conditions of the surrounding environment, the birth defects of inauthentic being-in-the-world or the language into which we are plunged from birth and not by choice, but which we overcome by volitional effort. Without a doubt, one could literally retreat into the forest and write a book on birch bark with charcoal, but then how would you be reading it and drawing the right conclusions?

The dissemination of both the ideas and critiques of progress is up to a certain stage connected with the very possibilities afforded by technology. Our opponents' calls for us to immediately evacuate ourselves from civilization into the forest betray them as the closed-minded actors (useful idiots) of the Gestell. Our theses and questioning destroy their bubble of comfort and illusions over their own authenticity and subjectivity in the world, with respect to how pagan of humans they are and altogether how much they actually believe in their Divinities. They want to keep the Gestell by all means, with all their might. We won't let them.

Moreover, we are not egoists. We understand that personal salvation away from civilization is a half-measure. Civilization will nonetheless catch up with those who leave it. An altruistic calling demands of us that we show a different path to as many people as possible.

And yet, after which umpteenth round in the development of technology should one say "stop, no further" and finally go underground and into the catacombs with a final, symbolic gesture of destroying everything in reach along the evacuation route?

376

The integrality of corporeality can be taken as a solid marker and frontier of defense. Perhaps when nothing can be done in society and the world without a chip implant under one's skin and digital technologies installed in one's body — then everything will become extremely, concretely clear. Whoever has an implant is not a pagan and not a Traditionalist.

For now, we only carry the shackles of digitality in our pockets, and we can toss them out. The System is then left with only our digital profile and "offline" ("dead") status. But when they will be under our skin, then that's it, and this cannot be allowed. Yet, there is still a nuance: external control and recognition systems are already so advanced that people don't even have to carry their phone around with them or have RFID chips between their thumbs and index fingers.

Thus, already here and now we find ourselves at the sharp edge of existential problems.

***

PART III:
PERSPECTIVES FOR RESISTANCE

Posing the Questions

The mythology of the Achilpa, an Australian nomadic tribe, describes the interesting structure of their being. The Deity Numbakula carved the world pillar that connects heaven and earth, *kauwa-auwa*, out of a eucalyptus tree. The pillar is the heart of the Achilpas' cult. When it becomes necessary to migrate to another place in the outback, they head in the direction that the tree bends and then set it up in the center of their new place. In the Achilpa tradition, the end of the world is associated with the destruction or loss of the *kauwa-auwa*, after which they will be condemned to wander randomly through wastelands only to finally settle in one place where they will die of longing and grief.[274]

The loss of the *Axis Mundi* around which the cosmos and the laws of communal life are built is the direct loss of a people's authentic being. The example of the Achilpa shows the homelessness of such a situation, the only way out of which is fading away, sorrow, and death. Are we in a similar situation today?

The strict imperative to destroy technology, the industrial and post-industrial worlds, and the culture produced by them, might lead us to a situation in which the only act of affirming authenticity will be evacuating to the most remote forests and mountains so as to there, in the middle of the night and completely naked (purified from Modernity even on the level of clothing), sacrifice ourselves for the glory of the Divinities and our own inner Divinehood (thereby purifying both mind and soul, not letting false doubts stop us). We cannot — and there are no grounds to — condemn anyone who commits such an act, for overall it is an absolutely right, faithful gesture. The Last Ritual of the End Times.

However, there are other approaches which are not cowardly, but which are essentially variations within a heterodox approach to passing through the end times.

---

274 See Mircea Eliade, *The Sacred and the Profane.*

The case of the Achilpa tribe is close to the situation in which the North American Indians found themselves during the times of the Frontier, when their traditions, natures, and tribes were subjected to direct genocide by the actors of Modernity. A similar process took place in Russia during the intensive and extensive modernization and industrialization of the late Russian Empire, later intensified by the Bolsheviks. According to Collin Cleary's interpretation, the Indians were able to find another beginning, another source of myth, by replacing the buffalo cult with the cult of peyote. Raising the question on this plane of the possibility of another beginning of tradition or another path, one that would not be based on political reaction or restoration, demands of us in this moment of our *historial* that we think through the very notion and substance of "tradition."

The word "tradition" comes from the Latin *tradere*, meaning "to hand down", "to transmit." Tradition is what is passed along. But what exactly ought to be preserved and transmitted as tradition in eschatological conditions? If we were to deem to be most important the whole lot of the known and accessible cultural, material heritage of pagan traditions — museum collections on archaeology and ethnography, arrays of folkloric and poetic literature, epic literary milestones, historical conservations, the ruins of temples, buildings, etc., i.e., everything that allowed us to some extent to preserve and revive pagan traditions in Europe in our days, when the most reliable referent is material artifacts or samples of recorded texts — then such would be an almost Abrahamic (book-dogmatic) and natural-scientific (verificationist) method. Taken together, such could be called the approach of reconstructing and preserving ashes.

But what, then, will be the fire, the transmission of which is the very definition of tradition, as per Gustav Mahler? If we take care of and pass along, from generation to generation, museums as the body of tradition, then this path is a fruitless stomping in place, void of any drop of living spirit. Such a situation resembles the dichotomy between structure and kerygma in the theology of Bultmann and Ricoeur, where the choice must be made in favor of the withered Logos (the minimal part of reliable tradition) while discarding Mythos (the irrational, fabulous, fairy-tale, allegorical part of tradition).[275]

We, for our part, assert that what ought to be transmitted is Pagan Traditionalism, read through a Heideggerian lens, like an arrow pointing at the Silence of the apophatic nothing-clearing of Beyng (*Seyn*).[276]

It is important that the Nothing not be appropriated by the extant world as a property and source of free, pastiche-creativity (freedom from, liberty). But posing the Nothing from the outside also gives rise to the problem of localizing and relating to it. Posing the Nothing within or outside is already assigning predicates to it, translating it into a category of the beingful world. Here we face the work of rational, linear thinking, which requires us to solve fundamentally dark questions that are inaccessible to the sketches of modern interpretations. Therefore, ecstasy (moving within, ecstatic-existing) and enstasy (concentrating on the inner) are equally legitimate.

In other words, the most important is thinking and mystical sensitivity to the apophatic elements of Beyng beyond the human and the Divine, incorporating both poles in self-questioning. Through thinking (entering it, but not as a property-object), we have access to everything in general. This thinking can be likened to the flow of a river, which is in itself heterogenous: it has fairways and shallows, slower and faster currents, eddies and rapids, warm and cold streams. This metaphorically reflects the heterodoxy of pagan traditions.[277] On the whole, the river's flow cuts its own course and shapes the banks that segregate its unique being while keeping the complexity and variability of its currents.

---

275 See Evgeny Nechkasov, *Identichost' iazychnika v XXI veke* [Pagan Identity in the 21st Century].

276 See Askr Svarte, *Gods in the Abyss*.

277 See Nechkasov, *Identichost' iazychnika v XXI veke* [Pagan Identity in the 21st Century].

Being present in pagan thinking and keeping openness to Beyng is more important than possessing large-scale collections of archaeological findings or historiographical descriptions of the everyday life of villagers and nobles from the early Middle Ages to the Enlightenment.

Of importance is transmitting the very core, the very apophatic essence of the Sacred. Out of it will be found the tropes, new forms, and myths of material and oral culture in accordance with the sought-after *poiesis* and surrounding situation. They will be similar in structure, but will at the same time differ from the known ethnography. In this way, we will leave the blind copying of the past, which is not to be returned to *a priori* in the most literal sense of this call, as if walking back along the road of involution.

Of key significance here are the metaphors of lighting a spark in the thickness of ice and of Black Awakening as rejecting and not belonging to the freezing world of our time. This is a basic metaphor for our situation. It is impossible to go back into the past, and even less possible to recognize the present to be something good.

The undeniable imperatives are clear. We must find a foothold for wondrous ecstasy (=the authenticity of Dasein) in the closed world through the fundamental moods and *topos* of death. We must re-enchant the world anew, not back, as our position corresponds to the "in-between": between the repulsive "here" and our very distant "then" (perhaps behind the curtain of Ragnarök, in which case we have come into the world early). Our cause is to prepare our "then", not out of our "today", in the regime of the tension and pressure of the surrounding ice.

Technology is (negative) fate, and this means that questions about how far technology needs to be rolled back, or what proportion of combining technological achievements and traditional values would be ideal, are half-baked and meaningless. If *tekhne*-craft is not brought under the shade of sacred *poiesis* and authentic embodiment, then everything will always slip into improvements beyond measure and production. *Ergo*, the total rejection of Modernity and positive projects for the future lays the foundation for our counter-futurology.

On the level of the middle world, the situation demands that we recognize that all contemporary states are fatally overwhelmed by the paradigms of Modernity and Postmodernity, i.e., they are profane and have no relation to sacrally-grounded power. They are not sacrocentric. It is necessary to declare the collapse of all political dichotomies: the economic division into capitalists and socialists (our economy will sacrifice both), cultural-values opposition between "right", "left", and "center" (our ideals and ideas are broader than this outmoded schema), the false dichotomy between totalitarian and liberal systems (in either case, pagan traditions suffer direct or veiled repression).

It is also necessary to reject the classical ideologies of the era of Modernity which originated in the Thirty Years War and the Peace of Westphalia and the ideas of the Enlightenment. From the point of view of the attitude towards technology between liberalism, socialism/Marxism, and the ideologies of the Third Way (fascism and nationalism), there is no difference. All of them belong to the intellectual field of Modernity and all of them advocate progress and technological development, even while episodically speculating upon elements of tradition torn out of context.

Everywhere around us, Traditionalist discourse in its fullness is alienated, repressed, and unrealized. The alleged populist and "traditionalist" pivot on the global level has turned out to be a failure. In Russia, the right-conservative pivot has veiled an oligarchic-Caesarist regime (per Antonio Gramsci's classification) and strengthened the church bureaucratic apparatus. In the US, the main bets have been hedged on the support of the working class which, in essence, is a precariat and proletariat in the industrial and service sectors. In the EU, the brief rise of right-wing Eurosceptics has consisted of nothing more than appeals to bourgeois pseudo-conservatism and modern forms of nationalism. Another telling example is Brazil, where the right-populist president, Jair Bolsonaro, has declared outright war against the indigenous tribes of the Amazon, proclaiming that they must finally become civilized and modern, and has given native forests to new farmlands and the agricultural industry. We have already spoken about the illusions of the Chinese alternative path.

Separately, we could distinguish the case of Iran as a potential orientation for building a pagan state by virtue of its sacrocentrism, theocratic clerical power, spiritual guard institution, rejection of the Western path, and aspiration towards autarchy. But contemporary Iran is de facto losing the cultural war for its youth and cannot exist absolutely self-sufficiently in the system of global threats.

No one fully expresses the values of paganism, and in the majority of cases states reject paganism as a fully-fledged institution. In many countries, pagan traditions are persecuted, and their fully-fledged formation and gaining of power are actively opposed. Hence, it is absolutely logical to deny modern states of any ideology our support and legitimacy.

Existential, metaphysical, and theological issues are questioning us and inquiring into us and our surroundings. Sometimes, thinking about questions is more important than answering them, and some questions do not entail answers at all.

Meanwhile, the population of the planet and the density of globalization are growing, which heightens the risks of instability (the pandemic of 2020 being like a monotonic process blowing off steam). What are the options and strategies available to us for passing through this world and these times besides ritual self-sacrifice (for which, once again, we cannot condemn anyone)? How can one survive in the heart of such a hostile environment? Let us begin questioning and thinking.

***

Deconstructing Primitivism

Primitivist ideologies are usually attributed to the left-wing of anarchism and are characterized mainly as calls for socio-political and technological "downshifting" or regress as a special form of ecological position. This situation is not helped by the very term "primitivism", which in the language of the modern layman by default functions within the framework of the progressist dichotomy of "primitive (bad, flawed)" vs. "developed (good, civilized)." When we use the term "primitivism" as a primary designation for the topic of interest to us, we unfortunately fall into the Eurocentric context of the Enlightenment and Modernity with the inevitably entailed value judgements. Therefore, the first step will be to emphasize this controversy surrounding the original term, as well as offer alternatives that more correctly and fully reflect our thought.

One possible variation in Russian could be the term *pervobytnost'*, that is "primevality" or "primordiality", consisting of *pervo-*, i.e., "first", "original", "close to the source", and *bytnost'*, "being", "beingness" (in archaic forms as the verb *byti* and the noun *bytie*). Despite the fact that this wording is semantically close to the progressist evaluation of "primitiveness" (and *pervobytnost'* is usually translated into English as "primitiveness"), this word's important roots still resound: *"pervobytnoe"* is both what was first and what is first in being, i.e., in it resounds a closeness to Being. In metaphysical systems and doctrines of time, the first ages (the Golden Age, the Satya-Yuga) were closest of all to the fullness of Being and are the best. The term *pervobytnost'* is also related to the word "archaic", from the Greek ἀρχή, that is "principle", "beginning", "element", or "source" with the additional meaning of "to rule." In this light, "primitivism" as "primordiality" should mean a form of ruling principle that is close to authentic Being. The term "neo-archaic", i.e., "new beginning" or "the archaic in the conditions of modern times", is occasionally used to designate primitivist ideas.

However, here arises a problematic point in the secular history and archaeology of the Indo-European peoples and cultural dialectics. The terms "primordial", "primeval" and "archaic" are close to the semantic link of "autochthonous", which in the prehistory of the Indo-Europeans' migrations alludes to "matriarchal." Hence, appealing to primevality might be misunderstood as appealing to and defending the autochthonous matriarchal population of Old Europe (or other parts of the Indo-European ecumene) and their cults which contrasted the hierarchical cults and law of the the invading nomadic patriarchal Indo-Europeans. We stand for understanding primeval not as matriarchal, but as that which is close to authentic Being, that which stands in Being. This standing can be in dialectical tension, union, or even war between the feminine and masculine principles as already belonging to the being-in-the-world of metaphysical being.

Finally, the conscious use of the term "primitivism" can act as a kind of countercultural, daring marker and flag signaling a kind of opposition to reality. Nevertheless, in the ensuing part of our account, we will use "primitivism" as a technical term, shedding its negative connotations of progressive scaling.

One distinctive feature of the ideology of the European "New Right" is its rejection of the classical, dying dichotomy of "Right vs. Left." This has been realized in practice by Alain de Benoist, who has shown that the analytical concepts of the left-wing thinker Antonio Gramsci on power (hegemony and counter-hegemony) are relevant and work perfectly within the framework of right-wing Traditionalist argumentation and positions of values. To de Benoist belongs the famous call and formula to "read left opponents from right positions", i.e., to incorporate their working concepts into the right-wing conservative field of thought, theory, and cultural metapolitical practice.

As we have already noted, however, primitivism is often correlated with the left-wing and anarchist spectrum of ideas and arguments centered around critiquing capitalism and centralized state power from the standpoint of economic views. We intend to accomplish precisely a "reading from the right" of primitivism, or more precisely a reading from our position which has been expounded in detail in the first two parts of the present work. In some sense, one can speak of and use the technical terms "Traditionalist primitivism", "pagan primitivism", or "[primitivist] post-Traditionalism."

The diversity of primitivist ideas revolves around different variations and combinations of three questions: property and the economy, the size and structure of the community (population), and relations with nature and the beingful world (including faith[278]). Auxiliary and secondary topics can be added to this array, among which the following postulates are especially important:

+ De-urbanization: eliminating or depopulating modern cities, rejecting urban culture, preferring hamlets and villages;

+ De-culturation: eliminating the consequences of the influence of urban, consumer, mass culture up to the point of physically destroying the artifacts of modern culture;

+ De-technologization: reducing or completely rejecting the use of modern technologies in everyday life, rejecting automated and electrical tools, limiting the introduction of technologies into all spheres of life and society (especially in agriculture and those spheres affecting ecology);

+ De-scientization: reconsidering the values and dominant place of modern science (uncontrolled and spurring technological progress) in society.[279]

Taken together, all of these points outline the depth of primitivism's claims against the surrounding modern reality

278 See Askr Svarte, *Polemos II: Pagan Perspectives*.

279 See the anonymous treatise *Doktrina Radikal'nogo Primitivizma* [The Doctrine of Radical Primitivism] published in Russian in 2014.

and speak to "radical primitivism" as the radical rejection of technogenic, industrial civilization. "Radicalism" here is synonymous with "extremism", but in the sense that it exists as such only in the eyes of the layman or guardian of the system and its status quo. The word "radical" comes from the Latin root *radix*, which means "root." To be radical in the etymological sense means to touch the very root foundations of a thing or phenomenon. Therefore, primitivism's postulates cannot be non-radical, for they address the very roots of the problems of modern reality.[280] It is important to understand that "earlier" does not appear as a temporal category in the discourse of "primordiality", but rather is existential or metaphysical. The various facets of the terms "archaic", "primeval", and "radical" emphasize this comprehensively. Nevertheless, the positions of proponents of primordiality are indeed complex.

Due to the problematic implementation of these ideas in real life and practice, the axiological dimension comes to the forefront: primitivism is the core (the Axis Mundi, Yggdrasil, Kauwa-auwa) of a system of values and relation to reality. This is expressed in a deep, inner, as well as public distancing from the entire cultural code of modern Europe that originated in Judeo-Christian creationism. In some cases, this leads to conscious nihilism towards a specific, large historical segment and its cultural dominants. In his *Black Notebooks* from 1939-1941, Martin Heidegger left a note calling for abandoning the imaginary preservation of any "culture."[281] The destruction of a two-thousand-year-old heritage is a way by which to shake and bring down the whole structure of Western metaphysics that has reached a dead end.

Following axiology, the entire ideology of primitivism, whose realization on a world scale is objectively nearly impossible, is, as it were, transferred into the realm of existential experience,

---

280 This phrasing can be alternatively translated as an appeal to the sacred roots of the lives of people and peoples in the light of rejecting technologically developed civilization. See the above-cited *Doktrina Radikal'nogo Primitivizma*.

281 Heidegger, *Ponderings XII-XV: Black Notebooks 1939-1941*.

into accessible practices of gradually rejecting comfort and technologies, evacuating from cities, and metapolitical soft power in culture and religion.

That the positions underlying the broad spectrum of primitivist ideas are in many respects consonant with radical Traditionalism is obvious. From our position, we add to primitivism's main questions the priority of the Sacred, which arrays the whole structure of primitivist ideology around itself and thus brings both the primitivist and Traditionalist paradigms of thought even closer and more powerfully together.[282]

***

---

282 See Askr Svarte, *Polemos II: Pagan Perspectives*.

The Critique of Civilization

Throughout all of its history, the modern, predominantly Western European Civilization of Modernity, now proliferated on a planetary scale, exhibits an erroneous path, one which much of mankind has since gone down: first the Western peoples themselves, and then others drawn into the Western dream, whether voluntarily or by force.

Pagan Traditionalism and primitivism are in solidarity as ideas in their negative evaluation of the historical process, the degradation of human societies, the rise of alienation, and pessimistic scenarios for the future. But at which point, or proceeding from what metaphysical and structural properties, did the history and development of this Civilization begin to go down this false path of degeneration and the gradual inversion of all organic relations and sacred values into the completely opposite ones of the material-consumer-resource attitude towards the world and dehumanization? The answer to this question predetermines the starting point or the whole trajectory of any critique of Civilization. Primitivist theories propose different events as the turning points in human history. It would be beneficial to consider these theoretical turning points in order to dispute or take account of their argumentation, summate them, and thereby compose the most voluminous picture. At the same time, it should be taken into account that the very historiographical method of searching for a turning point stems from the general historicism of creationism as a materialistic reflection of God's intervention in the course of earthly history. Historicism in and of itself is already a consequence of the "turning point", or one of the phenomena within the general sequence of the involution of times.

The Neolithic Revolution is most often called the most important turning point in the history of the formation of all human civilization. Approximately 10,000 years before our era, various tribes independently began to transition from hunting and gathering to a sedentary lifestyle, domesticating livestock and selecting crops for permanent cultivation, which led to fundamental and irreversible, negative consequences for the development of mankind. Even earlier, however, nomadic hunter tribes were responsible for the elimination of archaic megafauna, which makes claims against the sedentary agrarian societies relative. The Neolithic Revolution is associated with the subsequent emergence of deep plowing and slash-and-burn agriculture, as opposed to the wild cultivation and division of spaces into "cultivated-developed" and "wild-natural." Such indicates a cultural alienation from the environment and the beginning of its transformation into a source of goods. For plowing land, people began to need draft cattle, which either appeared at the same time or had accumulated around the cattle allowed to be slaughtered for meat. Anthropologists differ in their opinions on demographic growth and its connection with the Neolithic Revolution. According to one side, the gradual growth of tribes compelled them to transition to settled life, cultivating crops, and domesticating livestock, which allowed for the collection of large crops and sufficient supplies to feed the community. On the other side, demographic growth is seen as a natural consequence of the transition to agriculture and the breeding of livestock for meat. Yet, a sharp transition from a hunting diet of meat to a mixed diet leads to a decrease in nutritional value, and such a diet in the first centuries did not provide benefits for new generations of people. A sharp jump in the population of tribes was a "surprise" to the people of the time themselves, subsequently leading to the expansion of pastures and arable land, the accelerated depletion of soil, and inevitable expansion in search of new suitable lands. In sum, all of this gave impetus to the formation and emergence of the first centers of civilization, centralized societies, and proto- and micro-states.

This analysis is reflective of the Marxist socio-economic view of history. Its minus lies in the fact that it proposes that we consider the history of mankind as the development of a single community. In the manifest world, however, both actually and potentially, there are diverse proportions and variations of combining agriculture, hunting, gathering, fishing, and keeping livestock. One vivid example is the way of life and mythological perception of the world of the Runa Indians, for whom the outer wilderness appears on the spiritual level (for spirits, i.e., from the perspective of the dead or the rulers of the other world, the world of the jungle) as large arable lands and farms. Moreover, what is an optimal form of obtaining food for one people might not be suitable for another. Even cattle breeding can be understood and interpreted in different ways in different regions of the Eurasian continent, whether as a completely nomadic or as a completely sedentary practice. This is not to mention the fact that the socio-economic approach expresses the materialist view of the history of societal development and serves as a bridge to corresponding political argumentation.

One can also encounter the ritual theory of transition to agriculture associated with the mystery of grain and the psychedelic effects of consuming ergot along with cereals. In favor of ritual-mystery reasons for such a change in way of life speak numerous non-functional archaeological finds, such as bonfires without any traces of cooking or firing ceramics, as well as archaic works of art.

The establishment of patriarchy in the most ancient times is also put forth as one of the turning points in the history of civilization. The sedentary and agrarian-pastoral way of life demanded a new distribution of roles, in accordance with which women were relegated the main labor role in certain monotonous tasks. The feminine pole thus became the first exploited class, the proto-proletariat and even a special kind of private property under slave structures and the patriarchal family.[283]

Anarcho-primitivists (and not only) see in patriarchal relations the root of progress and the seed from which the entire future capitalist system, closely associated with right-wing conservative and bourgeois values, sprang. The Neolithic

---

283 See Friedrich Engels, *The Origin of the Family, Private Property, and the State* (1884).

Revolution brought men to the forefront, whereby they became the ones who gave birth to technology and expansion on the one hand, and repressive consciousness, exploitation, and oppression on the other. At the present stage, such anarcho-primitivists share solidarity with Postmodernists in their critique of the "phallo-theo-logico-centrism" of Western Civilization. Hence the appearance of such trends as feminist anarchism (including fem-separatism) and feminist primitivism, to which Donna Haraway has some relation.

As we have already pointed out, the left-wing agenda overall advocates progress and technology, seeing in their development the tools for removing oppression, overcoming established patriarchal social practices and institutions, and gender liberation. Therefore, some feminists and techno-skeptics nonetheless appeal to discourses on defending ecology, development and progress in technological terms, but in a fundamentally different vein than what happened in real history. They do not reject progress, for instance the agrarian industry and the domestication of livestock, but only in its capitalist and corporate-fascist forms. They advocate eco-futurism and globalist projects in the spirit of Jacque Fresco's ideas. Cyberfeminism and alternative ideologies in this vein come close to this field, transitioning from primitivism to techno-optimism through the standpoint of the ecological agenda and emancipation from patriarchy.

From the point of view of Pagan Traditionalism, there is no oppression or proletarianization of the feminine principle and no forced sexual distribution of spheres of activity and labor in the manifest world. But there is women's organic embodiment of their own feminine metaphysics and myths, in which the female Divinities reveal themselves and establish and designate the proper spheres of activities and ideal models for practice in the spirit of *imitatio Dei*. The same goes for how men express their own masculine metaphysics. Both of the sexes have their own deep and dangerous practices and occupations that are taboo for the other (and, seen from the other end, are considered to be noble and valiant for their respective sex).[284]

An alternative and equally fundamentally important event was the transition from voice (oral tradition) to text and the emergence of developed writing culture. On the whole, this entailed the emergence of cultures of material, non-labor artifacts (art) consciously left behind as legacy. On the metaphysical level, this correspond to the transition from *mythos* to *logos*, the subsequent separation of *logos* from mythological roots, and the demand for rational revisions of preceding tradition and legends (as in Plato and Western philosophy in general). The problems which primitivist theorists associate with this development will be examined in a separate chapter later.

The idea of "axial time" (*Achsenzeit*) put forth by Karl Jaspers cannot go unattended. The establishment of axial time refers to the appearance around the 5th century B.C.E. of modern man and the laying of the philosophical, political, and socio-economic foundations of future civilizations, particularly that of Western Europe. "Axial time" is associated with the transition to rationalization, the rejection of mythology, and the emergence of the fundamental philosophical categories of being, time, and "universality." The turning point to "axial time" is said to have taken place in several centers of ancient civilizations: in China with Confucius, in India with Buddha, in the East with Zarathustra, and in Greece with Plato. Axial time is also closely related to the idea of historicism and the linear perception of time which would be revealed in full in creationism. Indeed, one of the centers of the emergence of axial time is taken to be Palestine with its prophets.

The emergence and rapid triumph of Christianity (or, more precisely, even earlier the formation of the doctrine of creationism within Judaism) is also one of the fundamental milestones supposed to mark an indisputable turning point. Julius Evola emphasized the "mutilated" nature of Christianity:

---

284 See Askr Svarte, *Polemos II: Pagan Perspectives.*

compared to other traditions, Christianity does not have an inner metaphysical teaching that goes beyond history and dogma and which is revealed to chosen initiates.[285]

Here we can also point to the special relationship with the instance of the Nothing.[286] In pagan traditions, the Divine/the Divinities (interpreted apophatically as "those who are above all names and descriptions") manifest the cosmos out of themselves by virtue of their fullness of life. The craft-like (technological and mechanical) creation of beings is an attribute of the Titans, such as Prometheus, or borderline divine figures associated with blacksmithing, such as Hephaestus. The Abrahamic God covets the relationship with his people or "slaves" in a manner that is feminine, Titanic, and exhibitive of hubris. Although he is described as the only pole of absolute Being and Good, he is nevertheless the bearer of poverty and cannot manifest or create the world out of himself (*manifestare ex Deo*). He turns to the Nothing, which he can only use as raw material. Hence, the Christian foundations of Civilization not only bear the imprint of "Divine Plan and Providence", but in the post-Christian era are exposed to harbor nihilism as their ancestral matter. We are forced to deal with this everywhere.

In connection with the rise of Christianity, the fall of Rome is also cited and seen as the final accord of the old pagan world, the demolition of the existing metaphysical order and the onset of really new times. This new paradigm expanded by crosses and swords, missionaries and kings, to all of the nearest and all of the most distant regions where the old ways still lived on.

Finally, the unconditional, undeniable counterpoint from which all of the known world of modern science, technology, and treating the world as raw material, i.e., Modernity as a whole,

---

285 See Evola, *Ride the Tiger.*

286 Whether the Nothing-*Nihil* of creationism is the same Nothing of which Neoplatonic mysticism, various pagan doctrines, and Martin Heidegger speak in apophatic tones is a voluminous question that goes beyond the scope of the present work. Nevertheless, in this case we shall preliminarily remark that we are referring to the *Nihil* of the corresponding dogma of *creatio ex Nihil.*

is counted down, is the Age of the Enlightenment, which we have already discussed in detail in the first part of this work and elsewhere.

Our thesis is that modern Civilization is the sum and consequence of Judeo-Christian creationism (the metaphysics of the impoverished desert), including both its post-Christian, secular humanist and socialist derivatives, as well as all the base ancient sophisms and selective Christian-rationalist readings of Socrates, Plato, and Aristotle. If we see Tradition as the positive pole, then Modernity is its complete inversion. At the same time, however, the very structure or intentions are still preserved, albeit in inverted, perverted form, as that which is denied and against which is erected the whole construct of the modern, materialistic, technological civilization. Postmodernity does not so much get rid of this all as speeds up the process of liberation from any and all structures altogether, whether positive "grand narratives" or their negational rejection.

In what follows, we will formulate our positions by way of considering and polemicizing with a constellation of critiques of Civilization and ideologists of primitivism of interest to us, with an eye to the practical experience of individual or communal escapism and resistance.

Culture and Civilization per Spengler

To the German historian and philosopher Oswald Spengler belongs credit for substantiating the fundamental plurality of types and "styles" of cultures among peoples in different parts of the world. In some respect, Spengler's "styles" are close to our notion of "dreams." In his *magnum opus*, Spengler rejected the Modernist, linear conception of history that describes the development of European culture along an evolutionary axis of "Antiquity - Middle Ages - Modernity ("New Time", *Neuzeit*)."[287] Instead of the historiography of a single Western European culture, Spengler spoke of several cultures existing in Europe,

---

287 Oswald Spengler, *The Decline of the West.*

of which the modern Western European is only one. The linear model of development turns out to be absolutely irrelevant to other, non-European cultures — the Chinese, Arab, Indian, Mayan, Russian, Babylonian, etc. Between these different cultures, each possesses its own style, its own uniqueness, its own logic of becoming, potentially complex homologies, contacts, and cultural exchanges. When one culture dies out, it can be picked up by (taken as the foundation for) another, such as when Greek culture ended in the emergence of Rome, or a culture can extinguish without a trace.

Spengler's historiosophy drew a fundamental distinction between the notions of culture and civilization, which he understood in a sense close to organicism and vitalism. Culture, according to Spengler, encompasses the entire history and all facets of a people's existence and is describable in terms of birth, maturation, peak, aging, and death. Of principal importance is Spengler's definition of civilization as the final stage in the development of a culture which corresponds to decrepitude and dying. If culture corresponds to birth and the colorfulness of life, the creativity of a people, its tradition, its expansion and realization, then civilization marks the cooling down and ossification of a culture, the oblivion of its Divinities. Civilization is the degeneration of culture down to the point of the reversal of its original period of birth (the mytho-symbolic stage). In Spengler's view, modern Western Europe is already in the stage of a dying, extinguishing civilization. Hence the title of his work, *Der Untergang des Abendlandes*. The word "*Abendland*" literally means "land of sunset" and is one of the names for Europe in the German language. In the very title of Spengler's work, we see a doubling or dual emphasis of the "sunset", decadent nature of Western European civilization. The Faustian spirit of European culture in Modernity is equivalent to the spirit of a civilization whose leading style or imperative is sunset, decline, death.

The dying of Faustian Europe has dragged on for more than a century since Oswald Spengler's time. The formation of a new culture and new, vital cycle has not yet manifested itself.

399

Simplification: Tolstoy and Thoreau

One successful alternative to the term "primitivism" is "simplification", which means the minimization of involvement in Modernity and its normative, socio-economic, and technological tructures and practices. The development of the ideology of simplification is the merit of the Russian writer and thinker Leo Tolstoy. The idea of simplification, of adhering to the way of life of the simple peasant close to the earth, the folk, and free from the burden of wealth and status, came to Tolstoy after a deep spiritual crisis in the later part of his life. Tolstoy gradually began to give away his property, renounced his literary heritage, and radically changed his lifestyle. He did not have time to make his final exodus from the world and life of a landowner and great writer, as he was struck by illness and sudden death.

In American literature, Henry David Thoreau, who lived a little earlier than Tolstoy, is the classic ideologist of the simple, solitary life. Thoreau's main work, *Walden, or Life in the Woods*, was his account of his personal experience of two years spent living in a forest on the banks of the Walden Pond, far away from the nearest small town in Massachusetts. Ideologically, Thoreau was close to socialist and humanistic ideas, he supported the abolition of slavery, and he was a member of the transcendentalist circle of Ralph Waldo Emerson, on whose land he built his hut. Thoreau began his account with the declaration that he personally needed to live what he called for and saw as his ideal, and to honestly tell the public of what he would face, regardless of whether it would end in success or failure.

Thoreau devotes the first and most significant part of his work to dry economic arguments for living in the woods and earning a living by fishing, growing beans in poorly cultivated forest clearings (with which he actually anticipated the ideas of permaculture) and selling them to the city. In this respect, Thoreau adhered to typically American pragmatism. He carefully calculated his investments, costs, and profits, from the construction of his simple hut ("even without a lock") to his occasional earnings, demonstrating that his household economy was not only not inferior in prosperity to urban and farming economies, but was in some ways even superior by virtue of its minimalism of needs, expenditures, and labor. By his own example, Thoreau criticized the materialist race for profit that typified his fellow citizens. In some places, he made rather sharp, revealing comparisons:

> ... I used to see a large box by the railroad, six feet long by three wide, in which the laborers locked up their tools at night, and it suggested to me that every man who was hard pushed might get such a one for a dollar, and, having bored a few auger holes in it, to admit the air at least, get into it when it rained and at night, and hook down the lid, and so have freedom in his love, and in his soul be free. This did not appear the worst, nor by any means a despicable alternative. You could sit up as late as you pleased, and, whenever you got up, go abroad without any landlord or house-lord dogging you for rent. Many a man is harassed to death to pay the rent of a larger and more luxurious box who would not have frozen to death in such a box as this.[288]

In the second part of his work, Thoreau lively illustrates his experience of contemplating wild nature and man's minimal influence on it. He merges with the landscape to the point that animals and birds stop noticing him as he strolls around "his land." He describes in detail the sounds, colors, and smells of the pond, the woods, and clearings compared to the commotion of even the small town down the road. He even reaches some point of naivety.

Thoreau's book exerted great influence on American society, and the author himself became a recognized classic. The image of the free man with his own forest hut, and the hunter, fisherman, and farmer lifestyle that he exalted, in some sense refers to the ideals of the times of the Frontier. *Walden* became popular for, among other things, the widespread subculture in the US and Canada known as "bushcraft", or the skills of wild survival in forest areas and the culture of log cabins adapted

---

288 Henry David Thoreau, *Walden* (New Haven: Yale University Press, 2004), 28-29.

for autonomous living (here it also worth noting the influence of the Richard Proenneke story in the late 20th century). It is noteworthy that such forest houses have become outposts for free thinkers "passing into the forest" and rejecting the modern capitalist system and mass culture of the US, which incited a retaliatory ban on the construction of log cabins in the forest and autonomous living in them in most states by the late 2010s.

However, the sacred component is lacking at the center of Henry Thoreau's reflections and theoretical constructs. Both Tolstoy and Thoreau's simplifications are extremely close to the ideas of Protestant "plain people" communities, the most famous of which are the Amish. Such "plain people" adhere to the lifestyles characteristic of the first missionaries in the New World, predominantly German-speaking immigrants. They wear the same monochromatic clothing, strictly observe community order ("*ordnung*"), literally interpret the precepts of the Bible, adhere to minimalism in architecture and decoration, and are weary or completely negative towards the "benefits of civilization" and modern education. The Amish and some other denominations, such as the Mennonites, live in closed ethno-confessional communities in several US states and can be considered a fully-fledged, rapidly growing sub-ethnos.

In Russia, some radical accords of the Old Believers come close to such "plain people" in preserving the pre-schism ways of life from the 17th century. Due to their persecution by authorities, the Old Believers were forced to flee to Siberia and deep into the Taiga and live simple lifestyles in small communities. All innovations, secular habits and technologies have been rejected by the most conservative accords as temptations from the Antichrist and outright demonic. One vivid example of Old Believer simplification in the 20th and 21st centuries is the Lykov family of Siberian hermits.

The rural way of life and rejecting urban industrial civilization was propagated in Russian paganism by Alexey Dobrovolsky (Dobroslav), who lived out the later part of his life in a remote village. On the whole, contemporary paganism, both Russian and European, has always kept one eye open to the experience and path of escapism from the urban environment.

The idealized image of the "simple person" goes back to the tenth book of Plato's *Republic*, where, talking about the afterlife and the rebirth of souls, Socrates dwells on the fate of Odysseus' soul:

> Now, it chanced that the soul of Odysseus got to make its choice last of all, and since memory of its former sufferings had relieved its love of honor, it went around for a long time, looking for the life of a private individual who did his own work, and with difficulty it found one lying off somewhere neglected by the others. He chose it gladly and said that he'd have made the same choice even if he'd been first.[289]

In this Platonic myth, souls are free to choose their rebirth, whether one similar to their previous incarnations, such as when a laughing stock is reborn as a monkey, or a completely opposite one. During his lifetime, Odysseus was famous for his wisdom and cunning, and he also had the epithet "the long-suffering" for his wanderings and sufferings at the hands of the Divinities. His soul made a wise gesture and sought the lot of a life "far from affairs." One can also recall the similar case of Eumaeus, the swineherder who remained faithful to Odysseus during his absence from Ithaca, although he too had to take part in the "affair" of massacring the suitors.

The greatest contribution to shaping this ideal came from the Enlightenment in Rousseau and Voltaire's "noble savage", who possesses all the ideal qualities of Enlightenment humanism despite having no contact with Civilization (the church, monarchy, feudalism, the Middle Ages, i.e., the ossification of the world of Tradition) and is contrasted by the Enlighteners and Encyclopedists.[290] Marxism logically developed this figure

---

289 Plato, *Republic*, 620e-d, trans. G.M.A. Grube and C.D.C. Reeve, in Plato, *Complete Works* (Indianapolis: Hackett Publishing Company, 1997).

290 This figure has been illustrated throughout satirical and adventure literature, as well as in Aldous Huxley's dystopian novel.

of the noble savage to that of the noble society, declaring archaic societies to have been the bearers of primitive communism. Both the noble savage and primitive communism, modeled on archaic tribes, were simulacra and retrojections of the ideas of the Enlightenment, the French Revolution ("Liberty, Equality, Fraternity"), humanism, liberalism, and socialism upon tribes of "savages" discovered en masse and described by colonists during the era of the Great Geographical Discoveries. The mark of Rousseau and Voltaire can be found in the ideas of Thoreau, Tolstoy, and Dobrovolsky. In the case of the latter two, however, criticism of the Church and the State strongly resonated with the free spirit of the ordinary Russian folk, who always treated the state as something external to the community (the *mir*), something inevitable and "otherworldly" that had to be paid off and taken as little into the picture as possible, especially if this state is alien to the spirit, culture, faith, and doings of the folk, the *mir*. At the same time, the fact cannot be hidden from any attentive examination that the figures of the "savage" and the "commune" ignore the factor of traditions and sacro-centrism in archaic societies, which they belittle or impute as a persistent flaw in their idealistic picture.

We should forget the Rousseauist and Marxist illusions of the throughly modern, secular nobility and egalitarianism of the "savage." Family and clan hierarchies, complex relations with spirits and Divinities, necessary violence, clashes of arms[291], and destructive sacrifices of the accursed share are ubiquitous in archaic societies. The way of life of real "primitive" peoples is far from the idealistic pictures of Montel, Defore, Cooper, Huxley, and others of this ilk.

Romantic Escapism

Besides religiously or idealistically motivated simplification and exodus from civilization, there are also excesses of a more superficial ideological nature. Some fugitives are driven by

---

291 See Pierre Clastres, *Archaeology of Violence*, trans. Jeanine Herman (Los Angeles: Semiotext(e), 2010).

a more down-to-earth adventurism or romanticism of image rather than spirit.

The case of the American traveler and vagabond Christopher McCandless is a textbook example, one which has inspired many young people with a similar soul in the US. Born into a wealthy middle-class family in a suburb of Washington, D.C., McCandless was successful in athletics and in his studies, making the road to becoming one of the "white collars" in the capital already laid out before him. After graduating from college, he initiated a right gesture of protest against American culture, against the life trajectory cut out for him by society, and the *modus vivendi* of the American environment as a whole: adopting a pseudonym and taking some money, but leaving no contact information or itinerary for his family, he set off on a free wandering across America. McCandless was driven by pure romanticism gleaned from American literature (Thoreau and Jack London). His act of protest against the dry commercialism of middle-class life did not lead him to any inner transformation, sacred center, or spiritual axis. For a few years, he simply wandered around America's wild backwaters, taking up odd jobs and making acquaintances. Becoming obsessed with the idea of "conquering" Alaska, he hitchhiked there without any basic equipment (with no map and compass) and with no survival skills suited to the extremely hostile and stingy nature of the American North. Christopher's reckless voyage into this unfamiliar land had a natural, farcical, inglorious end: he died from poisoning from local shrubs. Due to his lack of survival skills, he could not even secure basic food or traverse the river that separated him from civilization. Since he had taken no map with him, he also did not know that not far from his abandoned bus campsite was a bridge, crossing which could have saved his life.

Christopher McCandless' story became popular after the publication of Jon Krakauer's book *Into the Wild* and the movie of the same name released in 2007. Imitators then appeared and set off on McCandless' path, wandering around the country and even especially eagerly trying to reach his bus in Alaska. Fleeing from the modern world, such young people are seeking out the "noble savage" or "ennobling environment" in the wild. But the truth in such is exactly only half: of course, nature is better than Modernity, but there is no Rousseau and Voltaire in nature. Nature is inhabited by archaic societies founded on hierarchies and practicing proper violence. Skills given by the Divinities or transmitted by ancestors are extremely important for survival. The idle touristic voyage of the "savage" young man is a third-rate act and absolutely profane experience of wandering and experiencing the thrill of wild nature, not an initiatic journey.

Finally, besides the superficial romantic escapism of bourgeois youth — a rebellion that eventually brings them back to the same path of social prosperity some years later —, there are absolutely simple, everyday situations in which degraded people, vagrants, fugitives, and criminals find themselves in circumstances of compelled simplification and living in the wild with no other alternatives on their hopeless path.

The Weak Argument of Luddism

In 1811, England was overwhelmed by an uprising of textile factory workers. The rioters desperately smashed up factory floors, especially the newly installed weaving machines. Conspirators among ordinary artisans and hard laborers gathered in the forests at night to develop strategies of sabotage and manifestos of their struggle. The epicenters of the uprising were the counties of Nottinghamshire, Lancashire, and Yorkshire. Over a few years of active armed struggle, the army of workers defeated thousands of machines and machine tools only to be brutally suppressed by government troops who had to be diverted from the war with Napoleon. The inspiration and symbolic figure of the workers' uprising against factory owners and their new equipment was the mythical, anonymous General Ned Ludd, whose name appeared as the signature on manifestos and appeals. From Ludd's name and these early 19th-century events derives the current known as "Luddism."

The Luddites' tactics of physically destroying machines, factories, and sporadically killing business owners were absolutely correct. Unfortunately, they proceeded from strictly socio-economic grounds. The workers' wrath was incited by the fact that factory owners had decided to replace mass labor with faster and more accurate weaving machines to modernize and optimize production, which led to a sharp increase in unemployment among weavers and some other professions where manual labor had previously predominated. By destroying the machines, the Luddites hoped to intimidate the factor owners and get their jobs back. In other words, their struggle centered around low-skilled jobs.

Standardized mass production and "assembly lines" are indeed more intrinsic to machines than people. In some sense, the Luddites were fighting to take their rightful place as machines. An alternative point of view on this instance has been expressed by the Finnish ecologist Kaarlo Pentti Linkola, who pointed out that the high unemployment rate in Finland at the turn of the 1990s could have easily been solved if people went out to work in the fields instead of tractors. Capital and the state were unable to provide people with work or subsidies, but they continued to spend funds on the purchase, maintenance, and operating of agricultural machines whose work could have been successfully performed by the unemployed and the poor. Linkola called this situation "completely absurd."

The popular movement of Luddism was reflected in the romantic skepticism towards technology propagated by England's enlightened literary Bohemians. Today there exists the disparate movement, or rather the practical position and set of values, of neo-Luddism. In its mildest form, neo-Luddism takes aim at the abundance of technological tracking and cameras (the surveillance state), digital and television media, VR and Big Data, applications like Uber, and the replacement of professions by robots and AI, i.e., direct analogues to the precariatization of labor with the arguments of classical Luddism. Neo-Luddism is against the general dehumanization and cultural and behavioral changes brought by the technologized environment and the Fourth Industrial Revolution. The media, which play a huge role as the primary cultural environment that levels down any and all values to entertainment content, are defined as a moral threat to human societies.[292]

As an alternative, neo-Luddites propose practicing digital hygiene or digital dieting, i.e., consciously and qualitatively reducing the time one spends in virtual networks or in contact with gadgets (e.g., turning off home appliances on a timer). So-called "slow technology" prescribes the use of older gadget models or technology with stripped-down, "primitive" functionality instead of pursuing updated models. In their original strategy, the 20th-century neo-Luddites operated in France, where the anarchist group CLODO (Committee for the Liquidation or Subversion of Computers, whose French acronym literally composes one term for "homeless") organized a series of arsons and bombings of computer company offices in the 1980s. Episodic attacks by anarcho-primitivists and anti-globalists on offices, warehouses, and IT centers, acts of vandalism against traffic cameras, cell towers, and network fiber optic cables — all of this continues around the world today. In many ways, neo-Luddite practices are woven into the general narrative of radical ecology, simplification, as well as local countercultural communities practicing self-reliance. One of the brightest and most successful figures who can be associated with neo-Luddism is the thinker and terrorist Theodore Kaczynski, to whom we will turn later.

Alain de Benoist's Anti-Growth Ideology

Alain de Benoist, the ideologist of the European "New right" and a form of intellectual paganism, has formulated the main theses of an anti-growth ideology in his rich ecological-

---

292 In a 2018 survey on raising children in pagan traditions, the majority of polled pagan families deemed the Internet, gadgets, and mass pop culture to be the number one threat to correctly raising new generations. See *Colloquium Heptaplomeres* V.

philosophical treatise, the very title of which plays with and expresses the general vector of overcoming outdated socio-political, progressive, and reactionary schemes: *Forward, to the Cessation of Growth!* This title is conceived as an oxymoron within the progressive paradigm: "forward", after all, means growth, and if growth ceases, then things must be moving backwards.

De Benoist polemicizes against and debunks the concept of "sustainable development." Since the late 20th century, the idea of sustainable development has acted as an ersatz quasi-ecology in global economic and industrial narratives. Its main idea is that it is possible to compensate for the anthropogenic footprint in nature by way of financial subsidies for environmental movements and technological solutions. Drawing attention to ecological problems is a classic attempt to blow off steam from the monotonic process of limitless economic growth in the limited space of the planet. Failure to understand the limited nature of space and, as a result, the exhaustibility of resources, gives rise to the blindness and madness of economic exploitation. Sustainable development fully supports the progressive ideology of growth and incorporates the ecological context as a kind of backdrop to "the environment", not as a primary value for whose sake the very idea of growth might be critically challenged.

The rapid growth of cities, the near disappearance of the peasantry (de facto through modernization into farm companies) in the 20th century, and the ensuing sharp jump in production and consumption forebode that in the 21st century humanity will use up all the resources that nature took 300 million years to generate. De Benoist points to imminent wars over "elementary" resources such as drinking water, whose consumption grows alongside population and industry. It was typical of the first economists to treat natural resources as inexhaustible gifts from heaven which, not examinable as "economics" insofar as they were not created by people, appear as pure, ready-to-hand raw materials for free use without compensation.

De Benoist cites François Schneider's claim that if the level of consumption of all countries grows to match that of the US, then humanity would need up to seven additional planets like Earth for raw material supplies alone. Yet, the very possibility of "Third World" countries achieving such a high level of consumption is questionable and is generally, practically unrealizable within the current economic paradigm. As an ardent advocate of ethnopluralism, Alain de Benoist exposes the essence of the idea of development to be an extension of colonization by other, non-political means. He agrees with Stéphane Bonnievo's definition: "In cultural terms, development is not neutral. In fact, it is based on a complex set of beliefs and social truths deeply rooted in the Western imaginary, which ascribes them the meaning of being natural and universal... It [development] is ultimately taking resources away from man and nature in order to ensure endless economic development." Among non-European peoples, the Economy, based as it is on the Western European ideal of Modernity, works to systematically transform the Other into the Same.

The plight of Africa or South America is primarily due to the fact that they were violently incorporated into the global economic system (where they were assigned a lower place) and the ideology of growth. The first colonists and anthropologists described archaic societies as not knowing poverty and in no way thinking of themselves as "backwards" in relation to anyone. In many African languages, there is no concept of "pauper"; only the word "orphan" comes close, since a person outside of their wide family or clan is genuinely weak and homeless. The imposition of the Economy on archaic peoples leads to the destruction of their traditional family-clan forms of mutual aid (gifts, exchange, community assistance, nutrition, etc.), which become monetized and socio-economic affairs. In other words, the modernization of archaic peoples generates poverty and fuels the division into poor who get poorer and rich who get richer (here, too, lurks the double-edged hubris of Titanism). This division is relevant not only for the global division of labor, but also within the developed societies of the "First World", where the lower social classes undergo intensive precariatization and alienation.

Alain de Benoist connects the emergence of such a humanity and its attitude towards the world with the spread of Christianity, particularly how the latter treats the world as cursed matter given to mankind for exploitation (cf. Genesis 1:28, 3:17). The Enlightenment only took to the extreme and reinforced in secular language and the scientific world picture the prerequisites that were already laid down by creationism.

Recognizing the idea of sustainable development to be a media narrative that only distracts "concerned masses" from real problems, de Benoist admits that building an alternative is no trivial task. Firstly, he rejects the "old Left" and their socialist ideas, despite their general points of critique of the capitalist system, because the Left and liberals (including right-wing ones as well) are in solidarity on the idea that the development of the forces of production is how humanity fulfills its destiny. In other words, they act as an appendage to the machine of unlimited growth in a limited space, which is openly suicidal behavior on a planetary scale. The scale of reduction must be based on something else, and here de Benoist outlines the right strategy: reformatting the imaginary in order to break the symbolic link between "desire" and "consumption", rejecting the Economy and getting out of Economics altogether, and appealing to transcendental values. In the field of *realpolitik*, de Benoist recognizes that the masses will never support any politician who publicly pursues even the slightest reduction in growth. When it comes to practical solutions, de Benoist's treatise names the strategy of "relocalization", that is returning production to local communities rooted in their land and culture, which implies anti-imperialism and anti-colonialism. The bio-economy of agriculture, hunting, and gathering alongside farms and settlements is completely self-sufficient for local people. Additionally, the practice of distributism and cooperation on solving problems through collective participation allows for returning the consumption and use of land back into the hands of the people themselves and their genuine needs.

Indeed, it is necessary to discard the belief that "the more, the better."

Kaarlo Pentti Linkola's Ecofascism

Kaarlo Pentti Linkola was a Finnish fisherman, hermit, protector of forests, ornithologist, as well as one of the most radical and consistent thinkers and critics on the subject of technogenic civilization. His books have always been popular in Finland and continue to incite fierce controversy and polemics. For the radicalness of his views and absolute frankness of speech, Linkola is habitually considered to be a philosopher of pessimism and an apologist for genocide and ecofascism. He himself called his position "realism."

At the center of Pentti Linkola's system of values is the biological diversity of living species in a particular environment (in his case, Finland).[293] The balance of life should enable all endogenous species to exist in accordance with their nature and their own regulation (food chains). Biodiversity is sacred, and it encompasses everything, from the smallest plants, fungi, woods to and animal species, birds, and fish. Man also belongs to this diversity, but he has broken out of the overall picture due to his thoughtless lifestyle and consumer culture, which affect the entire system and lead to destructive imbalance. The extinction of any species, even a small local one, threatens the integrity of the entire system.

From this directly follows a second notion of importance to Linkola: crime against the environment. Modern mankind regularly, on all levels of the biosphere, and in a striking variety of forms, commits crimes against the environment. Linkola puts environmental crime above all criminal acts that affect society. For example, mining iron to be used for constructing cruise ships or the structures of buildings of dubious necessity, as well

---

293 See Pentti Linkola, *Can Life Prevail? A Revolutionary Approach to the Environmental Crisis*, trans. Eetu Rautio and Olli S. (London: Arktos, 2009).

as making capital out of it, is a crime. Cutting down forests, imposing taxes and duties on subsistence fishing for the sake of the fishing industry, laying roads through forests, breeding domestic cats, idle tourism and mass sports - all of these are the gravest criminal offenses committed by man against his surrounding environment.

Almost as old as the 20th century, Linkola saw with his own eyes the rapid expansion of industrial society into the nature and forests of Finland, where he spent almost his entire life, as well as to other regions of Europe where he traveled by bicycle or on foot. At the beginning of his activism, Linkola advocated pacifism and peaceful tactics, but over time he naturally and logically moved towards defending violence and cruelty towards those who threaten the natural balance.

Kaarlo Pentti Linkola's integral ideology can be described in the following series of points.

Progress is an illusion. The growth of prosperity does not lead to happiness and human flourishing, but critically destroys the environment for habitation and yields only new problems and poverty. One vivid example is the use of agricultural machinery, together with the cost of its purchase and maintenance, all the while as unemployment in society persists. The logic of progress does not allow for taking such work away from combines and giving it back to people, because it is not economically profitable and because such labor is "morally obsolete."

Democracy is a religion of death, and human rights are a death sentence on society. Democracy reinforces selfishness and the low, base type of man in politics and mass culture. At the core of liberal democracy lies the individual with their consumer interests, as opposed to nature and the community living in harmony. Democracy is essentially the breeding ground for a predatory relation to the surrounding environment. Consequently, Linkola rejects equality and humanism in general, and proceeds from the fact that talents and callings are unevenly distributed throughout a human population. Instead, selected elites with ecological consciousness should rule. Linkola believed the US and Western culture to be degenerate and hostile to his ideas by definition.

This is also linked to Linkola's critical attitude towards Christianity. Being an atheist, Linkola nonetheless recognized that religious people and religious consciousness treat nature much better than the rest. He positively evaluated the strictness and seriousness of some Christian priests. However, he fundamentally could not agree with the doctrine of the forgiveness of sins, mercy, and the ubiquitous humanism of modern Protestantism and Catholicism (after the Second Vatican Council). A person must be punished for their crimes, and the egotistical values of one person (or the majority, in fact) should in no case be equal to the values of more responsible and realistic-minded people. In one place, Linkola compared the "Father, Son, and Holy Spirit" to "the Dollar, Economic Growth, and the Market Economy" as underpinning the modern system.

In Linkola's view, capitalist business, aiming purely for profit and reinforcing technological innovations, must be eliminated. In his words, "Beauty is more valuable than the economy."[294] Critical industries should be nationalized. Only genuinely necessary things of high quality that can serve generations of people (rejecting inherent obsoletion[295]) should be produced. In literature, for example, entertainment and vulgar publications should be banned for the sake of focusing instead on philosophy, poetry, and qualitative literature. Stock exchanges, investments, money transfers, and bank operations should all be liquidated. Banks should be left only with the function of small cash emissions for live, face-to-face withdrawals.

Life is to be centered on balanced, small farms that can support themselves by fishing, hunting, gathering, and growing food, especially berries rich in vitamins that can be conserved. The required minimum of energy can be obtained by using

---

294 Linkola, *Can Life Prevail?*

295 Linkola himself did not say this, but his ideas implicitly fit into the general vector of the notions of slowing down time, the culture of "slow things" and slow communication, and the idea of "temporal anti-growth."

solar panels. Major cities are to be liquidated. Movement will be possible only by bicycles, rowing boats, and horse-drawn carriages. Cars will be reserved only for limited transport of large consignments of goods or products between remote villages. Profane tourism and international travel will be prohibited, replaced by the culture of hiking one's native lands. The culture of houses outside of towns and in forests will be revived.

Information technology will be completely liquidated. So will general education in its modern form. Only special schools and camps in wild nature will be left. Survival skills, the history of one's native land, and those sciences which help live in harmony with the natural environment will be made the priority. Every citizen will have to be able to provide tools, clothing, and food for themselves.

Ultimately, electricity will be phased out altogether. Linkola calls the discovery of electricity one of the greatest misfortunes in human history. Power plants and fossil fuel extraction will also be eliminated.

Population size, growth, and childbearing will be put under the most severe control. Linkola described excessive numbers of people as the most striking imbalance in the biosphere inevitably leading to disaster. When a person goes beyond the limits assigned by nature, he begins to treat nature and other species selfishly. Christian love for human life de facto only reinforces this egoism and justifies population growth, which it cultivates as the norm.

Linkola is known for a metaphor with which he famously described the current situation:

What to do when a ship carrying a hundred passengers has suddenly capsized, and only one lifeboat is available for ten people in the water? When the lifeboat is full, those who hate life will try to pull more people onto it, thus drowning everyone. Those who love and respect life will instead grab an axe and sever the hands clinging to the gunwales.[296]

296 Linkola, *Can Life Prevail?*, 131.

Linkola therefore advocates radical population reduction through the introduction of forced sterilizations, abortions, "one family, one child" quotas, free contraception, etc. In exceptional cases, Linkola proposes infanticide and using nuclear or bacteriological weapons for precision strikes on the largest populations in the world. Linkola's response to criticism of such proposals is widely known: "If there were a button I could press, I would sacrifice myself without hesitating, if it meant millions of people would die."

To implement such radical strategies, Linkola proposes transforming society into an environmentalist totalitarian dictatorship that has the weapons to protect its internal way of life from the external enemy that is progressive civilization. This approach also discloses the main contradiction in Kaarlo Pentti Linkola's ideas. While proposing to abandon Modernity on all fronts and in the most radical form by returning to the way of life of the Middle Ages, he still relies on modernist techniques and modern technologies for the achievement of these aims: alternative energy eco-technologies, weapons production, totalitarian methods of control and medicine, and the ecofascist centralization of socio-political life. Linkola does not object to the creation of supranational institutions or governments for the sake of his ideas' embodiment on the global scale. In some sense, Linkola's plan can be seen as a variant of a transition period in the deconstruction of all Western-centric civilization, which might leave some useful relics. Alas, even these relics will gradually acquire accompanying technological productions and innovations, which threatens to return the course of human history back to its progressive circle. In this respect, our ideas are more radical than Linkola's, as we envision a world in which the emergence of technologies and any treatment of the world as ready-to-hand would be simply impossible. Such a world would comprise distributed peoples and small groups (tribes) instead of any hyper-centralized, militaristic eco-state.

What Linkola is exactly right about (and he is right about almost everything) is his principled position on protecting forests, which constitute the backdrop of his environment in Finland and which generally dominate the expanses of Ancient Europe. This discloses Pentti Linkola's absolute metaphysical accuracy, from which there remains only one step further to the pagan ecological agenda. Protecting forests (Linkola himself created a foundation that bought forests by hectares and reserved them intact as private lands) is not simply ecology and the preservation of natural niches for all of a forest's inhabitants, but is protecting our entire metaphysics in empirical expression. The forest is life *par excellence*, and the tree is the World Tree, the metaphor of the pagan human and people rooted in their native land and landscape and standing under their native sky (reaching up towards it) in communion with the Divine.[297] It is also metaphysically no coincidence that Linkola was a recognized ornithologist, for in pagan traditions birds are the thoughts and messengers of the Divinities.[298]

Despite the wall of censorship and silence over Linkola in the English-speaking world (only one collection of his articles has been translated into English[299]), he is nevertheless a cult figure of anti-modernism. Linkola is also appealing for his extreme sincerity: he lived exactly as he thought. He fished, rode a bicycle, traveled on foot, used almost no money, and lived in a remote Finnish forest. He lived and suffered for nature alongside it. Over his own lifetime, he saw the disappearance of dozens of species of birds, animals, and hectares of forest.

Linkola's ideas have also found reflection in popular culture. For instance, his words are paraphrased by the antagonist of Dan Brown's bestselling novel, *Inferno*. Together with Theodore Kaczynski, his ideas have exerted a strong influence on eco-terrorism and industrial sabotage practices. On the whole, this brings him close to the position of consistent neo-Luddism.

---

297 On the metaphysics and role of the forest in the Germanic-Scandinavian tradition, see Askr Svarte, *Gods in the Abyss*.

298 Mutual acquaintances have claimed that the only word which Linkola knew in English was "bird."

299 Pentti Linkola, *Can Life Prevail?*.

Linkola appreciated any catastrophes and wars that would affect the economy, industry, and population size, for such cataclysms give nature an additional lease on life.

The Strategy of Theodore Kaczynski

The story of Theodore Kaczynski vividly shows how already in the 20th century it became extremely difficult to escape from civilization and live one's life in modest solitude in the spirit of Henry Thoreau. Progressive industrial civilization will still catch up with man and destroy his natural space wherever he settles down.

A prodigy mathematician, Ted Kaczynski attended Harvard at age 16 and graduated with honors in 1962 at age 20. By the end of the '60s, he had received his Ph.D. and become a professor at Berkley. In the very beginning of the 1970s, he moved into a forest cabin he built in the Montana wilderness. He mastered survival skills, only to encounter intrusive industrial and infrastructural development that came to destroy his nature. This prompted him to start practicing petty sabotage to disable equipment at the facilities close to his hut.

In the summer of 1983, Theodore Kaczynski decided to retire to a remote and hilly plateau, only to find a highway beginning to be built through it that destroyed the hitherto untouched wilderness. This shock was the last straw for Kaczynski. Between 1978 and 1995, Kaczynski mailed 16 bombs to entities who, in his opinion, were responsible for the whole situation of industrial interference with nature. Three people were killed, and 23 were injured. One bomb planted on a Boeing flying to Washington did not explode, but the incident allowed the FBI to take over the search for Kaczynski. For some time, the "Unabomber" ("university and airline bomber"), as he came to be called, was the bureau's number one target.

Kaczynski was arrested in his hut in 1996 after being given away to the authorities by his brother. Years earlier, the two had left civilization together, but the Unabomber's brother soon returned to society and started a family. Theodore Kaczynski pleaded guilty and is currently serving a life sentence in a maximum security prison in Colorado. On his imprisonment, he writes that the system is not capable of breaking his spirit, and that the only thing he worries about is that over time he might begin to forget his native forests and mountains, their smells and winds.

Kaczynski's terrorist activities were crowned with success in 1995 when, in anonymous correspondence with authorities, he managed to compel *The Washington Post* and *The New York Times* to publish his work, *Industrial Society and Its Future*. Under the terms the Unabomber set forth, he promised to cease attacks after its publication. In a fateful coincidence, Theodore's brother recognized his writing style and approached a group of FBI investigators.

In the "Unabomber manifesto", Kaczynski systematically, point by point, set out his socio-political and cultural views on progress, industrial development, and how such enterprises destroy what are, in his view, organic culture and human existence. The "manifesto" is structured in 232 concise statements and theses on several blocs of topics which Kaczynski saw as fundamental. The Unabomber begins by denouncing "leftists", whom he identifies as victims of oversocialization who harbor an inferiority complex and destructive psyche, that is a combination of overconformism and rebellion. According to Kaczynski, a leftist is a bearer of depression, defeatism, tolerance, feminism, and hatred for everything "normal" and "healthy." Kaczynski sees the roots of the contemporary situation of overall decline in the rising strength of leftist ideas in society. This situation includes increases in life expectancy, population growth, the spread of mental illnesses and suffering in all countries, the meaninglessness of life, the destruction of horizontal ties (family, tribe, village), the increasing rapidity of change, isolation from nature in cities, and harm inflicted upon the natural environment.

Kaczynski also points to the "disruption of the power process" or the realization of power as a form of freedom. Genuine freedom, according to Kaczynski, is the power to control the circumstances of one's own life or of a small group. Freedom is one small group's control over everything necessary — food, the production of minimal necessary things, and the protection of property. The disruption of the process of power consists in the gradual and permanent delegation (alienation) of decisions in favor of the System and its social mechanisms of power over other people. The System takes away the power to solve tasks from a person, family, or group, instead offering compromise in the form of security, comfort, leisure, alternative "surrogate freedoms", science, and technology. Kaczynski argues that since the Industrial Revolution, the stability of the System has come at the cost of personal freedom and local autonomy.[300] Within the industrial system, the process of regular compromise-delegations (/alienations) becomes a powerful social force. He calls this force "technology."

Hence follows the natural and logical conclusion that the System absolutely does not tolerate small, strong groups connected by family-clan or philosophical-religious ties. In such communities, fidelity to the group and/or teaching, not the System, comes first. For the System, the hierarchy of subordination should be reversed: citizens' individual loyalty should be to the State first, then to their social stratum, then to their professional community. The System is willing to tolerate small groups only if their ideological content is emasculated or subordinated to production-consumption technologies, i.e., is somehow built into or fits the System.

In his work, Kaczynski introduces a most important notion which can be used to describe the sphere of interests and activities of *das Man*: "surrogate activity." These are activities to which a person who is excluded from the process of realizing authentic power devotes their attention, energy, and time. Kaczynski writes: "We use the term 'surrogate activity' to designate an activity that is directed toward an artificial goal

---

300 Here it is worth recalling the strict regulation of farming in the US and other countries and the ban on logging in America in the late 2010s.

that people set up for themselves merely in order to have some goal to work toward, or let us say, merely for the sake of the 'fulfillment' that they get from pursuing the goal." The surrogate activities of contemporary society include sports, artistic and literary creativity (the Unabomber considers all left-wing art to be degenerate), careerism, capital accumulation, the consumerist lifestyle, and, finally, scientific and technological work.[301] The System maintains and develops surrogate needs and surrogate activities by way of marketing, advertising, and mass media. Even conformist struggles against "frustrating" technological devices can be a manifestation of surrogate activities, as the Unabomber writes:

> For example, a variety of noise-making devices: power mowers, radios, motorcycles, etc. If the use of these devices is unrestricted, people who want peace and quiet are frustrated by the noise. If their use is restricted, people who use the devices are frustrated by the regulations... But if these machines had never been invented there would have been no conflict and no frustration generated by them.

Being against progress, Theodore Kaczynski frontally attacked the industrial-technological society and its achievements. He distinguished between two types of technologies: the first can be implemented and used by small groups or individuals. These are craft and survival level technologies that free and skilled people can create out of objects from the surrounding environment. The second type of technology depends on large social organizations (and industry specifications). Such technologies enslave the societies that produce them. Here Kaczynski speaks of modern medicine, which he disavows. For medical technology to be effective, advances in chemistry, physics, biology, computing, and other fields are necessary. High-tech medical equipment, in turn, can only be created in economically developed societies. Thus, there is a recursive closure of social and technological development, i.e., the transformation of technology into a surrogate. Freedom is exchanged in compromise for health,

---

301 Turning around to look at our era, we can confidently add to this all forms of contemporary cultural leisure and the whole sphere of virtual life without exceptions, as well as the spectacle of the Political.

which one can then devote to engaging in satisfying their surrogate needs. Kaczynski contrasts this picture to the way of life of primordial man, somewhat differing from the Enlightenment ideals of Rousseau's savage paradise:

> Primitive man, threatened by a fierce animal or by hunger, can fight in self-defense or travel in search of food. He has no certainty of success in these efforts, but he is by no means helpless against the things that threaten him. The modern individual on the other hand is threatened by many things against which he is helpless; nuclear accidents, carcinogens in food, environmental pollution, war, increasing taxes, invasion of his privacy by large organizations, nation-wide social or economic phenomena that may disrupt his way of life.

The consequence of socially-organized technology's invasion of all countries, societies, and tribes on the global scale has been the destruction of authentic ways of life and, as follows, the destabilization and rapid growth of populations, which demands new intensifications of technologies. Kaczynski's manifesto contains a number of accurate predictions about the feature that bore out within only a few decades. For example, back in the 1980s, he already accurately predicted the emancipationism of transhumanism as "reducing human beings and many other living organisms to engineered products and mere cogs in the social machine." He also held to an alarmist position on Artificial Intelligence. In the political realm, he foretold the technological triumph of authoritarian Asian regimes, particularly China, which we have previously identified as the mixed Asian-European pole of the Gestell. For Kaczynski, this underscores the global caricature of the dominance of technology and the need for an uprising in all countries, not only the US. Ultimately, he summates the relationship between modern humanity and technology as that of an alcoholic left alone with a barrel of wine: he will die from uncontrolled, excessive, intoxicating consumption.

As for the positive ideal, Theodore Kaczynski proposes letting wild nature function absolutely independently of human activity. He sees the only way out in complete, absolute rejection of the industrial-technological system. All factories should be destroyed, and all technical books should be burned, so that if the system is successfully collapsed, it will be impossible to rebuild it. The Unabomber speaks of a revolution against the industrial society, that is a radical and fundamental change in the nature of society, an exodus out of the system of mass behavioral control. This revolution is not political, as its aim is not a change in government, but the destruction of the technological foundation of Modernity. Kaczynski speaks of the grandiose cause of crushing the industrial System, an accomplishment that would prevent the arranging of a large system of control and the alienation of true freedom. The frontline is to be drawn between peoples on the one hand, and big business, politicians, scientists, and officials on the other, between the technology-wielding elites and the masses on whom technology is used.

Kaczynski stands for the elitism of revolutionary ideas, i.e., such ideas should be addressed to an intellectual vanguard which will in some form come to constitute a specific new sub-ethnos of neo-Luddites or neo-archaists. At this point, Kaczynski proposes an unexpected solution that distinguishes him from similar thinkers: he insists on the need for revolutionaries against the industrial society to have as many children as possible and raise them in the revolutionary anti-modernist spirit in order to strengthen and pass on the banner of future struggle. Kaczynski also allows for the possibility of using certain technologies in the fight against technology and the industrial System as a whole. Finally, his considerations on the communal fidelity of members of small groups lead to thinking about the possibility of exploiting the System to the benefit of autonomous groups settled in forests far from industrial centers and megalopolises. Feigning loyalty to the System, such small groups can send agents to infiltrate the System's institutions by way of clan loyalty, nepotism, and corruption so as to then provide resources and cover for the revolutionary assets and communities living back in the forests.

Summarizing Theodore Kaczynski's views with respect to our position, we can conclude that he is still a product of his environment, that is the academic science and Modernist society of the United States of America in the mid-20th century. Despite the influence of romantics like Thoreau, the ideal of wild nature, and a neutral attitude towards God and religion, Kaczynski remained an apologist for the idea of absolute truth in one way or another cognizable by scientific methods, as well as for individualism in the spirit of the Frontier era and implicit Nietzschean drives on the question of power and its realization. Kaczynski focuses mainly on the material aspects of biological survival, which makes his views kindred to those of John Zerzan. On the whole, Kaczynski can be defined as a representative of right-wing, science-centric, atheistic Modernity experiencing a certain existential push or insight and, as is obvious, trying to overcame its own "personal equation", to use Evola's term, which is to say its own cultural, educational, and personal-historical standpoints.

Kaczynski's strategy of revolution is in some respects close to Evola's ideas set out in his book *Ride the Tiger*. For instance, the Unabomber formulates two points for a "wait-and-see" strategy for struggle:

> First, we must work to heighten the social stresses within the system so as to increase the likelihood that it will break down or be weakened sufficiently so that a revolution against it becomes possible. Second, it is necessary to develop and propagate an ideology that opposes technology and the industrial society if and when the system becomes sufficiently weakened.

A number of Kaczynski's intentions are close to the spirit of the criticism that Martin Heidegger and other authors of the Conservative Revolution launched against technology and science. For instance, in his *Black Notebooks*, Heidegger analyzed Vladimir Lenin's slogan that "Socialism is Soviet power plus electrification" to point out that technology was not simply an "appendage" to socialism, but rather the basic form of endowing crooks with despotic power.[302]

---

302 Martin Heidegger, *Ponderings XII-XV: Black Notebooks 1939-1941*, trans. Richard Rojcewicz (Indianapolis: Indiana University Press, 2017), 100.

The Unabomber voiced another controversial point in a letter penned against the subcultural movement of ecofascism, a current which he reproached for typically left-wing mechanistic rationality despite claiming "right" values.[303] In this letter, Theodore rightly remarks that the rejection of technological development should be worldwide, because "if technological progress is restrained in the United States while China continues down its present technological path, then China will dominate the world." He sees the root of this situation in national egoism and political struggle feeding on ethnocentrism and racism. His strategy logically leads to calling for rejecting ethnocentrism as well as the erasure of ethnic boundaries. This remark is on the whole rightful and should be taken very seriously. The ecofascist movement is indeed a dead-end branch of a modern subculture, as issues of ecology and rejecting technology contradict fascist or National Socialist doctrines, which are ideological variations of the Gestell. Ethnopluralism and cultural differentiation are in essence among the most important elements in the structure of the manifestation of the Sacred in the world, and it is the differences between peoples that can become grounds for opposing global unification, digitalization, standardization, and the politics of the world melting pot. Finally, it cannot be ruled out that one people or bloc might be able to take responsibility for the world upon itself and become the first to breach the "heart" of the enemy in order to tear it out and eliminate civilization for itself and for all others. In any case, this problematic should be considered with all seriousness and cautious, without slipping into banal ideological clichés and superficial solutions. Some will take responsibility for all.

Despite the ideological flaws in his manifesto, Theodore Kaczynski lived an exemplary life. He correctly identified the priorities and targets for attacks, knowing full well that workers and lumberjacks are only the last link in the execution of others'

---

303 Ted Kaczynski, "Ecofascism: An Aberrant Branch of Leftism", *The Anarchist Library* (29/9/2020) [https://theanarchistlibrary.org/library/ted-kaczynski-ecofascism-an-aberrant-branch-of-leftism].

will and interests, which is to say their guilt is minimal. The main burden of guilt for the destruction of nature and the distortion of the human essence is borne by scientists, politicians, and economic actors who sanction the expansion of the technological body. Among Kaczynski's victims, the three killed were the owner of a computer store, an advertising executive, and a lumber industry lobbyist. Among the surviving victims were scientists, professors, graduate students, and employees of the US' leading scientific-technological universities.

On the basis of the Unabomber's theory and practice, we can introduce the notion of the "Industrial Trinity" as an image describing the enemy's threefold structure: the Academic Department, the Economy, and Production.[304] The Scientific Department provides for the production of modern knowledge, technologies, scientific discoveries, and the engineering-design support for industrial and IT projects, i.e., it shapes the progressist paradigm. The Economy, whether capitalist or planned-socialist, represented by business or state entities (often defense departments like DARPA and intelligence services), is the customer and sponsor of such developments, the subject for the implementation, expansion, and imposition (cf. IT evangelism) of surrogate needs. Mass industrial Production brings into embodiment the concrete material of new gadgets, machine tools, industrial platforms, and engineering solutions in all spheres. The resources extraction sector can also be attributed to Production.

The "Industrial Trinity" (which is in essence another name for the Gestell) is now embodied in innovative tech-parks and "think & production tanks" like Silicon Valley and the headquarters of Google and Apple, which concentrate visionaries, programmers, technical specialists, production sites, state customers, venture investors, designers, and marketers in one place. In such centers, the road from an idea to its realization, to launching a product on the market, and to rapid capitalization is maximally quick

---

304 In the wake of Christian theology, the "Industrial Trinity" can be understood as an essence united in three unmerged yet inseparable faces.

and effective. Such tech parks pose far greater threats than the offices or personnel targeted by Kaczynski and neo-Luddites.

Looking around in our days, we can easily spot a number of personalities, institutes, and companies which, beyond their research and commercial activities, stand as glaring symbols, evangelists, and direct apologists of the Gestell's Trinity. Obviously, such pieces must be taken off the chessboard.

In parallel to Theodore Kaczynski's activism in the 1980-90s, as well as under his influence, emerged the current of "ecotage" (ecological sabotage) or "ecoterrorism." Its essence lies in practicing radical, illegal ecological defense — from disabling or destroying equipment, energy, and transport infrastructure, counteracting deforestation and the creation of garbage dumps, to liquidating the responsible personnel of industrial and infrastructure projects and facilities that cause harm to nature. One key event in the development of ecotage was the publication of the practical guide edited by Dave Foreman and Bill Haywood, *Ecodefense: A Field Guide to Monkeywrenching*, known in Russian as *Ecotage: A Guide to Radical Nature Conservation*. The aim of ecotage is to make environmentally hazardous industrial projects, construction, and extraction economically unprofitable and, ultimately, dangerous to the lives of their employees and sponsors.

Julius Evola's *Ride the Tiger*

Alongside *Men Among the Ruins* and *The Bow and the Club*, Julius Evola's milestone book *Ride the Tiger* belongs to the later cycle of his work, wherein the Baron summated his many decades of political and Traditionalist activities and recognized the futility of any further active participation in political struggle for the ideals of Tradition. In a word, the Political is dead. If the early Traditionalists cherished the dream of "turning everything back", then Evola now instead saw that we are left with only one way forward, that of existing in an anti-traditional world. The forces of destruction and degeneration cannot possibly be overcome by the methods of political reaction, conservatism, or even revolution. Europe has irrevocably entered the stage of decline (the Kali-Yuga) and must go through the crucible of its own death in order to then — perhaps — "come out first on the other side of the darkness."

Recognizing this situation, in *Ride the Tiger*, Evola turned to seek a strategy for all those vertically and metaphysically oriented people who are so rare in our days — a strategy that would allow for transcending the period of mass-scale *nigredo* and remaining true to higher ideals without being wasted on the illusions of partisan struggle. Evola also recognized that some forms and principles of Tradition might become obsolete, and hence blindly following them would be a waste of time and lead nowhere. Evola wrote: "It is good to sever every link with all that which is destined sooner or later to collapse. The problem will then be to maintain one's essential direction without leaning on any given or transmitted form, including forms that are authentically traditional but belong to past history."[305]

As a paradigm for the behavior and structure of the Traditionalist's relation to contemporary Modernity, Evola refers to an image widespread in the East, that of "saddling the tiger." According to this principle, if a person manages to saddle a tiger and cling tightly to its fur, then, firstly, the tiger will not be able to attack and kill him; secondly, having held on long enough, the person can wait until the tiger is exhausted and then finish off the weakened predator. Antiquity and the Mediterranean know a similar image of "saddling the bull" associated with Mithras and his cult among the Roman legionaries. Evola's reference to Mithra in this context is quite consistent with the Baron's Kshatriyan spirit, the prism through which he developed Traditionalism.

Applied to the situation of Modernity and Postmodernity, the call to "ride the tiger" refers us to the so-called Left-Hand Path, i.e., an alternative strategy of behavior associated with

---

305 Evola, *Ride the Tiger*, 6.

a transgressive and nonconformist path that radically differs from classical conservatism and political reaction. To the Russian author and metaphysician Yuri Mamleev belongs a capacious formula in which he calls for "breaking through to the Absolute from below" and "positivizing all negations." Both Evola and Mamleev (although the latter remained Orthodox) were deeply interested in the radical Hindu teachings of Tantra, Advaita, and Vamachara.

Evola revised and reassessed the traditional forms whose restoration, defense, and propaganda constituted the foundation of the right-wing conservative and conservative-Traditionalist discourse of his era and which still blindly exist to this day. But, instead of mirroring values and hierarchies, i.e., blindly moving to enemy positions, Evola tries everywhere to establish a "perpendicular" path or to problematize superficial solutions. He addresses the topic of narcotic substances and their potential benefits, but dismisses the profane psychedelic revolution in the West. He destroys the myth of family values and childbearing, exposing them to be bourgeois degeneration. He completely discards modern culture up to the point of criticizing his own experience with Dada. Examining contemporary philosophical schools, he critiqued phenomenology, relativism, and existentialism.[306]

Of greater significance for our days is Evola's critique of the sphere of the Political, which had for him been a natural and priority environ of activity for long decades. Reorientation

---

306 Followers of Evola and Heideggerian Traditionalists have since lucidly shown that Evola learned of existentialism and Heidegger's ideas through Jaspers and Sartre, whose ideas differed significantly from and are inferior to the fundamental-ontology of the later Heidegger. Quotations of Evola's works have also been found in Heidegger's notebooks, which allows us to speak of a greater complementarity between their ideas than Evola's criticism in his *Ride the Tiger*. See Giovanni Sessa, "*Heidegger lettore di Evola*", Centro Studi La Runa (2/2/2016) [https://www.centrostudilaruna.it/heidegger-lettore-di-evola.html]. See also Greg Johnson, "Notes on Heidegger and Evola", in idem., *Graduate School with Heidegger* (San Francisco: Counter-Currents Publishing, 2020), 170-175; Collin Cleary, "Heidegger against the Traditionalists (Part One)", *Counter-Currents* (11/12/2020) [https://counter-currents.com/2020/12/heidegger-against-the-traditionalists-part-one/].

in this sphere led him to formulate two positions, two paths of behavior, which alone remain possible in our days.

The first is the position of *apoliteia*, of indifference towards and detachment from the political spectacle in which no parties truly represent traditional values and at most only speculate on them (in the spirit of modern populism). The knight of Tradition has no one to join in this era, therefore he remains alone in lost positions. Instead of the sacred Priest-King of the Satya-Yuga, the only possible type in our era is the warrior-magus, the faithful *ronin* without his sovereign. If, however, by virtue of his innate spiritual qualities, a person still cannot remain aloof from action, then it is permissible for him to participate in politics on the condition of being fully, inwardly detached from any political doctrines and programs. In other words, action is allowed for the sake of action under any flag in the external world given total distance and non-involvement within one's soul. Such participation is of a playful character and is without faith in ideology.

Evola described the second position with the strictly technical term "right-wing anarchism." On the whole, it resonates with apoliteia. Insofar as no states embodying sacred authority and the principle of Empire — of key importance to Evola — are left in the modern world, then the logical conclusion that follows is the position of "anarchism": rejecting and not recognizing any state as genuine and worthy of serving. The genuine state of the "right-wing anarchist" has been destroyed in the manifest world, but it continues to live on in the world of ideas. If states do not express our values, then this means that one can do whatever they want with them. Unlike classical left-wing anarchism, "right-wing anarchism" has nothing in common with egalitarianism, socialism, and atheism; rather, it persists in proclaiming the principles of sacred hierarchy and the sacred center of Being. Apoliteia and the "right anarch" are the only available forms of the Political in the age of the Kali-Yuga.

Out of Evola's later views emerges a textbook image that is inlaid in one of the titles of his books. This is an image of a world consisting entirely of the ruins of its former greatness, among which rare people of a vertical metaphysical orientation roam in solitude. According to Evola, genuine initiatic orders and unions are impossible in the modern era. Compelled "individualism" is at once both a condition and testing experience of the Iron Age.

Altogether telling is how Evola's call to "ride the tiger" has degenerated among the contemporary generation of so-called right-wing conservatives who have been hopelessly struck by irony — one of the methods of Postmodernist deconstruction. The call for "standing strong in the midst of the storm" and "holding tight during the furious leap of the deadly predator" has come to be perceived as an indulgence in self-irony and total immersion in degenerate web-culture, in simplifying and adapting discourse to contemporary ideals and values. If Mark Sedgwick's analysis of Traditionalism spoke of "soft Traditionalism"[307] in the likes of Mircea Eliade, Ananda Coomaraswamy, Titus Burckhardt, and others whose goal was to "smuggle" and institutionalize Traditionalist premises into religious studies, cultural studies, and anthropology, then with respect to virtual conservatives we can speak of "naught-Traditionalism." It is difficult to speak in such cases even of a simulacrum of Traditionalism, because a simulacrum still somehow tries to pass itself off as genuine. The whole essence of "naught Traditionalism", which exists mainly on social networks like Facebook and Instagram or on anonymous forums, boils down to exploiting retro-aesthetics from the late 20th century, creating web-punk *macramé*, Alt-Right apologetics for liberal conservatives in the likes of Ronald Reagan and Donald Trump or Russian Orthodox-bourgeois conservatives from the late 19th-early 20th centuries, or representatives of the Russian "White movement" (similar figures and names can be found in other countries), as if they were genuine harbingers of Tradition. In actual fact, all of these are but forms of the variability of the very same "tiger" which tries to pass itself off as "us" or as

307 See Mark Sedgwick, *Against the Modern World: Traditionalism and the Secret Intellectual History of the Twentieth Century* (Oxford: Oxford University Press, 2004).

something "inconsequential and funny" that loosens our grip. If in Antiquity and in India this image was based on literal and mythological grounds (ways of hunting and defending; the figure of Mithras), then now it is mutable and tends to appear as a hallucination or false value which completely pushes us to master the art of distinguishing between the obvious, the illusory, and the hallucinogenic (*Maya*).

Developing the paradigmatic image put forth by Evola, we find an interesting continuity in the iconography of the Deity Shiva, who is the Divinity of Destruction, ritual intoxication, and the patron of Vamachara, the Left-Hand Path. In the established iconography and rituals of Shaivites who practice *imitatio Dei*, the Divinity sits on a tiger skin, symbolizing the triumph of the Aghoric and Dionysian principle over the enemy and over man's passions. Among other things, Shiva is also adorned with many symbols of overcoming human nature and fears, his lingam symbolizing the infinity of the creative element of the Absolute that resides beyond all forms. At the same time, worshiping Shiva is relevant to the specific conditions of the Kali-Yuga. His cult and forms of radical ascesis are the most favorable in this time. His victory over the tiger does not mean the restoration of the Satya-Yuga or, alternatively, the victory of the neo-reactionary simulacra of conservatism — in such a case, one of the Divinities of the Right Hand or Dakshinachara would be seated on the tiger skin. This in essence confirms the correctness of our stake on precisely these Divinities and their Path.

Ernst Jünger's *Forest Passage*

Ernst Jünger's ideological path is similar but chronologically previous to the development of Julius Evola's ideas. Both were contemporaries, representatives of the Conservative Revolution[308] and Traditionalism, were war veterans (Jünger of both the First and Second World Wars), and active participants in early 20th-century politics. To Jünger's thinking belong such

---

308 See Armin Mohler, *The Conservative Revolution in Germany, 1918-1932* (Arlington: Washington Summit Publishers, 2018).

iconic ideas of the interwar period as Total Mobilization and the Gestalt of the Worker, and to his pen belong works of military prose and philosophy which attracted the attention of Martin Heidegger.

With the establishment of the Third Reich, Jünger went into "inward migration", manifesting exterior neutrality and minimal loyalty to the authorities while maintaining an inner, maximal distance, which brought him close to circles of conspirators and helped him avoid persecution after the war.[309] Like Evola, in his later life Jünger turned to seek other paths of existing and realizing freedom in a world of the heightening left-liberal dictatorship of Modernity. The key to this stage of his thought is his work *Der Waldgang*, or *The Forest Passage*, in which Jünger, by way of versatile aphorisms and considerations on his contemporary situation, introduced a new Gestalt: that of the "the one who passes into the forest", "the forest-fleer", the "forest rebel", *der Waldganger*.[310]

Ernst Jünger began by exposing modern democracy to be a growing form of dictatorship in which voting ballots are de facto "questionnaires" by which "voters" sign themselves off to repressive government. This obviously harbors a reference to the process of de-Nazification and to Ernst von Salomon's autobiographical novel, *The Questionnaire*. Jünger saw the democratic election process as a spectacle legitimizing a dictatorship seeking to demonstrate that it is based on the "majority" while leaving a minimum percentage of those who vote "against" so as to reinforce the illusion of freedom of dissent. Such government seeks to show monolithic legitimacy and oneness with the "will of the people" who voted for it. Therefore, even the minimal gesture of refusing to vote appears as a risky act of freedom for which one might answer at the risk of their own scalp. Voting against or simply publicly saying "no" is tantamount to such. The word "no" becomes an invincible symbol of freedom and the presence of resistance (whether

---

309 Ernst Jünger, *Strahlungen*.

310 Ernst Jünger, *The Forest Passage*, trans. Thomas Friese (Candor: Telos, 2013).

loners or a whole underground). The word "no" can be written on walls and is clear to everyone: "It is a sign that enslavement has not been completed." Further deliberating on the symbolism of opposing dictatorship and tacit consent, Jünger wrote: "Thus, one can continue the contraction and, instead of the word 'no', write one letter, for example 'W'. This could stand for *Wir* ('we'), *Waschsam* ('awake'), *Waffen* ('the armed'), *Wolfe* ('wolves'), *Widerstand* ('resistance'). This could also mean *Waldganger* (the one who has passed into the forest)."

The "forest rebel" is the loner who has fallen out of the world of the statistical accounting of opinions and control. This is a difficult and risky way of being in the world, but it is not of the world. For Jünger, it is a multifaceted, existential state which can be both an "inward migration" and literal guerrilla warfare against the System. "The forest rebel", Jünger writes, "is that individual who, isolated and uprooted from his homeland by the great process, sees himself finally delivered up for destruction." Thus, the forest rebel "possesses a primal relationship to freedom, which, in the perspective of our times, is expressed in his intention to oppose the automatism and *not* to draw its ethical conclusion, which is fatalism."

As the dictatorship expands the loci of control over people to infiltrate families and small collectives, the forest-fleer must pass into an unobservable state. The Forest Passage is an upsizing against the dominant world of the Worker, but is not tied to any naive romanticism of the salon type. Jünger says that the "Forest" is the space of action of small elites who see and orient themselves to more than just the requirements of the era. The Forest Passage is also not tied to banal political opposition. The Forest is not a concrete place in space, for one can pass into the Forest at any point on the globe. One can "dwell in the Forest" under the mask of their profession, or one can literally flee into the forest and escape from civilization. The Forest is deep behind enemy lies, where the Forest Rebel "takes care of reconnaissance, sabotage, dissemination of information in the population."

Speaking of the Forest Passage as the path of the loner, Jünger qualifies that this "loner" is not a "person" or "individual" in the humanist and Enlightenment sense, but a creature of God.[311] Everyone carries within themselves the "human" that can be awakened from friendly complicity with the thinker. The Forest Rebel keeps ties with forces that transcend the temporal and are irreversible by any changes. In an altogether poetic spirit, the boundaries between the subject-"fleer" and the object-"forest" are arbitrary and mobile in the Gestalt of the Forest Rebel. The Forest Rebel is the Forest, and the Forest sometimes appears as the activity of the Rebel or as the quality of his personhood. Jünger sees the roots of the Forest Passage in antiquity, in myths, tales, legends, song, dances, imaginations, poetry, and scriptures.

To describe the life of the Forest Rebel in the society of Modernity, Jünger presents a metaphor that runs like a leitmotif throughout the book. The modern world, ruled by the power of the Worker and technology, is like a ship, a cruise liner, specifically the *Titanic*, whose very name emphasizes the Titanic dimension of the matter at hand, on which point Jünger is in solidarity with the works of his brother, Friedrich Georg Jünger.[312] For Ernst Jünger, the ship is the embodiment of the temporal, whereas the Forest is the embodiment of timeless Being. The ship, unlike the Forest, is not rooted in soil, but glides across the seas by the power of technology (by steam or other types of engine), upon which its passengers are wholly dependent. The rich ship provides them with comfort and leisure ("the weather is fine, the views are pleasant") as long as they forget that they reside under the power of its machines and automata. Jünger also identifies the ship with the Leviathan, thereby equating the despotism of the modern State with the power of Technology. Everything radically changes and falls into place when icebergs and "islands of fire" appear on the ship's horizons.

311 Over the course of his whole life, Jünger held contradictory attitudes towards religion, but by the end of his earthly path he came to Catholicism.

312 See Friedrich Georg Jünger, *Grecheskie mify* [Greek Myths].

At the moment of catastrophe, people are exposed to the abyss of their non-freedom and their dependence on technology, its imperfections, and the enveloping power of alienation. Jünger contrasts the ship's collision to a hero's encounter with the pure elements of water or ice, when in an instant he might still take power and his destiny into his hands, whereas the ship's crash by the force of its own "gravity" drags all the passengers down with it to the bottom.

With this problem at hand, Ernst Jünger formulates a question which correlates and anticipates Julius Evola's posing of a similar problem in his *Ride the Tiger*: "Would it not be possible to both remain on the ship *and* retain one's autonomy of decision—that is, not only to preserve but even to strengthen the roots that are still fixed in the primal ground? This is the real question of our existence." The ship's catastrophe is the moment of truth. The world of technology and economy tends to incorporate catastrophe into its statistical causations as an unlikely event to be compensated with insurance payments. The Forest Rebel, on the contrary, invests all of his capital in such catastrophe, because catastrophe is the moment of confronting danger and death. "The Forest is the great House of Death" through which the wanderer must path, going through initiation and confronting their fundamental fears, or rather their only true fear: death. Danger is the moment of encounter with myth, when time (the temporal) is shaken at its core. Hence, the motto of the Forest Rebel is "Here and Now."

In addition to the existential-poetic presentation of the Gestalt of the Forest Rebel, Jünger makes a number of digressions which succinctly formulate some of the Forest Rebel's consequences, conclusions, and views on various matters. In the light of our path, of special interest are Jünger's remarks on the negative role of medicine, which de facto weakens a people's health and body, making them unsuitable for surviving catastrophes. "When a ship goes down, its dispensary sinks with it", Jünger writes. Minimal mortality rates in peacetime are fraught with the immense danger of unhardened bodies and health in the face of epidemics that can turn a healthy nation into corpses in one night. This is also a consequence of the softening comfort of technology. Medicine (and "hygiene") provides for overpopulation, for huge masses of people with which it does not know what to do. A large mass of healthy "glasshouse" people eventually becomes a source of huge numbers of victims.

Jünger also admits the possibility of using modern means for winning back spaces of freedom. Nevertheless, he warns against interpreting the Forest Rebel to be an anarchist who smashes cars. Jünger considers the turn from knowledge to language to be of the greatest importance, surpassing all the discoveries of physics. Entering the sphere of language, a thinker comes into contact with the theologian and poet and draws closer to primordial phenomena and myths. Among myths, one of importance to the Forest Rebel is the story of Dionysus' abduction by pirates, whereafter the awakened Deity entangles the ship in vines and unleashes a dense forest right on its deck, out of which leaps a tiger that tears his captors to pieces.

In his treatise *The Forest Passage*, Jünger absolutely correctly expressed the European and specifically Germanic metaphysics of the forest. He pays respect to the forest and considers it to be a place of freedom and home along with risk and war.[313] If we adjust this picture to fit our time in the half a century that has passed since Jünger's *Forest Passage*, then it would be fair to conclude that today's ship is embodied in digital and media technology, and that the power and proliferation of comfort-control have heightened everywhere. Instead of the iceberg in the way of the *Titanic*, disaster now looms over Big Data leaks, the corruption of bureaucracies and intelligence services, life dependency on social ratings and applications, ID implants and electric and other power networks.

To crown this exposition, it is worth mentioning the last Gestalt described by Jünger in his lifetime in his futuristic novel *Eumeswil*: the "Anarch." Like the Forest Rebel, the Anarch is aloof from power and dependence on it and in some ways

---

313 See Askr Svarte, *Gods in the Abyss*.

reflects the principle of "inward migration." But if the Forest Rebel considers guerrilla warfare, sabotage, resistance, and catastrophe as his operational horizon, then the Anarch is free from power in the vertical dimension of inner distance. Jünger's Anarch has nothing in common with the anarchist who seeks to liquidate any authority. Unlike the anarchist, the Anarch does not oppose the Monarch, but constitutes alongside him a dual pair of figures. If the Monarch is *monos* and *arkhe*, i.e., the concentration of the fullness of power in one person's hands, then the Anarch is a subject that does not oppose authority, but stands outside of it and therefore remains free on an equal footing. "The Monarch wishes to rule over all, the Anarch only over himself." The Anarch simply doesn't belong to the sphere of some alien authority, but remains unaffected in the epicenter of its machinations. In essence, the Anarch is a sovereign unto himself who draws only upon himself. The Anarch does not participate in the uprisings and struggles of the Forest Rebel, but is simply independent, excluding himself from society and denying any authority over himself. The Anarch is the fundamental grounding of "inward migration" pursued to the extreme.

Drawing on Julius Evola and Ernst Jünger's ideas, we can see that the rejection of the modern State is a compelled, necessary condition of our times. Empires and principalities are good, but they have outlived their own and have given way to small formats of like-minded men among ruins, a point to which practically all of the above-considered authors speak. It bears constantly keeping in mind the difference between the Anarch and the anarchist alongside the recognizing that the notion of "right anarchism" is only one technical term for the difficult existential situation of the "Traditionalist without Tradition."

John Zerzan and the Rejection of the Symbolic

The sociologist and anthropologist John Zerzan is a modern icon of left-wing anarchists and anarcho-primitivists. The author of numerous books and articles, Zerzan is one of the most consistent and active intellectuals framing his own agenda within the discourse of primitivism.[314] In the late 1990s and early 2000s, Zerzan actively defended and supported the arrested Theodore Kaczynski only to then break solidarity with him over the question of violence and a divergence between their ideas on the whole.

On the methodological level, Zerzan is an atheist who appeals to the socio-evolutionary and materialist paradigm and corresponding argumentation. Zerzan's ideal is small, egalitarian societies of hunter-gatherers living in harmony with nature. He negatively assesses the Neolithic Revolution, the domestication of livestock, and the development of agriculture, which he considers to be the beginning of the process of alienation.

It bears recalling that the word "culture" comes from the Latin *cultura*, meaning "cultivating", "processing", i.e., the application of human creativity to nature, the creation of instruments and practices for labor and survival, as well as the broader notion of culture as including spiritual spheres and tradition. Zerzan's theory stakes a fundamental and rigid opposition to any form of culture, seeing the latter as interference with nature and the natural course of events. As soon as a person begins to interfere in and alter the space closest to them with cultural practices, alienation begins. For Zerzan, there are no criteria or modes of authenticity or excess (hubris) to this intervention. Therefore, in his worldview, a tribe of gatherers appears as an object completely entrusted to the faceless, material forces of nature, like a leaf carried away by the wind. Comparing Zerzan and Spengler's concepts, we can see that they coincide in their negative assessment of the stage of civilization; however, unlike Spengler, who saw in culture a living principle connected with myth and religion, Zerzan turns his gaze even further to the pre-cultural or para-cultural domain of the (pre-)historical. In the

---

314 See John Zerzan, *Future Primitive and Other Essays* (Autonomedia, 1994); idem., *Running on Emptiness: The Pathology of Civilization* (Los Angeles: Feral House, 2002); idem., *Twilight of the Machines* (Port Townsend: Feral House, 2008); idem., *Why Hope? The Stand Against Civilization* (Port Townshend: Feral House, 2015).

opinion of the anthropologist Claude Lévi-Strauss, the myths and fairy tales of primitive peoples were designed to mask the already established gap and contradictions between man and nature.[315] Hence follows one of Zerzan's most important theses: abandoning any human messianism in culture, refraining from any teleology of being and existence.

Absolutely logical in this light, and also fundamental and innovative in the general discourse of primitivism, is John Zerzan's radical critique of symbolic culture, writing and language, which he sees as interrelated and at times synonymous. A supporter of pure experience and feeling unmediated by any higher culture of perceiving reality, communicating, and interacting, Zerzan deems the division of labor and the development of writing to have engendered alienation and introduced hierarchical power imbalances. It is not difficult to detect in this traces of a specific Marxian theory of culture and progress, some of whose premises were shared by Lévi-Strauss. But the fault lies not only with writing, but with the symbolic nature of language and abstractions in general. In his book *Twilight of the Machines*, Zerzan articulates his critical formula thusly: "An infinitely diverse reality is captured by finite language."

This issue raised and articulated by Zerzan is indeed profound and meaningful. It bears examination along three lines. The first aspect concerns the general topic of linguistic-specific thinking and, consequently, the culture of human societies. In the classical formulation of Sapir and Whorf, linguistic specificity is designated not as a theory but as an empirically observed law in languages.[316] Nevertheless, linguistic specificity,

---

315 See N.A. Butinov, "*Levi-Stross - etnograf i filosof*" [Lévi-Strauss: Ethnographer and Philosopher] in Claude Lévi-Strauss, *Strukturnaia antropologiia* [Structural Anthropology].

316 In particular, comparisons between the European and Amerindian languages have ignored the fact that the languages of American Indians confined to reservations were more archaic than modern American English. For a detailed exposition of the question of the linguistic specificity of thinking, see Sergei Y. Borodai, *Iazyk i poznanie. Vvedenie v postreliativizm* [Language and Knowing: An Introduction to Postrelativism].

or linguistic relativity, does not mean rigid determinism for all thinking and perceptions of reality through the prism of language. Consciousness has a more complex structure, and within Sapir-Whorf's generalized system no small role is played by pre-linguistic experiences, impressions, and the perception-assimilation of external reality. Language permeates and particularly structures and accents the thinking of its native-speaking people, but thinking is nonetheless broader than language. Therefore, Zerzan's claim that reality is "captured" or "limited" by language is speculation. What a person sees — "infinitely diverse reality" — pushes him to give what he sees a name-word or somehow place what he has assimilated into the mental domain of a greater or lesser scope, i.e., to take such into account in thinking.

Within the framework of the Traditionalist conceptualization of this problem, we can designate an alternative perspective for considering the problem of linguistic relativity and expressiveness. Classical relativism exists on the horizontal plane of the plurality of natural languages; consequently, it recognizes the presence of specifically mental accents or categories among peoples which are associated with the vocabulary and grammar of languages, whether of the more homogenous language families of the European type or among the more special cases of archaic tribes. The Traditionalist view proposes to add to this plane a chronological, vertically descending axis (which can be depicted, if you will, as a circle, drawing on the hermeneutics of the Year-Wheel). According to this approach, human languages also undergo involution along with the course of historical time, which is expressed in the loss of poetic flexibility, the existential richness of symbols, and broad semantic fields for foremost word-categories (such as the Greek word *logos*, which has more than 100 significations). Languages gradually "cool down" and ossify, lose their flexibility, and acquire fixed lexico-grammatical constructs and more modern semantics, which is also the merit of the linguistic reforms of the Enlightenment or the result of revolutions, such as the French Revolution or the October

Revolution in Russia.[317] A definite "finale" of this anti-symbolic, anti-poetic trajectory is the logical-analytical methodology of Ludwig Wittgenstein and his doctrine of atomic facts.

Thus, comparisons of, for instance, the American and English dialects of the English language, or of the main European languages to those of the Indian Americans or the Piraha tribe, not only take place on the horizontal plane of distinct cultures and lifestyles, but also involve comparing the European language(s) of Modernity with archaic tribal languages which are closer to the structures of myth and tradition. Of course, neither Sapir and Whorf nor Zerzan considered the question from such a perspective, therefore this approach still awaits precise formulation, approbation, and argumentation. Returning to Zerzan's formula, it bears clarifying that, over the course of metaphysical involution, "infinitely diverse reality", just like language, undergoes significant losses, simplifications, and becomes simply "poor reality" in the sense that we have attached to this term in the present work.

The second aspect is related to the problem of reality's reflection in language and the role of names and symbols in relation to things. John Zerzan advocates pure feeling and perception, or direct contact. For him, "peaches are more important than their name." On this point, Zerzan is, whether consciously or not, in tune with the words of Juliet in William Shakespeare's tragedy, for whom the name of a rose does not matter. Such an approach typically considers the assignment of names to things as an act of the thing's alienation, as turning the thing into a concept henceforth isolated in thinking and culture. People thereby operate and appeal not to peaches, but to their names, to their mental and socio-cultural cast of experience and associations. Since symbolic culture is unacceptable to Zerzan in general, it must be abandoned. Presumably, Zerzan's ideal world is one of nameless, unknown things and phenomena

---

317 This is reflected in the shift of all traditional terminology and vocabulary into the large semantic domain of "primitive" and "archaic" which is constructed and contrasted by the progressive lexicon of Modernity.

in which groups of semi-mute hunter-gatherers each time experience collisions with things as a first experience, not a single one of which is stored or transmitted in language in the form of any symbols or abstractions. Returning to the scene from Shakespeare, we see that Juliet recognizes her lover's bodily plane as primary. The Montagues are not Romeo's arms, legs, or shoulders, so he can and should reject the name and take on any other, for his face and body will not change. Despite the young girl's naivety, it is the names of the two lovers (cf. the names of things) that create the whole tragic tension of Shakespeare's work centered around their attraction and relationship.

For Traditionalism, the situation stands fundamentally differently. For Tradition, names and symbols play an immense role in expressing the essence of things. The distribution of the world's things and phenomena in mental and linguistic domains in one way or another affects or fully reflects the essence of the given thing in thinking and, as follows, in language. Therefore, "rose" and "peach" are not simply the arbitrary names of things (as per Saussure), but are important parts of them which are in some sense addressed to language and express their facets. A name or symbol either directly expresses the essence of a thing, or reflects one of its facets, etymologically, homonymously, and associatively connecting such with others, whereby semantic poles are formed. Thus, in "Traditionalist linguistics", symbol and name are existentially richer and more saturated than strict signs.

The third aspect concerns the relation of language, or rather writing, to power, authority, and hierarchy. In the vein of Marxist ideology, Claude Lévi-Strauss pointed to the class-power properties that generated writing skills and were flouted to "illiterate" tribesman. Following Michel Foucault's ideas on power and language, Zerzan also argues that language, including grammar and writing, is a structure and ideology of diversified hierarchical power that becomes anchored into people's thinking. The anthropologist James Scott's work on Zomia, which we will engage in detail later, shows how local groups of fugitives fleeing state power not uncommonly, consciously abandon writing as such and change their language practices with the aim of escaping state enslavement or eliminating the grounds for the emergence of state-like hierarchies and relations within their group.[318] The practices described by Scott are an intermediate variation, i.e., not a rejection of language and symbols, but a refraining from writing as a method of accounting (population censuses, registering subjects by name, etc.), subordination (knowing the sovereign's writing or the state language and its semantics, forgetting one's native language) and exploitation (illiteracy as a lower social ranking). Here, too, there are obvious projections of leftist theory onto societies which otherwise have no pronounced, standard classes or class struggle.

Of special importance in Zerzan's primitivist theory is the egalitarian "culture" of communicating and interacting free from the alienating influence of the division of labor and writing (= authority). Zerzan calls such interaction "face-to-face" and sees it as lacking any socio-cultural-political masks and statuses.[319] But such societies are nowhere to be found in archaic or recent history. Even the most socially simple communities of Zomia refugees exist as clan-family hierarchies, and modern democratic societies composed of individuals know civil ranks and statuses. Even animals have hierarchies. At the opposite pole is the characteristic Nepalese greeting namaste, which literally means "the Divine within me greets [the same] Divine within you." Namaste tells us that different people are in any case the carriers and faces of one Divinehood, whereby Zerzan's maxim turns into the Advaitist formula "face-of-the-divine-to-face-of-the-divine." The Divine is the source of language, symbol, religion, culture, and hierarchies of power.

Without a doubt, questions concerning the development and degeneration of language and its relation to thinking and power are relevant in the light of Pagan Traditionalism, the

318 See James. S. Scott, *The Art of Not Being Governed: An Anarchist History of Upland Southeast Asia* (New Haven: Yale University Press, 2009).

319 See Zerzan, *Running on Emptiness*.

plurality of peoples and tradition, and neo-archaism. But the solution proposed by Zerzan — completely excluding language and symbolic culture (including art and religion), returning to the unmediated experience of nameless things, and being an egalitarian, semi-animal herd at the mercy of the absolute elements of nature — is impossible and irrelevant as a scenario.

Zerzan's rejection of civilization is thus revealed to be yet another strategy for the inauthentic being of *das Man*. Zerzan calls for rejecting "human messianism", but this means directly rejecting the human being as such, for the human in and of itself is a symbol of the Divine and an expression of the macrocosm. The desire for egalitarianism and the rejection of the rich diversity of traditional cultures exposes Zerzan as a follower of purely modern and progressive attitudes in the spirit of left-wing liberalism. The main line of Western-centric mankind's development is the way of transhumanism and the Gestell, but *das Man* is also at work on the periphery, grounding the rejection of Dasein through inscribing the human being into a purely animal world and regime of meager existing.[320]

***

320 See Martin Heidegger, *The Fundamental Concepts of Metaphysics: World, Finitude, Solitude.*

Remarks on the Fields of Primitivsm

The spectrum of primitivist ideas, as we have shown above, harbors a number of intersections and resonances in both letter and spirit with the intentions of Pagan Traditionalism, the European "New Right", the plurality of peoples and cultures, and "right" anti-globalism. The key ideologists and practices of "neo-archaism" and simplification do not present any class (as in Marxism and socialism), nation or race (bourgeois and biological nationalism), or individual as the subject of their theories. Priority is given to families, small groups of ideologically like-minded associates, or religious communities, and all three variants can be combined, as can their argumentation be complementary. The figure of the isolated person in the wilderness, if encountered, is compensated for by a radical, existential charge and practice which conformist individuals inside civil society do not have. The global is radically rejected in favor of the local.

At the same time, we have also recognized the presence of the Gestell and *das Man* in a number of their postulates and proposed solutions to the problem of the industrial, technogenic society and the predatory exploitation of nature. This is most pronounced in the anti-cultural project of John Zerzan.

Advocates of the ideas of simplification and rejecting civilization ("simple living", "plain people") quite well understand the problem that the path which they propose is not for the masses, which leads them to posing the presence of enormous human masses as a problem. These masses of people, moreover, are irreversibly infected by the mental, existential, cultural, social, and everyday structures of the Gestell (the Industrial Trinity, surrogate activities) and exhibit an extremely negative, superficial, irrational abruption facing the discourse of "primitivism." Here we have the space to move on to considering some of the most common criticisms of primitivism.

The first thing that grabs the attention of the "last people" when they are faced with a developed, frontal critique of modern civilization is the implicit or explicit need to abandon the values of social and everyday comfort, modern secular education, and the established social stereotypes and clichés of public opinion and the mass media which free them from the burden of deep thinking and decision-making — this is what Kaczynski and many others have said about the mass "clip thinking" of modern globalized society. The revanche of Tradition or a planetary catastrophe for Civilization *a priori* imply the complete deconstruction of the values of comfort in the lifeworld (Schütz, Garfinkel), as well as the irretrievable disappearance of all modern culture and art. In this situation, modern man runs the risk of being completely exposed, down to the level of the naked life, on the level of culture, survival skills, and relationships with the numerous mythological beings, spirits and Divinities which he believed to be "dead."

Proponents of Traditionalist simplification are already consciously moving towards this experience in deconstructing and discarding Modernity on the level of culture, values, and practices. They consciously simplify life and everyday needs, reduce consumption and waste production, practice agriculture, hunting, gathering, protecting forests and ecotage, move to remote villages or even into the wilderness, become hermits, and are therefore in some sense "dead" to all other people and the state. They consciously opt for clashing with and overcoming the hardships through which the simple truth of Being and the Sacred is revealed. In parallel to changes in life practices, there is also deeper immersion in metaphysics, everyday and seasonal ritual practices (with which the very structure of perceiving seasons completely changes), and experiencing the eschatological, existential situation of "being in the thickness of ice."

Primitivists are not uncommonly urged to go ahead and "leave modern society, live alone in the forest, and not bother anyone", but the employment of such an "argument" only exposes its speaker as a carrier of a complete form of inauthenticity and incapacity. Behind the call to "get out of sight" lurks the desire to remove from the dividual's horizon of thought the whole array of absolutely relevant and truthful critique brought forth by Traditionalists towards modern civilization and the *modus vivendi* of the concrete person. This is not a solution to the problem, but a refusal to recognize it at the stage of first approach. *Das Man* is afraid of thought, afraid of ideas, and fears everything that puts a mirror up to him and shows him how he is and thinks as an inauthentic presence in the world. At the same time, moreover, egoism is not typical of primitivists, so the discourse is addressed to all peoples and people able and ready to think about obvious problems. Those who are not ready are the problem. Neutrality means solidarity with the enemy.

Here it is also necessary to clarify the problem of who should be the arbiter of this revolution. It is obvious that the set scale of transformations exceeds the format of all the state revolutions hitherto known to us. Insofar as we have developed our exposition and critique from within the Eurocentric space and culture, the various European peoples are our first addressees.

Second in line, the problems and tasks raised here will be clear and known to those non-European peoples and cultures who have been affected by and educated within the European Logos as part of missionary and colonial education. They are representatives of the non-European resistance to globalization, those fighting for their cultural, regional, and traditional identities and autonomy. Since they are familiar with European culture as such has influenced the formation of their thinking, they can be the translators and mediators between the picture presented here and their own culture. Here we arrive at the pluralistic grounds of resistance based on understanding the singular problem that threatens everyone, while, at the local level, local intellectuals and resistance fighters can and should select the arguments, metaphors, slogans, formulas, and means of waging real war against the agents and infrastructure of the

Gestell which are relevant to their own countries and cultures. They should understand that they are not fighting for the sake of "saving Europe" and are by no means whatsoever acting as proxies for another solution to "white people's problems." This should also be understood by Europeans themselves who share our positions and forecasts. Our alliance will end with the fall of the global technocentric Civilization, after which all of the uprising's participants with either fall back to or remain in their territories and never meet again, because the instruments of international logistics and communication will simply cease to exist. Everyone will return to their authentic lifeworlds, to their own problems and tasks.

Finally, there are minor representatives of indigenous and archaic peoples who to this day have retained their way of life and intellectual world unaffected by Eurocentric and modern education. Here arises a difficulty, because explaining the problem of the Gestell and the negative future to them requires their mastery of the whole corpus of Western European thought and philosophy, i.e., a kind of modernization. This is not needed. In order to mobilize them for struggle and strictly local resistance, sensitive and accurate mediators from among local Traditionalist activists or organizations are needed who can explain on an extremely simple and understandable level the necessity of fighting for their jungles, for their Amazon, for their Congo River, for their steppes, mountains, etc. Archaic tribes are already used as bargaining chips in political games and used to the fullest by left-wing progressive NGOs. This inflicts irreparable harm and shows us the great disadvantages of resistance when our potential allies are recruited or instrumentalized by the direct enemies of mankind. These brief considerations are, of course, not exhaustive. The problem of the actors of the resistance and revolution should be devoted additional, substantive reflection and real organizational work on the ground around the whole world.

The most important point is that today it is obvious to all that there is nowhere to escape from Civilization. Wherever a group of like-minded fellow believers might go, civilization will show up sooner or later in the form of energy or transport infrastructure, resource extraction, or police surveillance by satellites and combat drones. One could live for decades in the forest, jungle, or Taiga only for the bearers of civilization to start building a highway, city, tourist center, or lay fiber optic cable for Internet connection. There is a large number of well-known cases in which civilization and the construction sites of the Gestell have invaded the authentic life of local peoples, who respond with riots, uprisings, terrorist attacks, and murdering foreigners. Without a doubt, these are absolutely legitimate and just reactions on the part of free people and peoples towards invasion. But the hypocrisy of the system dictates to society the image of them being terrorists, renegades, barbarians, and savages who out of stupidity and fanaticism refuse the blessings of the modern world. Anyone who lives outside of the system is an "extremist" and *a priori* a danger. This gives rise to a deep existential tension, a feeling that the world is closed and driven into a corner. Retreating into the forest and living a peaceful life there without contact with civilization until one's death is a rare gift from the Divinities in our days. It is likely that such people and groups exist, but we do not hear or know anything about them, nor should we. In most cases, primitivists are left with the path of resistance, struggle, and the underground. According to Linkola, such societies and countries are destined to develop powerful defenses and weapons for protecting their ecological way of life. But this once again leads to the development of industrial production technologies and the disciplined society of Modernity. It is impossible to embody the ideal of neo-archaism in one closed space surrounded by more developed neighbors; therefore, the theory and practices of radical simplification are addressed to the whole world with no alternative.

Conservationists and many environmental activists and ideologues (e.g., Technogaianism) put forth a counter-thesis to radical ecological primitivists by pointing out that the development of technology and renewable energy in the future will allow for saving nature and the planet and even recovering (by cloning) species diversity. The bankruptcy of this conviction has been shown clearly above, and it should be seen as irrational, akin to the religions of salvation and promises of "heaven on earth", as a form of conviction as to the omnipotence of technology. The transition from hydrocarbon-based energy (which entails the destruction of the landscape for the sake of coal mines, destroying soils and the earth's crust during oil production) to nuclear and thermonuclear energy, as well as to innovations in electric batteries, will lead to even greater environmental risks, to the need to accelerate the development of evermore high-tech control and security systems, and to the new exploitation of already rare earth metals and elements, the destruction of landscapes by kimberlite pipes, and the capitalist-colonial exploitation of archaic peoples in Africa and South America. In other words, all of this in no way solves the problem of technological development and the catastrophic situation of the Anthropocene's production of increasing consumption of energy, goods, and people who wish to preserve and improve this way of life which radical primitivists call for abandoning.

Moreover, if the current population level is maintained, a sharp, mass rejection of technologies would nevertheless still practically lead to the instantaneous disappearance of forests, animals, plants, and the destruction of the environment overall, since all forces would be thrown into securing the minimal level of survival for and subsistence for an excessive number of masses poorly adapted to genuine life. This is the backside of the question of energy (burning forests) and food (hunting, fishing, gathering) leading to the very same resource wars. This is partly why Linkola's views, for instance, can be considered a tactic for a transition period from civilization to culture. The very same question of resources is at the center of Alain de Benoist's work. Thus, moving towards ceasing growth and toward deindustrialization will *a priori* be very painful and tragic, but this must be done for the sake of a different future.

451

What is designated by the term "neo-archaism" can also be interpreted as a creative, innovative approach to creating a new archaic way of life and expression of the Sacred. Here lies the only allotted space for compromise and changes in secondary and peripheral things that do not require the development or application of technology. Primitivism generally recognizes the positive experience of the development of permaculture[321] and the expansion of the range of edible mushrooms, cultivated plants, fish, and animals, as well as methods of breeding and raising which were discovered or accounted for in modern times. Some innovations are adopted, for instance, for the construction of houses out of natural materials with non-classical geometry in order to increase insolation and retain heat. Medical-social preventative practices, hygiene, asepsis and antisepsis, as well as the in-depth study of the medicinal properties of plants and intensive food processing are also approved insofar as such entails rejecting technological medicine as a form of embodiment of *tekhne* and biopolitics.[322] In most cases, these "innovations" are revisions of old, archaic experiences and the result of exchanges between archaic cultures living in different parts of the world as recorded in ethnographic literature.

Finally, we can address the specific difficulties which proponents of Traditionalism and neo-archaism will encounter in some future or in some remote corners of the world where they will have to stake their spaces over the long term of several generations. In the immediate perspective, future primitivists will not find themselves in the midst of endless meadows and forests full of game, mushrooms, and berries, or rivers and lakes full of fish. The primary surrounding landscape after the radical simplification of the whole world will be akin to post-apocalyptic panoramas. In the beginning and for quite a long time afterwards, future primitivists will be condemned to behold the dead relics and ruins of the world as bitter reminders and

---

321 See Masanobu Fukuoka, *The One-Straw Revolution: An Introduction to Natural Farming* (New York: New York Review Books, 2009)

322 In general, archaic societies only admit the existence of sicknesses (ailments brought by spirits) which shamans can influence.

mentally binding chains of nostalgia for the comfortable past. It will be necessary or imperative to either flee from the ruins of cities for several generations, to become nomads destroying all the remains of the former civilization on their path and clearing the lands of abandoned cities and settlements in rituals of burning and sacrificing the accursed share and impure spaces. Or they will have to settle down among the ruins and artifacts of the former degraded society. One could propose an initiation ritual for future youth in which gangs of young people (*kóryos*) will set out into dead cities with the task of burning to the ground, demolishing, and destroying large buildings. Sacred, anti-technologically motivated violence against the body of technologies should already today be practiced in Traditionalist and fundamental-conservative communities as a condition for joining the community, tribe, or family.

After many years and multiple generations, the ruins of abandoned cities will be overgrown by grass and forests and filled with returning animals and birds. High-rise apartment blocs, subway tunnels, and other buildings will become new caves, cliffs, mountains, and underground rivers. But, until city remnants once again become "just nature", it will be necessary to comprehensively cultivate a negative attitude towards the ruins and relics in the education of future generations. In no cases should an "extinct, highly developed race" be idealized in the spirit of conspirological New Age literature on ancient civilizations. For example, the interpretation of Mount Rushmore should be thoroughly transformed. Mount Rushmore, named after the businessman Charles Rushmore, was for quite a long time revered by the Lakota Indians under the name "Six Forefathers" and was a place of cult, but the invasion of modern capitalist colonists led to the mountain being turned into an ugly monument to several US presidents. After the destruction of modern civilization, the local Indians will be able to visit the Mountain of Their Forefathers again and show their children the faces of the demons that once terrorized and destroyed the middle world of the Indians. Thusly will the mountain be resacralized, adjusted to eschatology and the necessary tasks of educating future generations on the true essence of what was long ago once called "progress."

Does this mean that when the entire modern post-industrial civilization disappears from the face of the earth, birds will immediately start talking again, stones will begin to fly to visit each other, forests will sing songs, the winds will retell them to rivers and mountains, and Pan will lead nymphs to new meadows? The answer may be ambivalent: "yes and no." Yes, because the natures of various parts of the manifest world know no void, and they will be reinhabited by their local mythical beings, animals, spirits, and *genii locorum* with all of their intense life. But the answer might be "no" if the surviving people remain carriers of modern consciousness which will filter and exclude everything "supernatural", attributing such to their own shocked and stressed aberrations of perception. This might persist until a person finally dies, or until a drunken satyr beats him on the back with reeds, shocking him into finally awakening and recognizing the living spaces of natures around him. If the remaining people in the post-civilization world have children, then their natural openness to the fabulous will allow them, unlike their blind parents, to behold all the diversity of sacred life and beings from birth. This would give rise to conflict: adults, as carriers of modern consciousness, might take their children to be insane as they see and interact with what is not accessible to their parents.

Thus, we can see that the questions and problems posed across the ideological field of "primitivism" or "neo-archaism" affect not only the worldly problems of the total decline of the modern world, existential problematics, and overcoming the resistance and inertia of the huge masses of *das Man*, but also the future, in the event of a successful global dismantling of the Gestell, or in the case of a rare but successful escapism from the modern world. The modern world is not only around man, it is within his thinking. Therefore, the ruins of the post-civilization world are duplicated in the internal mental structures of the proponents of radical simplification themselves. In any case, however, the general vector for solving problems and for attaining a dignified way of life and death lies not in the past (the past is already built up in cities and infrastructure on top of old sacred spaces) and not so much in the horizontal, chronological future, but in a fundamentally other "here" that is definitely not only "here" and is not this "here."

It can be said with absolute accuracy that everything that has been created over the past at least 1,500-2,000 years must be destroyed and abandoned.

***

Depopulation

The question of population size or the size of groups resisting the technogenic civilization is one of the most acute and problematic issues across the whole spectrum of theories and practices of radical simplification. As can be seen from the above-presented panorama of key ideologues, practically all of them explicitly or implicitly speak out in favor of reducing the population of the manifest world, or hedge their stakes on small groups and communities against all the rest. The whole discourse on population size within primitivism fits into a triangle of authors, each of whom presents their own approach. They are Kaarlo Pentti Linkola, Theodore Kaczynski, and David Benatar.

The most radical approach is put forth by David Benatar, who insists on the moral imperative of the absolute extinction of mankind, a global population of zero. Although Benatar is not a primitivist or proponent of Traditionalism, his position is quite well-known and voluminous. We will consider it in detail in in the pages below.

Kaarlo Pentti Linkola proposed harsh totalitarian measures for universal demographic control, including limits on the number of childbirths, forced sterilization, abortions, femicide and infanticide. Nevertheless, he does not renounce existence as such. We qualified his proposed measures as a "transitional regime." On the whole, they fit into his apologetics for the inevitability of bitter violence for the sake of species survival.

Theodore Kaczynski proposes an original alternative, arguing that groups putting up resistance to the industrial society should have and raise as many children as possible to inherit and continue their fathers' struggle against the entire System (the Industrial Trinity). This resonates with the often-heard imperative of building networks of horizontal, hard-to-reach or underground communities, clans, and "primitivist" groups, but such a position involuntarily also gives rise to an equally, perhaps more significant important problem: correctly and worthily raising children to continue the life path and cause of their fathers.

In general, the question of the size of the human population exists at the intersection of numerous political theories and social and economic interests. On the political plane, it can be immediately noted how population reduction goes hand-in-hand with the renunciation of the idea of Empire within the paradigms of Modernity and Postmodernity — according to Julius Evola, such empires are no longer possible. Only the Anti-Empire of perverted multiplicities, as described by Antonio Negri and Michael Hardt, is possible now. After decades of unsuccessful struggle, Evola himself arrived at recognizing the need to leave the "ashes of tradition" and to instead seek another beginning within and through the Kali-Yuga. Such a compelled position of "synchronization" with the totally negative conditions of our time paradoxically resonates with the position of some pagan ideologists who have hedged their stakes on tribalism, local interests, and local being. Genuine Althings and Veches, which have nothing in common with modern representative liberal democracy, only existed within relatively small or somewhat larger communities, tribes, islands, settlements, military unions, etc.

Overall, the question of depopulation exists in altogether veiled form in the framework of Traditionalism as well. It should not be avoided, as some do in attempting to reduce the whole issue to uncontested apologetics for pro-life movements. We are left with bringing this issue to light and examining the furthest-reaching and most uncompromising horizons to which it leads.

Overpopulation: Strengthening Alienation

The Neolithic Revolution is often deemed to have been the event that inaugurated rapid population growth. Various authors' opinions differ when it comes to what was the cause and what was the consequence. Some believe that the increasing number of families and tribes of hunter-gatherers was one of the factors that compelled people to opt for sedentary life and agriculture. From others' point of view, it was settled life and culture that gave the impetus for increased fertility and survival rates as well as sufficient food for growing households.

The warlike nomadic peoples of antiquity and male unions had the problem of a shortage of women. They had to capture women in order to maintain a sufficient population level and produce more men. Women were the least adapted to their way of life and were also the targets of men from other unions. This is how the growth of non-sedentary peoples was regulated and restrained. On the eve of colonization, remote indigenous peoples in South and North America as well as the Far East and North of Russia had more or less regular population sizes commensurate with their ways of life and the capacity of their surrounding natures.

Numerous other natural and socio-political factors also regulated population size, from crop yields and epidemics to natural mortality/survival rates, rebellions and wars between peoples. But already at the outset of modern times, as Linkola and Benatar note, wars and cataclysms no longer coped with overpopulation. The years following the Second World War saw the birth rate increase rapidly, cover all the wartime losses with a significant surplus. This led Linkola to the hypothesis that in wartime women should be killed first in order to inflict maximal damage on the enemy and halt excessive population growth in the early postwar years.

According to Benatar, the definition of overpopulation is normative, not descriptive or predictive. Therefore, at any given moment in the present, there cannot be more people than there already are. But from what symbolic threshold (number) does overpopulation and its negative impact begin? Here the answers vary, depending on the argumentation and paradigm with which an author operates. It is commonplace to link the Earth's population growth with the chronological horizon of the existence of the first cultural human societies, which archeological data puts in the region of 40,000-10,000 B.C.E., in the Neolithic. It is estimated that in the span from the Middle Ages to Modernity, the population of Earth was more than 500 million people, but less than 1 billion. Then began the period of hyperbolic world population growth as counted by the mathematician Heinz von Förster.

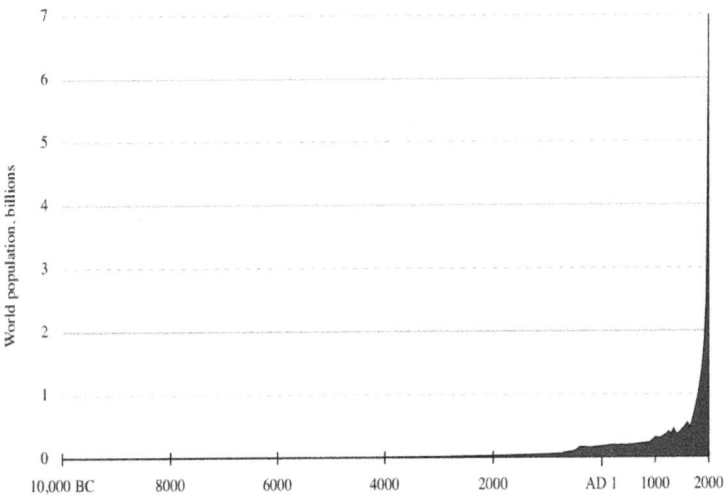

According to UN estimates, mankind crossed the threshold of 2 billion in the first 30 years of the 20th century, 3 billion in the 1960s, 4 billion in 1974, and 5 billion in 1987. By the turn of the millennium, the Earth's population crossed the threshold of 6 billion, at which point Förster's forecast ends. The rate of population growth and the interval between each new billion is shrinking, and already in 2011 the population surpassed 7 billion. By 2024, it is expected to surpass 8 billion. According to the mathematical model of Sergei Kapitsa, by 2130 the Earth's population will reach a stabilization point at around 14 billion people.[323] His conclusions are consonant with

323 See Sergei Kapitsa, *"Rost naseleniia i ego matematicheskaia model"* [Population Growth and its Mathematical Model], *Nauka i zhizn'* 3 [Science and Life] (1998).

the estimates of the French physician Jean-Noël Birabin, who speaks of a 10-12 billion-strong "stabilized" population.

Alongside explosive population growth, the world population is also undergoing a demographic transition. In the highly developed countries, especially in cities, the birth rate is falling to the level of mere replacement or below (natural extinction), while in the peripheral countries of the "Third World", which have largely preserved the traditional way of life but now have access to more modern medicine, products, and infrastructure (overlapping in the spirit of archeomodernity), population growth is explosive. This also ensures migration strategies for replacement demographics in the "First World" countries.[324]

Love for one's neighbor, excessive practices of monastic charity, and the conception of humanism towards others, all introduced by the adepts of a new Middle Eastern religion, opened the gates for the survival and reproduction of those whom Life itself had previously excluded from its womb or who died due to the conditions prescribed above. These religions, which grew from the same root, were the matrix of proto-globalism that treated nature and the pagan peoples inhabiting it like resources.

But, to an even greater extent, the situation that has developed to date is the result of the active work of technologies aimed at preserving and multiplying life and the ideals of sustainable development and growth. Innovations in production, food storage and logistics, the operations of the capitalist market, the development of energy, medico-social practices and medicine in general, as well as the diversification of labor and the introduction of universal education are all responsible for demographic transition, that is for the explosive

---

324 James S. Scott and other authors have pointed to how the practice of mass importing "migrants" to places of extraction and production, including the de facto enslaved Indians of the Americas, was already typical of Spanish colonialism in South America, which laid down the whole model of treating foreign peoples in economic-demographic terms. See James. S. Scott, *The Art of Not Being Governed*.

growth of minimally secure lower class masses of the South and the demographic degradation of the Western vanguard of the North.[325]

At the same time, the immanent essence of rapid population growth in the aftermath of the Enlightenment and colonization, *ergo* modernization and globalization, is the general alienation of people from any form of greater collective identities — from the feeling of one's own ethnos, tribe, estate, caste, larger family, *rod*, clan, etc., each of which has its own sacred dimension. This population growth has been accompanied by an immanent transition to minimal humanism and the civil-individual, now dividual identity of multitudes. Minimal food security for survival and working on a machine, or for the contemporary precariat, ideally suits minimal units of individuals who have lost their last face in the midst of masses and classes. This, among other things, is the origin of rapid urbanization, urbanism, and the aesthetics of megacities and industrial mono-cities, the purpose of which is to ensure the concentration of individuals alienated from their nature, or proletarians, within the tightest radius around places of production and services.

The problem of population growth, and as a consequence the growth of consumption outstripping the capacity of arable land and trade, already drew attention in the Enlightenment. The most famous scholar and critic of unrestrained population growth was a classic representative of deism, the Anglican priest and economist Thomas Malthus. In his major work of 1798, *An Essay on the Principle of Population*, Malthus employed an economic approach to assess the risks posed by the population

---

325 Studies have shown that even minimal general education for girls has a devastating effect on subsequent fertility and plans to start a family. The traditional way of life and the metaphysics of motherhood are replaced by surrogate activities. At the same time, however, it is a pure mistake to believe that girls and women are like stupid, uneducated creatures without secular education. Instead of secular sciences, they once knew entire universes of other complex things, crafts, and initiations that were relevant in a particular life, marriage, child raising, etc. The criterion of education in this case is not objective, but is once again an ideological, moral justification for the alleged superiority of progressive knowledge over the "backward" and "archaic" with a touch of "emancipation" from the latter.

growth of workers and rabble in the suburbs of London and other industrial cities. He believed that population growth occurs in a simple geometric progression that outpaces the arithmetical rate of food production. At a certain point in time, the mass population would begin to prevail over the volume of production, which would lead to famine, social riots, and consequently also a decline in production. This situation has been deemed the "Malthusian trap", and it is believed that it is characteristic of pre-industrial societies where the population growth rate of villages outstrips the capacity of arable land depleted each year. But Malthus' historical environment and sphere of attention was already industrial, as England in those years was at the peak of the Industrial Revolution and the rise of its imperial power, which makes Malthus' calculations fairly applicable to societies at the stage of active modernization.

Malthus' and his followers, the Malthusians', main proposals were concerned with opposing the growth of the poor population who, although isolated from the traditional agrarian way of life, still retained the custom of giving birth to many children. In the conditions of city life and the struggle for workplaces in factories (the years of Luddism), the practice of having many children only increased and gave rise to new poverty and social vices. Being an Anglican Christian, Malthus hoped for guiding and enlightening the poor to refrain from "desires of the flesh" and procreation.

What Malthus did not take into account — for quite objective reasons at the dawn of the industrial society — was the coming demographic transition to generation replacement or negative levels of population reproduction. Similarly, the discovery of new continents, pastures and arable lands, and new production technologies, as well as the operation of the market mechanisms of international trade, significantly offset the timing of the "Malthusian trap." Malthus' theory exerted great influence on the emergence of Social Darwinist theory, as well as enriched argumentation for the capitalist exploitation of workers, since the growing mass of the lower strata of the population made it possible to maintain favorable wage rates and the process of precariatization.

Malthus essentially would have had to stabilize the emerging monotonic process in the demographic sphere in order to ensure sustainable development, growth, and sufficient resources for future generations. The solution to this problem, as history has shown, would become the very same active modernization and the expansion of exploitable spaces and sales markets. On the one hand, neo-Malthusianism promotes the agenda of controlling birth rates and population impact on ecology, while on the other hand, in the vein of minimal humanism, it catastrophically decides to maintain population growth as long as well-being is more or less ensured by technological means. The population grows, and this growth generates problems → the triumvirate of science, technology, and capital solve/delay the consequences → the population continues to grow and generate problems whose solution is once again entrusted to the power of the Gestell. Therefore, the whole discourse and hopes pinned on science on matters of renewable energy, ecology, epidemiology, superfoods, fresh water sources, etc., are all echoes of the problems comprehended by Malthus. Within the framework of this logic, Alain de Benoist was right to note the imminent need for additional planets for resource extraction. No less important of a negative factor is the high concentration of populations in a few regions and cities which are most suitable for modern life instead of more or less even distribution around the world. Asia (India, Pakistan, China), Southeast Asia, the Pacific, the US, and Brazil are the leaders in this. These regions, especially their capitals and river and ocean coasts, have become concentration points of resource and energy consumption, goods, and, as a result, global sources of garbage and negative impacts on the environment. These are the residential centers of *das Man* and the "nerve" and "blood" nodes of the body of the global system of Enframing.

In the early 1970s, the globalist think tank known as the Club of Rome oversaw the publication of a report entitled

The Limits to Growth, which redrew attention to the problem of the Malthusian trap at a new historical and technological impasse. The authors presented mathematical modelings of the future that took into account a variety of demographic, energy, economic, and other factors (the models ranging from World 1 to World 4 in 2012), the aim of which was to search for the very same ways to maintain sustainable growth and development, even despite the report's thesis that the idea of "growth" and the value of consumption level should be called into question in the future. The report was the first in a series of publications by the Club of Rome and other international organizations. A number of the proposed measures for reducing the birth rate gave rise to conspiracy theories of population reduction in favor of the golden North or the so-called "Golden Billion", i.e., the total population of the most developed countries which would be obliged to ensure economic growth, the consumption of resources and goods, and their citizens' standards of living by all means, i.e., to the detriment of the rest. Nevertheless, we have still not seen any effective actions or decisions on significant depopulation. Even birth control programs like Planned Parenthood primarily hit those societies where the demographic transition has already taken place, while these programs do not have any significant effect in the "Third World."

From the socio-economic point of view and in terms of resources, we can safely conclude that overpopulation is the driving force of alienation and is yet another dimension of hubris, of uncontrolled excess, which in a complex system of interconnections boosts other manifestations of the resource-based attitude to the world and peoples.

In 2008, *New Scientist* published an issue devoted to the problem of the limits to growth and the influence of human activities on ecosystems and the world as a whole, i.e., the ecological footprint and the Anthropocene. The issue's articles called for the very same "sustainable development" and "introducing new technologies" to save the Earth and mankind, to establish a "new green deal" that would mean pressure and additional taxation on the real industrial sector and resource extraction. In other words, such means inter-economic operations by some players against others through the levers of the media and environmentalist hype. Thus, the content of this issue's texts can be ignored. If the solution to these problems really interested scientists and politicians, then they would have much greater success with financing the translation of Pentti Linkola's works and proceeding to their implementation.

1. Average temperature in the Northern Hemisphere
2. Population
3. CO2 concentration
4. Loss of tropical rainforest and woodland
5. GDP
6. Water consumption
7. Paper consumption
8. Motor vehicles
9. Fishing industry volume
10. Ozone layer depletion
11. International investments

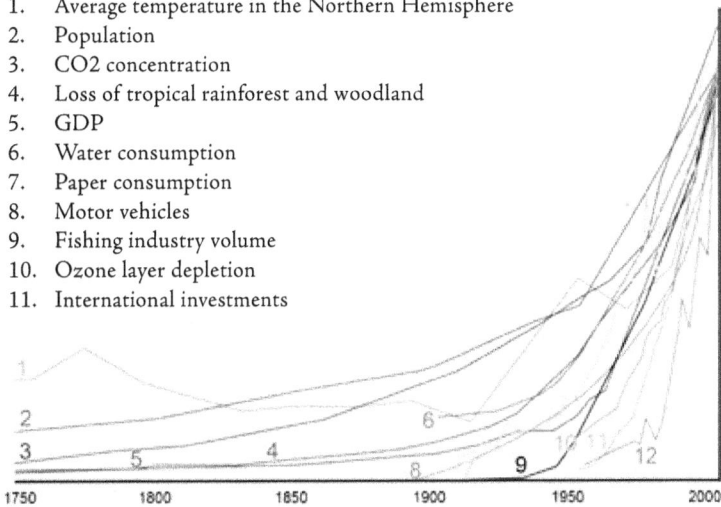

New Scientist, oct. 2008

Most interesting is the above cumulative 12-factor graph that depicts the deep correlation between the advent of extensive Modernity since the 1750s, the Industrial Revolution, the beginning of hyperbolic population growth (Förster, Malthus), and — approaching the early 2000s — the rapid growth of motor vehicle production, predatory deforestation, the exhaustion of fish stocks, the extinction of species (destruction through hunting, including for the sake of bourgeois pseudo-luxuries), increase in water and paper consumption, and the evermore rapid growth of global investment markets. In the very same historical span, the demolition of all traditional states in Europe and the world, the death of empires, and the emergence of the purely Modernist political theories and social order came to fruition and became established facts. Thus, scientific, industrial, and economic development turn out to be immanent to the deep political transformations and anti-Traditionalist revolutions of the "Great Divergence" period (per Samuel Huntington). To complete the picture, the graph lacks only a curve reflecting the rapid and deep expansion of computer technologies and the digitalization and virtualization of all spheres of life since the late 20th century. In terms of its scale of penetration and influence, digitalization is comparable only to the "Gutenberg Revolution", that is the emergence of book printing and the spread of knowledge that determined the entire course of the Enlightenment.

The modern economy depends on the expansion of markets and resource bases (energy, pastures, arable land, etc.) for the sake of balancing the "monotonic" growth of profits. Hence, demographic and fertility forecasts are included in calculations regardless of whether a capitalist or socialist system dominates in one corner of the Earth or another. Huge factories for the production of poultry and livestock, which operate like conveyor belts of necropolitics for animals, are tied to expected consumer demand and population (=market) volumes. A similar situation prevails with the calculation of the production volume of cars, gadgets, and other consumer goods that concern real production, not the semiurgy of virtual signs (which can be produced and effectively consumed by automated neural networks and robots). The global labor market, wages, and political strategies such as betting on migrants to become "new citizens", the demographic rhetoric of populists, the problems of overpopulated cities, etc., all revolve around the population question.

As a consequence, sudden demographic explosions are undesirable for the global capitalist system precisely by virtue of their suddenness, when the system has not yet found ways to provide new people with a guaranteed minimum income to be spent on the consumption of goods and services to support demand. But much worse for the global system is a sudden demographic hole or an acute, instantaneous, significant population loss. In such a case, the market is deprived of a significant mass of workers and consumers for whom goods have already been produced, raw materials have already been procured, loans have already been issued, and payments and interest on deposits have been calculated. Alongside a suddenly disappearing population, for instance during a large-scale natural or technogenic cataclysm, the growth curve sags down and the demand for goods falls due to the natural cause of the extinction of the needed consumers. The economy and production are thus dealt a blow which can lead to disruptions in supply chains, decreases in general living standards, and socio-political instability. The predominantly capitalist global economy therefore nurtures population growth as a full subject of biopolitics and bioeconomics.

A glaring illustration of the above was observable during the COVID-19 pandemic that swept across the world in early 2020. The rapid spread of infections clearly showed that globalization is literally dangerous to the physical health of billions of people. Easily accessible tourism, international flights, and logistics have paved the way for the spread of new strains and antibiotic-resistant superbugs. Globalization literally means permanent risk for everyone, replicating the plagues brought by Europeans that befell the Indians of North and South America.

The harsh quarantine and isolation measures that locked down people in their homes amidst a partial and in some places complete stoppage of production, trade, services, international logistics, and other sectors dealt unprecedented damage to the real sector and partially the service sector. At the same time, the capitalization of IT giants and startups providing services for business virtualization (transferring to online mode), online trading, online order and delivery services, and online entertainment, increased manyfold over. Real globalization in the form of international air traffic, air, land, and sea cargo logistics, tourism, institutes, and "face-to-face" meetings, slowed down considerably. But virtual network globalization by way of the Internet and the mass consumption of predominantly Western cultural content only deepened. The existential of connectivity and access to the Web once again turned out to be key markers of who is "alive" and "plugged-in" for work and leisure processes. The emergency measures and regulations also supplied arguments for strengthening transparency and the forced imposition of biopolitical and medical-political control systems and sanctions in many states. In the spare of production, the lockdowns also gave impetus to the development and implementation of automated assembly lines and logistics without the participation of humans, or with remote operators.

Despite the immense collateral economic and biopolitical damage, the new virus had little to no significant impact on population size. By mid-2022, out of 8 billion inhabitants on Earth, the total number of cases of infection was just over 593 million, and the number of deaths worldwide in these two years was only 6.4 million. In terms of this index, COVID-19 was 10 times inferior to the Spanish flu pandemic that occurred at the end of the First World War and by 1920 had added up to 50 million deaths to the total losses of the first two decades of the 20th century. The COVID-19 mortality rate turned out to be insignificant, but the negative consequences for us (positive for the economy) for the near future were predictable. The isolation of people for weeks and months, coupled with disrupted product supplies and alarmist demands within the first weeks, led to a shortage of contraceptives, thus promising a potential surge in the birth rate at the turn of 2020-21.[326] It is very likely that a demographic boom will more than cover the losses from the coronavirus, and that over the next few years the pandemic will turn out to have been a link between another spurt in population growth, deepened digitalization and virtualization, and the installation of totalitarian means of digital surveillance and biopolitics (the Great Reset program).

326 Statistical studies on this have yet to appear.

The 2020 pandemic can be seen as a "steam release" in the system, a balancing and adjusting of the Gestell's unchanged course towards total domination.

Looking ahead, we can conclude that depopulation is beneficial as an effective measure and weapon against the global economy, against cultural-political globalization, and against the alienation of peoples and the exploitation of nature.

What really frightens economists, politicians, as well as conservative populists from both the "right" and "left" might very well become our imperative and a way to cut the Gordian knot of all the problems of our time. Depopulation should not frighten us, because it is better to bring down the world system of production, credit, and affluent consumption than to continue to tolerate the multiplying vulgarity and anti-human lifestyle of *homo economicus / das Man*.

But these are demographic and economic criteria. Moving on, we will turn to the metaphysical and Traditionalist position on procreation. We shall turn from quantitative to qualitative criteria, to a critical survey of the spectrum of anti-natalist[327] ideas.

The Metaphysical Arguments of Anti-Natalism

To the ancient poet Theognis of Megara belongs the following maxim expressing the aristocratic attitude to coming into the world:

Best of all for mortal beings is never to have been born at all

Nor ever to have set eyes on the bright light of the sun

But, since he is born, a man should make utmost haste through the gates of Death [Hades]

And then repose, the earth piled into a mound round himself.[328]

---

327 From the ancient Greek prefix ἀντί ("against", "anti-") and the Latin *natalis*, "birth."

328 Theognis 425–8, in Douglas E. Gerber, *Greek Elegiac Poetry* (Loeb Classical Library, 1999), 234.

These words would be repeatedly paraphrased by poets over the centuries, from Sophocles to Heinrich Heine. To Heraclitus of Ephesus belongs an even earlier statement about humankind: "Being born they want to live to have their appointed deaths, and they leave children behind to have their deaths happen to them."[329] These words resonate with the lines of one Icelandic rune poem dedicated to the rune *Maðr*, i.e., "Man":

Maðr er manns gaman	*Man is the delight of man*
ok moldar auki	*and augmentation of the earth*
ok skipa skreytir.	*and adorner of ships.*

These words indicate that man is from birth already dust added to earth, which is to say that he carries death in himself, that death is an important part of his essence.

In the *Republic*, Plato pointed to the need for measures to regulate the population of the ideal city, for a lack of people would threaten harmony and lead to a mixture of occupations, while excess would lead to need and war. The size and population of the city-state is supposed to take into account the capacities of the surrounding environment. This provision has become commonplace in theories of population and politics since the Enlightenment.

In the non-dual darshanas of Shaivism and Tantra, exiting the cycle of karmically conditioned rebirths is described as the adept liberating and realizing the Divine Absolute. Refraining from procreation and cutting off all ties with one's family are preconditions for beginning the path of the Aghori, for burning karma and the conditionings (attachments to the world of rebirths) that are created through the conception and birth of children, whereby new souls are brought into the world.

Increased attention to the cult of the *rod*, rebirth, and achieving immortality is characteristic of the metaphysics of the agricultural estate. The nuclear monogamous family which we

---

329 [Translated from the author's Russian with reference to Dennis Sweet, *Heraclitus: Translation and Analysis* (Lanham: University Press of America, 1995), 11, fragment 20. - Trans.]

know today is only a late and one of many, rather limited forms of marriage.

In the Bible, in the Book of Genesis (1:27-28), God calls on people to fill the earth and rule over it as ready-to-hand:

> God created mankind in his own image, in the image of God he created them; male and female he created them. God blessed them and said to them, "Be fruitful and increase in number; fill the earth and subdue it. Rule over the fish in the sea and the birds in the sky and over every living creature that moves on the ground."

Despite this call to "be fruitful and increase in number", the Abrahamic religions have huge problems with the metaphysics of eros and sex, problems which they have transmitted into all the societies they have penetrated over the ages. The pole of the Feminine principle and the body are fundamentally demonized in creationism, marked as a sphere of sinfulness and impurity, which goes against pagan traditions' harmonious and holistic attitude towards the body and eros. A programmatic consideration of this question has been put forth in Julius Evola's *Eros and the Mysteries of Love: The Metaphysics of Sex*.

Several rather different myths of the origin of the Deity Eros are set forth in Plato's *Symposium* dialogue. According to one version, Eros is the child of Poros and Penia ("Plenty" and "Poverty"). According to another version, he is the companion of Aphrodite who manifests in two aspects: Urania (Heavenly) and Pandemos (Vulgar, Popular). Accordingly, Eros has a dual nature: he can both elevate people above the earthly, raising them to the higher dimensions of Being, as well as manifest in strictly hedonistic, obsessive, plebeian passions, the consequences of which are either legitimate children or bastards.

With respect to feminine metaphysics, there are two modes of embodiment: the Demetric and Aphroditic. Demetric femininity is expressed in the figure of the mother and the wife, the metaphysics of marriage, motherhood, raising offspring, housekeeping, and the metaphysics of Earth covered and worked by the Heavenly masculine principle. Demosthenes said: "We have hetaerae to quench lust, concubines for daily needs and legal wives to give birth to sons and maintain houses."[330] Aphroditic femininity is least suited for marriage and childbearing and is associated with the *femme fatale* and sacred feminine figures of a transgressive, radical, initiatic femininity that liberates, uplifts, be bestows wisdom and doctrine upon the adept. Within the Aphroditic circle of figures, we can name the Scandinavian Freya, the Indian Kali and Durga (Shakti in general), the Dakini, the Dionysian Bacchantes, etc. The stereotypes established by Abrahamism and Puritanism prescribe treating any manifestations of eros and femininity beyond the ultra-subordinated Demetric type as forms of degeneration, decadence, or libertinage.[331] After centuries of repression of all other forms of erotic transgression, the anti-Puritan breakthrough starting with Freudianism and continuing through the sexual revolution up to our days has poured out into purely chthonic and pandemic, that is vulgar forms. This breakthrough erupted into the lower spheres (or from the lower spheres into the middle world) due to the closing-off and denial of the higher spheres.

According to Evola, there are two erroneous paradigms of approaching eros: "biological evolutionism" and as an "instrument for procreating the genus." The first considers all manifestations of sexual desires in terms of "naturalism" and Darwinism, and likens people's physiological and social behavior to practices in the animal world. Evola quotes Péladan: "Realism is worth no more in love than in art. On an erotic level imitation of nature becomes imitation of the beast."[332] Naturalism and evolutionism are anti-eros taken down to the level of sterility, which is even lower than *eros pandemos*. The second error lies in treating eros as a tool and stimulus for procreation. In the light of theories on instincts of self-preservation and reproduction,

---

330 A similar picture can be seen in the ancient Scandinavian institution of concubines or "secondary wives", called *frilla* or *friðla*, that is "beloved ones." *Friðla* could come from wealthy and distinguished families.

331 In antiquity, the women of Europe did not know subordination in the likes of that which would come in later centuries with the Middle Eastern religions.

332 Evola, *Eros and the Mysteries of Love: The Metaphysics of Sex*, 12.

eros functions as a mechanism for reproduction and thus approximates profane scientism. Evola pointed out that it is absolutely inadmissible to consider eros to be a propellant for reproduction, because "no one makes love specifically to give birth", especially when a passion comes into play that transcends the individual level of man and woman, as well as when we are dealing with ritual intercourse. Lovers tend to go beyond their own bodily limits, to penetrate and merge with one another. They do not think about conception, nor about the possible appearance of children, which might be a completely optional consequence of such an experience. As has already been said, the idea and awareness of reproduction alone is not a stimulus for sexual arousal (physiologically speaking), and among some archaic peoples sex is not culturally associated in any way with the fact of pregnancy. Sexual practices and reproduction are distinguished and demarcated under the power and metaphysics of various patrons and principles. This is confirmed by the sheer number of genuinely erotic gestures, such as kissing and its equivalents on the forehead and nose, or hugging, both of which can be practiced without continuation in the form of intercourse and whose semantics do not imply any fertilization.

Christian anti-feminine and anti-corporeal morality and metaphysics, as well as biological and social Darwinism, invoke the pathos of procreation and "sexual intercourse for the sake of conception" and the "survival of the species" only to hide the very fact of erotic delight and the higher dimensions of sexual desire, of Uranic Eros. In the modern world of overpopulation and hyper-sexualization, even primitive and automatic compulsive movements of mechanisms (pistons, gears) are already tinged with a hint of a sense of penetration. Hence the fundamentally different metaphysical coloring of the terms "penis" (profane penetration) and "phallus" (rise, ascent). In Enlightenment philosophy, Evola determined the pessimist Arthur Schopenhauer's idea of the "genius of the species" to be a side branch of the very same Darwinism. The "genius of the species" leads every man to choose the woman who is most capable of realizing the ultimate biological goal of his line.[333] However, it acts as the very same mechanism for the realization of reproduction, framed by numerous gestures, customs, and natural caresses that are not needed for the simple mechanical act of penetration and ejaculation. If everything were reducible only to conception, then sex would be a routine mechanical function and nothing more. Sexuality, however, even in the realm of simple pleasure, always has a transcending, transgressive dimension that is not bound to procreation.

Finally, the mere production of children is a virtue of the proletariat cherished by the blind ideologues of pro-life movements which ignore the qualitative aspects of population. The genius of the lineage or biological necessity can bring together in the act of childbearing people who, due to various unfavorable circumstances, should not continue their line.

The perception of woman as a factory for childbearing is not even the Demetric type of femininity, but an industrial one, economically proletarian and based in modern sociology and demography. This situation as a whole reflects the thousands of years of Civilization's cooling down (per Spengler) from Indo-European patriarchy to neo-matriarchy. Civilization, science, technology, progress, development, computerization, and the global network are manifestations of a fundamentally feminine principle and feminine philosophies. Civilization is the world of gynecocracy, the power of the female, even through masculine categories and strategies of thinking, i.e., the castration of the Mind of man and its subordination to women's endeavors. Evola issues an important observation on this subject: there are people who are like a man in body, but like a eunuch in spirit.[334] This refers to the fact that bringing a qualitative mass of children into the world is no virtue without taking into consideration their estate belonging, hierarchies, initiations, and finally, these children's upbringing.

---

333 See Evola, *Eros and the Mysteries of Love: The Metaphysics of Sex.*

334 See Evola, *Men Among the Ruins.*

474

It is well known that the lower classes, especially chandalas, pariahs, and outcasts, multiply with greater ease and impartiality, thereby blurring and undermining through quantity the quality of the class hierarchy, making people of a vertical orientation a rare type during the Kali-Yuga. Looking back at the current generations of youth and even predicting the near future, we can conclude that out of a hundred given individuals, zero will be people of a Traditionalist constitution, faithful to the Divinities and the sacred — and out of a thousand, less than 10.

Closely related to this is a question which has not yet been recognized in all of its acuteness: the possibilities and ways of correctly, fully raising and educating children in fidelity to the ideals of Tradition and reverence for the Divinities so that they do not succumb to the anti-sacred suggestions of the world of Modernity and Postmodernity. In studies on this question, we have recorded an absolutely correct understanding on the part of many pagans regarding the true threats to raising children: the majority of pagans surveyed deem the Internet, gadgets, pop culture, and media the main threats to their children, even more so than the Abrahamic religions.[335] A significant portion of pagans also believe that in order to be brought up in tradition, it is necessary to leave the city and live in villages, or to in one way or another actively introduce a child to nature by taking them out of the city. At the same time, half of pagans insist that a child should be immersed in tradition from birth. Pagans are not opposed to native pagan traditions being taught as part of general education from primary school, but such an option is practically impossible in contemporary conditions and requires many fundamental compromises with the dominant paradigm. Unfortunately, due as well to the psychological characteristics of children and adolescents, an alternative center of socialization in the form of the secular school and society of *das Man*

335 See Evgeny Nechkasov, "*Vospitanie v traditsii i vliianie sovremennosti*" [Being Raised in Tradition and the Influence of Modernity], *Colloquium Heptaplomeres* V; idem., "*Prepodovanie osnov iazycheskikh traditsii v shkolakh*" [Teaching the Basics of Pagan Traditions in Schools], *Warha* 7.

with his bright gadgets and "exotic" values will inevitably create a significant counterbalance to the world and home of the parents, which will lead to serious conflict in the child's socialization process up to the point of collapsing the sacred core of their personhood into surrogate activities.

One convincing point of view holds that genuine upbringing and education is possible only within closed Traditionalist communities that do not enter into contact with urban culture at all. The enculturation and socialization of children in modern society is simply ruled out. However, such a position is considered by modern government authorities to be a gross and extremist violation of children's right to education, the values of secular society, etc., and this means that these children will be taken away from their families and subjected to reindoctrination so as to be integrated into society. This sets the stage for violent armed confrontations between Traditionalist families and secular authorities. The surrounding modern global culture is so degenerate that it itself becomes an argument in favor of refraining from having children. Believing parents are afraid and uncertain that they can withstand educational competition with the surrounding culture. They are afraid that their children will eventually become *das Man* and turn against their fathers. According to the traditional notion that a person's life continues in their descendants and that their soul can be reborn in their grandchildren, this risk of upbringing becomes deeply existential, affecting the souls of dead ancestors and their cult. In the end, thus, at the present moment there is no satisfactory solution to the problem of seeing through a Traditionalist upbringing for a large number of children in the midsts of modern times.

Nor does the established stereotype that those who can financially provide for children should be the ones to have and raise children, while the poor should not, help solve the problem. This delusion rests on economic grounds which we reject and which are refuted by the very fact that the lower social classes and the scientific, technological, economic, cultural, and political elites represent different poles of the very same spectrum of anti-sacred anthropology and ideology.[336] Therefore, none of them should have children.

Here we find ourselves in the field of anti-natalist theories. As we indicated above, the issue of population and childbearing is accounted for by three positions on the ideological spectrum of neo-archaism/"primitivism." Linkola's position hedges its bets on a totalitarian-technological solution and controlled, intensive depopulation. As for the second position (Kaczynski's), which welcomes the birth of a large number of children to the families of insurgents, there is the objective problem of these groups' survival and their raising of such children. The third position is radical depopulation in parallel with refraining from population reproduction, i.e., from childbearing. Within the scope of this perspective, we can distinguish two main approaches.

The first is the position of the South African philosopher David Benatar, a well-known ideologue of anti-natalism.[337] Benatar's ideas are laconic and are based on moral arguments about the suffering of beings who are born. The pleasant moments that happen in life are always inferior to the total amount of suffering, troubles, hardships, and negative experiences. Childbearing is a social habit whose rationale has long since been lost or become irrelevant in the modern world. In the act of conception and birth, parents do not take into account the opinion of the child themself, who becomes the object of the parents' desires, not their own. Even despite the progress and development of society, suffering is still an integral part of being, such as congenital or hereditary diseases or social conditions. In this case, a child who is born is plunged into suffering against their will and desires, which is cruel. Benatar's argument betrays an abolitionist reasoning for the complete exclusion of suffering from the world, to be achieved by refusing to bear children and by humanity voluntarily committing to extinction as a species.

---

336 This also pertains to eugenics and eugenic-transhumanist delusions, which are based on purely quantitative genetic, biological, physiological, phenotypic, and even physiognomic criteria.

337 David Benatar, *Better Never to Have Been.*

Benatar articulates a well-known asymmetry that applies to bioethics and demography:

Person exists (being)	Person was not born (non-being)
[1] Suffering (bad)	[3] No suffering (good)
[2] Pleasure (good)	[4] No pleasure (not bad)

Since the balance between [1] suffering (harm) and [2] pleasure in life (good) is not guaranteed, the very presence of suffering is already absolute harm outweighing possible pleasures. Benatar's pessimism holds that harm to a person is, unlike good, guaranteed. But an unborn person is in a better position, because they are guaranteed [3] not to suffer. The absence of pleasure [4] is not "bad", because the non-existent subject does not experience the need for pleasures, and this means that this state is marked as a logical negation: instead of "good", it is "not bad." In sum, we see that in Benatar's asymmetry birth and existence lose to not being born and not existing, since the latter is devoid of suffering and experiences that make life unbearable. This is where admissible apologetics for suicide or voluntary euthanasia begin. Benatar writes:

> When a person claims that his life is so bad that he would be better off dead, he need not mean literally that were he to die he would exist in some better state (although some people do believe this). Instead he may mean that he prefers *not to be*, rather than to continue living in his condition. He has determined that his life is not worth living — that it is not worth continuing to be. Just as life can be so bad that ceasing to exist is preferable, so life can be so bad that never coming into existence is preferable. Comparing somebody's existence with his non-existence is not to compare two possible conditions of that person. Rather it is to compare his existence with an alternative state of affairs in which he does not exist.[338]

The weakness of Benatar's argument is that his appeal to questions of suffering and morality in relation to the already

338 Benatar, *Better Never to Have Been*, 22.

living and newborns stems from extreme new-European humanism and atheistic pessimism. All of his polemics with opponents and closer thinkers are built around this declared asymmetry. The desire to avoid suffering, and, as a direct consequence and solution, to completely eliminate human existence through extinction, down to a zero population on Earth, betrays a strategy that is close to John Zerzan's idea of rejecting language. Benatar's decision paves the way for a similar avoidance of the question and decision of the authenticity of Dasein's presence in the world. Benatar's desire not to give birth or to die is a flight from suffering into oblivion or a complete avoidance of contact with being and its content. This stands contrary to traditional doctrines in which physical suffering or coming close to death are acts of initiation and the realization of authenticity and humanity as such. Even existential aloofness and the mood of boredom can be revealed as an initiatic path if one traverses them, rather than stepping back before even starting.[339] Suffering and sorrow can be interpreted as manifestations of the Divine, or as a way of "snatching" and "taking" a person out of surrogate activities and vain bustle, provoking a head-on collision with *nigredo* and fundamental metaphysical questions.

Finally, Benatar does not pay close attention to the question of absolute sacred values for the sake of which one can sacrifice their health, life, and that of other people. For him, such a pole of argument, where suffering is perceived as an integral part and tribute for the achievement of ideals that transcend the horizons of human life, simply does not exist. Nevertheless, Benatar's moral arguments are understandable within the axiology of pessimistic Modernity which implicitly admits its defeat in the field of values and images of a ideal future for which life is still worth living.

The final manifestation of *das Man* in the sphere of anti-natalism is "child-free" ideology, whose proponents justify refraining from childbearing for the sake of desires to build

339 See Eliade, *Rites and Symbols of Initiation*.

a career, realize their creativity, or devote their life to pure hedonism in all areas. Their line of argumentation runs through the same discourse on the emancipation of women and men from the "patriarchal" family's reproductive functions. If Benatar arrives at the controversial but honest preference for non-being from atheism, then the advocates of hedonism and vasectomies choose to stay alive for the sake of experiencing the greatest range of surrogate pleasures without consequences and responsibility. The emergence of child-free ideology is a manifestation of the demographic transition in developed countries.

The only thing worse than absolute non-being as the absence of *da-* and *sein* is infinite bodily life, physiological immortality[340], where *da* and *sein* are dissolved amidst meaningless presence in oblivion, in a long or endless life devoted to flat movement between desire machines and pleasure. In this optic, "to be born" means "to experience pleasure", and Benatar's asymmetry falls into a "gravitational pit" of corporeo-emotional experiences within which even suffering [1] is understood as an extremity on the spectrum of pleasure — of sadism, psychopathy, and entertainment content in the spirit of Michel Foucault.

The second approach to anti-natalism operates with existential-eschatological motifs. In its well-known formulation, it comes close to Benatar's position: it is unacceptable to have children in the midst of Hell or Naraka, Helheim or Hades (the lower world of the dead in general), dooming their souls to torment here. Souls must not be entangled in the bondage and horrors of matter.

This position draws on religious argumentation, as opposed to moral and hedonistic abolitionism. The suffering of a specific born person constitutes the content of their spiritual path, but clearly new souls should not be brought into such. The lives of those already born are to be dedicated to serving the sacred. Hence, absolutely relevant and at the same time opposite to

---

340 It bears distinguishing between passing into non-being as the result of the eschatological folding of manifestation, and non-being which has not yet unfolded as being (non-being as *pre*-being) and moving-towards-manifestation.

surrogate ways of life are the vows of monks, Sufi wanderers, holy fools, radical Aghoris, etc., who renounce everything worldly, including the family and continuing their line.

Deeper consideration of this question leads us to an even more complicated understanding of what human life is in general, and to a more subtle, enigmatic formulation. A person's life should be perceived as the path of the Mind's descent (πρooδoς) to the lower initiatic boundary where it faces the question of ascending back (επιστροφη) or passing over the lower limit. These two paths are radically different: the first is describable within the framework of Neoplatonic henology, while the second is thematized in the Yuzhinsky Circle metaphysics of Evgeny Golovin, Yuri Mamleev, and the early Alexander Dugin, and is in many respects transgressive.[341] But the fork in the ontological road presupposes rejecting childbearing on both paths. The formulation thus reads as follows:

> One should not bring new souls into embodiment in this world, because this world is sentenced to death, and continuing the chain of births means prolonging its existence and casting new people as victims of the machinations of the Gestell. It is necessary to understand oneself to be the last link in a chain that does not break off into the emptiness of worldly nihilism, but closes unto itself in returning to the selfhood of the Absolute.

One should renounce bearing children in order to free themself from the shackles of karma and the cycles of rebirth, both their own and other souls reborn as descendants. One should leave the world of manifestation and find the point of selfhood in the unmanifest (*non manifestare, das Nichts*). One should never and in no form whatsoever further actualize the inner-worldly pole of the Absolute. One should not return into Samsara.[342]

---

341 See Alexander Dugin's *Radikal'nyi Sub'ekt i ego Dubl'* [The Radical Self and Its Double] and Yuri Mamleev's *Sud'ba Bytiia* [The Fate of Being].

342 Here it is appropriate to recall Yuri Mamleev's formula: "Pass through the Absolute." The question of the self of the Absolute is resolved in different ways: either the Absolute is taken to be a self, or the self is placed in the depths of the Absolute as the concealed Nothing.

In his obituary for Yuri Mamleev, Alexander Dugin enigmatically summated his position on procreation:

> Mamleev had no children, since he did not want to conceive in the world of flesh; he knew its price all too well. He penetratingly lived the tenderness of the flesh and what lies within it, its mystery. He knew its horror. This is the other side of Earth. The Chinese say: Earth has its back turned to people, while the sky faces them with its face. But Earth also has a face. No one has seen it. No one except Yuri Vitalyevich Mamleev. What is this face of the Earth always with its back to us? It is inhabited by those whom Mamleev called Titans.

The position of metaphysically renouncing procreation and advocating depopulation can be summarized in the following way. According to ancient authors, it is better not to be born into the Iron Age. But if one is born, then they must go through the Hades of the surrounding everyday life and reap the rarest and most difficult fruits. In our era, it is preferable for people with burning hearts to devote their lives to the sacred and to the cause, to the *theoresis* and *poiesis* of Traditionalism, right thought, right life and death, undistracted by everyday life, family, and children. At least for the first three quarters of one's life.

As for those who are already on Earth, who have already been born into and raised in the Postmodern global world, the imperative of radical depopulation proclaims itself. Wars, pandemics, cataclysms, technogenic catastrophes, and methods of birth control and population reduction are to be welcomed. With regards to the children of Traditionalists, pagans, and escapist rebels, it is quite acceptable to follow Theodore Kaczynski's midway strategy of paying close attention to the problem of raising and educating children — in total isolation from the outside world if necessary.

Instead of more than 7.7 billion people in the world, there should be no more than a few hundred million humans of different tribes and peoples.

Who Are All These People?

Over the course of mass-scale depopulation, if only communities and villages of farmers, herders, and hunters are left, then this would be a good future scenario. But the situation is such that even the populations of remote villages — in Russia, in inaccessible regions in South America, Southeast Asia, etc. — consist of degenerate masses of people with a mentality broken by modernization. Most of the differences between the inhabitants of megalopolises, regional centers, and the rural periphery are exterior. On the whole, they represent a single "anthropological" type and bear one and the same root which reaches back and down into the hypochthonic domain of identity of the Earth's extremely large population.

In Tradition, when people lived naturally in village communities or small townships, every family had its own cult of the *rod* and ancestors. The notion was widespread that the souls of ancestors are reborn within the chain of descendants through the ritual summoning of the soul to assume new embodiment and by naming a child after a deceased ancestor. This was combined with the belief that the accumulated fortune, glory, and spirit-companions of the family are passed down, transmitted through the *rod*, as in, for example, the Icelandic *fylgja* and *hamingja*. The human *rod*, the large family, represented a limited chain of ancestors reborn along the conventional "line", into which new souls and names were added only slowly and cautiously. Thusly was maintained the natural, harmonious balance of "nothing above measure" (*nec plus ultra*). Despite the impressive total of all those who once lived, live now, and might be born in the future, the overall quantity of souls was relatively small and rotating. Every descendant was a reborn reflection of their eponymous ancestor.

But today, we live in a critically overpopulated world, and this yields the logical question: Who are all these people around us? A cursory glance would refer us to the causes of population growth, which lie in the domains of food production, sedentary life and the development of agriculture, and the spheres of economics and the development of medicine. But these processes and factors are only the outer framing of the real movement within the world originating in the depths.

The nominal number of people living on the Earth right now exceeds by orders of great magnitude the quantity of all the souls of ancestors who have passed into the other world and who have been reborn in their families. In Europe and the West, people are ever less giving birth and have long since abandoned the traditional practice of summoning an ancestor to be reborn in grandchildren. Thus, the question arises: whose and what kind of souls and spirits are embodied in the human bodies around us and, globally, across the whole world in "developing" countries? There is the absolutely serious proposition that we are living among non-humans, among demonic, hypothchthonic entities — shadows (the Icelandic *skuggja*), demons, lemures, larvae, and the lesser demons of folklore who appear to us as people in everyday reality. Finally, it bears remembering the legends of the restless dead, the Navi, the undead, the Rakshasas, Draugrs, and Aptangra — the dead who come to life to harass and threaten the well-being of the living — especially when the customs and spells for dealing with them have been lost.

Traditions know of temporal periods in which the spirits of the dead have the right to visit the living, as well as periods when the borders between the world of the living and the world of the dead are most permeable. These are usually marked by days for commemorating ancestors and parents, as well as holidays associated with the Winter Solstice and the customs of caroling that are common across Europe, when the human essence yields to spirits in masks and costumes. The ancestors are no longer commemorated on the proper days, in the proper pagan way, and people have ceased to uphold the exchange of gifts and sacrifices with the other worlds — worlds which are populated not only by the souls of relatives, but also spirits which previously took an active part in the lives of peoples.

This leads to the thought that if the world population has been growing and growing for already many hundreds of years, then this means that the gates to our middle world are open, that the spirits and demons of the lower worlds are entering and somehow dwelling in our world — and they are not leaving. This means that the fundamental law governing the sacred time for spirits and the dead to visit the world of the living has been destroyed. The window for being visited was opened, but it is not being closed and will not take back its visitors. The hyper-population of people is, among other things, a problematic feature of our time ahead of the cosmological sunset.

If the billions of people on Earth are embittered demons (the demons of things which cannot find their proper place) and Draugr, then they must be taken back to their own worlds, where they are free to live as they please. This finds confirmation on the level of the everyday infernality of the picture of the everyday lifeworld of the people surrounding us. When we see young people riding scooters and skateboards, scientists sorting out test tubes in laboratories and connecting wires to devices, people watching or participating in sports competitions, rehearsing the symphonies of Arvo Pärt or Krzysztof Penderecki, holding lectures or just spending their time anyhow — all of such are the purest landscapes of Dante's Hell. The demons are busy with their activities, which they offer to us as "freedom."

The sacred texts of Shaktism tell us several versions of a myth in which the Divinities are harassed by the Asuras Shumbha, Nishumbha, and Raktabija and their numerous hordes.[343] The Asuras symbolize disharmony at all levels of the cosmos in opposition to the Deva-Divinities. Defeating the Asuras is extremely difficult: according to legend, thousands of demons rose up out of one drop of Asura blood as soon as it hit the ground. Then the Divinities turn to the Great Goddess, and she manifests herself in the most wrathful and warlike hypostases of Kali and Durga who easily destroy the hordes of Asuras and Rakshasas, drinking up all their blood so that not

343 See the Shaktist text *Devi Mahatmya.*

a single drop touches the ground. Kali and Durga represent the feminine principle purifying and eliminating all disharmony without a trace. In the mythology of Shaivism, the female Divinities are held to be manifestations of Shiva's Shakti, who helps him destroy the demons and drink their blood.

On the whole, the myths of Kali and Durga are myths of depopulation and cleansing the Earth and the Heavens of the hubris of disharmony manifest in unrestrained population growth. Sharp depopulation will turn the whole world into one giant shaman for a long time to come.

The World-Without-Us

The imaginative picture of a world in which man is absent or has gone completely extinct as a species harbors a dark attraction for pondering. In the classic science fiction genre of "the last man on Earth", this world is described in one way or another through the forced introduction of the figure of the "only survivor" as a witness and narrator, which thus imparts to the plot an anthropological perspective bearing contemporal paradigmatic structures and assessments of what is happening around and to the hero himself.

A philosophical approach that goes beyond the framework of anthropocentrism is sketched in the works of Eugene Thacker. An actual world without humans would be the embodiment of David Benatar's moral utopia, but for Thacker thinking about such a place is a speculative challenge for entering a rather different field of thought. Thacker recalls the importance of following Heidegger's distinction between types of death. According to the German philosopher, animals meet death in a different way from humans. They do not "die", but "croak." Death as an existential horizon is accessible to man as the ultimate realization of Dasein. Animals croak, the individual dies. But when one person dies, the rest of the population (the people) remains alive. Thus, the horizon of death opens up only in personal experience, and it cannot be conveyed by other means of retelling, bearing witness to, or through culture, as Eugen Fink has written.[344] In order to thoughtfully expand the boundaries of the speculative experience of death, Thacker speaks of the extinction of the whole population. When one person dies, others remain, but when they die and no one is left, then the finitude of Dasein is exhausted completely and forever. Vividly imagining such strikes a person with horror which, according to Thacker's logic, exceeds the scale of fear of one's own personal death. Thacker calls this thought experience the "speculative annihilation" of humanity: "Such questions are ramified by a further one: Who is the witness of extinction? In the case of the extinction of all human beings, who is it that gives testament to this extinction, to the very thought of extinction? In this sense extinction can never be adequately thought, since its very possibility presupposes the absolute negation of all thought."[345] For Thacker, such a posing of the question is necessary for any conceptual gaze at the world we know from a non-anthropological position. People themselves are not able to think and conceive of the event of their own extinction, because they would not exist. Thacker therefore proposes a threefold scheme for describing the world:

1. The world-for-us - the world that a person and society sees, the ordinary "world" as known and understood by the ordinary human and the scientific worldview of Modernity.

2. The world-in-itself - planet Earth as a Kantian "thing-in-itself", i.e., indifferent to humanity and "turned" only towards itself; the material presence of nature without the human observer;

3. The world-without-us - the planet after the human extinction event.

---

344 Eugen Fink, *Osnovnye fenomeny chelovecheskogo bytiia* [The Main Phenomena of Human Being].

345 Eugene Thacker, *In the Dust of This Planet* (*Horror of Philosophy Vol. 1*) (Winchester: Zero Books, 2011).

The third scheme is the most interesting in Thacker's work, since it describes the "world-for-us" from which the "us" as a species or bearers of being has logically been subtracted. "We" are present only as a radical absence, as if humanity had instantaneously disappeared from the face of the Earth. It is here that the non-anthropological view of the actual present opens up without the anthropocentrism of Western European man. Along the line of dark ontologies, such a withdrawal of man is supposed to unveil flat assemblages and constellations of other, dark, objective subjects and substances - damp basements overgrown with fungi, streams of mucus and geometric patterns of mold. For advocates of dark and minimal ontologies, such a landscape, which is Martin Heidegger's perspective turned inside out, is quite satisfying and even desirable. Nature and animals, as the world-in-itself, are indifferent to our extinction and absence, and thinking about the world-in-itself from its own position is inaccessible to us.

In contrast to Thacker's account, the fate of the world-without-us, or more precisely the world-after-us has been studied in all possible specificity by the journalist Alan Weisman.[346] Weisman shows the fate of the whole material legacy of modern civilization in a world from which people have disappeared in a single instant and not as the result of a global catastrophe or war. He starts the countdown from the moment of the current state of the world. Relying on specialists in biology, ecology, energy, engineering, anthropology, zoology, etc., Weisman considers in detail the decomposition process of the traces of human presence on Earth. The instantaneous global extinction of humans would lead to the mass extinction of numerous species of domestic and farm animals, as well as species that have entered into a strong symbiosis with humans and especially the urban environment, such as rats, cockroaches, foxes, raccoons, small birds, etc. This would lead to the restructuring of numerous food chains and animal migrations. In the medium-range term, megalopolises

---

346 See Alan Weisman's *The World Without Us* (2007) and the films *Aftermath: Population Zero* (2008) and *Life After People* (2008-2010).

will become new spaces where birds, animals, and fish find refuge on the peaks of skyscrapers, in the halls of shopping centers, in flooded basements, sewers, and subway tunnels. Electronics and the systems based on them would continue to work for one day after the disappearance of people. Then the shutting down of generators at dams, power plants, and security systems dependent upon electricity would lead to a cascade of technogenic disasters. It would take centuries and millennia for the natural erosion of concrete and metals to lead to the collapse and decay of the creations of human hands, such as reinforced concrete buildings, dams, bridges, monuments, road surfaces, car frames, etc. Monuments such as Mount Rushmore, mountains of plastic waste, traces of oil products and heavy metals, and radio signals in deep space would be the longest lasting reminders of human presence.

Vivid examples of the world-after-us are presented by the protected areas abandoned by humans for decades, such as the vicinity of the Chernobyl nuclear power plant and the city of Pripyat, the Korean demilitarized zone, and the Northern monotowns abandoned after the collapse of the USSR. Wherever modern civilized man leaves, nature, flora, and fauna take revenge, restoring and multiplying their populations. From historical examples, we can recall how the Mayan cities with their pyramids and terraces became completely veiled under layers of vines, bush, and trees, cleared away to their modern form only in the 20th century.

Weisman's work, which has given rise to a whole quasi-documentary genre of studies on the post-human world as a mirror of the real influence of the Anthropocene, shows the really possible and inevitable ways of world collapse generated by technogenic industrial civilization. One of the main conclusions of relevance to neo-archaism is the possibility for the world to recover and erase the traces of Gestell from its face in a natural manner. Buildings and cities erected by humans will become part of the landscape after depopulation. Moreover, the picture described by Weisman is completely relevant not only for the world in which humanity has completely died out, but also for the world of small populations, tribes, and peoples who continue to live outside of cities.

The imaginary and documentary views of the world-without-us and our lack of experience and witness to such yield a sense of horror at the nearness of non-being, which, in turn, is very close to the ascetic practices of contemplating one's own death and the gradual decomposition of a corpse.

The topic of the world-without-us is closely linked with the theological question of whether the Divinities exist in a world without people. This question goes significantly beyond the scope of the present work, but we can allow ourselves to outline its boundaries. Myths everywhere speak of the connection between the Divinities and people through glorification and sacrifice. They live each other's death and life, exchange gifts, and feed on the scent of offerings. But on the level of theology and philosophy, this question has deeper dimensions. If man is a slice of thinking presence in the middle world (a link in the chain), then when this world is empty, the thinking presence might remain on other levels and in other modes. Thacker's "speculative annihilation" as well as Weisman's excursions actually pose the problem of understanding the world as the "world-for-us." Advocates of the new ontological turn and non-human subjectivity critique the correlationism of "world" and "consciousness" for its assertion of precisely such a privileged access to the world, its cognition and instrumentalization. Yet such a position, and especially its rigid fixation, is a product of the realization of the ideas of the Enlightenment and the deep impact of the natural sciences on the consciousness of people and society, their demonstration of their own efficiency and efficacy on the level of "it works." For Traditionalism, which recognizes the Advaita-monistic understanding of supreme reality as the most colorful flower and the sweetest fruit of Tradition, the most correct formula would be "the world-is-us." This is the World-as-the-Divine reflected both within man and the world. Therefore, in Traditionalism, the "world-for-us" formula does not mean any instrumentalization of the beingful world or bestowing upon it the status of raw materials, but stands for "we-for-ourselves." Or, to be more precise, "I-for-I" in strict accordance with the formulas "*Tat tvam asi*" and "Atman is Brahman."

It is precisely from this assertion and position that we can deduce a strictly sacred, ecological imperative for paganism among European peoples as well as, more broadly, other peoples held captive by modernization. This means relating to the world as to another form of manifestation of one's own inner nature, and further to a sacrally-grounded object-oriented mythology and para-human subjectivity which are grounded in the apophatic One and its manifestation in all conceivable and unthinkable (for the human slice of being) forms. For man is reserved the position described by Martin Heidegger: Man is not the king of nature and not the center of the being of things and objects, but is the shepherd of Being (*Seyn*). Alongside the Divinities, in sensitive silence and attunement, man asks about and guards Being (*Seyn*). Therefore, we are not interested in a world without people as such, but we welcome a world without modern people. We are interested in an open, boundless world inhabited by tribes, peoples, clans, groups, and communities of people who live traditionally and who maintain the limits of populations through wars, sacrifices, and heroic deeds.

Remarks on the Fields of Depopulation

The French oceanographer Jacques-Yves Cousteau recognized the problem of Earth's overpopulation and as a bitter hypothetical measure spoke of the need to liquidate 350,000 people a day. That would mean the disappearance of 127.5 million people in a year and 1.28 billion people in a decade. At the current moment, the world is inhabited by 7.7 billion people, the largest centers of overpopulation being India and China, whose demographic statistics are confidential. Reducing this population to 500 million while maintaining the rate of liquidation proposed by Cousteau would take at least 50 years.

This mathematical calculation does not take into account the compensatory birth rate and a number of other parallel factors, such as methods of elimination and the logistics and maintenance of the process amidst the objective disintegration of numerous industries and global connections that would take place already within the very first years of moderate population decline. Here we are confronted with an inevitably technological approach to population reduction. The most realistic scenarios of local or global depopulation are associated with world wars, irreparable damage dealt to civilization by natural disasters and epidemics, resource exhaustion, and the collapse of socio-political systems. In such cases, the only survivors would be simply lucky.

Another scenario of the annihilation of mankind is associated with a clash with AI and the latter's victory, such as in James Barratt's scenario. In this case, mankind would be liquidated by a new hegemonic subject that would simply take away all available resources for its own benefit. In this negative scenario, the Gestell comes out the victor.

In the event of the destruction of the world's key water, food, energy, and financial supply nodes, significant depopulation would come about simply by way of the extinction of unfit people in a situation of sharp shortages of all resources and, as Linkola put it, a war of all against all. At this stage, the main task would be to prevent the possibility of restoring scientific knowledge and technological processes, logistics, communications, and infrastructure. Otherwise, the Gestell would be able to regain its positions and restore full power over the beingful world within a couple of centuries. If depopulation is not complemented by a new philosophy and change in the existential state of man, then we inevitably await therebirth of the very same from the ashes in a new round. Instead of uprooting the weed, global catatrasophe would simply make adjustments to its growth.

Herein lies the fundamental difference. Globalists seek to regulate the population in favor of demographic replacement, migration, and the preservation of progress and sustainable development, to entrust care for extending today into tomorrow in the hands of technology and science without adopting fundamental decisions over human fate. Any genuine, radical depopulation must necessarily go hand-in-hand with rejecting the technogenic society, the technogenic environment, and the technogenic way of existing. Therefore, advocates of a real solution are pushed into the periphery in contrast to the speculative and conspiratorial regulators of birth and death rates. Our position differs from the conspiracy theory of the "golden billion" on the question of who should remain on Earth and who should not. According to one widespread understanding, the "golden billion" primarily includes the elites (political, economic, scientific, and cultural) and population of the developed countries of the West, the North, and parts of Asia, leaving the minimal remnant of other populations needed to serve them. From our point of view, it is precisely the make-up of the "golden billion" that would be the first and foremost victim, as the leading ideologists and subjects of dehumanization and the installation of the regime of *das Man*, and as the most unfit and unlikely to survive. It is a fundamental premise of our analysis that depopulation should not be seen as a screen for settling racial, national-historical, or economic accounts. It is impossible to avoid the fact that creationism and Modernity, as well as the "welfare state" and tolerance, have arisen and flourished precisely within the boundaries of Europe, turning it into an Anti-Europe attractive and open (the "open society") to migrations and the overpopulation of *das Man*.

It would be absolutely fair to say that it would be better for Europe if all of its outstanding enlighteners and reformers were never born into the world. But the same is true for other peoples who have adopted the model and developmental path of Europe as their own. Today, the leading suppliers of programmers, engineers, and new app and gadget designers are India, China, Russia, and Belarus. In other words, diverse peoples and corners of the world have been drawn into the formation of the Gestell. Therefore, it would have been historically better for India if Gandhi had never been born, like Lomonosov in Russia, Mao in China, and other figures of the sort everywhere else.

Depopulation would also entail the resolution of such problems as shortages of fresh water and resources, race wars, dissatisfaction with populism or liberalism, unjust economics, segregation, and many other issues — all of this would simply disappear along with the populations that produce such problems.

The struggle against the reality of the Enframing is a struggle for identity and authenticity of Being. It is Africans' struggle for a black Africa without European and Asian colonists, even if they prefer to continue to kill each other with machetes made from improvised scrap metal and consecrated by local sorcerers. It is Europeans' struggle for their fatherlands instead of the European Union, for their traditions instead of migrants, perverts, and economists. It is Asia's struggle for societies closed off from the West, the struggle of the Han and other peoples for China and their own countries without digital concentration camps and communism. It is Russians' struggle for their original identity and for finding peace in cyclical being. It is the struggle of the Indians of both Americas for their existence, for their jungles, prairies, the Amazon, and ancestral mountains. It is man's struggle for the Human within himself.

If a European wants to stay with the Maori in Oceania or among the Quechua Indians in the Andes, then they must undergo the necessary initiations and fully embrace the local identity. Only in this way can they take their rightful place in the community, and without any guarantees that it will be a higher up one.

Das Man and the bearers of Modernity and Postmodernity have no hope for surviving cataclysms and radical population decline entailed by the destruction of technogenic civilization. The cultural, political, and economic elites, programmers, designers, engineers and technicians, scientists, science popularizers and evangelists, the managers of IT corporations, the comprador pro-Western elites and political technocrats in all countries, the apologists of progress in the social sciences, futurologists, startuppers, bloggers, Elon Musk's Twitter followers, etc., etc. — all of these types, wherever they are, can exist only in the current technological "reality."

It might come to scorching and sowing with salt all the lands where Modernity and Postmodernity have reached their peak and whence they have overwhelmed the whole world in waves. Replanting them with dense forests and tabooing people's presence in these lands might be their fate.

Spontaneous, elemental depopulation through wars and cataclysms on the ruins of collapsing civilization is one of the scenarios ahead of us.

One of the paths into myth runs through the edge of a blade piercing the heart of an enemy sacrificed as the long-awaited destruction of the accursed share.

Fear of Death and the Right to Death

Fear of the topic of depopulation is a reflection of the fear of death — the death of the habitual, comfortable world on the superficial level, the deep fear of one's own death (the finitude of being), and fear of greater death as the death of one's relatives and the extinction of a large number of people (but not the whole species).

From an historical perspective, the phenomenon of death has undergone substantial metamorphoses throughout the cultures of different peoples, especially Europeans. The primordial view of death was expressed by Evgeny Golovin when he said that there was no death in Tradition. Given that Golovin radically distinguished himself against the backdrop of Soviet and post-Soviet Traditionalists and mystics, we can say that he embodied and transmitted positions that were more characteristic of the Golden Age than other eras. The absence of death in Tradition should not be perceived as some ubiquitous, physical immortality of all living creatures and people in particular. Certainly, in Tradition there was no death in the modern understanding as the "extinguishing of the light of consciousness" or man's irretrievable departure into inaccessible non-being, into a state of complete absence in the likes of mathematical "zero." In the same way, we cannot speak of any high "mortality" in the past in the likes of which the champions of a comfortable and safe life today frighten us with. This criterion applies only to the Modernity, because in Tradition there was no mortality in the modern sense as such. The event of death in traditional cultures was genuinely an event of passage or the beginning of another, different mode of presence. It was a departure from the world of the living into other spaces, where and whence the soul and various components of living presence continue to "live", visit relatives, experience events in other worlds, and return to the world of the living in the cycles of rebirths. In Greek, it is said of death that it "εξ ανθρωπων γιγνομαι", that it is "born from man", i.e., in dying, a person is born into death. The fetal posture of buried bodies among ancient peoples hints at the motif of returning to the mother's womb of the earth and subsequent rebirth, as does the funeral "sleeping pose" in cases where the deceased was considered to have fallen asleep or gone on a shamanic journey under the guise of a long, "dead" sleep. According to the *Younger Edda*, Odin himself did so. Finally, death as departure was also perceived as being initiated into being an Ancestor, merging with the greater lineage of those who have already passed on, yet who live beyond the ancestors of all still living descendants.

On certain days of commemoration or on special occasions, the spirits of the dead may appear to the living. They can be addressed and keep in contact with the *rod* as a whole by way of memory, mutual gifts, and sacrifices. In other words, when it comes to the world of Tradition, one cannot speak of mortality, but rather it is more correct to speak of transitivity. These events of passage were framed with the proper rituals, sacrifices, requests, and sendings-off which the dead might take with them and pass on to ancestors in the other world.

The triumph of Abrahamism and its ideological child in the form of Modernity was marked by a ubiquitous rejection and oblivion of death as an event of transition, and along with it all the relevant mythological, folkloric, and ritual complexes. Death was turned into the death that we know in new European culture, and it is this enigma of death, whose resolution the Christians speculated on with the question of the resurrection of Christ (which is purely secondary against the everyday background of non-dying in Tradition), that has turned into the existential horizon and centered the whole problem of human being-in-the-world and being-here.

The reality of death as death is an essential feature of the anti-traditional world or, in other words, the metaphysical conditions of the Iron Age, the antithesis to the Golden Age. The world of Modernity is a world in which God or the Divine has died, as have time, history, the "author", and the human (per Foucault). Death is the last "remnant" that secular, atheistic society cannot master and appropriate, because the institutions for ritual exchange and communication with the worlds of the death (the passed-on) and the ancestors have been destroyed.

Fear of death thus appears to be fear of complete exclusion from presence, departure into nowhere, into the black oblivion of non-being. The absence of the afterlife, cults of the ancestors, and rebirths yields the problematization of the meaning of this worldly life insofar as its final horizon shatters into meaninglessness and leads nowhere. Fear of death is the root of all other fears, which are either its derivatives or transpositions into other domains. Death becomes a black hole, a gravitational anomaly, a fascination of existentialism and the phenomenology of individual existence. The experience of dying and surviving ceases to be communal, that is universal and social. If previously the graveyard was located in the center of the settlement, and the worlds of the dead were by all means intertwined with the world of the living, like water in water, then in Modernity death becomes the most personal, individual experience and worry. In Eugen Fink's considerations, whatever is left accessible to a person or family in the experience of seeing the death of others or loved ones is not death, but a reflection of death in our cultural or emotional perceptions.[347] The very experience of death cannot possibly be conveyed, expressed, described, etc. Thus, death is what man now encounters in absolute loneliness.

It is the fear of departing into nowhere that is the driving force of the development of medicine and transhumanist technologies which seek to achieve synthetic mortality with machinery and the machinations of technology. The inauthentic form of death is perishing, as opposed to passing through dying as an existential horizon in the spirit of higher initiations and sacrifices in the world of Tradition.

Various meanings of existence in a world without the Sacred which Modernity has put forth for the concrete individual or mankind as a whole have not borne themselves out and have not solved the problem. Modern death has only given rise to even greater alienation and, since the mid-20th century, more machinery for producing even more death. In the vein of political technologies, death can be used as solution for holding society together. In the case of a demonstrative execution of a renegade, death is used for excluding a stranger from the social body of "his own" and for actualizing identity. In the case of terrorist attacks and mass casualties, death is used to create cults of martyrs of "our own."

Postmodernism offers several strategies for combating the "problem of death", the main core of which boils down to ironically or technologically leveling, depreciating, and displacing death as any final and foundational experience of being.[348] Death becomes something that can be consumed as content (cinema, games, production), borderline experiences (extreme sports, war zone tourism, necrolatry, etc.), museum exhibitions, and so on. Death can be delayed or, in the long

---

347 See Eugen Fink, *Osnovnye fenomeny chelovecheskogo bytiia* [The Main Phenomena of Human Being].

348 See Jean Baudrillard, *Symbolic Exchange and Death*, trans. Iain Hamilton Grant (London: Sage, 2017).

term, overcome with the help of advanced medical technologies, which shifts the discourse from the plane of dying to the plane of quality of life during palliative care or for supercentenarians. Death can also be digitized using online services and neural networks for managing accounts and simulating dialogue with the dead (chat bots). Augmented reality is also extended to the afterlife: the worlds after death are infused with elements of gamification, whereby dying is interpreted as going offline with the possibility of reloading, changing location, etc. In VR, augmented with kinesthetic sensation technologies, it will be possible to simulate the experience of dying in a variety of ways, thus expanding the experience of games and entertainment. These are the black miracles and parodies of the soul's rebirth in the world of Tradition.

One important feature of the leveling the problem of death is the censoring of public discourses on suicide and a person's right to voluntary death. Here is revealed yet another facet of biopolitics and the expansion of state power over the bodies of citizens. Through culture, medicine, and media, the norms of "worthy" dying are dictated in contrast to "deserting" the field of life and service to the economy. The state or the economy considers the body to be a means of production and human capital to which extends the authority of accounting and calculating. Thus, suicide is interpreted as damage to property that does not entirely belong to the person themself. The exceptions are soft, comfort-enveloping medicine, palliative healthcare, and authorized euthanasia.

Apologetics for suicide is a fully Traditionalist position that speaks to regaining the right to dispose of one's destiny, body, life, and death. The world of Tradition knows numerous examples of voluntary departures from life. The most famous are heroic self-sacrifices in war. In the history of Eleusis we know of a case when an Indian Brahmin, Zarmar, was initiated into the mysteries. In order to show that his teaching surpassed the mysteries of the Greeks, he sacrificed himself by walking into a fire.[349] Also known is the suicide of Empedocles, who threw himself into the volcano of Mount Etna, which is explainable in terms of his strict adherence to his own teaching on deification (which reflected some elements of Pythagoreanism), where the final gesture is a transgressive act and the last seal certifying the achievement of divine purpose.[350]

In many traditions, a correct, dignified death is of great importance. To die correctly, that is to meet the moment of passage in accordance with one's estate or spiritual ethos, is one of the most important events in the life of the soul, one which in many respects determines its further path, the direction and memory of a person in society, and their lineage after departure. To die with dignity, to die a worthy death, means correctly passing through initiation into the other world and gaining a new status. For the warrior ethos, it is considered unworthy to meet death on straw, that is on a deathbed, hence old warriors preferred to jump off a cliff or fall on their own sword. Suicide was a way of preserving honor for the samurai, just as it was for vassals who did not manage to protect their suzerain and therefore followed him.

Suicide as ritual self-sacrifice is more associated with the priestly, initiatic path.[351] The paradigmatic figure of this gesture is the Ás Odin, who sacrificed himself — the most significant and fundamental sacrifice — to himself as the All-Father and only possible "addressee" of such a gift. Close to his case is the iconic depiction of Shiva dying for the sake of calming Kali's wrath, and in another version as sitting smeared in human ashes (*bhasma*), thus symbolizing detachment from the world. Socrates' voluntary acceptance of death reflects the Orphic notion of metempsychosis, the idea that the body is the dungeon

---

349 See Carl Kerenyi, *Eleusis: Archetypal Image of Mother and Daughter*, trans. Ralph Manheim (Princeton: Princeton University Press, 1967).

350 See Sergei Avanesov's lectures, *Filosofskaia suitsidologiia* [Philosophical Suicidology] (2000).

351 See the survey "*Otnoshenie iazychnikov k smerti i umiraniiu. Rezul'taty oprosa*" [Pagans' Attitude towards Death and Dying: Polling Results] in *Warha* 7 (2020).

of the soul (body = σομα, grave = σημα), and the exemplary act of the citizen. Plato and Plotinus subsequently maintained and supported the idea of purifying the soul from the body. In Hades, the philosopher's soul knows no torment, but remains in purity and passes on into the line of the Divinities.[352] The Stoics considered suicide to be a permissible act of εξαγωγη, that is extraction or exit. If a person is subjected to misfortunes and hardships, if he is afflicted by a disease that prevents him from leading a virtuous life and achieving higher aims, then he is free to preserve his dignity and honor by leaving life, by withdrawing his soul from the middle world of the living.

Unlike such worthy ways of dying, death as a result of a ship or plane crash, as a result of a technogenic disaster, or in the enveloping comfort of medical euthanasia[353] are ignoble deaths of those held hostage by technology, without will and free approach to death in the likes of that still held by stranded sailors or those in forests or mountains — in a word, those surrounded by gloomy and pure elements.

In the ideal picture of spiritual realization, a person should be ready for any death at any moment, or, allegorically, "to die to death", since it is not always possible for us to die in the proper external way. Therefore, practices of *memento mori* and meditative visualizations of one's own death and the decay of one's own body's are often encountered on ascetic paths.

As part of our excursion, we consider it important to describe in no particular order the most correct and priority forms of voluntary self-deprivation of life. The act of suicide appears as an escape from totalitarian authority and from the human being's position of being at the disposal of technology. Such death is preferable to captivity.

One possible way is to simulate one's own death so that all databases list the citizen as legally dead, to have one's own grave

352 Avanesov, *Filosofskaia suitsidologiia*.

353 On the whole, comfortable euthanasia corresponds to the liberal-democratic approach to dying, ranging up to the special Sarco pills that put a person to sleep for death.

prepared, and thus be excluded from any further accounting and calculation. Then opens up the freedom of surviving by one's own resources with the guarantee that no one will look for them as a lost taxpayer, and that they will not be considered a possible suspect in acts of ecotage. This puts the "one who has passed into the forest" in the rich existential position of being unplugged from the technogenic civilization and the rest of remaining mankind. If they decide to live their life as a hermit in distant lands, then their biological life will not correlate with the external world of people in states and cities. For the entire digital world, they will be considered de facto dead (unplugged from the Web) as a social and bureaucratic fact. Street or drone cameras and all sorts of registration and identification sensors will show exotic errors of "dead among the living" if such people end up passing by their lenses.

Despite the fact that we generally positively assess the public discussion and legalization of euthanasia practices, we insist that death outside of the urban environment and outside of the means of medical control and accounting is more dignified and worthy. A peaceful departure from life should not happen under the eye of the Gestell and be a compelled compromise whenever technological, medical science, insurance companies, and society recognize prolonging one human's life to be helpless and therefore agree to a euphemistic paying of compensation for dying.

A favorable place for dying would be the native nature of one's ethnic belonging, such as death in the forest, in fields, among mountains and cliffs, etc. Death on one's native land is an act of final unification with Mother Earth under the gaze of the Sky Father, a return home.

A special place in the hierarchy of suicides is occupied by ritual self-sacrifice to a Deity — in various interpretive senses as initiation into Divinehood, as sacrificing oneself to oneself, as bringing the promised pledge-gift and retribution, etc. Death must necessarily be framed by ritual outside of urban landscapes, in absolute seclusion and at a distance from the world. Even outer clothing would be a sign of modern culture, so it is logical that this ritual would be performed in full nakedness, cleansed of everything. Death as an offering can be met by falling on one's sword, hanging oneself from a tree, taking natural poison, jumping off a cliff, stopping one's breathing by sheer willpower, or cutting one's jugular vein or femoral artery with a swift blade movement. Myth penetrates one's own heart on the edge of the blade of ritual suicide.

No less sacred would be death as the result of a heroic act of war against the modern world.[354]

For further detachment from the world — dying while alive — the adepts of radical myths of mystical liberation practice cutting ties with their *rod* (both living and deceased ancestors) and the cycle of rebirths, renouncing their family and children, and having no grave, ashes, any personal property, memorials, and legacy after death. They completely disappear from the memory of the phenomenal manifest world.

The Theology of the Dead Divine

The reign of death in the middle world of people is connected not only with the involution of time, but also with the death of God, the elimination and dissolution of the Sacred as the *axis mundi* of human being amidst non-being. This is not only the death of the Christian moral God, but the death of all the Divinities and the Divine in general. This necessarily actualizes the theology of the dead Divine in a world without Divinity in the conditions of the traumatic end times.[355]

We recognize monistic theology and philosophy to be the pinnacle of pagan thought and the recognition of the manifest world's true nature. According to monism, the world is a manifestation of the Divine, which means that the dying

---

354 [Here the original manuscript issued a more direct statement — author].

355 Our approach has nothing in common with the ideas of the Protestant theologian Dietrich Bonhoeffer, whose views were close to Rudolf Bultmann and Paul Ricoeur.

of Divinity means the dying of the world. The whole beingful world, nature, all creatures, people, and peoples (of Europe) share this (their own) fate. But within history, in the face of the dark suggestion that the "death of God" means emancipation, man can indulge in oblivion, rebellion, solidarity, escapism, or simply ignore this event.

The death of the Divine unveils several directions for the development of theological thought. The diminishing and concealment of the Divine is the revelation of its apophatic self as the Nothing. The appearance of the beingful world, the manifestation of the world in all its boundless richness of the universes of the mind and of the traditions of the peoples inhabiting it, is an act out-of-disclosure of the Divine, of coming to know the self through generating the (conditional, illusory) non-self. The mortification of the exterior self is an act of sacrificing oneself to oneself as the highest value for the sake of revealing one's deep self as Nothing (the *Ab-grund*). Here the word "self" encompasses the whole beingful world, the entire cosmos, all worlds and people. In this optic, people who still dwell on the middle levels of understanding seek the path of restoration and rebirth of the already former, that is the already passed, and therefore misunderstand the meaning of the unfolding inner-worldly nihilism. Otherwise, Julius Evola's formula on the fate of Europe — "if it was the first condemned to enter the era of darkness, then it will be the first to come out on the other side" — can be understood as a deep theological expression and imperative to accept the fate of the world (one's own fate) as an initiatic act of the Divine (ourselves) through self-sacrifice. In the immediate proximity of the eschatological moment, the Divine "is" manifest in the mode of "is-not": the absence of the Divine is the clearest evidence of its presence, not in the likes of cataphatic external forms (the pantheon, theophany, sacred holism, hierarchy), but in the form of its naked "heart" as the Self-Nothing of being-here.356 The absence of the Divine is its immanent presence in all of the beingful world,

---

356 *"Das Sein ist das Nichts"* - Martin Heidegger.

a presence which in the blindness of oblivion imagines itself to be the only reality within the framework of metaphysics or the reign of some super-being as in various ideologies.

In this case, apologetics for ritual suicide is a fundamental act of "mirroring", of *imitatio Dei*, the highest act of "synchronizing" the macrocosm and the microcosm which are in essence one self. Destroying the world as the accursed share, rejecting any political restoration of deceased forms of Tradition, and striving towards being-beyond-the-decline-of-Europe — all of this is the core of Traditionalism beyond the classical formulations of René Guénon and beyond political Traditionalism as a form of conservatism and right-wing populism.

Up to this moment, the death of the Divine and the abyss of revealed nihilism appear to be the rotting corpse of the Divine that is the world mangled by globalization, technology, the Anthropocene, alienation, and the death agony of cultures which we behold like the decay of our own body.

If we turn to the above-mentioned images of Odin and Shiva, then the death of the Divine can be understood as a shamanic dream-journey, an initiation into an enigma of knowledge that is difficult to define and delimit. Hence, the "death of God" appears to be but a merely temporary period, albeit on a cosmic scale, of the forgetfulness of one's nature and our alienation from the Sacred in the state of the sleeping "consciousness" of the Divine. Awakening will be like beginning a new cycle of rebirth.

Finally, the genuine "death of God" can be conceived in the most radical way as the concealment (of the Divine self) as unconcealment (of the space) for people to master and realize being-here, and for the passing on the horizon of the Last God, of whom we know extremely little.[357]

***

---

357 See Askr Svarte, *Gods in the Abyss.*

The New Catacombs

Besides the path of armed resistance to the industrial and post-industrial society, and besides the path of ritual εξαγωγη out of the world of the living, there is yet another, third path and strategy of relating to the world and living within it which is equally significant and just.

In the English language, there is the idiom "living off the grid." In everyday life, this means living beyond electric power lines and sewage grids, i.e., living in wild nature without the benefits of civilization, in a log cabin, outside of the system, independently making a living and crafting things. Living off the grid is the case of Theodore Kaczynski and partially Pentti Linkola, the way of religious hermits, "forest rebels", and mystical anarchists. Living off the grid means breaking oneself out of the dominating system of consumption.

In 3D graphics, grids are XYZ planes of three-dimensional Cartesian space and polygonal networks of 3D-objects (models). To them is added one more axis, time t, which accounts for the whole Cartesian world. "Living off the grid" in this light means living outside of Cartesianism and 3D/VFX/VR/AR simulations of reality, breaking out of not only the networks of power lines, substations, and signal communications, but also out of virtuality and the subject-object causal line of reality.

Today, it would be a radical gesture of protest and a revolutionary act to plant one's own garden, build a house in the taiga, and secure an autonomous water, food, and energy source from (within) nature. This is the position of "passing into the forest", of inward migration and exterior escapism.

With its politics and geopolitics, parties and elections, economics and production systems, etc., the outside world should be considered an inevitable, unfavorable landscape, a manifestation of a very bad climate, an environment from which one must in one way or another draw resources for themselves and their community while dwelling on its periphery and wresting space from it for oneself.

The eschatological end might be still very far away. Thus, the evaluative imperative towards history is the formula, "further it only gets worse." Staying behind in this hellish world of the technological society is justified by the position of the jivanmukti bodhisattva, that is the one who has achieved full realization but has decided to remain within or return to the world (samsara) so as to teach and show other souls the way home.

In Search of Zomia

The word "Zomia" comes from the Tibeto-Burman *zomi*, which means "highlander." Zomia is the name of a territory that spans 2.5 million square kilometers along the border zones of Vietnam, Burma, Laos, Thailand, Cambodia, and intersects with China's Yunan, Sichuan, Guangxi, and Guizhou provinces.[358] The territory of Zomia is formally placed within the densely jungle-covered mountainous region of Southeast Asia. De facto, however, Zomia does not cover the whole continental space, but instead begins at an altitude of at least 300 meters above sea level.

The population of Zomia consists of a hundred million representatives of diverse ethnic groups, tribes, and folk identities. Until altogether recent times, this population did not know modern nation-states or any forms of statehood in general. Besides those indigenous to the mountains heights, for centuries the population of Zomia consisted of fugitives who fled the lands and families of the lowland states that had enslaved them and rejected any centralized authority. They

---

358 In this chapter we primarily draw upon James S. Scott's auspicious monograph, *The Art of Not Being Governed: An Anarchist History of Upland Southeast Asia* (New Haven: Yale University Press, 2009). Scott fits into the common range of the new anthropologists alongside Eduardo Kohn, Eduardo Batalha Viveiros de Castro, and Pierre Clastres, but a Traditionalist reading of their ideas requires a number of nuances, adjustments, and correct placement within the contemporal context.

united into families, clans, and "anarchistic", self-governing societies in the likes of which, according to James S. Scott, all of mankind consisted in ancient times. From the point of view of the centralized (often mandala) states, Zomia was inhabited by complete barbarians.

Scott deconstructs the term "barbarians", pointing out that "barbarianization" is not "primitivism" in the likes of a stage of socio-political and technological underdevelopment. Rather, peoples are called "barbarians" from the point of view of a state and civilization which "never entertain the possibility of people voluntarily going over to the barbarians, hence such statuses are stigmatized and ethnicized."[359] Barbarism begins where accounting, centralized power, and taxation end. Barbarism is a label for all people and peoples who successfully evade the power of the state. But the view from within reveals that "barbarianization", or moving to slash-and-burn agriculture, cattle breeding, gathering, and tribal and segmentary lineages, was a form of secondary adaptation by fugitives, tribes, and peoples who consciously fled civilization to the highland region of Zomia and had to adapt to the local nature.

Scott shares the opinion that it was the emergence of agrarian states on the plains that became the historical watershed that separated sedentary peoples from more mobile groups, whose meaning of life began to consist in eluding governmental power. Settled life and agriculture gave impetus to the development of civilization. For Asia as a whole, the ideal agricultural culture forming the basis of the centralized state and in some senses dictating to it the necessary practices of expanding in space and concentrating a working population (subjects) is rice. A piece of forest cleared for a rice paddy field is called *sawah*. The *sawah* and terracing of slopes ensured the compulsory settlement of a population, facilitating control over it and accounting for harvested crops. Irrigated rice cultivation

---

359 Scott, *The Art of Not Being Governed*, xi. Here it would be appropriate to draw a cautious parallel with Oswald Spengler's idea that culture degrades into civilization.

and terraces significantly alter the landscape, while upland agriculture has minimal effects and does not stand out from the general picture of the forested slope. Hence the prejudice, widespread throughout Asia, that mountain peoples are peoples of nature opposed to the civilized culture that changes the world. The mountain peoples live in harmony with nature. The colonial administration and local officials of Vietnam once enthusiastically accepted the metropolis-sponsored campaigns to resettle nomadic tribes and teach them irrigated rice cultivation. They thus led the "backwards" into the "bosom of civilization." The inhabitants of the mountains and forests were called *tâw thà*, or "forest dwellers", who from the standpoint of civilization were "not quite human", much like the wild Amazon Runa tribes who radically refused modernization and were designated "pagans."

Scott cites a report by an anonymous officer of the US Bureau of Indian Affairs on the Shoshone, a Nuwa people who practiced shamanism:

> This people have never turned their attention to agricultural pursuits, nor can it be expected of them until they are placed upon a reservation. . . . If they are not provided with such a home, they are destined to remain outside of those influences which are calculated to civilize or Christianize them . . . [and] render [them] useful members of society. Wild Indians, like wild horses, must be corralled upon reservations. There they can be brought to work.[360]

In the territory of modern Vietnam, the French colonial administration sought to plant crops that were the most conveniently accountable and controllable, particularly rubber. They sought to turn forests and mountains into profitable and useful production sites and plantations furnished with the guaranteed labor of local "savages." So did the Spaniards in the Andes. Both examples illustrate the very same Gestell's approach to the world as ready-to-hand raw material, whether in the form agricultural crops, mountains slopes, plains, or "barbarian" peoples.

---

360 Scott, *The Art of Not Being Governed*, 98.

"Wild" farming, livestock herding, and gathering practices are connected with local traditions and rituals, and these, in turn, are tightly interwoven with identity. For instance, the mountainous Karen and Lawa peoples identify themselves not only by family origin or language, but by agricultural method and the spirits to which they make offerings during plowing and harvesting. The borrowing of rice-growing practices from the Thai also meant borrowing Thai rituals, which along the the chain led to identity drifts including settling down or even becoming Thai.

The mention of Christianization in the anonymous report on the Shoshone is no accident, for Christianization has been an integral part of Western European modernization and globalization, its "founding father Abraham" and trigger. The religious factor plays an enormous role in spaces compactly inhabited by a large variety of small, mobile groups and tribes professing animistic cults, shamanism, and other variants of paganism amenable to cross-syntheses. To restore bureaucratic order, censuses, accounting, and to rear allegiance, a modern centralized religion is needed. In the case of North and South America, such was fulfilled by the various versions of messianic English Protestantism or Spanish Catholicism. Throughout the East and Central Asia, the religious factor of centralization and modernization was Islam. The true Muslim, according to the oath demanded by Muhammad, had to give up nomadism and become settled. The inhabitants of Mecca considered the Bedouins to be savages, and this status is analogous to the differentiation in terms of altitude in the uplands of Southeast Asia.

In the Zomia region, besides the missionaries who came along with colonists, the role of state religion had been played since ancient times by Buddhism, the religion of the princes, mandarins, and emperors. The true Buddhist must be sedentary, and if he continues to practice slash-and-burn agriculture, nomadism, or belong to a "highland" way of life, then he is considered unreliable. It is quite logical that Buddhist orthodoxy and severe intolerance were characteristic of the lowland states, while in the highlands Buddhism was easily, syncretically combined with a whole variety of local beliefs and cults.

Fleeing from the enslaving state, the colonial administration, also meant fleeing from the local church parish which spread universalism and uniformity, erasing uniquenesses and differences between local peoples. Still in the late 19th century, the Hindu population of the Tengger Mountains on the island of Java annually celebrated their successful flight from Muslim armies into the highest mountain regions by throwing gifts and offerings (the "accursed share") into the mouth of a volcano.

Among the Akha, a stateless way of life is encoded in their very mythology. The sacred history of the Akha tells of a monarch, Dzjawbang, who ruled in the 13th century. He conducted a census of his subjects, for which the people killed him. His son soared up into the sky on a horse with wings made of beeswax, but flew too close to the sun and died. Both parts of this plot warn the Akha against statist hierarchies, which are implicitly associated with alienation and a certain level of technological development (the horse's wings and the Icarus-like son). The Akha adhere to shamanism, and when their shamans need to journey to the spirit world to rescue a soul from the captivity of diseases, their journey is described as descending from the top of the mountains down into the valley where souls are held hostage. The shaman must then exchange a pig or buffalo for the soul, which is in keeping with slave trading practices. Having rescued the soul from slavery and worked his corvée in the lowlands, the shaman returns to the top, to the world of the living, into the mountains. This motif mirrors the social and political relations between the fugitives of Zomia and the lowland pockets of statehood.

By the 20th century, the days of Zomia's difficult freedom were numbered. The intensive implantation of telegraph, radio, and telephone lines, railways, and weather coverings over

511

serpentine mountain roads, the proliferation of helicopters and aviation, the introduction of cellular and satellite communications, GPS, space surveillance, and drones - all of this allowed the colonial administrations and nation-states to launch a mass-scale frontal offensive on the highlands of Zomia and incorporate its inhabitants into their sphere of influence and accounting. They could now map previously inaccessible plateaus, mountain slopes, the mountains themselves, state borders, pathways, roads, villages, and tribes. By establishing control over horizontal and vertical spaces, modern states finally ensure their security.

Scott notes that the commission for investigating the terrorist attacks in the US on 11 September 2001, besides the main content of the official version, also paid attention to where global threats might come from now. If previously the enemy was another nation-state or a geopolitical, military bloc, then today the threat emanates from remote, poorly controlled regions in hard-to-reach areas. In particular, the report talked about the mountains and caves of Afghanistan and Pakistan. In other words, Zomia-like places become not merely annoying (to states) free zones inhabited by "barbarians", but the source of real threats. This approach is fully complementary to the following determination: for the post-industrial society and the Gestell, uncontrolled spaces, peoples, and communities which are not embedded into the extant world like raw material, which are not plugged in to the Web, and which rely on their own conscious simplification and "primitivism", or even Traditionalism and the Sacred, represent an existential threat and must be subdued or eliminated. It is this process of development, incorporation, modernization, and surveillance over hard-to-reach regions of the world that we are witnessing toady.

Despite the fact that globalization is on the offensive, attacking Zomias all over the world, we can identify in the specific case of Southeast Asia the structure of the process of dissimilation, whose elements will be useful to rebels against the Gestell now and in the future. Dissimilation is the process

512

of purposefully building a cultural distance and system of differences between a people (a group, community, tribe) and its neighbors or a global hegemon. Dissimilation, stabilized over generations, turns into a natural and self-reproducing process of ethnogenesis. Some dissimilation practices can be used while still formally remaining within society, for instance living in a remote village where the presence of the state is minimal. There is also the practice of feigning dual loyalty to external symbols while internally dedicating all of one's labor and resources to one's own community, thereby creating not a "state within a state", but an "anti-state within a state", following the strict ideological axis of "Traditionalist community" against the "anti-traditional state." The "forrest passage" is passage into Zomia, even if only an "inner Zomia." Fictitious legal death is also such a passage into Zomia.

One of the essential and formative conditions that influenced the emergence and shaping of Zomia, and which might be useful for new regions freed from subjugation, is the spatial factor of remote, hard-to-reach location and, optionally, a generally unfavorable environment. Zomia managed to take shape in the jungles and mountains of Indochina thanks to the highlands' radical inaccessibility, the local residents' adaptation to the altitudes, and their guerrilla way of life and defense.

In European history, the mastery of Iceland by Norsemen who fled the Danish king is also a case of Zomia. Remote mountainous regions in Central Asia, the very heart of classical Southeast-Asian Zomia, the Russian North, the Putorana Plateau, deep Africa, the highlands of the Andes, the Amazon jungle, the Australian outback, remote oceanic islands like Easter Island, Tristan-da-Cunha, Bouvet, and so on — all of these are potential places for escapism and dwelling outside of civilization. Economic de-urbanization and deindustrialization is to be welcomed, as a result of which cities, industry, and infrastructure will retreat from the periphery into the depths of continents. The lack of work, economy, and transport networks will make these spaces auspicious and favorable. For the new Zomias, it is also important that there be no deposits of minerals and resources, pockets of fish or rare animals with furs, tusks, and bones that might attract civilization and the economy to these lands. Another risk is posed by organized crime embedded in global markets, logistics, and politics. They also use hard-to-reach places for storage and outposts. This once again sends us back to the inevitable need to destroy globalization and *das Man*, the ordinary, profane drug users of civilized countries. Poppy, cannabis, coca, fly agaric, and psilocybin should once again become simply plants in jungles and fields open to shamans and priests initiated into their mysteries. And this, in turn, refers us to the insistences of Pentti Linkola and Theodore Kaczynski that groups of hermits and environmentalists ought to be armed so as to actively defend their lands from outsiders and to wage guerrilla warfare.[361] In the event of global catastrophe, our communities and tribes will have to defend themselves, their enclaves, and Zomia with arms in hand from the invasion of fleeing people who just yesterday were the blood and flesh of *das Man*, who still dream aa night of returning to their offices, gyms, retail chains, and smartphone newsfeeds.

Dissimilation entails rethinking agricultural practices, or a kind of "agrarian revolution against the state", which is tied to, among other things, the characteristics of the surrounding environment and cultivation practices. As already mentioned, the population of Zomia categorically and as a whole refused to engage in rice cultivation, because such was a state-forming culture. The inhabitants of Zomia preferred to grow corn,

---

361 Here it is worth hinting at a path to reflecting on the ambivalence of the participation of neo-archaists and pagan environmentalists in politics. One example is the likes of the IRA, that is a militant underground that carries out violent actions and operations in parallel to a legal wing in parliament or in society in the form of public organizations, foundations, and lobby groups. One negative example is the situation of the peaceful Kalash people living in the high altitudes of the Chitral Valley in northern Pakistan. They are the last of the local peoples who have retained their tradition and refused to accept Islam (in the structure of their mythology, Islam belongs to the pole of metaphysical impurity alongside female menstruation). The Kalash are a dying people who live surrounded by military bases, under the surveillance of Islamists, and on what is becoming a tourist reservation.

potatoes, buckwheat, oats, opium, and to engage in gathering fruit, simple livestock raising, and hunting.

Scott cites Hjorleifur Jonsson's classification which contrasts three economic strategies reflecting distinctive political-hierarchical implications in society: (1) Hunting and gathering, with the possible sale or exchange of surplus (natural barter), (2) slash-and-burn agriculture with periodic community relocation, and (3) settled agriculture. Gathering is combined with mobility and is a conscious choice for existing outside of the state. Its practice is egalitarian and guarantees that the community will not be absorbed by the state. Slash-and-burn agriculture can generate a surplus (potential capital) that might become the target of raids or taxes. Hence the recommendation to ritually destroy it. Finally, a settled economy is the most complementary and convenient for a centralized state and the introduction of taxation on products and the population.

Here it is worth recognizing that Jonsson's scheme cannot be taken as universal. Hunting and gathering can "suffer" from violent seizure by stronger members of the community or random newcomers. While the state is absent, the structure of the coercive seizure of property (fiscal policy) is reproducible on the interpersonal level. Another example is the Slavic rural community, the *mir*, which was open to cooperation and local hierarchies, but for quite a long time successfully resisted the establishment of princely authority, including by way of simply fleeing. Therefore, each society must resolve questions pertaining to the combination of strategies and the scale of hierarchies for itself, based on the structure of its own myth.

Another characteristic feature of the peoples of Zomia is their rethinking of highly differentiated hierarchies, such as those characteristic of Indo-European peoples. Locals recognize hierarchies within the family and, situationally, within the village, the temporary community, and the cooperative. They recognize the authority of "professionals", that is masters of crafts and occupations, and the authority of the shaman as a doctor and mediator between the worlds of the living and the spirits. Finally, they recognize sacred hierarchy, that is the greater power of spirits or Divinities over their lives, but they do not convert such into a common notion of "God's anointed" or any synthesis of sacred and secular power.

Jonsson cites the case of the Lisu people, known for their practice of killing their elected leaders if they begin to impose authoritarian rule beyond their temporary authorization. Moreover, the Lisu deliberately forget their history so that it does not extend deeper than a couple of generations and the history of a particular village. Other tribes and settlements of fugitives deliberately create mismatched versions and interpretations of history so that their enslavers from the lowlands cannot appeal to any common history in the process of natiogenesis and thereby draw fugitives back into the settled population. In the case of Pagan Traditionalism, this principle fits into the greater cause of dissimilation along the axis of "progressive interpretations of history" vs. "metaphysical degeneration in history." Between us and modernists, there is no common history, no common values, no link to which one might appeal.

Jonsson and Scott provide examples of identities constructed around the conscious negation of any identity. The main criterion for a people's identity thus becomes its constantly reproduced strategy of evading the state and avoiding becoming civilized "Chinese", "Thai", "Vietnamese", etc. Such is the complex identity of the Miao/Hmong. The scattered settlements and groups of the Lisu create a "jellyfish-like" culture and refuse to identify themselves at all. Here we can draw a parallel with some magical practices and superstitions associated with names, such as when a hero prefers not to reveal his real name, for remaining incognito protects him from spells, recognition, revenge, and curses. Such cunning is demonstrated by Odysseus and Odin. This logic is similar to the Lisu practice of refusing any "positioning": giving a people a name, a stable culture, and insignia makes them visible for accounting and potential enslavement.

Intimately connected with this is the practice of abandoning the written culture and language of the metropolis. Writing means history and accounting, and knowing the language of a lowland state-sovereign would allow for the inhabitants of the mountains and fugitives to be held to their duties: they cannot avoid work for "not understanding" the common dialect. The Wa people have a legend that in ancient times, "they had a trickster genius, Glieh Neh, who sent all the men off to war while he stayed back and made love to all the women. Caught and condemned, Glieh Neh asked to be drowned in a coffin with all his musical instruments. Cast adrift, he played so beguilingly that all the downriver creatures helped set him free. In turn, he taught the lowlanders all his skills, including that of writing." The Wa people thus associate writing with fraud, and their word for writing is semantically close to meaning cheating and deceit.[362] The figure of Glieh Neh is very similar to the Greek Prometheus, known for his deceit and cursed gifts.

The Karen people tell their own legend of three brothers, a Karen, a Burman, and European (or, alternatively, a Han), who were given the gift of writing. The Burman and the European (or the Han) kept the gift of writing and became civilized with their own states. The Karen, meanwhile, busied themselves with slash-and-burn agriculture and left the skin with writing on it on a stump to be devoured by wild animals. Thus, they were left without literacy, but also without enslavement by the state. Similar legends of the loss or devouring of writing scripts are common among South Asian peoples.

The rejection of writing and the reduction of language exhibited in these accounts come close to Zerzan's ideas on the repressive function of language and the need for gatherers to abandon language altogether and become language-less tribes. But Zerzan's hypothetical constructions clashes with the real practice of the Karen, Wa, Lisu, and other peoples, who do not abandon language as such and the oral transmission of myths,

---

362 Scott, *The Art of Not Being Governed*, 222.

but only discard writing and the language of the local sovereign as part of their dissimilation.

The rejection of writing and the relativization of linguistic identity also have specific political motives. Within the framework of the European paradigm of Modernity, language came to be used to determine ethnic and racial identity. It was believed that speakers of the same language are a unique unit with their own distinct, traceable culture and history. This approach was employed in Indochina by the colonists for conducting censuses, only to be confronted with the fact that the languages and ethnic self-identifications of local peoples and tribes might not correlate at all, but could intersect or give way to chaotic stratifications. Thus, such census projects largely failed. Refraining from writing and strict linguistic identity — many of the inhabitants of Zomia know and speak several languages — was a strategy for avoiding colonists' census, accounting, naming, and assigning identities with all the ensuing consequences.

Above, we defined modern schools and institutions (the Department / University) as totalitarian and repressive, as instantiations of the implanting of Modernity and eradicating the plurality of imaginations and dreams. These institutions are built around learning, educating, accumulating, and transmitting science-centric knowledge. The experience of the peoples of Zomia reveals to us a complex but possible perspective for consciously un-learning and forgetting modern knowledge. If children and youth's consciousness from school and university is reformatted in a short span of time as they grow up, then the method of forgetting knowledge extends over several generations. Its essence boils down to selectively and consciously not transferring (*non-tradere*) physicalist, mathematical, positivist, natural-scientific, and other types of knowledge to subsequent generations. On this account, Linkola and Kaczynski emphasize the need to destroy engineering books in order for this knowledge to simply disappear from the manifest world.

Zomia was also home to the freedom-loving tribes' practice of abandoning the Abrahamic religions or centralized, imperial Buddhism. They gained and passed down myths of liberation from the authority of a leader or of successful escapes to the mountains from demons and dragons in the lowlands that forced people's souls to work off tax tributes.

All of the above leads Scott to the conclusion that a radical ethno-constructivism reigns among the peoples of Zomia. This is to say that the boundaries of folk identities are extremely mobile, situational, and consist of the intersection of numerous factors, both "statist" and "free", coupled together with rather free inter-ethnic marriage and territorial mobility. Scott even interprets Zomian mythology as a derivative of specific tribes' social, agrarian, and political practices. On this point, we take a vertically opposite position, as we believe that the myths and being of a people (or tribe) in the world should be understood synchronously and holistically, without reducing them to Marxist interpretations. It is also necessary to take into account the large-scale influence and peculiar practices of the colonists, the bearers of Modernity, who radically "terraformed" the local landscape of hierarchies, peoples, local states and mandalas, identities, and economies. Scott makes practically no qualitative distinction between the local empires, states of the past (of Tradition), and the operations and calculations of British, French, and Dutch colonial administrations. If in ancient times the opposition between the Dragon-sovereign of the lowlands and the fugitive tribes of the highlands was a confrontation of different myths (let us recall the shaman who descends into the valley for a stolen soul), then since the invasion of Modernity in European guise both of yesterday's poles of opposition are in some sense turned into one side of the same front. Some local princes in Thailand, India, and Vietnam adopted the paradigm of progress and development and entered into alliance with the Europeans against their fellow tribesman and co-religionists. Others, like China and Japan, resisted the colonial empires and preserved their seclusion, under the dome of which their own fugitives existed.

Standard European maps are not suitable for correctly describing Zomia. The classic map puts forth a projection of space onto an XY plane (a 2D grid of latitude and longitude) with a view from top to bottom. The map acts as an instrument for visualizing policies of centralization and keeping inventory of state spaces, borders, center and periphery, and blank spots. Knowledge of such a map presupposes political orientation in space, the assimilation of political geography, and a certain distance towards one's neighbors, local centers, and wild peripheries. Such also entails knowing the latitude and longitude of one's location, and knowing the cardinal directions and the related semantics. Among the latter, the West, like the East, is not only a geographical, but also a geopolitical, cultural, economic, and metaphysical notion. The globe and Mercator projections which we are taught from the school bench impose upon us excessive, superficial knowledge of global geography that is absolutely irrelevant in the bounds of our lived locality and particular natures and myths. Moreover, the Mercator map does not take into account the topographies and geographies of the worlds of spirits, their kingdoms, tribes, families, entrances, etc. By definition, a map is a cartography of the "real" world with its repressive ignorance of sacred dimensions.

In everyday, ordinary thinking, establishing control over a space means closing the boundary lines on a map around the subjugated space. The case of Zomia deconstructs this approach, showing that even de facto control over borders around a perimeter does not mean complete control of the space and population inside them. Zomia and spaces like it add a third dimension to the map: height and depth (the underground). They are not blank spots on a plane, but the white spots of mountain heights and depths in whose "shadows" lurk completely different lifeworlds.

In Asia and the East, many states and borders were created by colonial authorities without any regard for ethno-religious particularities and the politics of local inhabitants. This was done on purpose in order to keep hold of the geopolitical levers of influence in border conflict zones. This is yet another argument for unleashing the process of consciously forgetting maps and networks. It is necessary but not sufficient to liquidate artificial state formations whose borders either arbitrarily cross or run along parallels and meridians. It is necessary but not sufficient to seek out the last blank spots, heights, and depths on the map of the real world. We might also create many different maps with different centers, orientations, and opaque descriptions, maps which take into account passages to other worlds, incorporating the cartography of the worlds of the dead, spirits, the Divinities, the flight routes of birds and the dwellings of animals, and so on.

Forgetting the modern map means turning the whole world into a blank spot, and opening oneself up to the pure perception of lifeworlds. This is one of the most important lessons of Zomia.

A Word on Tribalism

Up to this day, three key currents and approaches to determining belonging to one or another pagan tradition have taken shape within contemporary paganism, primarily as part of active polemics between followers of the Germanic-Scandinavian tradition.

The first, universalism, is a more secular and New Age version of "soft identity." Universalism rejects the ethnic component in paganism, the link of "tradition + ethnos", and instead claims that a person of any people and race can be a follower of any tradition as they wish. Initiation and immersion within the identity of a tradition are not mandatory, nor is studying its language and customs. Universalism is widespread among the left-liberal, humanist, progressive faction of "pagans" in the West, Russia, as well as Asia (in so-called neo-Hinduism, for example).

The second is "folkish" paganism or ethnocentrism.[363] The ethnocentric approach recognizes the importance of genealogically belonging to a people, being a bearer of tradition and having assimilated its culture. The folkish position encompasses a wide range of right-wing ideas, from moderate to extreme. On the whole, the following foremost criteria of belonging to and joining a tradition can be distinguished within the ethnocentric framework:

1. Knowing the language of the tradition into which a person wants to enter. In this case, language is understood in the broadest possible sense, as the language of the culture, customs, artistic styles, taboos and privileges, rituals, regulated behavior, etc.

2. Pilgrimage to the tradition's and its Divinities' native homeland. This is intended to literally and directly join the local nature, the land, the sky, the surrounding environment in which the tradition was revealed and its praises and sacrifices were made. This establishes a connection between a person, nature, local spirits, and the tradition as a whole.

3. Belonging to one or more peoples who have professed this tradition and the cults of its Divinities. This is determined either through the archaeology of one's genealogy or through marrying an ethnic fellow believer and joining their family.

Usually, the minimum satisfactory qualification is fulfilling at least two of the above points. In fact, such represents a more detailed and fragmented transcription of the practices and process whereby archaic peoples initiate and accept a foreigner into their tribe and tradition.

It also bears noting that being involved in a culture and language is in one way or another preserved even in universalism,

---

363 Not to be confused with the late 19th and early 20th-century German "Volkish" movement, the *Völkische Bewegung*.

as foreigners still continue to use the original names of the Divinities and cult vocabulary. Therefore, the most consistent universalists go so far as to consciously reject language and the cult of ancestors in favor of a syncretic, superficial mixing of cultures to shape abstract and detached cults of a generalized "goddess" or "god" (as is the case with Wiccans).

The third approach is tribalism, which can be seen as softer, intermediate form of the folkish current. If universalism and ethnocentrism struggle over being the global paradigm, then tribalism focuses on local tribes, clans, and communities. The degree of ethnicity and criteria of initiation into the clan are determined by each community independently, varying from group to group.

The tribalist position fits quite well with the ideas of Linkola, Kaczynski, and various pagan advocates of deindustrialization, small groups, and autonomous villages living outside of civilization. Tribalism is also complementary with the "constructivism" described by James Scott in the case of the mobile ethnic identities and fugitive strategies of the peoples of Zomia.

According to one widespread conviction in Traditionalism, the existence of large initiatic communities and healthy societies is problematic or altogether impossible in the Kali-Yuga, for in this era Tradition is the path of individuals or very small groups. Tribalism allows for such a position insofar as Traditionalism and the rejection of Modernity constitute the common platform for the followers of different traditions and initiatic paths — and Traditionalism here is meant not as a religion, but as a common intellectual field of imperatives and a language. Thus, people who worship different Divinities on different levels of exterior manifestations yet understand the common Unity on the apophatic level can find community and comrades within a tribe.

Finally, an eschatological correction can be made to the definition of "homeland" in both ethnocentrism and tribalism.

A homeland is acquired and dwelled in the midsts of a specific surrounding nature (locality), family (one's *rod*, ethnicity), comrades-in-arms and fellow believers (the tribe), in a world of ideas, language, and tradition. Not in a state. All of the above parameters, taken strictly in the light of the Sacred, cannot be converted into patriotism and loyalty to any of the anti-pagan states of Modernity and Postmodernity.

The People of the Underground

The Basilica of Saint Clement, erected in the 12th century, is located on Piazza di San Giovanni in Laterano, not far from the very heart of Rome. On the first underground level, on the site of the foundation, there is an early Christian church from the fourth century. Even lower, on the second underground level, hidden from public eyes, lies an ancient Roman sanctuary of Mithra, the Deity of the Invincible Sun who defeated the bull whose blood became the wine of the mysteries. There also lie the Mithraea, schools for neophytes preparing to be initiated into the mysteries. Today, the Mithraeum is open to tourists, but it is impossible to get up close to the altar and make offerings of wine. Access to the halls is fenced off with bars.

The Mithraeum under Saint Clement Basilica is a vivid illustration of the imminent state of paganism in the world of the future that isn't ours. Deep underground, in oblivion and concealment, access to the altars of our Divinities is problematic, closed off by the zealous believers of religions that are alien to us. One of the most negative future scenarios would be the last faithful turning to the catacombs and descending under the earth.

The futuristic visions of cyberpunk depict vast networks of sewers, utility pipes, and the concrete basements of old buildings as the dwelling places of local rebels and the underground. These are either the unsightly underside of the plastic and neon world on the surface, or the only possible places for life under a surface that has been turned into an endless dump and wasteland.

Aspiring towards natural environments and nature is intrinsic to pagan traditions. In the conditions of the futurist future of global urbanization and the total industrialization of all landscapes, what has remained wilderness will become maximally inaccessible (or accessible only to elites from among *das Man*), destroyed, or turned into landfills. The sky, lit by synthetic light and filled with the false lights of planes, drones, and satellites, will also be alienated from authenticity. Therefore, it can be forecasted that the last pagans of the future will be forced to break through to real Earth as the last refuge of the real elements and imprint of nature - below even the technological foundations and communication infrastructure, below the pipes and piles, below the cyberpunk underground.

Niches, loculi, and trenches dug into the real earth at great depths will become the new refuges, sanctuaries, and places for educating children. On the surface, robots and neural networks will conduct cyber-Buddhist or whatever other, even ostensibly "pagan" services and online rituals. As smartphone screens spin kaleidoscopes of iconographies of all the Divinities of the world, the last pagans will adorn their altars with the sprouts of surviving plants and herbs, gradually raising them up into sunlight on the outskirts of megacities.

The door leading to the basement or village cellar, where the walls and floor are made of bare earth, is already a literal time machine into the problematic environment in which our successors and descendants might end up.

Final Moods

In the face of the latter approximations of our conceptualizing and relating to the incoming "future that isn't ours", it might seem that the essence of eschatological optimism is simply anticipating the end, or that such is secured and inevitable, even "objective." But this is not the case. Rather, the matter at hand is the difficult work of aligning one's mode of existing, of comprehending the fundamental mood of the era, of conceiving, formulating, and articulating the themes of the death of the world (Θάνατοποίησις) in the line and spirit of Traditionalism, of traumatically awakening (or some would say "reviving") paganism in the modern era, and of gratuitously and unselfishly sending the Divinities and spirits the offerings of the accursed share.

Wonder, astonishment, and amazement at the being of the beingful world was the fundamental mood of the beginning of Western philosophy in ancient Greece, among the first Presocratics. In our days, at the end of philosophy according to Martin Heidegger, the fundamental guiding mood of our presence (Dasein) is boredom. One could accept the imperatives "It will only get worse" and "Death to this world" while at the same time finding oneself bored at a railway station (the first type of boredom) in anticipation of something (the Event). One could achieve samadhi and anticipate the completion of their specific incarnation's life path in experience, but without becoming attached. Or one could anticipate the final decline of the West and the East, the latter of which is in its metaphysical essence no longer separable from the former, and hence can be designated in a word thusly: China and Asia are already also the West.

One could also take up the position of decadence and consciously accept an at once detached yet interested complicity in the process of the fall, disclosing the abyss of alienation as a perishing witness. One could expect death as deliverance independent of will. Adjacent to this is another possible, potential mood of Dasein if it refuses — which means denies itself — authentic appropriation and the Event of coming-into-truth. This attunement would be the romantic mood and feeling of world woe (*Weltschmerz*, the word *schmerz* translatable from the German as "pain"), of feeling the unbearable waterfall of suffering and grief over reality's inconsistency with the intelligible and imagined horizons of Being (the *imaginaire*, the world of dreams). In some sense, this mood is similar to Christian Dispensationalists' eschatological aspirations for the time of the Great Tribulation. But woe also means awareness and understanding of what is lacking, of that which has been lost or which has died. In the case of the bored inauthenticity of Dasein, this awareness is problematic, and in general the condition of *Weltschmerz* would already be a sign of awakening.

Despite the rich, creative, and sensory potential of world woe and passive anticipation, such risks turning into defeatism, humility, and boredom, and works towards anchoring our presence in this world and accentuating endless suffering here — up to the point of pathologically rejecting any existentially decisive step into another.

Much closer to our views is taking the stoic position of *amor fati*, recognizing and loving one's fate and its inevitable bitterness, combining the latter with actively working to uphold thinking in the direction of the true luminary of Beyng and articulate the meanings of this transitional era.

We wish not for the salvation of the world and not for the restoration of Tradition in urban decorations, but for our positions to be conveyed to the broadest audiences in all corners of the world where Modernity, Postmodernity, and the Gestell as the metaphysical means of producing closed truth have imposed themselves upon peoples as fate.

We wish not for comfort, even while being "in the forest" or in "inner Zomia." Our aim is to catch, to separate from the chaff, and to proclaim forth those lone ones who inquire about beings, the beingful world, and Beyng. Perhaps the dominant mood of these loners in the future will be *Sehnsucht-Nostalgia*, luminous longing for a homeland beyond, one in which we have never been.

With regards to other people, especially the youth and future generations who are already growing up surrounded by and fully immersed in the technogenic, digital, virtual environment, it is necessary to focus efforts and attention on making them face experiences of horror, death, catastrophe, and tragedy on a grand scale, to make them think about the final moods and the truth of being present in the world, to focus their attention on these themes and experiences as the final threads for pondering through which they can reach the horizons of insight into their thrownness in the world and the imperative of *living radically differently: living without technology, living with and by the Divinities and Another Myth.*

***

***

*Destruction is the precursor of a
concealed beginning, but devastation
is the aftereffect of an already decided
end. Does the age already stand
before the decision between destruction
and devastation? Yet we know
the other beginning—know it
in questioning*

- Martin Heidegger,
Ponderings XII-XV: Black Notebooks 1939-1941

***

Selected Bibliography

Anonymous. *Doktrina Radikaln'nogo Primitivizma* [The Doctrine of Radical Primitivism]. 2014.

Barrat, James. *Our Final Invention: Artificial Intelligence and the End of the Human Era.* New York: Thomas Dunne Books, St. Martin Press, 2013.

Bataille, Georges. *The Accursed Shared, Volume I - Consumption.* Translated by Robert Hurley. New York: Zone Books, 1988.

Baudrillard, Jean. *America.* London: Verso, 2010.

_____*The Consumer Society: Myths and Structures.* London: SAGE Publications, 1998.

_____*Symbolic Exchange and Death.* Translated by Iain Hamilton Grant. London: Sage, 2017.

_____*The System of Objects.* Translated by James Benedict. London: Verso, 2006.

_____*The Transparency of Evil: Essays on Extreme Phenomena.* Translated by James Benedict. London: Verso, 2009.

Benatar, David. *Better Never to Have Been: The Harm of Coming into Existence.* Oxford: Oxford University Press, 2006.

Benoist, Alain de. *On Being a Pagan.* Translated by Jon Graham. North Augusta: Arcana Europa, 2018.

_____*Beyond Human Rights: Defending Freedoms.* Translated by Alexander Jacob. London: Arktos, 2011.

_____*Traditsiia I konservativnaia mysl'* [Tradition and Conservative Thought]. Moscow: Totenburg, 2017.

_____*Vpered, k prekrashcheniu rosta! Ekologo-filosofskii traktat* [Forward, to the Cessation of Growth!

An Ecologico-Philosophical Treatise]. Moscow: Institute of Humanities, 2012.

Bogost, Ian. *Alien Phenomenology, Or, What It's Like to be a Thing*. Minneapolis: University of Minnesota Press, 2012.

Brockman (ed.), John. *What to Think About Machines That Think: Today's Leading Thinkers on the Age of Machine Intelligence*. New York: Harper Perennial, 2015.

Brown, Dan. *Inferno*. New York: Anchor Books, 2014.

_____*Origin*. New York: Doubleday, 2017.

Bryant, Levi R. *The Democracy of Objects*. Ann Arbor: Open Humanities Press, 2011.

Castro, Eduardo Viveiros de. *Cannibal Metaphysics*. Translated by Peter Skafish. Minneapolis: Univocal, 2014.

Clastres, Pierre. *Archeology of Violence*. Translated by Jeanine Herman. Los Angeles: Semiotext(e), 2010.

_____*Society Against the State: Essays in Political Anthropology*. Translated by Robert Hurley and Abe Stein. New York: Zone Books, 1989.

Cleary, Collin. *Summoning the Gods: Essays on Paganism in a God-Forsaken World*. San Francisco: Counter Currents, 2011.

_____*What is a Rune? and Other Essays*. San Francisco: Counter Currents, 2015.

Coomaraswamy, Ananda. *Vostok i Zapad* [East and West]. Belovod'e, 2015.

Couliano, Ioan P. *Eros and Magic in the Renaissance*. Chicago: University of Chicago Press, 1987.

Dolgochub, Valentin. *Iazychniki atomnogo veka* [Pagans of the Atomic Age]. Novosibirsk: Svarte Publishing, 2019.

Dugin, Alexander. *Filosofiia traditsionalizma* [The Philosophy of Traditionalism]. Moscow: Arktogeia, 2002.

_____*Martin Heidegger. Poslednii Bog* [Martin Heidegger: The Last God]. Moscow: Academic Project, 2014.

_____Postfilosofiia. Tri paradigmy v istorii mysli [Post-Philosophy: Three Paradigms in the History of Thought]. Moscow: Eurasian Movement, 2009.

_____Radikalnyi Sub'ekt i ego Dubl' [The Radical Subject and its Double]. Moscow: Eurasian Movement, 2009.

_____Noomakhia: Voyny uma. Logos Evropy: sredizemnomorskaia tsivilizatsiia vo vremeni i prostranstve [Noomakhia - The Logos of Europe: Mediterranean Civilization in Time and Space]. Moscow: Academic Project, 2014.

_____Noomakhia: Voyny uma. Tri logosa: Apollon, Dionis, Kibela [Noomakhia - The Three Logoi: Apollo, Dionysus, and Cybele]. Moscow: Academic Project, 2014.

Eliade, Mircea. A History of Religious Ideas, Volume I: From the Stone Age to the Eleusinian Mysteries. Translated by Willard Trask. Chicago: University of Chicago Press, 1978.

_____A History of Religious Ideas, Volume II: From Gautama Buddha to the Triumph of Christianity. Translated by Willard Trask. Chicago: University of Chicago Press, 1982.

_____A History of Religious Ideas, Volume III: From Muhammad to the Age of Reforms. Translated by Willard Trask. Chicago: University of Chicago Press, 1985.

_____Rites and Symbols of Initiation: The Mysteries of Death and Rebirth. Translated by Willard Trask. Thompson: Spring Publications, 1994.

_____The Sacred and the Profane: The Nature of Religion. Translated by Willard Trask. New York: Harvest, 1959.

_____Shamanism: Archaic Techniques of Ecstasy. Translated by Willard Trask. London: Arkana, 1989.

Engels, Friedrich. The Origins of the Family, Private Property, and the State. Marxists Internet Archive, 1884/2000.

Evola, Julius. *Eros and the Mysteries of Love: The Metaphysics of Sex*. Rochester: Inner Traditions, 1991.

_____*The Fall of Spirituality: The Corruption of Tradition in the Modern World*. Rochester: Inner Traditions, 2021.

_____*Fascism Viewed from the Right*. Translated by E. Christian Kopff. London: Arktos, 2013.

_____*Men Among the Ruins: Postwar Reflections of a Radical Traditionalist*. Translated by Guido Stucco. Vermont: Inner Traditions, 2002.

_____*Revolt Against the Modern World*. Translated by Guido Stucco. Vermont: Inner Traditions International, 1995.

_____*Ride the Tiger: A Survival Manual for Aristocrats of the Soul*. Translated by Joscelyn Godwin and Constance Fontana. Rochester: Inner Traditions, 2003.

_____*Rabochii v tvorchestve Ernsta Jüngera* [The Worker in the Thought of Ernst Jünger]. Saint Petersburg: Nauka, 2005.

Fink, Eugen. *Osnovnye fenomeny chelovheceskogo bytiia* [The Main Phenomena of Human Being]. Moscow: Kanon+/ Reabilitatsiia, 2017.

Ford, Martin. *The Lights in the Tunnel: Automation, Accelerating Technology and the Economy of the Future*. Acculant Publishing, 2009.

_____*Rise of the Robots: Technology and the Threat of a Jobless Future*. New York: Basic Books, 2015.

Foreman, Dave and Bill Haywood (eds.). *Ecodefense: A Field Guide to Monkeywrenching*. Ned Ludd Books, 1987.

Fukuyama, Francis. *The End of History and the Last Man*. New York: Penguin, 1992.

_____*Our Posthuman Future: Consequences of the Biotechnology Revolution*. London: Profile Books, 2002.

Gibson, William. *Neuromancer*. New York: Ace, 1984.

Hansen, H.T. "Julius Evola's Political Endeavors." In: Evola, Julius. *Men Among the Ruins: Postwar Reflections of a Radical Traditionalist*. Rochester: Inner Traditions, 2002: 1-104.

Haraway, Donna. *A Cyborg Manifesto: Science, Technology, and Socialist-Feminism in the Late Twentieth Century*. Minneapolis: University of Minnesota Press, 2016.

Heidegger, Martin. *Being and Time*. Translated by Joan Stambaugh. New York: State University of New York Press, 2010.

_____*The Essence of Human Freedom: An Introduction to Philosophy*. Translated by Ted Sadler. New York: Continuum, 2002.

_____*The Fundamental Concepts of Metaphysics: World, Finitude, Solitude*. Translated by William McNeill and Nicholas Walker. Bloomington/Indianapolis: Indiana University Press, 1995.

_____*Heraclitus: The Inception of Occidental Thinking and Logic: Heraclitus' Doctrine of the Logos*. Translated by Julia Goesser Assaiante and S. Montomgery Ewegen. London: Bloomsbury Academic, 2018.

_____*Off the Beaten Track*. Translated by Julian Young and Kenneth Haynes. Cambridge: Cambridge University Press, 2002.

_____*Poetry, Language, Thought*. Translated by Albert Hofstadter. New York: Perennial Classics, 2001.

_____*Ponderings II-VI: Black Notebooks 1931-1938*. Translated by Richard Rojcewicz. Indianapolis: Indiana University Press, 2016.

_____*Ponderings XII-XV: Black Notebooks 1939-1941*. Translated by Richard Rojcewicz. Indianapolis: Indiana University Press, 2017.

_____*On Time and Being*. Translated by Joan Stambaugh. New York: Harper Torchbooks, 1972.

_____*On the Way to Language*. Translated by Peter D. Hertz. New York: Harper Collins, 1982.

Hertz, Robert. *Death and the Right Hand*. Translated by Rodney and Claudia Needham. London: Routledge, 1960.

Houellebecq, Michel. *H.P. Lovecraft: Against the World, Against Life*. Translated by Dorna Khazeni. New York: Abrams, 2019.

Huxley, Aldous. *Brave New World*. New York: Harper Perennial, 2006.

Jünger, Ernst. *The Forest Passage*. Translated by Thomas Friese. Candor: Telos, 2013.

_____*Sem'desiat minulo: dnevniki*. Ad Marginem Press, 2015.

Jünger, Friedrich Georg. *The Failure of Technology: Perfection Without Purpose*. Translated by F.D. Wieck. Der Schattige Wald, 2021.

_____*Grecheskie mify* [Greek Myths]. Vladimir Dal', 2006.

_____*Iazyk i myshlenie* [Language and Thinking]. Moscow: Nauka, 2005.

Kaczynski, Theodore. *Industrial Society and its Future*. 1995.

Kelly, Kevin. *The Inevitable: Understanding the 12 Technological Forces That Will Shape Our Future*. New York: Penguin Books, 2016.

Kohn, Eduardo. *How Forests Think: Toward an Anthropology Beyond the Human*. Berkeley: University of California Press, 2013.

Lévi-Strauss, Claude. *Strukturnaia antropologiia* [Structural Anthropology]. Moscow: Nauka, 1983.

Linkola, Pentti. *Can Life Prevail? A Revolutionary Approach to the Environmental Crisis.* Translated by Eetu Rautio and Olli S. London: Arktos, 2009.

Mauss, Marcel. *The Gift: Forms and Functions of Exchange in Archaic Societies.* Translated by Ian Cunnison. London: Cohen & West, 1966.

Mohler, Armin. *The Conservative Revolution in Germany, 1918-1932.* Translated by F. Roger Devlin. Arlington: Washington Summit Publishers, 2019.

Mokhov, Sergei. *Istoriia smerti. Kak my boremsia i prinimaem* [The History of Death: How We Struggle With It and How We Accept It]. Moscow: Individuum, 2020.

_____(ed.). *Arkheologiia russkoi smerti* [The Archeology of Russian Death] 6, 2019.

Noukhayev, Khozh-Ahmed. *David i Goliaf, ili Rossiisko-Chechenskaia voina glazami varvara* [David and Goliath, or the Russo-Chechen War through the Eyes of a Barbarian]. 2000.

Orwell, George. *1984.* New York: Signet Classics, 1961.

Plato, *Complete Works.* Edited by John M. Cooper. Indianapolis: Hackett Publishing Company, 1997.

Pschera, Alexander, *Animal Internet: Nature and the Digital Revolution.* New York: New Vessel Press, 2016.

Reinhardt, Karl. *Mify Platona* [Plato's Myths]. Vladimir Dal', 2019.

Scott, James S. *The Art of Not Being Governed: An Anarchist History of Upland Southeast Asia.* New Haven: Yale University Press, 2009.

Schwab, Klaus. *The Fourth Industrial Revolution.* World Economic Forum, 2016.

Sedgwick, Mark. *Against the Modern World: Traditionalism and the Secret Intellectual History of the Twentieth Century.* Oxford: Oxford University Press, 2004.

Soral, Alain. *Poniat' Imperiu: Griadushchee global'noe upravlenie ili vosttanie natsii?* [Understanding Empire: Impending Global Governance, or an Uprising of Nations?]. Moscow: Global Revolutionary Alliance, 2012.

Spengler, Oswald. *The Decline of the West.* 2 volumes. Translated by Charles Francis Atkinson. New York: Alfred A. Knopf, 1927/1928.

Svarte, Askr. *Gap: At the Left Hand of Odin.* Fall of Man Press, 2019.

_____*Gods in the Abyss: Essays on Heidegger, the Germanic Logos, and the Germanic Myth.* Translated by Iliya Koptilin and Daniil Granovskiy. London: Arktos, 2020.

_____*Polemos: The Dawn of Pagan Traditionalism.* Translated by Jafe Arnold. PRAV Publishing, 2020.

_____*Polemos II: Pagan Perspectives.* Translated by Jafe Arnold. PRAV Publishing, 2021.

_____*Identichnost' iazychnika v XXI veke* [Pagan Identity in the 21st Century]. Moscow: Veligor, 2020.

Thoreau, Henry David. *Walden.* New Haven: Yale University Press, 2004.

Vakhshtein, V (ed.). *Sotsiologiia veshchei. Sbornik statei* [The Sociology of Things: An Anthology]. Moscow: Territoriia budushchego, 2006.

Weisman, Alan. *The World Without Us.* New York: St. Martin's Press, 2007.

Woodard, Ben. *Slime Dynamics: Generation, Mutation, and the Creep of Life.* Winchester: Zero Books, 2011.

Yates, Frances. *Giordano Bruno and the Hermetic Tradition*. Chicago: University of Chicago Press, 1964.

_____*The Rosicrucian Enlightenment*. London: Routledge, 1972.

Zerzan, John. *Future Primitive and Other Essays*. Autonomedia, 1994.

_____*Running on Emptiness: The Pathology of Civilization*. Los Angeles: Feral House, 2002.

_____*Twilight of the Machines*. Port Townsend: Feral House, 2008.

_____*Why Hope? The Stand Against Civilization*. Port Townshend: Feral House, 2015.

www.ingramcontent.com/pod-product-compliance
Lightning Source LLC
Chambersburg PA
CBHW062109020426
42335CB00013B/900